Cuban Transitions
At the Millennium

Edited by
Eloise Linger
John Cotman

D0209757

International Development Options

International Development Options
Largo Maryland, U.S.A.

Published in the United States of America in 2000 by
International Development Options
912 Falcon Drive
Largo, Maryland 20774

Manufactured in the United States of America
First printing August 2000

Library of Congress Cataloging-in-Publication Data

Cuban Transitions at the Millennium / edited by Eloise Linger,
John Cotman
    p.   cm
Includes bibliographical references and index.
ISBN: 0-9643624-1-4 (cloth)—ISBN: 09643624-2-2 (paper)
1. Cuban Transitions — Cultural Issues   2. Economic
and Environmental Issues   3. Theorizing Politics
I. Eloise Linger. II. John Cotman

Contents

Acknowledgments

The editors are deeply grateful for the work of International Development Options' Managing Director, Dr. Bamijoko S. Smith, for helping us revise a previous special issue of *Global Development Studies* into a well-rounded book that is appropriate for use in English-speaking classrooms. Both the original journal collection and this book share the title *Cuban Transitions at the Millennium*.

The editors are very grateful for the assistance of translators and graduate students who helped in the production of the special issue of *Global Development Studies*. The translators have made it possible to publish in English the ideas of Cuban writers, some of whom have not previously published their research in the United States. The translators include Jean Paul Borja, Maritza Colon, and Fernando Janvier, all from New York City, and Esther Pérez from Havana. The graduate students include Aretha Jones (Political Science, Howard University), Sara Lulo (Cornell University Law School), and Katia Perea (Sociology, New School for Social Research).

Two of the chapters in this volume were previously published in two academic journals. The Perseus Books Group has graciously granted permission for a revised version of chapter 6 to be published. The Inter-American Dialogue has also graciously granted permission for a revised version of chapter 18 to be published.

LIST OF CONTRIBUTORS

Holly Ackerman taught in the School of Social Work and the Center for Latin American Studies at Tulane University in New Orleans. Professor Ackerman is now a post-doctoral Fellow at Duke University. Her publications include *Five Meanings of Cuba's Political Prisoners* (1998) and "Protesta Social en la Cuba Actual: Los Balseros de 1994," which appeared in *Encuentro* (1997). She also has forthcoming chapters in *Nonviolent Struggle in the Emerging International Arena*, and *Reconciliation in Global Perspective: Theory and Practice*. She is currently working on the manuscript "Generations of Struggle: Opposition Political Culture and the Cuban Diaspora."

Benigno E. Aguirre is Professor of Sociology at Texas A&M University. His areas of specialization are collective behavior and social movements, sociology of disasters, and ethnic relations. Dr. Aguirre is the author of *Collective Behavior, Social Movements, and Social Change* (1993). Forthcoming articles include "The Caribbean and the Guianas" in the *Handbook of Latin American Studies*, and "The Reliability of Cuban Educational Statistics" in *Comparative Education Review*.

José B. Alvarez IV is Assistant Professor of Spanish at the University of Georgia. His articles include "(Re)escritura de la violencia: el individuo frente a la historia en la cuentística Novísima cubana," *Chasqui* (1997), "La generacion literaria sin trauma: mirada socio-histórica a los Novísimos narradores cubanos," *La Chispa '97: Selected Proceedings* (1997), and "Miguel Otero Silva," *Encyclopedia of Latin American Literature*.

Al Campbell is Assistant Research Professor at the University of Utah in the Department of Economics. He has published in the *Review of Radical Political Economics*. Articles on Cuba include "Cuba Today and the Future of Cuban Socialism," *Monthly Review* (1997).

Marisel Caraballo Sánchez is Research Fellow at the Juan Marinello Center for Cuban Culture in Havana. Ms. Caraballo's area of expertise is media studies.

Julio Carranza has been at the forefront of analysis on the Cuban economy. He carried out research at the Center for Studies of the Americas (CEA) until 1996. He now works at UNESCO in Havana, Cuba.

John Walton Cotman is Associate Professor of Political Science at Howard University. His book *The Gorrión Tree: Cuba and the Grenada Revolution* was published in 1993. Other publications include articles in *The Encyclopedia of Political Revolutions* (1999), and *Cuba's Ties to a Changing World* (1993). The article in this volume is part of his ongoing "Caribbean Convergence: Cuba and CARICOM" research project.

Jorge Ramon Cuevas is an internationally prominent biologist, and innovator of Cuba's environmental protection programs. He directs "Entorno" the popular Cuban television show on the environment.

Elvira Díaz Vallina is Profesora Titular (full professor) in the Department of History at the University of Havana. She specializes in the history of social and political theory, and in contemporary Cuban history. Published inside and outside of Cuba, she has lectured at several United States' universities as a Junior Visiting Scholar of the Latin American Studies Association. She was a founding member and serves on the council of Catedra de la Mujer (Women's Studies) at the University of Havana.

Elisa Facio is Associate Professor of Ethnic Studies at the University of Colorado at Boulder. A sociologist by training with expertise in Chicano and feminist studies, Dr. Facio's book *Understanding Older Chicanas: Sociological and Policy Perspectives* was published in 1996. "Ethnography as Personal Experience," appeared in *Race and Ethnicity in Social Research.* Current work on the connections between socialism, nationalism and feminism in Cuba includes an anthology in process with scholars from the University of Havana.

Marisela Fleites-Lear, who formerly taught philosophy at the University of Havana, was born, raised and educated on the isle. Currently she teaches Spanish at Green River Community College in Auburn, Washington, while pursuing her Ph.D. in Romance Languages and Literature at the University of Washington. Her most recent publications include "One Little Soldier: A Personal and Socio-political Analysis.

Victor Fowler Calsada is a researcher at the Biblioteca Nacional Jose Marti. His works include *Visitas* (1996), and two books of essays now in press *Rupturas y homenajes* and *La Maldicion Literatura y homoerotismo en Cuba.*

Julio César González Pages teaches courses in women's history and gender studies in the Department of History at the University of Havana. He has lectured in the United States, Mexico, Puerto Rico, and Colombia, and he has served as President of the Mujer y Paz (Women and Peace) Commission of the Cuban group Movimiento por la Paz (Peace Movement).

Tony Henthorne teaches in the Department of Marketing at the University of Southern Mississippi.

Emilio Ichikawa Morin has published essays in Cuba, Mexico, Spain, the United States, Switzerland, France and Uruguay. Since 1985, he has taught philosophy at the University of Havana, specializing in Cuban and Latin American Thought. His book *El Pensamiento agónico* won the Pinos Nuevos prize in 1995.

John M. Kirk is Professor of Latin American Studies at Dalhousie University in Halifax, Nova Scotia. He is author of *José Martí, Mentor of the Cuban Nation* (1983), *Between God and the Party: Religion and Politics in Revolutionary Cuba* (1988), *Politics and the Church in Nicaragua* (1992) and has co-edited *Transformation and Struggle: Cuba Faces the 1990s* (1990) and *Cuba: Twenty-Five Years of Revolution, 1959-1984* (1985).

Eloise Linger teaches Sociology and Latin America Studies at Tulane University. Articles and book reviews on Cuba have appeared in *Behavior and Social Issues*, *Sociological Forum*, *Contemporary Sociology*, *Cuban Studies* and *21st Century Policy Review*. Her latest work in publication is *Mirar el Niagara: Huellas culturales entre Cuba y los estados Unidos (*Mexico*:* Centro Juan Marinello*)*.

Sara Lulo is currently studying international law at Cornell Law School. She received her Master of Arts in Latin American and Caribbean Studies in 1999 at New York University. She has worked professionally in economic and political research on the Latin American region, and has completed several academic projects on Cuba, including a graduate thesis on the implications of Cuban economic reform.

Clarence Lusane is Assistant Professor in the School of International Service at American University where he co-directs the Comparative and International Race Relations sub-field. He is also an activist, journalist and commentator on the concerns and challenges facing African Americans. He has written five books on Black politics and social issues, including *African Americans at the Crossroads: The Restructuring of Black Leadership* and *Race in the Global Era: African Americans at the Millennium*, both published by South End Press.

Edward J. McCaughan is Assistant Professor of Sociology at Loyola University, New Orleans and author of *Reinventing Revolution: The Renovation of Left Discourse* *in Cuba and Mexico* (1997), co-editor of *Latin America Faces the 21st Century* (1994), and co-author of *Beyond the Border: Mexico and the U.S. Today* (1979). He is also on the editorial board of the journal *Social Justice.*

Peter McKenna is Assistant Professor in the Department of Political and Canadian Studies at Mount Saint Vincent University in Halifax, Nova Scotia. He is the co-author of *Canada-Cuba Relations: The Other Good Neighbor Policy* (1997) and *Canada and the OAS: From Dilettante to Full Partner* (1995). He has recently published articles in *Hemisphere,* and *The American Review of Canadian Studies.*

Julia Nevárez completed her Ph.D. in Environmental Psychology at the City University of New York (CUNY). She has participated in collaborative research projects with U.S. and Cuban scholars.

Sharon Oswald, Professor and Department Head of Management, holds the Colonel George Phillips Privett Professorship in Business at Auburn University. After a 10-year career in health administration, she joined the faculty at Auburn University in 1987. Professor Oswald has published more than forty articles, she has presented numerous papers at international and regional meetings, and has lectured in Japan and the Czech republic. She recently had the opportunity to tour health care facilities in Cuba. After several research-related trips to the Czech Republic, she established the College of Business' first international studies program in Central Europe in 1997. Her current research focuses on strategic international business issues.

Katia Perea completed her MA in sociology at the New School for Social Research in New York. She works with the Harlem Writers' Group. Focusing in cultural studies, Ms. Perea utilizes ethnographic research in the analysis of social problems.

John Peeler chairs the Department of Political Science at Bucknell University in Lewisburg, Pennsylvania. His book *Building Democracy in Latin America* appeared in 1998. For over twenty years his research has focused on the problem of democracy and democratization in Latin America. Currently he is exploring the political organization of indigenous peoples in the Andes and Guatemala.

Christina Proenza is a Ph.D. candidate in the Department of Sociology at the New School for Social Research in New York and Adjunct Professor of Sociology at Cooper Union College.

Peter M. Sánchez is Assistant Professor of Political Science at Loyola University of Chicago. His teaching and research interests include comparative politics, international relations, Latin American politics, and democratization. Published in *PS: Political Science & Politics, The Air Force Law Review, Journal of the Third World Spectrum, Journal of Developing Areas,* and *Journal of Conflict Studies*, Dr. Sanchez spent the 1997-98 academic year as a Fulbright Scholar at the University of Panama, Panama City.

Diane Soles is a Ph.D. candidate in the Department of Sociology at the University of Wisconsin at Madison. Her research is focused on Cuban film and cultural studies.

1

Introduction: Where is Cuba Headed? Implications of Research and Recent Events[1]

Eloise Linger

The "Elián phenomenon" has been marked by unprecedented and prolonged U.S. media attention, a fresh view of Cuba, and widespread public sympathy in the United States for Cubans on the island. In 1996, 49 percent of Americans supported reestablishing diplomatic relations with Havana, compared to 71 percent today. In September 1994, 35 percent of Americans wanted to end the embargo; the portion today is 51 percent.[2] "Polls show sympathy and understanding for Elián and his dad, Juan Miguel Gonzalez."[3] A CNN/USA Today poll released on April 25, 2000 reported public opinion about whether Elián should live with his relatives in the U.S. or his father in Cuba. In December 1999, 45 percent were equally for each position; however, by late April 2000, 27 percent favored his staying with Miami relatives, while 59 percent thought Elián should live with his father in Cuba.

It is not surprising that U.S. public opinion is changing as we deepen our exposure to real Cuban people and actual life on the island. With its in-depth views of what is happening on the island and in exile communities, this volume of research and analysis also can contribute to a better understanding of the changing and challenging realities of contemporary Cuba.

Over the past decade, Cubans have been forced to alter their daily lifestyles, places of employment, methods of transportation, and their ways of providing food for their families. As the U.S.S.R. and other Soviet bloc states disintegrated, the Cuban economy reeled from losing 85 percent of its foreign trade, most of its imported food (dairy, meat and other foods) and petroleum, so vital for all economic life. Cuba began efforts to insert itself into the global capitalist economy, while also seeking to maintain as many benefits as possible from its socialist welfare state. In the various countries of their Diaspora, Cubans also have been undergoing serious changes. Many have re-evaluated their attitudes toward the island, toward one another and toward the most strident exile groups that had been controlling political life and, amazingly, even determining what was permissible as cultural enrichment in South Florida.

The twenty-four chapters in this collection can help bridge the gap between the old Cold War images, political posturing, misinformation, and ignorance on the one side and the many layers of transformation taking place on the island since the mid-1980s, processes that accelerated in the 1990s.

Every few years a new edited volume on Cuba appears in English.[4] Fortunately, in the last decade more Cubans have had their research, analysis and opinions published in these anthologies. In this selection, eight voices are those of Cubans living on the island. Cuban voices from the United States include several contributions by the people who "live on the hyphen," the Cuban-Americans, while two more report research about Cubans in the U.S.

When the editors issued the call for papers,[5] we did not specify cultural studies, economics, Caribbean studies, Cuba-U.S. relations, gender studies, state-citizen or state-society relations, social science, contemporary history or any of the singular disciplines or inter-disciplinary divides of the academy. The responses showed serious work, sensibility and sensitivity. The reader can ascertain that most of the chapters are too critical to represent the official point of view from Havana, while most offer too much critical support of the Cuban system to represent the official views dominating in Washington. Furthermore, some authors challenge the "politically correct" canon of both the Right and the Left.

Many of the contributors' vantage points from which to view Cuba, plus their research methods and writing styles, form a combination quite different from those in previous anthologies. Besides the large number of Cuban voices, twelve of the authors are women. If the contributors, by their research interests and their own personal attributes tell us anything about the new century's Cuba, and the scholars interested in Cuban life, they would reinforce two old phrases: first, that change seems to be the only constant of social and economic relations and life on the island; and second that Cuba and scholarship about Cuba is multifaceted. We might also conclude that what happens culturally and politically inside Cuba often affects the thinking of Cubans on the outside, just as new trends abroad work themselves into Cuban music and other cultural expressions. Besides the flow of ideas and images, economic prosperity or hard times for Cubans in Miami or Madrid or Union City, New Jersey, may have some material impact on their relatives who live on the island.

The majority of research compiled here presents changes of the past ten years, since the collapse of the Soviet Union and COMECON external (socialist) support for the island. Elisa Facio is highly critical of the social impact of the economic crisis and certain changes in Cuba. In a poignant and very troubling piece, "The Devaluation of Women's Work: Jineterismo during the Special Period," she probes the depths of Cuban immiseration that has driven some young women (and men), to turn to forms of prostitution related to the tourist boom.

Life on the island, since 1959, has been neither a paradise nor a hell compared to life in the United States, neither a model for democratic political life, as some would claim, nor a model of tyrannical rule as others with an inordinate amount of media time have been screaming at us for decades. The comparisons made by people from other Latin American countries are the most relevant to appreciate the positive Cuban achievements. They say that over the last forty years, Cuba has achieved far more social justice, and improved every social indicator far beyond the accomplishments of their own (often larger and richer) countries. Both first-hand observations and United Nations data verify these evaluations.[6]

No matter their political viewpoints, no group or individual in the 1970s or 1980s could have imagined an economic distress so severe in Cuba that it could lead to the re-emergence of prostitution. That shocking development has been especially hard-hitting to the generation that eliminated prostitution, retrained the women involved, and helped them find stable jobs and reintegrate themselves into mainstream society. They actually saw the achievement of a better life for the general citizenry in terms of education, health, general welfare, and social justice. To see young Cubans now cozy up to foreigners, in order to help make ends meet at home, is a very bitter medicine for those who risked lives and sacrificed continuously so that future generations could lead dignified lives free of such humiliations from the past.

Thankfully, not all the recent changes have been unpalatable. Perhaps the least known yet most important issues are those concerning the life of the planet. Julia Nevárez, who informs us of the possible pitfalls and rewards of carrying out research in Cuba, gives a clear impression that Cubans are very concerned to do the most they can to protect and enhance environmental resources. Dr. Jorge Ramon Cuevas, an internationally recognized leader in promoting mass consciousness of ecological threats, directs one of Cuban TV's most popular shows, "Entorno." His contribution presents the rich quantity of Cuban flora and fauna, and shows that there are several opportunities for more U.S. and Cuban cooperation to stop the erosion and destruction of natural life on land and sea in the Caribbean (and northwards).

Readers in the United States may be surprised to hear that on the environmental scientific level, there has been cooperation for years between the two countries. Besides the biotechnology industry, Cuban efforts to forge sustainable and environmentally sound economic development are two of the most important yet undervalued efforts that should be more publicized in the United States. They hold great promise for future cooperation, because the time is approaching rapidly when our planet will depend on an environmentally conscientious mentality that can restrain the waste and destruction of the biosphere, a threat to all residents of the planet. It is imaginable that Cuba and the United States together might make a powerful team to pressure global economic and political elites to pay serious attention to sustainable and environmentally sound development.

2. Was the Decade of the 1990s More "Transitional" Than Others?

Since 1900, Cuba has seen so many transitions—wars, dictatorships, revolutions and foreign interventions—that it may seem artificial to refer to the social, cultural, economic and political changes reported in this volume as "transitions at the millennium." However, due to the coincidence in timing, the disintegration of the former Soviet bloc, structural adjustment and global neoliberalism have led to many big "transitions" with great social impact in several parts of the globe during the last two decades of the millennium. The forms of change and of insertion into a global capitalist network are widely varied from country to country. The analyses of cultural and socio-economic change, with the examples from daily social life, offer some visions of the many ways that Cubans have been dealing with the crisis.

If the calendar years were different, and we were not writing at the turn of the century and the millennium, we might have entitled the collection, "Globalization Hits Cuba" or something similar. However, such a title would not be quite right because it implies powerlessness and impending doom, as if those Cubans who support a humanitarian system of economic production and distribution had no internal recourse and no connections to other events and people from Brazzaville to Brasilia to Beijing. Hundreds of millions of people have been finding it harder to survive against the behemoth of growing inequalities on a global scale.

While Cuba has suffered deeply in the immediate aftermath of the collapse of the former socialist economies and states, its political leadership was able to mobilize sufficient numbers in the early 1990s to prevent starvation and turn around agricultural stagnation. The Cuban economy is almost midway in the slow climb out of its 1993 abyss by developing a mixed economy (see Campbell, Carranza, Cotman, and others in this volume as well as recent writings by specialists Carmelo Mesa-Lago, Pedro Monreal, and Jorge Pérez-Lopéz). Income from the jointly-owned or foreign-owned tourist industry has provided a counterweight to falling sugar prices and production levels in recent years. Survival of the population also has been aided by the *remesas* or money sent by relatives living in other countries.

The Cuban example of striving to maintain its sovereignty while also integrating its economy into the global system is not easy in the midst of a phrenetic global expansion of capital in search of investment opportunities where wages are low, lower and lowest. Cubans' caution may find echoes among other poor countries with long-standing needs for investment and sustainable development. Some of the rapidly-developing economies (Malaysia and Indonesia, for example) have had major economic crashes, corruption and massive civil unrest. Cuba seems to be weighing carefully exactly how to avoid these pitfalls as it re-integrates itself into the global capitalist economy.

3. Cultural Transitions?

Some of the drama of Cuba's adjustment to the global realities of a post-Soviet world is presented in this volume. It is clear that not all the readjustment is economic or political. In the cultural fields of film (Diane Soles and Jose B. Alvarez IV), literature and literary criticism (Victor Fowler) and philosophy (Emilio Ichikawa), we get a feeling of the expansion of new and challenging issues. Fowler speaks of more controversial themes in recent Cuban literature and the arts, for example, openly homoerotic and other sexual expressions. He claims it is long overdue, and chides the more prominent literary critics for being out of touch with the newer trends. His criticism of the literary establishment has been published on the island. Ichikawa's chapter, published in Spanish a few years ago, is interesting because it shows that, despite the economic hardships, some of Cuba's young intellectuals have maintained access to academic trends and social theory in Europe, the United States and Latin America.

One of the thought-provoking themes, approached from different angles in this collection, is the issue of the social construction of race in the United States and Cuba. Clarence Lusane raises theoretical understandings of "race," the ways in which race has been constructed historically, and the ramifications to this day on the island and among Cuban communities in the U.S. Christina Proenza, raised in a Cuban household that spoke Spanish in a predominantly Cuban urban area (Miami), observes the construction of Anglo whiteness, her father's self-defining identity before the Cubans in Miami became prosperous and dominated the region's politics. Her title, "What Color is Cuban?" aptly captures some of the attempts by young Cuban-Americans to come to grips with their puzzling multiple national and ethnic identities.

Katia Perea, also a "hyphenated" Cuban-American from Miami, alludes briefly to race and gender in her contribution "Black Beans and MTV."

While our selection on religious transitions is one-sided,[7] we are delighted to have Marisel Caraballo's interview with Monsignor Carlos Manuel de Cespedes, great-grandson of the nineteenth century Cuban patriot with the same name. With his love of Cuban culture, he explains its mixture of religiosity and national symbols. He insists that the Catholic Church is an indisputable part of that culture. "Personally, I think that the Virgin of the Caridad del Cobre is a symbol of Cuban nationality... present since the beginning of the Seventeenth Century.... It may be that she is the universal symbol that unites all Cubans." These are views rarely presented to U.S. readers—whose visual images of Cuban religiosity are generally limited to the coverage surrounding the January 1998 visit of Pope John Paul II.

It is important to realize that the Cuban Catholic Church began to emerge from its long slumber, not with the arrival of the Pope but, rather, in the mid-1980s. The number of people attending church services swelled into a far stronger tide in the 1990s, as they sought solace from the suffering of Cuba's economic crisis. The papal visit was more a culmination than an initiation of religious practice, and at the same time, the visit undoubtedly strengthened the Church on the island. Monsignor de Cespedes was highly instrumental in organizing the teams of people who carried out out the immense arrangements for the dramatic and successful visit of the Pope. One must also add that many Cubans profess a mixture of beliefs with origins in West Africa, Roman Catholicism, Protestantism and other forms of spirituality.

We move from one chapter on religion to seven on political developments. Perhaps the most salient to recent events in Miami, Havana and the U.S. legal system is Holly Ackerman's argument that processes of Cuban reconciliation have been underway since 1978. Her research combines interviews among different generations of immigrants within the Cuban exile community, survey data, and theoretical discussion of the meanings of national reconciliation. Her contribution reveals the stereotypes that beguile some Cubans to expect to become wealthy upon arrival on U.S. soil while others were disgusted with their government's constant showing of the U.S. in negative images over the years. The chapter is especially illuminating for those who have no contact with the Cuban communities in Miami and elsewhere.

Sara Lulo also synthesizes survey research with the interviewing of members of the Cuban community in Miami and emphasizes the importance of the Miami community for what has been going on in the politics of U.S.-Cuban relations. Her chapter is especially useful as a succinct summary of the various waves of emigration, and the relationship of each wave to U.S. policy toward the immigrant communities and toward the Cuban government. Any understanding of the journalist's theme "Elian the eye-opener for us about Cuba?" [see endnote 3] would begin with Lulo's summary of "Exiles in Action" and Ackerman's more detailed reporting on political actors on the island and in Miami, and both authors' discussions of the political spectrum within the Cuban-American communities.

Through the prism of Canadian political scientists, McKenna and Kirk criticize the woeful state of U.S. foreign policy. They seem amazed (yet remain polite) at the backwardness and self-destructive policies of Washington, and recommend Canadian policy as an example for their neighbors to consider.

Other contributions examine the Cuban regime and the island's internal political developments. Benigno Aguirre looks historically at the Castro regime and seeks to explain its durability. He employs the political sociological theory of Berger to account for Fidel Castro's popular legitimacy. Edward McCaughan, John Peeler and Peter Sanchez consider aspects of democracy in and for Cuba. While Sanchez and Peeler follow more traditional political scientific modeling for a democratic transition, McCaughan's research inside Cuba reveals the variation in several (competing) groupings and tendencies, and their degree of accordance with variants of Marxism and degree or type of democracy preferred. His contribution strongly suggests that U.S.—or any other—policy, to be successful with Cubans, must understand the subtleties of Cuban political theory and debates, and rise above the crass bi-polar posturing that used to pass as theory in the academies that trained people to work in U.S. foreign policy careers. As the world changes, the education to prepare people to make good policy must be more open-minded toward the entire world.

The Cold War is over, and somebody should be educating future Latin Americanists about Cuban and other Latin Americans' perceptions of Cuba's century of relations with the United States. Cubans fought hard and long (1868-1898) for the right to run their own affairs. The leaders of its early Republic were forced to agree to U.S. intervention into its affairs.[8] Over the course of the dictatorships of the 1930s and 1950s—and U.S. support for them— Cubans have developed mixed feelings toward their powerful Northern neighbor. The United States has not been seen by most Cubans, including those at different ends of the political spectrum, as a "good neighbor."

Thus, it is quite difficult to discuss Cuban political transitions without taking into account its relationships—the turbulent political past, the economic and non-economic embargo, as well as the positive cultural and familial ties—with the United States. Cuba, due to U.S. policy, has far better state-to-state and economic relations with Canada, Europe, South America and the Caribbean, as McKenna & Kirk,

Cotman and others document in the pages that follow. Yet Cubans have maintained networks of ties to the United States, which also has a very strong cultural presence on the island.

It may come as a surprise that Cubans have always watched Hollywood movies. One night in mid-week and on Saturday night, Cuban television shows many of the latest films from the U.S.—and two of them on Saturday night! Following the explosion in popularity of Cuban music throughout the United States, the increase in the scope of cultural exchanges, and most recently, the publicity around Elián, U.S. citizens are finally having the opportunity to take a better look at Cubans and their lives on the island.

4. So, Where is Cuba Headed?

The fate of the Cuban population over the past decade, and even over the entire twentieth century has been far kinder than what has befallen many others across the globe. But life has not been easy on the island, not even in relatively prosperous times. The human cost was excruciatingly high to defeat the forces of Spanish monarchy (1895-98), and the brutal dictatorships in the 1930s and the 1950s. The economic hardships of the 1990s were considered the worst of Cuba's many periods of food and material goods shortages since the triumph of the revolution in January 1959. Somewhat bruised and sore, yet, Cuba has survived. Its governing party is teeming with debate but intact. Many of its citizens are struggling very hard to survive while others are beginning to accumulate enough wealth to purchase simple material comforts. The saga of Elián Gonzalez shows that tens of thousands of Cuban citizens will mobilize on short notice to demonstrate, provided people feel they are struggling against a grievous social injustice.

Cuban transitions away from dependence on the Soviet bloc for foreign trade and technological development have already led to a mixed economy on the island. As capitalism makes greater inroads, material conditions of daily life worsen for significant sectors of the population; but they have improved so much for a few others that an observable social differentiation can be measured. Cuban intellectuals report that beginning in the mid-1980s, cultural and political space opened for more challenging and controversial themes; with minor setbacks the space continues to expand as the Cold War recedes.

Is Cuba headed for a rapprochement with the United States? In the 1999 edition of this volume, we said,

All signs would indicate it is, but certainly not fast enough for some contributors to this special [journal] issue. Will the United States wait until Fidel Castro is no longer on the scene before opening up its diplomatic doors? Not if the U.S. business community has anything to say about it. Cuba offers a wise investment opportunity, but European and Canadian competitors are gaining while their U.S. counterparts are losing out (unless they go illegally and at a cost through other international houses of investment).

Any news media or relevant governmental website in early Summer 2000 (date of this writing) confirm a change even more dramatic than what we predicted.

Is the Cuban-American community in the U.S. still a hindrance to improving relations between their two countries? We also pointed out in the earlier edition of *Global Development Studies,*

The research presented here shows how much the gap has narrowed between the two extreme opinions toward Castro and the Cuban state within the Cuban community in the United States. While the older generation, the most vehement against the Castro regime, now has a weaker input into the Cuban dialogue within the United States, the U.S. Congress has not yet caught up to the younger Cuban-American generation nor to the changes reported in this volume.

The events of Spring 2000 suggest that public opinion and members of the U.S. Congress are beginning to get a truer picture of the multiple views of Cubans, Cuban-Americans and the U.S. public regarding a whole range of issues, including the need to normalize relations between the two countries.

We close the introduction to readers with the hope that from the research presented in this volume they will gain knowledge and study further. Knowledge about Cubans and their culture is important to reach the goal of making life easier for divided families and for all those who seek freer travel and mutual exchange in an atmosphere of peaceful relations.

ENDNOTES

1. The author, who teaches Sociology and Latin American Studies at Tulane University, thanks her colleagues at Dickinson College, Professors Mark Ruhl and Sinan Koont, for their helpful suggestions on

an early draft of the introductory chapter for the 1999 issue. Co-editor John W. Cotman , Cuban colleague Rafael Hernandez and Tulane University colleagues Timmons Roberts and Holly Ackerman made helpful comments on the updated introductory chapter.

2. Sarah Wildman (2000) "Old Man and the Pea," *The New Republic*, issue date June 12, post date June 1, 2000.

3. "Elian the eye-opener for us about Cuba?" 05/26/00-Updated 08:28 AM ET, http://www. usatoday.com /news/comment/columnists/neuharth/neu041.htm.

4. Among them, Miguel Centeno and Mauricio Font (1995) (editors) *Toward a New Cuba? Legacies of a Revolution*, 1996; Ruth Behar and Juan Leon (editors) *Bridges to Cuba/Puentes a Cuba*; Mesa-Lago (1993) (editor) *Cuba After the Cold War*; Sandor Halebsky and John Kirk (1990) (editors) with Rafael Hernandez. *Transformation and Struggle: Cuba Faces the 1990s*; Dominguez and Hernandez 1989) (editors) *U.S.- Cuban Relations in the 1990s*; Irving Horowitz (1977) *Cuban Communism* (and revised editions since then); Rolando Bonachea and Nelson Valdes (1972) (editors) *Cuba in Revolution*.

5. All but one of the chapters were previously published as a special issue of *Global Development Studies*, Volume 1, numbers 3-4. Several of them have been minimally updated.

6. *United Nations Convention on the Elimination of All Forms of Discrimination Against Women (1999)* Fourth Periodic Report of Cuba, September 27. CEDAW/C/CUB/4 (in English or Spanish). Also, UNIFEM document *Perfil Estadística de la Mujer Cubana* (1999) La Habana: Oficina Nacional de Estadisticas and the Regional Office for Central America and the Caribbean of UNIFEM (Nations United for Women), February . For comparative observations see María Vigil López (1999) *Cuba, Neither Heaven nor Hell* (Washington, D.C.: Ecumenical Council of Central America and the Caribbean, EDICA).

7. In fairness to ourselves, we had solicited some other research about the religious revival among various branches of the Christian faith, but it did not materialize. We also have no article regarding a Jewish cultural revival, but can report from personal observation that the main synagogue in Vedado has taken on a new coat of paint and a new cultural life. Groups have traveled to the island from the U.S. in recent years to celebrate the traditional Passover Seder.

8. The Platt Amendment in 1902, which stated that the U.S. had the right to intervene at any moment it deemed necessary, was a bitter pill that Cubans had to swallow in order to have a nominally independent republic (Perez-Stable, 1994). Although several Cuban elite politicians themselves used the Platt Amendment until it was withdrawn in 1934, to urge U.S. intervention (on their side of an internal conflict), it is judged by most knowledgeable historians, e.g. Louis A. Perez, Jr. from the United States, and Cuban historians Jorge Ibarra Cuesta and Jose Antonio Tabares del Real that, by and large, the U.S.-imposition of troops at several junctures was resented greatly by Cubans in the first half of the twentieth century.

REFERENCES

Behar, Ruth and Juan Leon (1995) (editors) *Bridges to Cuba/Puentes a Cuba* (Ann Arbor, Michigan: University of Michigan Press).

Bengelsdorf, Carollee (1994) *The Problem of Democracy in Cuba: Between Vision and Reality* (New York: Oxford University Press).

Bonachea, Rolando and Nelson P. Valdés (1972) *Cuba in Revolution* (Garden City, New York: Anchor Books).

Centeno, Miguel and Mauricio Font (1996) (editors) *Toward a New Cuba? Legacies of a Revolution* (Boulder, Colorado: Lynne Rienner Publishers).

Dominguez, Jorge (1978) *Cuba: Order and Revolution* (Cambridge, Massachusetts: Harvard University (Belknap) Press).

Dominguez, Jorge and Rafael Hernandez (1989) (editors) *U.S.-Cuban Relations in the 1990s* (Boulder, Colorado: Westview Press).

Gunn, Gillian (1993) *Cuba in Transition: Options for U.S. Policy* (New York: Twentieth Century Policy Fund).

Halebsky, Sandor and John M. Kirk (1990) (editors) with Rafael Hernández. *Transformation and Struggle, Cuba Faces the 1990s* (New York: Praeger).

Horowitz, Irving Louis (1977) (editor) *Cuban Communism* (New Brunswick, New Jersey: Transaction Books) (and several revised editions 1984-1997).

López Vigil, María (1999) *Cuba, Neither Heaven Nor Hell* (Washington, D.C.: Ecumenical Council of Central America and the Caribbean, EDICA).

Mesa-Lago, Carmelo (1993) (editor) *Cuba After the Cold War* (Pittsburgh, Pennsylvania: University of Pittsburgh Press).

Paterson, Thomas G. (1994) *Contesting Castro. The United States and the Triumph of the Cuban Revolution* (New York: Oxford University Press).

Perez-Stable, Marifeli (1993) *The Cuban Revolution: Origins, Course and Legacy* (New York: Oxford University Press).

PART 1

CULTURAL ISSUES

2

The Self Emancipation of Women

Elvira Díaz Vallina and Julio César González Pagés

The historical roots of Cuban feminism were grounded in early complaints about the legal codes, and the authors report on a few of the voices of intellectual women who complained or acted for themselves in the nineteenth century through their first organized expressions in the early decades of the twentieth century. Concentrating on the role of women in the insurrection and the revolutionary process before and after the triumph of January 1959, the chapter discusses the potential threats posed by the current economic and social crisis to the great gains that women have achieved. The painful re-emergence of prostitution, its causes, and aspects of its dimensions as a social problem are discussed.

1. An Historical Sketch of Women's Emancipation in Cuba

The public and private lives of nineteenth century women help us to understand how and when Cuban men and women assimilated a set of ideas characterized as feminism. Throughout the nineteenth century, the paradigm of the saintly woman was restricted to maternal, marital, and domestic roles. Women were presented as if they were far removed from anything that deviated from the notion fostered by the "beautiful sex" or "weak sex." Nevertheless, questioning the value system imposed by men turned women into a subject of controversy in some intellectual circles which were forced to define criteria concerning education for women, marriage, the rights of children born out of marriage, and some measure of protection for working women.[1]

By the end of the first stage of the War for Independence (1868-78) many of the previously constructed female archetypes had become obsolete. Violence, starvation, and emigration contributed to changes in the ethereal-romantic ideal that had flourished during the 1850s and 1860s. Gertrudis Gómez de Avellaneda was a literary pioneer of the liberal female avant-garde. In the 1870s the views about special education for women allowed for a much faster assimilation of feminist ideas. The *escuelas para señoritas* (schools for young ladies) brought to public attention teachers such as Dora Galarraga and, above all, María Luisa Dolz, who incorporated in her school secondary education as a compulsory requirement for the enrollment of women in universities.[2]

Another influential element in the assimilation of feminism was the emigration of thousands of Cuban women to the United States and to Latin American republics, where they had to take on a double work shift: one at home and the other at the factory. Poems such as Luz Herrera's *El burgués de la casa*, which directly denounced the prevalent male chauvinism, were written at the time. The social, economic, and political involvement of emigrées was a crucial factor in changing the mentality of a huge sector of both female and male Cubans.[3]

The fact that Cuban women were able to preside over groups of women organized in clubs and carry out activities in favor of the future independent republic gave rise among them to a new vision of their own gender. The founding of more than one hundred women's clubs aimed at supporting the ideals of Cuban fighters for independence made it possible for women to be present in the public spaces where the future of the Island was being debated. The drafting of political speeches for patriotic meetings and women's economic contributions to the war effort were experiences that helped to strengthen their liberal ideas.

Thus the nineteenth century—mainly the 1890s—witnessed the emergence of the first feminist ideas in Cuba, which were voiced by women such as Elvira Martínez, Angela Landa, Martina Piedra Po, Fanny Galarraga, and Aurelia Castillo.[4] María Luisa Dolz wrote the most polemical female discourse of the decade: "*Feminismo injusticia de los códigos*" (Feminism, unfairness of the codes), published in around twenty different publications, among them the country's most widely read periodicals.[5] In an article entitled "*El movimiento feminista en Cuba,*" published in *El Fígaro* on May 1894, Cuban thinker Enrique José Varona acknowledged his astonishment. Varona admitted that the question had to be considered together with "very serious and respectable things such as, for instance, the Constitution, and the individual rights it guarantees or should guarantee."[6]

Throughout the nineteenth century, Cuban political movements used the image of the female body to express the principles of freedom and democracy, and as a symbol of individual rights. Yet this had only aesthetic implications: once the war and the U.S. intervention were over, the Constitution, which denied women the right to vote, was passed on February 21, 1901. Thus, women were disenfranchized from the new republic for which they had also fought. No wonder these same women, rejecting the male chauvinist notions of its first presidents, wrote hundreds of letters in which they asserted their rights, among other things, to public positions, voting, and compensations. This led to a rise in expectations around the question of women and to a considerable increase in the number of documents concerning feminism, legislation, and the right to vote.

The construction of United States-style Cuban nationalist ideals used the female work force as the bearer of its pedagogy through public education. This effort achieved a special momentum during the second U.S. intervention (1908) with its promotion of "modern ideas for women," which included training courses for thousands of Cuban teachers at Harvard University and the establishment of contacts with the Women's Club of Boston. Those contacts would influence the subsequent emergence of "U.S.-style" feminist organizations in Cuba.

There are some statistics concerning the gradual enrollment of women in universities during the first fifteen years of the twentieth century. During that period seventy-five women passed the entrance tests and 189 graduated in several specialties. Similarly, the number of female teachers increased to 4,244, representing 82 percent of all teachers in the country. The first suffragist organizations were founded during this same period. Many of their members were teachers, and Amalia Mallén de Oztolaza presided over the first three of them: *Partido Nacional Feminista* (Feminist National Party-1912), *Partido Sufragista* (Suffragist Party-1913) and *Partido Nacional Sufragista* (Suffragist National Party-1913).[7] These organizations centered their activism on the question of the right to vote, and their members came mainly from the middle-class urban sectors in Havana.[8]

The 1910s proved decisive in the change of female archetypes. On the one hand, World War I and its so-called "promotion of the female sector" and, on the other hand, the U.S. influence in the area of mores (dance, literature, dress codes) widened the range of expectations for middle-class and petit-bourgeois Cuban women. Domestic and marital roles lost some of their previous rigidity.

The passing of two important laws, the *Ley de Patria Potestad* (Law on the Rights of Parents) in 1917 and the *Ley del Divorcio* (Divorce Law) in 1918 signaled a boom in liberal feminism in Cuba. In 1918 women organized the *Club Femenino*, an organization that included among its members protagonists of the feminist debates of the 1920s. Women like Pilar Morlor de Menéndez, Pilar Jorge Tella, Mari Blanca Sabas Alomá, Ofelia Domínguez and Hortensia Lamar helped change the dynamics of journalism concerning women's subjects and focused on the concerns of working women, women prisoners, and other marginal female sectors.[9]   However, the members of the Club were always women from the intellectual elites who, as part of an educational endeavor, established contacts with the less privileged sectors.[10]

Its activism led the *Club Femenino* to establish in 1921 a *Federación Nacional de Asociaciones Femeninas de Cuba* (National Federation of Cuban Female Associations). The Federation held its First National Congress of Women, the first of its kind in Latin America. Topics of the Congress ranged from female gardening to such polemical subjects as the difference between legitimate and illegitimate children, the need to achieve equality between men and women in legislation on adultery, and the inevitable question of the right to vote. A second congress was held in April 1925; but if the first one had fostered unity among women, the second one did exactly the opposite. The Catholic Church, represented by several "ghost" organizations, boycotted the debates of the more polemical subjects and forced the *Club Femenino* to leave the sessions.[11]

The contradictions deepened during Gerardo Machado's administrations (1925-1933), since the right of women to vote became one of the populist slogans of his campaign. Thus feminists and suffragists became divided.[12]   The conflicts between Pilar Morlor and María Collado, leaders of the opposing sides, were used by the conservative press to try to prove that women were not yet mature enough to become full citizens and, consequently, to vote.

Other women's organizations were founded at this time, such as the *Lyceum de la Habana* (Havana Lyceum), which focused on culture and education; the *Unión Laborista de Mujeres* (Women's Labor Union), for working women; and political organizations like the *Unión Radical de Mujeres* (Women's Radical Union) and the infamous *Porra Femenina* (Women's Gang).[13]   By 1930, there were 320 legally registered women's organizations.[14]

On January 1934, during Ramón Grau San Martín's transitional administration, which followed Machado's overthrow, article thirty-nine on women's right to vote was finally passed.[15]   Paradoxically, after so many years of struggle for the constitutional acknowledgment of their rights, many of the feminists and suffragists who had been involved in the process were in exile, and others had died. The rest knew that this meant only the beginning of the legal battle for equality.[16]

The changed balance of forces, which favored the Left after the 1933 revolutionary movement, was reflected by the Third National Congress of Women which was held in April 1939. This congress signaled a shift from the liberal feminism of the 1920s. The greater part of the demands that had been previously posed had already been achieved: divorce, joint custody of children, the ballot, laws for working women, and a maternity law. What was still missing? That these laws would be effectively put into practice. The congress also discussed other subjects, such as the specific problems of young women, women and social laws, women and peace, women and the legal codes, and women and children. Other events taking place on a global scale, such as the conflicts that preceded World War II, the lack of protection for children and trade-union membership for women, were also given high priority. The presence of black delegates, headed by Inocencia Valdés, was an important feature of this congress, the last of its kind to be held during the republic.[17]

Echoes of the congress were felt in the conquests women achieved in the progressive 1940 Constitution. Many of the issues women had been struggling for were acknowledged in the new constitution. For instance, its fourth title established the equality of all citizens regardless of race, class or sex; and its fifth title dealt with family issues. Article forty-three consecrated the right of married women to administer their property, freely engage in trade, industry, a profession, or the arts, as well as to make use of all profits derived from their work without the need for spousal license or consent. The sixth title, which dealt with the issues of work and property, regulated the maternity rights of working women and extended them to all female employees. Additionally, no differences were established between single and married women concerning work.[18]

Nevertheless, some conservative sectors forcefully expressed their concerns: what else did women want? Did they want to rule the country? In fact, since 1936 women had been eligible to hold public positions. Between 1934 and 1944, women were elected to the following offices: two senators, three mayors, fifteen representatives, and two alderpersons. Women like María Gómez Carbonell, María Teresa Arrieta, María Antonia Quintana, and Esperanza Sánchez Mastrapa led successful political careers.[19] Even if their visions were very close to those of their male predecessors, they took a first step on the road to a wider social representation.

By the early 1950s feminism in Cuba, and in many other places, had stopped being "news," and women's reality became fused with a great deal of other questions. For women the end of World War II had meant a "return to the home" and the "American way of life," including the glorified role of the housewife. The more than eight hundred feminist and feminine associations then existing on the Island had branched into very different agendas. The golden age of liberal feminism, the Club Femenino, the women's congresses, and leftist feminism searching for a space was coming to an end.

General Fulgencio Batista's coup d'etat in 1952 inaugurated a new stage of confrontation for Cuban women. Again, as was the case during the wars for independence, women were asked to sacrifice their aims for a higher cause. It was not a struggle for gender demands, but one against dictatorship and in favor of an imagined revolutionary utopia. Old fighters from the 1930s and many young women from the 1950s joined revolutionary groups, such as the Federation of University Students, the 26th of July Movement, the National Revolutionary Movement, and the Revolutionary Directorate. Most of them were not in leadership positions. Only strong personalities such as Haydee Santamaría, Melba Hernández, and Vilma Espín, among others, were invisible in the media.

Few women's revolutionary organizations emerged in the period from 1952 to 1958. The most outstanding ones were the Civic Front of Women, inspired by José Martí,[20] and United Women of the Opposition.[21] Neither fought for specific gender demands: their priority was the overthrow of the Batista regime. *Frente Cívico*, a heterogeneous organization, was headed by well-known women, such as Carmen Castro Porta, Aida Pelayo, Olga Román, Rosita Mier, Maruja Iglesias, and Naty Revuelta. They appropriated Martí's ideals as their political discourse and participated in a great deal of the decade's revolutionary actions. In a letter dated September 1955, Fidel Castro suggested that they could become the women's branch of the 26th of July Movement, although this never materialized.[22] *Mujeres Oposicionistas Unidas* grouped well-known women members of the Popular Socialist Party, such as Clementina Serra, Esther Noriega, Zoila Lapique, Nila Ortega, and Marthe Fraide, its president. The prevalence of leftist women in its ranks, together with other contradictions, made other sectors, among them *Frente Cívico*, reject this organization.

The participation of women in the political actions that culminated in the 1959 revolutionary triumph included their joining the *Ejército Rebelde* (Rebel Army). On September 4, 1958 a platoon of women soldiers was organized in the *Sierra Maestra*; it was named after Mariana Grajales, a nineteenth century Cuban heroine, and was commanded up to the end of the armed struggle by officers Isabel Rielo and Teté Puebla.[23] In January 1959 there were more than 920 women's organizations in the country.[24] The revolutionary project demanded the unity of all sectors into a few like-minded organizations, which led to the founding of the Federation of Cuban Women, an organization in which the masses of women on the Island have participated for almost forty years.

2. Women and the Legal Codes in a Different Cuba, 1959-1998

On January 1, 1959, the Cuban Revolution came to power. Fulgencio Batista's overthrow had been bought dearly—after seven years of struggle, a heroic period in which women and men were equal in their willingness to accept all sacrifices, organizational and leadership responsibilities. The revolutionary government that seized power in 1959 had both the awareness and the political will to ensure respect for the equal rights of women. This would be possible only through changes in the societal structures and the building of a new social vision of justice. However, women had been forced to carry on a difficult and prolonged fight on another front as well, that of ideology, in order to transform conservative beliefs, habits and values concerning the traditional role of submission that women had been assigned by society and culture over the centuries. This battle is not yet over.

A review of present-day Cuban legislation allows us to understand objectively the achievements women have been able to make in their prolonged struggle for equal rights and to evaluate the degree to which these achievements have materialized during the revolutionary period.[25]

The Constitution of the Republic of Cuba passed in 1992 sanctioned all the principles consecrated by the 1976 Constitution in the field of women's rights and states that: (1) every man or woman who is able to work is entitled to the opportunity to find useful employment; (2) the state protects the family, as well as motherhood and marriage; (3) discrimination due to race, skin color, sex, national origin, religious beliefs, or any other consideration that diminishes human dignity is forbidden and punishable by law; and (4) all citizens, regardless of their race, skin color, sex, religious beliefs, national origin or any other consideration that diminishes human dignity, should have access to (a) all state and public administration positions, as well as employment in the areas of production and services, and that the only factors to be taken into account in this respect should be those deriving from merit and ability; (b) all ranks of the *Fuerzas Armadas Revolucionarias* (Revolutionary Armed Forces) as well as of the internal security and law and order bodies; (c) equal pay for equal work; (d) men and women enjoy equal rights in the economic, political, cultural, social and familial fields; (e) adult men and women have a right to free education; (f) everyone is entitled to be provided with free health care and protection; and (g) Cuban citizens, both men and women, who enjoy full political rights can be elected. They must be over 18 in the case of elections for membership to the *Asamblea Nacional del Poder Popular* or the People's Power National Assembly (Cuba's national congressional body-Editors).[26]

Other juridical regulations, laws, and codes complement these constitutional principles and guarantee that they are put into practice. For instance, the Social Security Law establishes that working women over fifty-five may retire after twenty-five years of work, although in cases of total disability they may retire at forty-six after only ten years on the job.[27] The constitution explicitly and implicitly reiterates that the protection of women and motherhood is compulsory. Consequently, the Work Code and the Maternity Law stipulate that not just pregnant women, but also those who want to bear children should not be employed in activities or jobs that may affect their reproductive system or the normal development of pregnancy.[28]

The Maternity Law establishes the right to eighteen weeks of paid maternity leave, twelve of them to be enjoyed after the delivery, and an additional two more weeks in the cases of multiple pregnancies or error concerning the delivery date. It also guarantees a non-paid additional leave when the mother is prevented from resuming her job because of the need to care for the baby—she maintains her right to return to her job after this leave.

Special mention should be made of the revolutionary laws designed to protect single mothers: the Constitution of the Republic, the Family Code and the Civil Marital Status Registration Law.[29] A single mother has the right, among others, of stating at the maternity ward to a marital status registration official the name of the father of her child. With the voluntary or compulsory (through a trial) admission of parenthood the father acquires the obligation of fulfilling his moral rights to contribute towards the child's economic well-being. If the father is absent or economically unable to fulfill said obligations, the state, through its welfare services, protects the mother and gives her child priority for enrollment in a day-care center, even if the mother is not a working woman.

The Civil Code protects Cuban women irrespective of their marital status in the areas of property, obligations and contracts, specifically with respect to property acquired and transmitted by law.[30] The Family Code benefits married women, single women involved in common-law marriages, widows and divorced women as follows: common-law marriages can be retroactively legalized, provided the couple agrees to do so, through the testimony of witnesses before a civil-registration official or a public notary. This retroactive formalization can also be effected by a single or divorced woman, or a widow, by presenting her witnesses before a competent court. Thus women in the above-mentioned situations enjoy all the rights accorded to married women by the Civil Code.

Concerning the rights and duties of married women, the Family Code proclaims the absolute equality of both spouses, a principle which entails the juridical elimination of all vestiges of subordination of the wife with respect to the husband. The code further establishes that if the woman happens to be a housewife and only the husband contributes to the economic needs of the family, the work she does is comparable to her husband's paid job, since domestic work contributes to the reproduction of the family. The provision was designed to support the rights of women who have historically been burdened with domestic chores and the care of children, an anonymous and arduous job men (very early) fled from in order to get involved in the more enriching and transcendent public spaces. It was during the process of social and cultural structuring of the genders, under male supremacy, that roles were assigned to each and that the enslavement of women to household duties was consecrated. The equivalency of a wife's work carried out in private spaces with that of the wage-earner husband is in present-day Cuba a juridical and ethical principle, but the need to advance its understanding and full implementation is still present.

Cuban women have massively joined the labor force since the early stages of the revolution; but they are still burdened by the responsibility of household chores, which implies that they engage in a double work shift. This has been worsened by the economic blockade the country is subjected to, as well as by the collapse of the Soviet bloc. The serious economic difficulties the Cuban people face have turned both social work and obtaining the resources for everyday life into strenuous tasks—this is especially true for women who are still responsible for day-to-day subsistence.

If a woman works or studies, her husband is required by law to share equally the chores and family responsibilities; unfortunately, this seldom occurs. The shaping of an awareness concerning the equality of the genders is a duty for public institutions, mothers, and wives.

Concerning economic issues, the Family Code establishes that the wife, as well as the husband, keeps the ownership of all property acquired before marriage as well as of that bought afterwards with her own money. Both spouses should administer all property jointly acquired during the marriage. In case of separation or divorce, common property is equally divided between both spouses or among the surviving spouse and the heirs of the deceased one. But if there are under-age children, some common property that may be deemed necessary for their education and well-being is assigned to the spouse—usually the mother—who retains custody. There are special legal provisions for divorced women who do not hold paying jobs—the former husbands are required to pay provisional alimony for a period of six months during which she must look for employment.

Lastly, on the subject of women and the law in Cuba, it should be pointed out that the penal code considers rape, statutory rape, and illicit abortion crimes against the female sex. The law states that rape and statutory rape do not damage either the honor or the modesty of women, but that they are, in fact, crimes against the well-being of society and the family. Illicit abortion is regarded as a crime against life itself. It has also been established that marriage does not exempt from punishment the spouse who physically assaults the other member of the couple, a provision aimed basically at the protection of women, the usual victims. The Cuban penal code also establishes that pimping, sexual enslavement and sexual offenses—activities that usually affect women—are crimes.

The Cuban code does not typify violence within the family as a separate kind of criminal conduct, the way other legislation on the continent does. Due to social, cultural, and historical reasons, domestic physical violence, although not unheard of, is considered to be rare in Cuban families. This helps explain why this crime has not been reflected as such in the penal laws, or the fact that shelters for battered women have not been created, or that statistics are not kept. At present, some lawyers are analyzing legal alternatives for the question of domestic violence.

To summarize, from January 1, 1959, the laws passed by the revolutionary government have had a deep popular content and have benefitted women both implicitly and, on many occasions, explicitly. Among many others, three of them, namely the laws that guarantee the right of both sexes to work, literacy and a free education, have opened to women public spaces traditionally reserved for men.

3. Liberating the Achievements of Women

Women's participation in the labor force is a striking reality. Statistics for 1996 show that out of a population of roughly eleven million (10,963,000), 42.3 percent of all civilian workers employed by the state were women, 65 percent of all technicians, 54 percent of all workers employed in the service sector, 85 percent of the administrative employees, 70 percent of the technical workforce involved in education, and 43 percent of all scientists were women.[31] These figures clearly denote the dramatic quantitative and qualitative changes Cuban women have experienced as a result of the process of emancipation from the gender stereotypes that previously subjected them. They have contributed to the country's development and, with their formidable presence, they have built, together with Cuban men, the nation's possibilities for the future.

It should be further emphasized that the social presence women have achieved has been at the expense of tremendous personal effort implied by shouldering a double work shift, since they have lacked the necessary support from their families in household chores. This has been an obstacle throughout the whole period for their cultural development and for a larger presence of women in leadership and key decision-making positions.

Special mention has to be made, when speaking of the struggle for equality, of the role played by the *Federación de Mujeres Cubanas* (FMC). This organization was founded in 1960, the result of a conscious expression of unity among women in different sectors. In its first congress held in 1962, the FMC stated that its basic goal was to "increase the ideological, political, cultural and scientific level of women so that they could massively join the process of building a new life."[32] If one takes into consideration the above-mentioned figures, it is easy to understand that the goal has been achieved. The statistics embody a feat carried out by women, based on a political will consistently nurtured and channeled by the systematic work of the FMC throughout its forty years. Nevertheless, social awareness about the full equality of women has proved more difficult. What one finds in this area is slow growth and occasional steps backwards.

One of the most important services provided by the FMC to Cuban women has been the establishment of a network of day-care centers, which guarantee the education and general care of the sons and daughters of working women. Thanks to day-care centers women have been able to join the gigantic tasks implied in the transformation of Cuban society. The FMC has implemented numerous initiatives aimed at supporting women's development. It has also carried out a great deal of research in order to substantiate proposals aimed at obtaining greater achievements.

The improvement in the life of women is clearly illustrated by their involvement in education. One has to remember that prior to the revolutionary triumph there were one million illiterate persons, six hundred thousand children deprived of schooling, and ten thousand unemployed teachers in Cuba. No wonder the revolutionary government immediately set itself to the task of reforming the educational system through the nationalization of private schools and the implementation of the 1961 literacy campaign. Women amounted to 59 percent of teachers and 55 percent of students in the literacy campaign, which meant that their participation was decisive in the heroic battle to end illiteracy in the country. Schools were built in the remotest corners of the island and an intensive training plan for teachers was organized. The enrollment of women was again very significant.

Three decades have elapsed in this continuous effort. In 1996 48.7 percent of all students in the country were women who enrolled in all levels of education from pre-school facilities to high schools and universities, including adult education.[33] In the forty-six higher education centers in the country, out of a total enrollment of 134,101 students, 58.55 percent were women.[34] Women have practically achieved equality in the educational field at large, and their numbers have surpassed those of men in higher education.

Of the utmost importance for women is the vast health system set up by the Cuban government aimed at providing free heath care to the entire population. Its sub-system devoted to women and newborns has saved the lives of thousands of mothers and of women, thanks to programs for the early diagnosis of breast cancer and cancer of the cervix and uterus. Approximately 96 percent of these cancers have been diagnosed at an early stage, thus leading to a very high rate of cure.

Another great ambition of Cuban women has been fulfilled: the safe birth of their children. One has to consider that in the five-year period from 1990 to 1995 infant mortality in Latin America was 41 per 1000 live births; in Cuba in 1995 the rate was already 9.4 per 1000 live births; this rate was further reduced to 7.2 per 1000 live births in 1997. These figures, similar to those achieved in developed countries, are a veritable feat of the Cuban men and women who practice medicine in a poor and blockaded country, marked by almost constant and universal scarcity. The U.S. embargo policy obstructed the normal flow of medicines, nutritional supplements, medical equipment, spare parts, disposable material for the care of children and for the population at large.

Another chapter in the prolonged struggle of women for equal rights relates to parity with men in the area of leadership and decision-making positions. After the revolution came to power important goals have been met, but the equal promotion of men and women to these positions is far from achieved. The road is open for the struggle in favor of one-to-one representation; that is, one man-one woman in key positions. In 1996 Cuban women were 29 percent of the leaders in the country; that is, less than a third of all persons in leadership positions, a much smaller proportion than that of women in the professional and technical ranks (64.6 percent).

Subjective factors such as the under-valuation dictated by prejudice, paternalism and self-limitation, still hinder the advance of women in spite of their active participation in the society's development. Objective factors also have a bearing on the problem, especially since the beginning of the "special period" during which material scarcities greatly increased. Electrical power black-outs and brown-outs, the breakdown of the transportation system, the scarcity of food, personal hygiene and cleaning products have made everyday life very difficult for women.

In statistical terms the presence of women in political and administrative leadership positions has been as follows: (1) In state ministries only two women hold posts as ministers, which amounts to 6 percent of the ministerial positions. Women deputy ministers have fluctuated between 5 percent and 9 percent. In 1996 there were seventeen female deputy ministers; (2) Fourteen Cuban women are ambassadors or heads of diplomatic missions, eleven are consuls and 133 hold other posts in the diplomatic corps; (3) Only 10.5 percent of the top positions in the Sugar Ministry are held by women, and only five are sugar-mill administrators; and (4) In the *Ministerio de la Industria Básica* (Ministry for Basic Industry) 12.9 percent of the top positions are held by women, while in the agricultural sector the portion is 11.6 percent, and in the cooperative sector 14.4 percent. In the elections for the Cuban Parliament held in January 1998, 27.6 percent of those elected were women, while for provincial assemblies the proportion was 28.61 percent.

When one analyzes the social participation of women in the country's history, one easily understands the essential roles they have played. But when one compares this role with the presence of women in leadership positions, it becomes obvious that Cuban women are far from achieving equality despite their achievements in the cultural, scientific, and juridical fields.

The economic embargo this small island has been subjected to by the most powerful country in the world has had several social outcomes. One of the most painful consequences of the scarcities experienced in the country during the "special period" has been the rebirth of prostitution, which had practically disappeared since the early stages of the revolution.

Who are the women engaged in this behavior? They are women who, faced with the economic crisis in the 1990s, have receded into the heart of alienation by selling their favors and companionship to foreigners for a few dollars. Those who visit Cuba and use their dollars for the favors of young women are making very opportunistic decisions to take advantage of people who are seeking to meet the needs of everyday life. The revolutionary government is unable to provide even basic needs and the country has many material scarcities, in part due to the brutal nature of the U.S. embargo.

In the Cuban Penal Code prostitution—a primarily female activity—is typified as a pre-criminal activity, an anti-social behavior that hurts the dignity of the person who practices it and impairs normal sexual relations and the family. This means that it is not typified as a crime since it is difficult and very hard to prove.

Pre-revolutionary prostitution was eliminated through the economic and social transformation that took place during the initial stages of the revolutionary process. The true implementation of the right to work, free education, and healthcare established the framework for the elimination of this ominous practice. On the other hand, the closing of bordellos, the care accorded to prostitutes' children, and disciplinary measures ranging from the internment of prostitutes in agricultural farms to prison sentences led to the gradual elimination of prostitution, which had previously been practiced by approximately 100,000 women out of a total population of six million in 1959.[35] It should be stressed that the majority of the women involved participated in the consensus brought about by the revolutionary triumph and also feared the open rejection of prostitution prevalent in the popular sectors of the population; thus, they voluntarily joined this process of social re-integration.

The re-emergence of prostitution precisely when the country is undergoing the most serious economic crisis of its history should make everyone think about its causes.[36] In fact, revolutionary processes which involve social transformation in order to achieve a new and more just society demand a change not only of the material and objective world, but also a transformation of the spiritual world, both collectively and individually. All those who have studied prostitution—among them Karl Marx in *Capital*—agree that the basic cause of its cyclical booms at a global level is economic depression. Cuba is undergoing such a depression. The economic crisis since 1990 has resulted in a sharp decrease of the population's well-being and has visibly affected certain values, which further deteriorated due to some measures the country was forced to implement in order to face the crisis.[37] These measures, which indirectly conditioned the emergence of prostitution, are the following: (a) the opening to foreign tourism and investments; (b) the free circulation of dollars within the Cuban economy; and (c) the establishment of market mechanisms. These measures, together with others, constitute the so-called emergent economy, aimed at stopping the ever-worsening economic crisis of the 1990s and saving the country, while attempting to maintain the revolution's great achievements such as free education and health, and a comprehensive social security system. Nevertheless, these new economic measures have generated social inequalities and unwanted effects that include the re-emergence of prostitution. Cuba attempts to fight prostitution through control and prevention, discretionary police warnings, and records for those who "stand out."[38] The measures designed to fight this new kind of prostitution are aimed at curbing its growth. However, it is obvious that it will disappear only as a result of the economic and spiritual advancement of the bulk of society and of each individual man and woman.

4. Conclusion

Despite the temporary crisis and the painful consideration of the re-emergence of prostitution in the economic crisis, the longer view of the achievements of Cuban women is an inspiring one. The statistics for educational and occupational advancement are coupled with a record of free and accessible health care for all Cuban women and their families. It is, taken as a whole, a glorious achievement from the 1950s to the end of the 1990s: fifty years of significant social changes by and for women. The self-emancipation of Cuban women is a reality that resulted from a prolonged and ongoing process of struggle. Fortunately, the struggle for women's rights was able to develop under favorable conditions due to the revolutionary government's political will and the steadfast work of women organizers at all levels of society.

ENDNOTES

1. Raquel Vinet de la Mata's preliminary research results about 1898 have brought us a new vision of women who were not Mambises. See "Cuban Women from 1895 to 1898," a discussion of the research (as of) 1996, available at the Institute of Cuban History, dated February 18, 1997.

2. The college of Maria Luisa Dolz was converted into the First Institute for Secondary Teaching in 1895. An important publication, *El Pais*, saluted the initiation of a new educational epoch for women: "The era is beginning when the doors of academies and universities will open to women who can cease to be a victim of ignorance." Seven Cuban women obtained university degrees in the two last decades of the nineteenth Century. They are Asuncion Menendez, Maria Pimentel, and Mercedes Rivas y Pinos in Pharmacy; Digna America del Sol in Natural Sciences and Pharmacy; Francisca Rojas y Sabater in Civil and Religious Law; Laura Mestre y Carvajal in Medicine and Natural Sciences; and Maria Luisa Dolz in Natural and Physical Sciences. Cuban National Archives, fondo Donativos y Remisiones, Box 68, Fo. 96.

3. This poem appears in a general analysis of patriotic emigration by Cuban women. See Estrada, Paul, "Los Clubes Femeninos en el Partido Revolucionario Cubano [Women's Clubs in the Cuban Revolutionary Party] (1892-1898)," in the *Anuario del Centro de Estudios Martianos*, Number 10, 1897, p. 191.

4. This speech circulated in the form of a pamphlet sent out by Dolz and other figures interested in feminist or women's issues. See the Prologue by Fernando Portuondo to "Maria Luis Dolz: La Liberacion de la Mujer Cubana por la Educacion [the Liberation of Cuban Women by education]" Office of the Historian of the City of Havana, Municipality of Havana, 1955, p. 15. We are grateful to Dania de la Cruz, a researcher at the Cuban National Archives, for calling to our attention the personality of Maria Luisa Dolz and for making available a copy of her biography. See de la Cruz, Dania, Marcos Arriaga Mesa and others, "Maria Luisa Dolz, Documents for the study of her teaching and social work." Havana: Editorial Academica, 1990.

5. The speech was reviewed by *Diario de la Marina, El Pais, El Figaro, El Eco de Gallicia, La Gimnastica, Las Avispas, La Lucha, Revista Blanca, La Discusion, Diario de la Familia, Cronica Habanera* and nine other publications. Cuban National Archives, Fondos Donativos y Remisiones. Box 428, Number 3-a.

6. Reflections about feminism formed a part and was a theme at the center of many debates in the extensive works of Enrique Jose Varona. See Varona, Enrique Jose: "El Movimiento Feminista en Cuba," in the Cuban National Archives, Fondos Donativos y Remisiones. Box 428, Number 3-a.

7. For a commentary about the suffrage organization in Cuba, see, Gonzalez, Julio Cesar, "El Voto Femenino en Cuba," presented to the event "Mujeres en los umbrales del Siglo XXI [Women at the Threshold of the 21st Century]," University of Havana, November 1995.

8. A logical comparison by theme, year and gender of this bibliography can be obtained to analyze the collections that exist about women in Cuba. See de la Cruz, Dania, *Movimiento Femenino Cubano*. Havana: Editora Politica, 1980; also Fernandez Robaina, Tomas, *Bibliography of Cuban Women*. Havana: Biblioteca Nacional de Cuba, 1985.

9. University professor Marial Iglesias has studied the theme of nationalism and public education. See Iglesias, Marial, "El Nacionalismo en Cuba 1895-1908," presented during the program "Debates in the Social Sciences," University of Havana, January 1997, in press.

10. For a general picture of the education of Cuban women in the first decade of the 20th Century, see Caraballo Sotolongo, F, *Mujeres !A las Urnas! [Women! Out to the Ballot Box!]*. Havana: Cervantes Books. Galiano 62, 1918, Chapters VII and VIII, pp. 173-216.

11. See Cuban National Archives, Fondo: Registro de Asociaciones. Leg. 346, 11299; Leg. 300, 8677; Leg. 400, 11886; and Leg. 305, 8882.

12. These reflections are part of the analysis by this chapter's author (Gonzalez) for his doctoral dissertation on the theme of women's suffrage in Cuba in the nineteenth and twentieth centuries.

13. Pichardo, Hortensia, "Liberacion de la Mujer," in *Documents for the History of Cuba*, Volume II. Havana: Ciencias Sociales, 1973.

14. We have not found a study of this organization, however, more information is to be found in the Information Center of the Federation of Cuban Women, and in the Cuban National Archives, Fondo: Registro de Asociaciones. Leg. 299, 8644.

15. See Cuban National Archives, Fondo: Registro de Asociaciones.

16. Ibid.

17. See material cited in note 6.

18. Pichado, Hortensia, "La Constitucion de 1940 es un camino y no una meta" [The Constitution of 1940 is a pathway and not a goal] in *Documents for the History of Cuba, Volume IV*, part 2, pp. 327-418. Havana: Ciencias Sociales, 1973, 411.316. See also, Funes, Reynaldo, "Cuba Republica y democratica, 1901-1940." Havana: 1915, in press.

19. See Cuban National Archives, Fondo: Registro de Asociaciones.

20. The author Gonzalez has interviewed many of the members of the organization, thanks to the work of Texidor Sabigne, author of an unpublished book, a history of *Women with History*. See Castro Porta, Carmen, Aida Pelayo and others, *La Leccion del Maestro*. Havana: Ciencias Sociales, 1990. See also Gonzalez, Julio Cesar, "La Lucha Revolucionaria de la Mujer Cubana," thesis of 1991, Library of the Faculty of Philosophy and History, University of Havana.

21. See Gonzalez, Julio Cesar, "Creacion de Mujeres Oposicionistas Unidas," in *La Republica Femenina*. Havana: Editora Abril, 1993, pp. 47-49.

22. Ibid., p. 46.

23. Ibid., pp. 78-89.

24. See Cuban National Archives, Fondo: Registro de Asociaciones.

25. Mesa del Castillo, Olga, "La Situacion Juridica de la Mujer en la Cuba de Hoy," [The juridical situation of women in Cuba today] paper presented to the Second International Meeting of Women, University of

Havana. The author teaches at the Faculty of Law and is President of the Cuban Society for Civil and Family Law of the National Union of Jurists.

26. Constitution of the Republic of Cuba, proclaimed February 24, 1976, and reformed by the National Assembly of People's Power in the Eleventh Ordinary Journal of Sessions by the Third Legislature, July 10-12, 1992. Both recognized the conquests that had been approved by the Constitution of 1940 but had not been implemented.

27. Law No. 24, August 24, 1979.

28. Law No. 49, December, 1984 (Code of Work) and Law No. 1263, January 14, 1984 (Law of Maternity Work and Leave).

29. Law No. 1289, February 14, 1975 (Family Code).

30. Law No. 59, July 16, 1987 (Civil Code).

31. Simeon, Rosa Elena, Minister of Science and Technology, speech to the opening session of the National Seminar on "Cuban Women from Beijing to 2000," July 5, 1996.

32. National Congress of the Federation of Cuban Women (FMC), Havana, 1962.

33. Center of Documentation of the Federation of Cuban Women (FMC).

34. Penate, Ana Isabel, "Feminization of the University of Havana," interview in the magazine, *Alma Mater*, April-June, 1997.

35. Center of Documentation of the Federation of Cuban Women (FMC).

36. Diaz Canal, Teresa and Graciela Gonzalez Olmedo, "Cultura y Prostitucion: una solucion posible," [Culture and Prostitution: a Possible Solution] en Papers 52, University of Barcelona, 1997.

37. Carranza, Julio, "Los Retos de la Economia," *Cuadernos de Nuestra America* [Notebooks of Our America], Volume IX, Number 19, 1992.

38. Teresa Diaz Canal and Graciela Gonzalez Olmedo, opus cited.

3

Women, Family and the Cuban Revolution: A Personal and Socio-political Analysis[1]

Marisela Fleites–Lear[2]

This chapter presents an analysis by a woman who was born, raised, and educated in Cuba after the revolution of 1959. The highlights of forty-one years of grand-scale social change and the psychological and familial impact on various generations of female members in one family are placed in the broader context of the revolutionary process. The chapter also takes into account the changes in the 1990s that now threaten to destroy the tremendous educational, professional, employment, and political participatory strides toward dignity by Cuban women. The legal codes enacted by the revolutionary state are examined in the context of the limitations of long-standing patterns of patriarchy and the absence of an independent women's movement to develop creative ways of challenging patriarchal norms. The chapter reveals both extensive social statistical results and a detailed personal experience.

One afternoon in the 1920s, the Tenerife civil guard came to look for my grandfather, Anselmo González. He was in big trouble for refusing to fight for the King of Spain in the African War. My grandmother Ernestina, seven months pregnant, watched as he slipped out the back door. Never knowing if Anselmo would return, she waited. The weeks turned to months, then years.

When the baby she was carrying (my Aunt Isolina) turned seven, Anselmo reappeared, telling stories of a "promised land" where white people were welcomed, a new republic rich with recent investment from the United States. With the money he had managed to save while he was away, the family pulled up stakes and moved to Cuba.

Ernestina and Anselmo established a homestead in Havana Province where they scraped out a rudimentary living by working the fields. Seven more children followed Isolina, but not one was able to attend a decent school. Their only education was from an itinerant teacher who offered lessons in exchange for milk and beans. During the Machado dictatorship, the family lived in constant fear of the Rural Guard, who were always threatening them for "contributions." Fed up, they moved to the big city, Havana.

When my mother was fourteen, the family bought a little *bodega* (corner store) in *Habana Vieja* (Old Havana). The sons helped in the store and the daughters worked, one as a telephone operator, another as a dressmaker; and the prettiest daughters got jobs as sales clerks in the fashionable department stores along Calle Neptuno. The family pooled their money and somehow survived, crowded together in quarters above the bodega.

Ernestina was a typical Spanish-Cuban woman of that day: Catholic, poor, illiterate. Her life was limited to the house, her children, and her husband. She had her babies at home and never went to the doctor. Ernestina accepted her lot without question or protest, as did the majority of peasant women in pre-revolutionary Cuba. Ernestina's youngest daughter Susana, my mother, was a beautiful, intelligent, and strong-willed young woman who learned easily and liked to read novels. Romantic and creative, she wrote naïve poems about love and castles. In 1956 she met the man who would become my father, a young doctor from a poor rural family who had just finished his studies at the University of Havana. After a year of courtship they married, and just nine months later, in 1958, my older brother was born. I was born in 1959, and my two younger brothers were born in 1962 and 1966, respectively.

When my mother was seven months pregnant with her first son, she stopped working as a sales clerk. In the Cuban tradition, my father told her that the house was her domain, and she accepted happily, ready to fulfill her role as wife and mother. My father had started a clinic in a working class neighborhood, a career move in keeping with his humanitarian ideals about the practice of medicine. Everything was going just right for my parents when, in 1959, the Revolution changed everything. My parents, never before involved in politics, but fully aware of the corruption and brutality of the Batista regime, readily supported the new leadership. My father joined with other doctors to set up free clinics in the Sierra Maestra Mountains, staying there for six months just after I was born.

As the revolutionary process became more radicalized, Cuban professionals were tempted by job opportunities abroad, and many opted to leave the island. My parents considered various factors—their social idealism, their nationalistic sentiments, their ties to family—before deciding to stay and raise their children within the Revolution. In the next few years nearly all their friends abandoned Cuba and my mother wondered if they had made the right decision.

The Revolution was not only a political and economic transformation of society as a whole, but a radical upheaval for the Cuban family as a social organism and for women in particular. Soon women like my mother found their roles and opportunities dramatically altered. The new social project, compounded by the influence of the sexual revolution in the western world, presented women and their families with difficult dilemmas. Suddenly, in the same homes where the preservation of virginity until marriage was seen as parents' sacred duty, parents were asked to let their daughters volunteer for agricultural brigades, where they would spend months living and working alongside young men. For the first time Cuban women, long accustomed to being dependent wives and dutiful mothers, were exploring the ideas of women's equality, a direct challenge to machismo.[3] It was a painful and paradoxical process.

Cuban women were incorporated into the intellectual, political and labor worlds as never before. Chapter VI, article 44, of the Constitution of the Republic, in its 1992 version, boldly declares:

> The State guarantees that women are offered the same opportuni-
> ties as men, with the goal of achieving their full participation in
> the country's development.
>
> The State organizes institutions such as day care centers,
> boarding and semi-boarding schools, homes for the elderly and
> services to facilitate the working family in the fulfillment of its
> responsibilities.
>
> Taking care of women's health and their healthy progeny, the
> State provides working women with maternity leave with pay,
> before and after birth, and some temporary labor options
> compatible with their maternal function...[4]

The *1995 Human Development Report* released by the United Nations Development Program recognized that Cuba leads the developing world in gender equality.[5] In the last forty years Cuba has implemented a gradual program to improve women's conditions. Our goal is to discuss here the contradictions that arose throughout this process of improving gender equality. In order to meet this objective, it is necessary to understand the gains achieved and their limitations. The figures give eloquent testimony to the success of Cuban policies toward women.[6]

(1) In 1981 about 50 percent of women between the ages of 25 and 44 were employed, a dramatic increase from the pre-revolutionary period when around 20 percent of women in this age group worked outside the home.[7]

(2) According to 1995 statistics, women comprise 40.6 percent of the Cuban labor force,[8] compared to only 15 percent prior to 1959.[9]

(3) In 1995 women constituted 57.7 percent of university graduates, 62 percent of middle and high-level technicians, and 42 percent of scientific researchers.[10] In the school year 1993-1994, of the 165,843 students enrolled in universities, 95,622 (57.6 percent) were women.[11]

(4) Since 1980, more than 12 percent of Cuban women above the age of 24 have earned college level degrees, compared with only 0.7 percent prior to 1959.[12]

(5) As reported by the United Nations Development Program (UNDP) in 1995, 48 percent of Cuban medical doctors were women,[13] as were 47 percent of hospital directors and 61 percent of the 12,000 general practitioners. This United Nations report states that these figures are "the result of a deliberate emphasis on sexual equality in educational policy..."[14] and finds that there is less discrimination against women in Cuba than in the majority of developing nations.

(6) Among the 589 members of the Cuban Parliament elected in 1993 (the National Assembly of the Organs of People's Power), 134 (23 percent) were women,[15] a figure that, though less than ideal, represents a significant advancement in a country where politics was virtually "men's affairs" before 1959. In comparison, in 1995 there were only seven women in the United States Senate and 47 women in the House of Representatives (7 percent and 10.8 percent, respectively). In the 1995 municipal elections for delegates to the municipal assemblies of the Organs of People's Power, 15.4 percent of the elected officials were women (that is, 2,144 women were elected at the municipal level).[16]

(7) By 1986 13.8 percent of Communist Party leaders were women.[17]

(8) Between 1984 and 1986, 38 percent of all Cuban women were members of the National Workers' Union (CTC), and 49.4 percent were members of the CDR (Committees for the Defense of the Revolution, a neighborhood social organization). In selective organizations, women were 21.5 percent of the members of the Communist Party, and 41 percent of *U Jota Ce*, the Communist Youth Union. In 1994 María Victoria was the first woman elected as the national leader of the UJC, a very important organization.

(9) Female athletes have enjoyed opportunities that would have been unthinkable before 1959. Cuban sportswomen and men enjoy equal support from the state and sporting events are free to the public, both factors that encourage large numbers of women to participate in athletics. Since 1960, for instance, Cuban women's volleyball, judo and track teams all have won international recognition. Names like Ana Fidelia Quirot, Liliana Allen, and the young archer Jacqueline Fernández have become models of Cuban athletes.[18]

Supporting these changes were the following elements:

(a) The availability of quality medical attention for all women and their children. The new health system drastically reduced the health problems families faced before the Revolution. Cuban women's life expectancy in 1995 reached 77.6 years, the highest in Latin America.[19] In 1993 the infant mortality rate in Cuba was 9.4 per 1000 births,[20] a rate on a par with the United States at (9 per 1000),[21] and in sharp contrast to the rates of Mexico (28 per 1000), Brazil (54 per 1000), and Haiti (87 per 1000).[22]

(b) Access to free education for every woman.

(c) The establishment of quality day-care centers, with access for all children regardless of race or social origin. This benefit gave women the option to stay in the workplace after starting families. In 1989, 136,000 children were receiving day care[23] in low cost centers subsidized by the state.[24]

(d) The founding of the Federation of Cuban Women (FMC) to advocate and organize on behalf of women (to be discussed later).

(e) The establishment, in 1975, of the "Family Code" advocating equal job opportunities and domestic responsibilities without regard to gender. For the most part this regulation has been successful, although until the Constitution was amended in 1992, there were jobs that, because of their physical demands, were not available to women (a paternalistic approach that, even if changed by law, persisted in people's minds).

(f) The creation of the Permanent Commission on Infancy, Youth, and Women's Equality of the National Assembly of People's Power (NAPP).

(g) The founding, in 1977, of the National Working Group on Sex Education (GNTES) within the NAPP. With many limitations, this group has been directing a massive sex education program to support the principle of sexual equality.

(h) The unprecedented decline of fertility rates, after an initial baby-boom in the 1960s, largely due to women's freedom to pursue education and careers. In 1971, for instance, the average number of children per woman in Cuba was 3.88, but just 10 years later, in 1981, the figure had dropped to 1.63.[25] Cuban fecundity in the 1990s is among the lowest in the world, with an annual population growth rate of roughly

10 per 1000 people.[26]   While developing nations struggle with rapid population growth, Cuba's demographic growth resembles that of developed countries.[27] Vilma Espín, the head of the Federation of Cuban Women, explained in the Fourth World Conference on Women (September 1995) that because of this decline in fertility rate, it has not been necessary to establish in Cuba an explicit demographic policy.[28]

The revolution also allowed for a positive sexual liberation for Cuban women. Several factors contributed to this phenomenon:

(a) The decline of the importance of the Catholic Church and its patriarchal values. Even though the Cuban population was never fanatically religious, conventional Catholic morality had weighed heavily on the socio–sexual behavior of pre-revolutionary Cuban women.[29]

(b) The increase in women's educational levels. In the first two years of the revolution, a nationwide literacy campaign raised the basic (first grade level) literacy rate from 75 percent to 96 percent.[30] This enlightened campaign, promoted through the media and supported by social and political organizations, was a precursor to free and mandatory education for all children through the 9th grade, and free night schools for adults. Subsidized publishing made books available to all. By 1988 the adult literacy rate had reached an astonishing 97 percent.[31]

(c) Not only did Cuban women learn to read and write, but in ever increasing numbers they pursued higher education, aspiring not just to "women's profes-sions"—teaching or nursing—but to fields traditionally dominated by men. By 1985, 28 percent of Cuban women were enrolled in higher education, compared with only 3 percent in 1960. The figures are similar to those in Argentina, Costa Rica, and other advanced Latin American countries, but as Francesca Miller points out, "... the critical difference in Cuba may be that young women are more likely to pursue studies in the hard sciences and technology."[32]

(d) The incorporation of women into social and mass organizations. Agricultural mobilization and political meetings allowed women to escape their parents, husbands, and "the mop and broom." In their new activities, women were valued not so much for their virginity or "decency" (in the traditional sense), but for their intelligence, diligence, and attitude as workers and students.

(e) The rejection of old values. The revolution, as the word implied, meant the radical turning around of all the previous structures. This subversion provoked a progressive transformation of the traditional idea of the *mujer virgen, mujer de su casa* (virgin woman, woman devoted to the home), especially for the younger generation. Changes were manifested not only in the attitudes of women but also in those of men, who began to consider virtues other than "purity" when looking for potential partners.[33]

Of course, not every woman took advantage of these changes. Many women of my mother's generation felt it was too late to change their lifestyles. My mother never went back to school or out to work; she stayed at home raising four children, as did most of her friends. However, she was one of my biggest influences to pursue ambitious goals in my intellectual life. She wanted me to have every opportunity she had been denied.

Women of my generation were given mixed messages; our mothers wanted us to behave according to the old Catholic mores, but at the same time encouraged us to take advantage of educational and cultural opportunities—the very things threatening those mores.

All of these new conditions set the stage for women to expect a better balance in their relationships with their husbands and lovers. Told they were equal, women rightfully looked to be respected and satisfied as individuals and not to subordinate their own needs to a relationship. For the first time, they had the option of breaking off an unsatisfactory relationship without stigma. However, the changes were filled with contradictions, and several paradoxes continue to affect women in Cuba.

Paradox One: While women gained the freedom to join the social process of the Revolution, this same freedom doubled (or tripled) their workloads.

The new jobs of women outside the home, their political work, or participation on committees did not automatically exempt them from traditional domestic tasks. Neither families nor the State was prepared to overcome the machismo that held the accepted patriarchal practices and structures in place. Women felt exploited in their own homes, while in their workplace and in political organizations little consideration was given to their family duties. The same revolutionary man who expounded on the equality of women at a 3:30 p.m. meeting would expect his *compañera* to have dinner ready at six. Such is the chasm between rhetoric and reality.

Cuban daily life has, for most of the last forty years, been extremely difficult and complex. While Cuba's economic woes are too complex to analyze here, the principle roots are: (1) the lack of essential natural resources, the most crucial being hydroelectric and petroleum; (2) the continuing United States economic embargo; (3) funneling of resources into military and civil defense spending ; (4)

inefficient systems of production and distribution; (5) increasing dependence on the CAME (Council of Mutual Economic Assistance, the socialist trade bloc) and less self sufficiency for basic foodstuffs and consumer products before 1989; and (6) with the collapse of the socialist trade bloc and the tightening of the U.S. embargo, the economic situation became desperate

Since 1991, the monthly ration of food and goods has steadily diminished, and as of 1997 lasted only 10-15 days. Cuban women have had to become "food-alchemists," making something from nothing; and the burden is probably four times higher than it was before the "special period" (after 1990). Without exaggeration, the same career/family balancing act requires three times the effort in Cuba today than in a developed country. For example, there are no disposable diapers. Cuban women have only a very short supply of fabric diapers, and they must be washed by hand (whether soap is available or not), disinfected by boiling, hung out to dry and then ironed.

Even if public opinion accepts frequent women's absences from work for family duties, their administrators and political organizers (often men) are not as sympathetic, which in practice (even if not established by law) imposes limits on certain jobs and leadership positions to women. In political and social organizations the problem is even more complicated because these activities presumably take place during women's "free time." To cope with all the demands on their time and energy, it is quite common for women to feign illness as a pretext to miss a mobilization or an internationalist mission.

The socialist state support of women and families is of undeniable importance. However, the State, so successful in encouraging women to get out of the house, has been unable to fully create the conditions that allow them to rest when they returned home. The fact that families have not been able to overcome machismo underscores how even the best intentioned educational programs and constitutional laws are not enough to change traditional human behavior, especially when the laws are not supported by a solid economic base, a non-patriarchal political system, and community structures in place to provide alternatives.

Paradox Two: While women gained sexual freedom, their family relation-ships became more unstable.

Increased freedom and mobility for women were accompanied by a secondary effect with negative ramifications; couples, both married and unmarried, were not staying together as long as they did in pre-revolutionary Cuba. Though statistics are hard to find regarding unmarried sexual partners, the figures on marriages and divorces demonstrate a marked increase in the divorce rate during this period:[34]

Roughly paralleling increases in population, both marriages and divorces increased steadily through the late 1960s. Then, in the 1970s, the number of marriages leveled off, but the divorce rate continued to rise, peaking in 1989. Interestingly, in the 1990s, the number of marriages rose again, while the divorce rate

Year	Marriages	Divorces	Divorce Rate
1956	29,094	2,818	9.70
1961	74,067	4,575	6.17
1966	48,664	9,696	19.92
1971	113,082	27,641	24.44
1985	80,193	29,182	36.38
1988	82,431	35,668	43.27
1989	85,535	37,647	44.01
1990	101,515	37,646	37.08
1991	162,020	43,646	26.93
1992	191,837	44,973	23.44

slightly declined, precisely in the years of great economic, political, and social crisis. It is possible that we are witnessing a phenomenon contrary to what happened in the 1980s, years of apparent stability and economic growth. It is, of course, premature to postulate a direct connection between the two trends, but it seems possible that the deep social crisis of the country is prompting young people to spontaneously return to the family and domestic stability as a refuge from "the street."

In response to the trend, organizations like the *U Jota Ce* (Union of Young Communists) started promoting stable domestic relationships through sex education programs that reinforced the family as a social institution, especially in the 1990s. The media[35] is also stressing the importance of stable relationships and sexual health, particularly in the prevention of sexually transmitted diseases, particularly AIDS.[36] These campaigns have also been stepped up in response to the increases in prostitution since the opening to tourism.[37] These are all part of larger social, economic, and political trends, beginning in 1990, as the revolutionary state struggles to adapt its structures to the global capitalist economy.

Certainly, the general trend throughout the first forty-one years of the revolution has been the decline in the stability of conjugal relationships.[38] It has been recognized that the average marriage lasts five years.[39] Other elements are very difficult to calculate—the systematic change in partners (especially among youth), and infidelity (in particular male, but also female)—which reflect the changing moral and sexual values within Cuban society.

There is another factor to consider in the analysis of this instability. In Latin American societies, where historically *caudillismo* (strongman leadership) has been especially prevalent, the way caudillos conducted their personal lives was seen as a pattern for the behavior of their followers. If we consider Fidel Castro not only as a political leader but also as a role model highly important to the formation of public opinion, it is important to note that he is a man without a family. He has embodied the archetype of the revolutionary, one who has placed society first, subjugating family and personal needs, justifying this as a necessary sacrifice for those who would attempt a social transformation on the scale of the Cuban Revolution. Consciously or not, his followers try to imitate him, many adopting his body language, his figures of speech, even his gestures. But Castro's archetype does not present a model of family unity or stability.

By the late 1970s some organizations were formed to create sex education programs, covering not only hygiene and family planning, but also promoting a new, more egalitarian and domestic partnership.[40] Despite good intentions, the programs have had limited resources and access to the younger generations. Well organized at the national level, the programs suffer from a lack of strong grassroots support. Since 1992, the Federation of Cuban Women (FMC) has been working on the gradual establishment of "Casas de la Mujer" (women's houses), neighborhood centers to build grassroots support for sex education and the discussion of women's issues. So far, the Casas have made little impact on the population at large.

To date, a new socialist family has not been realized in Cuba. It could be argued that Cuba is responding to the same trends in domestic instability found in the rest of the developed world. However, Cuba has a social system completely different from capitalist countries and, for that matter, distinct from the former socialist countries. Is it because the ideological and educational work has failed to change the daily interactions of the people? Or, is it because radically altering women's potentials outside the home has destabilized domestic partnerships? Is it also the case that any real challenge to patriarchy will require dominant men to relinquish power? It is safe to say that all of the above factors are true to a degree.

Paradox Three: Women gained freedom to participate in the political system on the one hand; but, on the other, they met continual barriers in creating their own organizations outside the system.

In the 1960s and 1970s, women in all parts of the western world were discovering feminism. Rich and poor, women of all races and ethnicities were reveling in their newly-found solidarity, attacking the existing power structures and organizing new ones. However, in Cuba even talking about some women's or more general gender issues—sexual harassment, domestic violence, homosexuality—was considered a taboo. The official Cuban organization for women took the position that we had no need for feminism since the revolution had made men and women equal by law.

People joined organizations because they felt they should, because it was expected of them, and not necessarily because they felt a real identification. This is more true in the case of the non-selective mass organizations (the women's federation, the FMC, the CDRs or Committees for the Defense of the Revolution and the CTC, the labor union federation) than in the selective political organizations, the UJC and the PCC (Cuban Communist Party). It is particularly true in the case of the FMC, *Federación de Mujeres Cubanas* (Cuban Women's Federation), which is a thoroughly official body. To quote the First Congress of the Cuban Communist Party in 1976:

> The Federation of Cuban Women, founded on August 23, 1960, through the unification of all the existing women's revolutionary organizations, has grown rapidly from a few thousand members, to 2,127,000 women workers, peasants, students, house-wives, professionals and members of FAR and MININT, and now comprises 80 percent of our female population over 14 years of age.[41]

On balance, the Federation of Cuban Women has been a positive force in improving women's lives. As a national organization, the FMC played the dominant role in organizing the Literacy Campaign of 1961 and instituted many social and rehabilitation programs to improve women's lives. The FMC created special schools to retrain former domestic servants for new employment and established programs to help prostitutes re-enter mainstream society.[42] Between 1960 and 1986, the FMC recruited over 58,000 women to work on hygiene brigades to improve rural sanitation and 13,000 women to serve as social workers. The FMC has been instrumental in encouraging women to pursue non-traditional work: in 1975, more than 20,000 women were working in construction brigades. In the same year Cuban women harvested 221 million arrobas[43] (2.7 million tons) of sugar cane. Vilma Espín, herself with a degree in chemical engineering, spearheaded the FMC's drive to integrate women into more technical fields. Rural women were encouraged to learn technical agricultural skills including tractor driving, specialized farming techniques, and animal husbandry. By 1986, 55.4 percent of Cuban technical workers were women. The FMC has also worked with older Cuban housewives to achieve a junior high school equivalency. Approximately 99,392 housewives had already obtained this level by 1986, and 18,048 were studying to achieve it.[44] In 1977 the FMC created the National Working Group on Sex Education (GNTES) to oversee the formulation and implementation of a massive sex education program with the goal of "establishing the individual's capacity for love, marriage, and the family on the principle of equality between the sexes."[45]

Undeniably, the FMC has accomplished much to benefit the lives of Cuban women. The fact that the FMC is an official arm of the Communist Party, admittedly a strength in terms of national organization and the establishment of policy, is, in other senses, precisely its weakness. However, the FMC is the only women's organization allowed, and all educational material and guidelines for discussion are published under the supervision of the Party. Therefore, real discussion and relevance on the local level are severely limited. Many young women feel that this organization, founded before they were born, cannot effectively give voice to their concerns.[46]

According to Cuban Law, no organization can be created for individuals outside the state and the party system, or at least not without the authorization of these institutions.[47] There is no forum for diversity or individual dissent. Without authorization, any meeting of more than three persons with political goals can be considered illegal and its participants subject to punishment. Vilma Espín's 1977 statement about feminism speaks volumes about the weakness of the FMC's ideological orthodoxy and its position as an institution of the state:

> ... we have never had a feminist movement. We hate that. We hate the feminist movement in the United States.... We see these movements in the United States which have conceived struggles for equality of women against men!.... That is absurd! It doesn't make any sense! For these feminists to say they are revolutionaries is ridiculous![48]

In more recent years, the FMC has adopted a more open-minded view about these issues, and hopefully that will become a political trend within the system.[49] Several academic seminars and conferences have been organized to discuss women's issues, like the Sixth Conference on Philosophy and Social Sciences at the University of Havana in June 1994. Eighteen papers were discussed with themes including, "The subordination of women within the Cuban family" and "Is there a sexual democracy in Cuba?" In 1994 the University of Havana established a Cátedra de la Mujer, a sort of Women Studies Program with links not only with national and international academia but also with the FMC. Since 1995, the existence of MAGIN was allowed, an association of women authors, artists, and journalists that focused on women's representation in the media; but it was denied an NGO status in 1997 and, therefore, it disappeared.

Paradox Four: The younger generation, women who grew up with the Revolution, gained new freedom and opportunities while women in middle age—their mothers and older sisters—felt somehow left behind.

While my mother's generation watched its daughters and younger sisters go off to schools, political meetings and volunteer work brigades, those women felt the revolution had come too late in their own lives. If it were not for the revolution, my mother probably would have been content in her role of wife and mother. For her, the social upheaval was very problematic, and in the end, she was not able to take full advantage of the opportunities offered by revolutionary power. As a wife and mother, she behaved according to the old paradigm and experienced the new paradigm vicariously through her children. She was stuck between past and present.

Nonetheless, my mother joined the CDR (Committee for the Defense of the Revolution) and the FMC during the 1970s, probably because of peer pressure, but also because her involvement could help assure opportunities for her children in school and youth organizations. Gradually, she became quite active. Through these neighborhood organizations, she gained not only a political education, but also a new place of respect in her community. For many years, my mother served as head of our neighborhood CDR, sort of a combination precinct captain and social worker. She helped people find jobs, organized vaccination campaigns, and mobilized the neighbors to keep our block safe and clean.

At some point, my mother decided that my father should help with domestic chores, but he did not share her obsession with the house. Theirs was a microcosm of the classic conflict between men's privileges and women's burdens that their generation could not overcome; and the younger generations are still struggling with these issues. In retrospect, neither of my parents was at fault. They were just not prepared for what happened on the island. No one was prepared.

This lack of preparation was aggravated by many psychological factors. Propaganda from the U.S. was attempting to undermine the goals of the revolution. The CIA's infamous Peter Pan Program[50] seduced many families into sending their children to the U.S.; most would never return. A period of severe scarcity, in the late 1960s, before the country finally joined the CAME, spread fears of famine. Nationalization affected nearly all families with property (including mine, although my parents were among those who felt it was necessary). For some, the very word "communism" conjured up images of the worst aspects of repression and dictatorship. The new consciousness of class and ideological struggle began to color even the most mundane of activities; it seemed daily life would never again be simple. Parents worried that their idealistic children would marry outside their race. Heads of households faced the rationing of nearly all necessities: food, clothes, gasoline. Overnight, even cherished traditions like the celebration of *semana santa* (Easter week) or Christmas were seen as bourgeois because of their religious ties. There was a constant fear of being politically "misinterpreted." The rules were changing; sociolismo[51] (cronyism) suddenly counted for more than good deeds. None of these factors made holding a family together any easier.

Women of my mother's generation who chose to stay in the home and maintain the old values faced another interesting paradox. Living lives that were not always happy or satisfying, these women nonetheless made sacrifices, persevered and ultimately succeeded in holding most of their families together. If all these women had disappeared at the beginning of the revolution, the Cuban family as an institution would be far weaker today. At the same time, they somehow reproduced within their families the same patriarchal patterns that enslaved and bound them to the house.

Paradox Five: In spite of all the educational work and laws to achieve women's equality, sexist language and images are still pervasive, even in Communist Party rhetoric.

In 1994 there was a billboard in Cuba that represented an eloquent example of this paradox. It said, "Where there are men... what is worthwhile goes forward." It shows a man's muscular torso, with the shirt open and the Cuban flag imprinted in the chest. The billboard was celebrating Cuban sovereignty and nationalism against outside aggression and was meant to encourage Cubans' confidence in their possibilities to overcome the crisis of the 1990s.[52] The billboard is not naïve or impartial. It depicts the masculinization of patriotism that offends women because it reinforces machismo. It ascribes to men the strength and the power to carry on the duties of the revolution, and it implies that men are the ones who can wear the Cuban flag on their muscular chests. In a survey conducted that year, 57.4 percent of the Cuban women interviewed rejected the billboard's message.

There are some particular elements within the Spanish language that make it difficult to reach a linguistic awareness about issues of gender discrimination. One of these elements is the use of the masculine as the "general grammatical gender." How can it be claimed that "hombre" (man) in some definitions includes women and in other definitions does not? It could sound childish to claim, after more than 500 years of using *los hombres del pueblo*, *los aquí presentes*, etc., that this is a sign of sexism, or that this contributes to sexist behaviors and to the masculinization of symbols in Cuba. Linguists might claim that the use of the masculine as the "generic gender" is nothing more than a linguistic marker. However, language is the most important tool humans have to form and express ideas. It helps create a person's ideas about her/himself and the world. If a society is serious about expanding opportunities for women, language must be addressed because it is a major mechanism for changing ideas and behavior.

Historically, men have been the soldiers, the political leaders, the priests, and the deep thinkers in Cuba. To change this reality, it is necessary to change the language through which social issues are addressed. It is also important to change the graphic language commonly used to represent women in the media.[53] It is extremely offensive to look at Cuban tourist brochures to find them full of provocative and inviting women as bait to sell the beauty of the island, converting them, once again, into sexual symbols.

Paradox Six: Some of the significant gains for women within the Revolution, particularly in the area of employment, are being jeopardized by the economic crisis of the 1990s.

No example illustrates this threat more than the resurgence of prostitution. Though prostitution was virtually eliminated by the Revolution, and exemplary efforts were made to retrain prostitutes for new careers, hard times have prompted many Cuban women to barter their affections for dollars. This is particularly ironic in light of revolutionary goals to give Cuban women back their dignity and eliminate the pre-1959 image of Cuba as the brothel of the Caribbean.

How is it possible that a society, with such a large majority embracing revolutionary values just ten years ago, now sees the return of prostitution? How is it that a state that usually exerts such a firm hand in suppressing illegal activity turned a blind eye? Who are these new prostitutes? It is impossible to examine this trend without considering the current economic crisis. To survive the *período especial* (the "special period" in the wake of the collapse of the socialist trade bloc) all Cubans, not just women, have been driven to extreme measures. For those without more socially acceptable means to earn dollars, there is always *jineterismo* (roughly: hustling, literally: bronco busting or horse taming).

A *jinetero* might sell coins depicting Che Guevara or craftily disguised counterfeit cigars, or offer his services as a guide, or he might offer to find the traveler a companion for the evening. His counterpart, the *jinetera*, is Cuba's new prostitute. Likely to be educated, working in a state enterprise, and living with her family,[54] the *jinetera* is a far cry from the illiterate and homeless woman who worked Havana's red light districts before the Revolution.

In this new form of prostitution, a woman gets friendly with a foreigner and parlays her charm into restaurant meals, a night at a disco, or possibly a pair of shoes for her child. More subtle than conventional prostitution, there may or may not be a quid pro quo, sex-for-cash transaction. Certainly for the *jinetera* the bottom line is cash, whether she needs the money just to get by, to afford modest luxuries like deodorant soap, shampoo, or a chicken for a family meal.

On my 1994-1995 trip to Cuba, I saw an indelible image as I walked along Havana's seawall promenade, the *Malecón*: foreigners slowing their rented cars to peruse the freshly caught pompano fish proffered by illegal fishermen, and the young women in provocative dresses, strolling alongside them—these were two forms of "meat market", unthinkable just three years before.

Until 1995, the Cuban state was dealing with *jineterismo* through education and media campaigns, ideological work and the pressure of public opinion, without using direct repression, since "being friendly" with a foreigner was not a crime. The control in hotels was minimum and more often than not, some of the hotel workers were involved or at least sympathetic to *jineteras/os*. Since the state had been forced to eliminate many jobs, it was clear that this situation was going to provoke a steady increase in prostitution, because for the first time, the state was not able to guarantee full employment to all citizens. The FMC created a group to help *jineteras* find solutions to their individual problems (many of them are divorced, single mothers, or have no other means of support). The FMC started to work with the tourist industry to limit images of sexually provocative women in their advertising.

For most Cubans, the new prostitution presents a double embarrassment. Cubans are confronted with the economic failure of the Revolution—these women cannot make decent a living from their legitimate jobs— and are reminded of the days before the Revolution when rich foreigners had their way with Cuban women. While in Mexico in 1990, I was mortified when an upper-class man told me Mexicans send their sons to the island to lose their virginity, since Cuban women are "easy" and the prostitutes are the cheapest, healthiest, and more educated in the world.

There is another form of prostitution in Cuba, that which might be called a "prostitution of values." One particularly pernicious effect of the dollar economy is that some of the best minds in Cuba are abandoning their posts as technicians, teachers, and scientists to work for dollars in tourism or joint venture businesses. This might seem pretty normal in any other developing capitalist country, but it represents a drastic change in Cuba. One of the principles that made the socialist labor ethic so different from the capitalist one was the idea that people had to work according to their capacities and abilities, and that the main goal of working was not the satisfaction of the individual's money earnings, but rather, the realization of their "human essence,"[55] their contribution to the solution of the problems of the society as a whole. I remember working as a professor at the university without ever thinking about whether or not I was accomplishing duties that I was not paid for. Nowadays, however, things are changing drastically.

Two young women in my own family have left their jobs as professionals (one has a degree in English literature and the other is an engineer), one to work as a sales clerk and the other to do odd jobs, respectively. A woman who studied philosophy with me quit her job at a university in Havana and is now working as a private massage therapist. One university English department has been decimated by the "brain drain," its professors now waiting tables at Varadero Beach hotels. Almost every day women ring the doorbell at my mother's house offering to do housework for dollars. This potential supply of domestic servants, so common in other countries, was non-existent in Cuba after the Revolution, since domestic service in private houses was considered to be degrading work.

A related phenomenon is that enrollment in higher education has actually decreased over the last decade.[56] For thirty years, those who reached higher levels of education enjoyed respect in Cuban society, but on a recent trip (July 1997), young people told me that it was no longer worthwhile to pursue a university degree. They saw no future for professionals since most state-sector jobs pay so poorly. This aspect of the "prostitution of values" is perhaps all the more disturbing since it erodes two of the pillars of the Cuban revolution, the importance of education and the expectations of a certain future. It affects women in particular since these two "pillars" that have allowed the empowerment of Cuban women in the last forty-one years are now jeopardized by the present inversion of values. The fact that a domestic servant could earn more than a female engineer is unfortunately going to affect all forms of female gains.

Conclusion

In this era when an economic and spiritual crisis has brought Cuba to the brink, to find solutions we must begin by recognizing and discussing Cuba's problems openly and without limitations. If Cuba is to make good on its promise of women's equality, Cubans will need the courage to envision change, and the economic, educational, and legal fortitude to make this vision a reality. A return to the traditional family is not what is needed: rather, women and men need the social and political freedom to envision a new type of family, free from the structures of patriarchy. My suggestion is for Cubans to work toward the following:

(1) The improvement of economic conditions that facilitate daily life. We are reminded of the old Marxist principle that the economy is the base of society, and human beings are integral to their material circumstances. The egalitarian discourse, without an economic base to support it, will never be more than talk.

(2) The opening of the political discourse to new ideas, new organizations, new non-sexist language. Cubans will need the freedom to rebuild their society without paternalism, authoritarianism or, for that matter, any kind of "ism."

(3) The amplification of men's participation in domestic duties. This should begin with effective legislation and be subsequently supported and endorsed through education and public relations campaigns to motivate real change. Cuba needs a new paradigm, one that values men for their nurturing qualities.

(4) The measured reduction of political and community commitments. Both women and men need free time to enjoy family and home. The family could then be a true stabilizing and mediating entity in Cuban society, helping to achieve a balance between "social participation and individuality."

It will not be easy to dismantle the patriarchal structures that have remained despite the socialist revolution. But men and woman, working together, could build a new society, a new family. Cubans could practice equality more efficiently and not just talk about it. I hope my mother can live to see that day.

ENDNOTES

1. This chapter was presented at the Latin American Studies Association Congress, September 1995, in Washington D.C. I would like to thank my father, Dr. Gilberto Fleites, for his assistance in gathering information for this chapter and Jaime Kibben, a San Francisco based film maker, for his editing assistance

2. The author is a Ph.D student at the University of Washington, Seattle, and is a professor at Green River Community College. She taught philosophy at a university in Havana from 1982 until 1991.

3. Machismo: the idea that men are superior to women and that they should dominate them socially, economically, physically, and sexually.

4. In *Gaceta Oficial de la República de Cuba*, 1992, p. 38. It is interesting that the focus in the Constitution is not on individual rights, but on the guarantees provided by the state, a characteristic that reinforces the "paternalistic nature" of the Cuban revolutionary state.

5. See Raquel Sierra, "Cuba Leads Developing World in Gender Equality" published in *Peacenet World News Service*, on September 1, 1995.

6. It can be argued that many of these achievements are due, in part, to international socio-sexual trends during the decades of the 1960s and 1970s. However, ordinary Cubans had little access to non-socialist foreign magazines, radio, or television until 1986. (A notable exception: U.S. propaganda via Voice of America and later on, Radio Martí.) Feminist literature was rejected as a form of "bourgeois ideology." The only systematic influence was through the cinema.

7. Federation of Cuban Women, *Statistics on Cuban Women*, Havana, FMC, 1985, p. 22.

8. *Cuba Update*, Volume XII, Number. 3, Summer 1991, p. 15; also see Raquel Sierra, "Cuba leads ..." and Vilma Espín Guillois, "Intervención en la IV Conferencia Mundial de la Mujer," organized by the United Nations, September 8, 1995 and published by Cuba-L, an Internet information service on September 16, 1995.

9. See Evenson, Debra (1994) *Revolution in the Balance* (Boulder, Colorado: Westview Press, Inc.), p. 89.

10. From Vilma Espín Guillois, "Intervención en la IV Conferencia Mundial sobre la mujer"...

11. See *Boletín de Inicio del Curso Escolar*, edited by Comité Estatal de Estadísticas, Habana, 1993.

12. See Marifeli Pérez-Stable (1993) *The Cuban Revolution: Origins, Course and Legacy* (New York: Oxford University Press), p. 33.

13. It is interesting to note that in the United States, only 22 percent of doctors are women. See Sam Roberts' article "Women's Work: What's New, What Isn't?" *The New York Times*, April 27, 1995.

14. Quoted in Raquel Sierra, "Cuba Leads Developing World in Gender Equality".

15. See *Areíto*, Volume 4, Number 14, p. 7, Miami, October, 1993.

16. *Granma*, Cuban daily newspaper, on July 14, 1995. Even if this figure is low, it is still amazing due the current economic crisis that has affected women and children the hardest.

17. See *Central Report of the Third Congress of the Cuban Communist Party*, edited by Política, La Habana, 1986, p. 78.

18. See the magazines *Bohemia*, March 31, 1995, No. 7, pp. B38-B47, and *Correo de Cuba*, agosto 1995.

19. Vilma Espín Guillois, "Intervención en la IV Conferencia Mundial sobre la Mujer"...

20. Compared to 46.7 per 1000 in Cuba in 1969. See *Granma*, January 5, 1994, p. 3.

21. See article by Susan Chira, "Study Confirms Some Fears on U.S. Children," in *The New York Times*, April 12, 1994.

22. See *Granma*, January 5, 1994, "Mortalidad infantil en período especial", La Habana.

23. See *Granma Weekly Review*, January 24, 1988, p. 4, La Habana.

24. My daughter attended a day care center where I paid roughly 10 percent of my monthly salary of

$340.00. For what amounted to a little more than a dollar a day, my daughter could receive care from 6:00 a.m. to 6:00 p.m., breakfast, two snacks and lunch, not to mention an organized program of pre-school education. Although children of low income single mothers are eligible for scholarships, demand for day-care is greater than capacity, so at times children must be wait-listed before being placed in day care. A child's eligibility also depends on the mother's work, with preferential treatment given to those working in industries considered high priority by the state.

25. Source: *Censo de Población y Viviendas 1981*, Publicación del CEE. Instituto de Demografía y Censo, 1982.

26. Source: *Revista Bohemia*, Number 16, 1993, p. B7 and Dalia Acosta, "La descendencia" in the weekly newspaper *Juventud Rebelde*, February 20, 1994.

27. In 1993 Cuban population was 10,922,187, and births had decreased by more than 5000 since 1992. This declining birth rate is a source of real concern for Cuban authorities since 10 percent of the population is now more than 60 years old and the current reproduction rate does not replace one daughter per woman (see Weekly Newspaper *Juventud Rebelde*, July 10 1994, "¿No creceremos?," by Dalia Acosta.

28. See Vilma Espín, "Intervención en la IV Conferencia Mundial sobre la Mujer",....

29. See Raúl Gómez Treto, *La iglesia católica durante la construcción del socialismo en Cuba*. Costa Rica: Editorial DEI, 1987. It is interesting that from 1990-1995 church attendance has increased rapidly, with the economic and social crisis and especially after the Communist Party discussed the issues of religiosity and accepted the idea that religious men and women could be elected as Party members. It is too soon for this new move to have an impact on sexual behavior and attitudes related to women's equality, but it should be observed carefully. Cuba, for instance, has one of the highest rates of legal abortion in the world; could that record be affected now as an increasing number of people return to the Church?

30. Max Azicri (1980) *Cuba: Politics, Economics and Society* (New York: Pinter Publishers), p. 177.

31. Azicri, op. cit,. p. XVII.

32. Francesca Miller (1991) *Latin American Women and the Search for Social Justice* (Hanover, New Hampshire: University Press of New England), p. 63.

33. Of course many of these old traditional values and attitudes remains, because forty-one years is not enough to change centuries of macho education. For instance, in 1985 the "Center for the Study of Youth" conducted a study with eleventh graders. When the question of whether boys prefer to marry a virgin was asked, 49.85 percent of the girls answered "yes" and 72.42 percent of the boys also answered "yes" (see Marvin Leiner, *(1994) Sexual Politics in Cuba. Machismo, Homosexuality and AIDs* (Colorado: Westview Press,), pp. 81-84.

34. Source: De la Riva, (1975) Juan, *Las Estadísticas Demográficas Cubanas*, Havana, Editorial Ciencias Sociales and *(1993) Datos Demográficos y Vitales*, Havana: Instituto de Inv. Estadísticas, 1993. Note: The Cuban population grew appreciably during these years. In 1953 Cuba's census was 5.8 million and in 1970 it was 8.5 million (plus the émigrés outside the island). By 1985 it had grown to 10.1 million.

35. During 1993 and 1994, several articles about love, family stability, prostitution, jineterismo, etc., appeared in periodicals like *Juventud Rebelde* and the weekly, *Bohemia*.

36. For a report on the incredible achievements on AIDS prevention, as well as the problems of Cuba's policy on AIDS treatment, see the bimonthly *Cuba Update*, Volume XV, Number 2, March-May 1994, from the Center for Cuban Studies, New York.

37. See Rosa M. Elizalde y A. del Pino, "Flores de 5ta Avenida", [The Flowers of Fifth Avenue] *Juventud Rebelde*, January 23, 1994, La Habana.

38. Of course, this trend has been seen globally. The influence of worldwide social trends on Cuban society has not been very obvious and this discussion does not examine them, focusing rather on forces within Cuba that can be addressed constructively once the problems are recognized.

39. See magazine *Bohemia*, Number 45, November 9, 1990.

40. See Debra Evenson, op. cit. chapter 5, and Marvin Leiner, op. cit., chapter 3.

41. *First Congress of the Communist Party of Cuba* (1976) (Moscow: Progress Publishers), p. 197.

42. See Max Azicri (1988) *Cuba: Politics, Economics and Society* (New York: Pinter Publishers), pp. 114-115.

43. One arroba equals about 25 pounds.

44. See *First Congress of the Communist* ..., pp. 198-199, and *Central Report of the Third Congress of the Communist Party of Cuba*, edited by Política, La Habana, 1986, pp. 7-79.

45. See S. Halebsky and J. Kirk (1992) (editors) *Cuba in Transition: Crisis and Transformation* (Colorado: Westview Press).

46. See Debra Evenson, op. cit., p. 94. Since 1991, the FMC has lost its active role in many communities.

47. In recent years some NGOs (non-governmental organizations) had appeared, most with less than whole hearted approval of the state. The first gay men's organization sprang from the concern over AIDS and the group "Cubans in the Struggle Against AIDS" was founded with the help of a Cuban-American academic from the USA. (see Reed, Gail: "AIDS, Sexuality and the New Man" (sic), in *Cuba Update*, May 1994, Volume XV, Number 2, March-May, 1994).

48. Max Azicri, op. cit., p. 115.

49. For instance, the organization Radical Women from Seattle, USA, received an invitation from the FMC to visit the country and to discuss women's issues in 1994.

50. The Peter Pan Program, launched by the CIA in the 1960s, was a propaganda campaign to create discontent inside Cuba. Essentially, it claimed that the communists were going to abolish the *patria potestas* and take the children from their families. Working through "legitimate" churches in Miami, the program brought Cuban children to the U.S. without their parents, to save them from the "terrible faith." Many of the children stayed with church families or in foster homes, some in orphanages. Although some were reunited with their birth parents years later, many never saw their families again.

51. Sociolismo is a play on the word socialismo, from socio (pal or buddy). In the 1970s, much in the same way as was manifested in the Soviet Union, personal connections became more important to success than hard work or political correctness. Sociolismo, though practiced by "revolutionaries," was distinctly reminiscent of the traditional politics of personality common in Cuba before 1959.

52. The picture of this billboard appeared in "Estereotipos sexistas. Póngase usted a pensar," [Sexist Stereotypes: Think About It] by Mirta Rodríguez Calderón, in *Bohemia* (May 1994), pp. B4-B7.

53. The group MAGIN (previously mentioned) was trying to work on media representation of women until the group was prohibited in 1997.

54. See *Flores de 5ta Avenida*, by R. M. Elizalde y A. del Pino, op. cit.

55. As Marx stated in his *Theses on Fuerbach* and in his *Economic and Philosophical Manuscripts of 1844*.

56. From 200,000 in 1983 to 165,843 in 1993. See Max Azicri, p. 178 and *Boletín de Inicio del Curso Escolar* (1993), CEE, Cuba.

4

Jineterismo During the Special Period

Elisa Facio

The emergence of *jineterismo* with the growth of the tourist industry, developments in the 1990s, is compared to the forms of prostitution that existed in Cuba during the 1950s. The historical background reveals the terrible contradictions for the revolutionary socialist state and the feminist women who organized the elimination of prostitution by providing viable economic and educational alternatives for women from the 1960s to the early 1990s. Finally, the arguments raised here imply a certain optimism for turning one of the worst of all imagined developments into a practice with some redeeming value, by stating explicitly that the new form of sex work has provided at least some children of *jineteras* some badly needed food, clothing and medicine that can be bought almost exclusively at Cuba's "dollar stores."

1. Introduction

In the early 1990s, many observers spoke of the imminent collapse of the Cuban Revolution. With the breakdown of the Eastern Communist bloc, political and economic relations between Cuba and its former allies were abruptly and drastically reduced. Few foreign analysts argued that Cuba had the potential to survive. This notwithstanding, Cuba marked the 41st anniversary of its revolution in January 2000, which also marked the ninth year of the "Special Period in Time of Peace". The continuation of the "Special Period in Time of Peace" essentially signified that existing policies could no longer operate within a "business as usual" framework.

Amidst the unraveling of Cuba's relations with Eastern Europe, there is also the overall realignment of the global economy and the continuation by the United States of its aggressive attempts to destroy the Cuban state and economy, namely with the Torrecelli and the Helms-Burton bills. Only the visit of Pope John Paul II and some home-grown relief from the devastating food shortages of the first half of the 1990s seemed to have offered hope and optimism. Throughout the 1990s, Cuba has sought to survive and adapt to the new international circumstances without losing sight of the revolution's past accomplishments and future goals for sustaining an adequate quality of life for its people.

One of the most controversial areas in Cuba's post-Soviet economic strategy has been the tourist industry. In urgent need of quick hard currency, the Cuban government turned to the island's greatest natural resource—its gorgeous beaches and glorious weather. Its campaign to attract Canadian, Latin American (particularly Mexican), and European tourists (Spanish, Italian and German) led to a major leap in the number of foreign visitors from about 250,000 in 1988 to some 400,000 in 1991 (Dello Buono, 1992, pp. 4-5). Gross income earnings during these same three years doubled from $150 million to $300 million. The largest foreign investment in Cuban tourism was cemented during the summer of 1996. Canadian hotel mogul Walter Berukoff and Wilton Properties agreed to split the cost of a $400 million investment in eleven hotels and two golf courses with a Cuban partner, the state-run Gran Caribe. Tourist development at the white sand beaches of Varadero (80 miles east of Havana), *Santiago de Cuba*, and *Holguin's Guardalavaca* is still in demand. Cuban Vice President Carlos Lage reported that in the spring of 1996, tourist visits were up 45 percent over 1995. Cuban tourism official Eduardo Rodriquez de la Vega stated that tourism revenues in 1996 exceeded the previous year's $1 billion (Falk, 1996), and future prognoses predicted significant increases in tourism's earning for several years.

Extensive debates have taken place in Cuba over the relative social costs and benefits of developing tourism. The renewed emphasis on tourism has been accompanied by a host of problems. First, tourism has created a two-tiered society in Cuba—the privileged foreigners and the unprivileged locals. In an effort to absorb tourist dollars, the government created tourist stores, restaurants, nightclubs, hotels, even tourist taxis that are accessible only to foreigners with hard currency. Some Cubans feel that this "tourism apartheid" subverted the whole purpose of the revolutionary state, which is to promote equality. Others counter that unlike other countries, tourist income in Cuba does not go into the hands of a few wealthy business tycoons but goes to keep up the health care system, the schools, and the food supply. But many Cubans who understand this argument are nevertheless highly bothered when they see the island's best resources going toward coddling foreigners while their own lives are plagued with serious daily difficulties. Second, with the inception of tourism there has been an increase in crime. Cuba was once known as one of the most crime-free societies in the world. While violent crime remains low, petty theft has increased dramatically.

Finally, and of particular interest to this discussion, tourism has led to a form of sex work called *jineterismo*. There is a new language to describe the range of behaviors ascribed to "*jineterismo*" (literally translated as horseback riding or breaking in a horse, or "gold digging" in its colloquial form), and the attitudes by and toward the *jineteras* who engage in it. *Jineterismo* is a range of behaviors, not only a direct exchange of sexual relations for dollars (Diaz, 1996, p. 4). Additionally, Cuban sex workers or *jineteras* can include pubescent girls to professional women. Unlike prostitution in the U.S., Cuban sex workers are not organized or integrated into networks controlled by "pimps." Cuban *jineterismo* has been described as having "advantages" over other places such as Thailand or the Philippines. The country is relatively free of AIDS, it is inexpensive, and the women themselves have an "innocent quality" (Lane, 1994, pp. 15-18). When *jineterismo* initially surfaced in the latter part of 1991, a very financially hard-pressed Cuban government, facing an anticipated $4 billion trade deficit by the end of 1992, appeared to turn a blind eye in hopes the dollars *jineteras* earned would help overcome the Revolution's worst economic crisis.

The government's initial acquiescence was at odds with one of the principal aims of the revolution: ridding the country of the vice that had turned Havana into the sin capital of the Western hemisphere at a time when casinos, cheap rum, and sex attracted thousands of North Americans to the Caribbean island. The revolutionaries aimed to free women from sexual exploitation in all sectors of society. Several older women recalled that during the early years of the revolution, the government did not use laws and punitive measures to sanction women in order to eliminate prostitution; rather, job training and a non-judgmental approach prevailed in contrast to the strong social taboos at that time from families, religious leaders, and the men who purchased sexual services. The new revolutionary leaders offered the compassionate combination of real economic opportunities and moral rehabilitation with the active mobilization of large numbers of female revolutionaries to assist less fortunate women in the transition from prostitution to gainful employment and social integration.

The Cuban government today—in what is known as "legalizing reality"—appears to be using dollars earned by *jineteras* and other illicit business to help overcome the economic catastrophe caused by its own mismanagement, the demise of the its Soviet ally, and the U.S. embargo. Given the existence of *jineterismo*, and the cultural images of Cuban women produced by the tourist industry, Cuba faces tremendous contradictions and complexities regarding women's lives.

Many social scientists argue that *jineteras* engage in sex work because of materialistic desire as opposed to any realistic economic necessity (Stout, 1995, pp. 13-18; Miranda, 1993, pp. 1-24). They propose that in a society where education and health care are free, and where people are supposedly secure with adequate foodstuffs and clothing through the *libreta* (ration book), women do not need to engage in sex work. However, since 1990 no Cuban household has been able to survive on the goods available through the *libreta*. The debatable question remains whether *jineterismo* is either a result of dire economic need or the desires for materialistic consumption, or both. Generally, government officials voice the notion that the phenomenon is clearly related to the material shortages as well as the increasing presence of foreign consumerist values. Furthermore, social scientists argue that while traditional prostitution was eradicated in Cuba in the 1960s, sex work appears to be practiced as a personal decision by young people otherwise capable of engaging in more dignified and less risky activities. Thus the Cuban government can conveniently label *jineteras* as social deviants while also maintaining a more lenient stance toward non-professional *jineterismo*.

The following discussion explores the phenomena of *jineterismo* in the context of Cuba's current economic crisis. The next section of this chapter focuses on some of the social realities for women in Cuba's declared wartime economy during peacetime. Then, Cuban tourism is highlighted, particularly how women's lives have been affected by both the inception of the tourist industry and the emergence of *jineterismo*. Finally, the chapter concludes on a speculative note suggesting that an analysis of *jineterismo* be placed in a context of patriarchy and international tourism.

2. Cuban Women During the Special Period

The shortfall in oil and other key inputs during this period began to have dramatic effects in Cuba's industrial sector, (these effects have been documented and discussed by Campbell and Carranza and other contributors—Editors note). Comprehending the economic realities of daily life is important in order to discuss the conditions from which women, in particular, became vulnerable to various forms of sex work or *jineterismo*. The curtailment of consumption and the implementation of a food self-sufficiency program provide a panoramic backdrop for viewing the daily struggles of Cuban life during the special period.

2. 1. Curtailment of Consumption

The drive towards rationing of food consumption was thrown into high gear with the failure of 100,000 tons of wheat to arrive from the Soviet Union in early 1990. Bread rations were initially cut in most provinces from 200 grams to 180 grams per person per day while the price of a 400 gram loaf of bread in Havana was raised from 30 to 35 cents. The price of eggs was nearly doubled, from 8 to 15 cents. Tens of thousands of tons of citrus fruits originally destined for export were poured into the domestic market, improving short-term availability, but at the expense of hard currency earnings (Dello Buono, 1995, p. 2). By mid-February 1992, the price of many food products including potatoes, carrots, tomatoes, beets and bananas had doubled, while increasing significantly for other fresh food products. Pressure mounted on the Cuban state to reduce its subsidies. Fuel saving measures within forty-five major industrial firms were likewise implemented beginning in 1990 with the aim to save at least 150,000 tons per year of oil (Dello Buono, 1995, p. 2).

Throughout 1992, more drastic measures of austerity became evident throughout the Cuban society, particularly in urban areas. Beginning in January 1992, work centers had begun to reduce their hours, street lighting was reduced, most regular taxis were taken off the road, television broadcasts were reduced to five hours on weekdays, night baseball games were suspended, and air conditioners in most government offices were ordered turned off. By September 1992, the nation's single biggest development project, a nuclear power plant being constructed near *Cienfuegos*, was ordered suspended. The project had employed some 10,000 workers and had cost more than $2.5 billion over its seven years of construction. Designed to significantly reduce Cuba's energy bill by cutting the island's oil needs by approximately 20 percent, the project was nearing completion. The abrupt cutoff of Soviet assistance meant that Cuba now would have to pay Russia in hard currency for completion of the plant.

2. 2. The Fight for Food Self-sufficiency

President Fidel Castro indicated on several occasions that the food crisis was Cuba's "Achilles heel", and that it could be alleviated only with the massive participation of all Cubans in the drive to achieve food self-sufficiency (Deere, 1991). Beginning in 1989 and expanding rapidly by mid-1990, Cuba's emergency food program (*Programa Alimentario*) was designed to rapidly increase domestic food production in the event of the continued disruption of food imports. Substantial effort was also placed on improving the yield of sugar cane fields to compensate for lower prices, a principal characteristic of the new reorientation of Cuban exports toward the capitalist world market. In addition, an increasing percentage of Cuba's sugar product was diverted to domestic import substitution via by-products that could be used for animal feed.

An important aspect of the emergency program was its sponsorship of labor mobilization to produce food. Particular attention was given to cultivating lands for food production in Havana Province, including in local communities and on lands pertaining to workplaces. One object was to lower transportation costs associated with the movement of foodstuffs from the provinces into the densely populated city of Havana. The program also sought in principle to divert workers who were idled in other sectors to the agricultural sector. Thousands of state employees in the construction and agricultural ministries were given leave of absence from their jobs and sent to new posts located primarily on state farms in 1992 and early 1993.

By March 1992 scant availability of vegetables and some fruits were reported in Havana, but the early successes with food production were insufficient to resolve the demand for food in the Cuban economy. By 1994, the state took even more radical measures to encourage production and increase the stock of food supplies by re-introducing private farmers' markets that would allow producers to sell their goods at whatever price the market would bear. By early 1995, food products in variety and high quality began to circulate on the now legal market as private producers responded to the growing stimulus, making products which had not been seen for almost a decade available for those who could afford to purchase them.

3. Tourist Industry: *Un Mal Necesario*

With the onset of the Special Period, Cuba also placed a high priority on foreign exchange earnings. Of the many concessions made to salvage the economy and the socialist project, the most controversial has been the inception of tourism to bring in freely convertible hard currency. The state invested in the physical infrastructure in order to expand tourism into untapped regions of the island. At the same time, Cuba diverted highly educated and underemployed labor to the tourism industry, established new training facilities in tourist services, and prepared to accommodate the anticipated influx of foreign investment capital.

In 1989 Cuba's 13,000 hotel rooms earned $200 million from 326,000 tourists. Key markets were located with Canada, West Germany, Spain, Mexico and Italy. In 1990 it increased its capacity to receive 334,000 customers largely from the

German and Mexican markets. A target of 500,000 tourists was set for 1992 for a yield of over $400 million in revenues. By 1993, as the quality of services improved, the over 560,000 tourists visiting Cuba generated a gross income of $720 million dollars (Diaz, 1996). The most recent figures hover around one billion dollars, an impressive fivefold increase in less than one decade.

While the Cuban state strived to maintain control over the tourist industry, joint venture capital entering the Cuban tourist industry now included major investors from Spain and Germany. For example, the creation of *Gaviota*, a major state enterprise based in the Cuban military, combined private enterprise flexibility with strong state financing and high worker discipline as it entered the tourist arena. By mid-1994 Cuba's Minister of Tourism projected that the island was quickly regaining its status as a tourist competitor and indicated that Cuba would break the one million tourist mark by 1996 with an annual income of $1 billion. Although the net profits are still low compared to the gross receipts, nevertheless such a drastic change in the economy was accompanied by several social changes.

4. The Special Period and Women's Lives

Scholars have given tremendous attention to the strides women have made since the triumph of the Revolution of 1959. Women have made substantial achievements materially and culturally, especially in professional status and in the struggle to change sexual ideology in the family (Smith & Padula, 1996, chapters 1-3). This view is shared by scholars such as Max Azicri, Carolee Bengelsdorf, Lourdes Casal and Margaret Randall. However, I would argue that these changes have not extended necessarily to larger political and economic policies nor to party practice. The overall quality of women's lives, which is in serious jeopardy, is overlooked by most revolutionary ideology. Thus women's existence as women has gone largely ignored. The issue of patriarchy has not been adequately considered by the revolutionary leadership. Therefore, it is not surprising that *jineterismo* has surfaced with a great deal of confusion inside and outside the political circles.

In this context I am defining *jineterismo* as a new form of women's work, and, therefore, the daily struggles of women's lives during the special period must be highlighted. First and foremost, women have been active in all the strategic programs initiated during the economic crisis. In 1992 women constituted more than 61 percent of the middle and upper level technicians, half of the doctors and 40 percent of all executives in the health and education areas. There has not been a reduction in female participation in the economy, but a reorganization of job sites. Women who worked in light industries which were subsequently closed were transferred to local industries closer to their homes. In addition to transportation problems, brown-outs (apagones) and the lack of kerosene and spare parts greatly affected women and families. There were difficulties in producing and procuring milk, meat, chicken and eggs, and even soap and detergent. The availability of rice, frozen fish, and canned meat was reduced to a minimum. Cuba even experienced a total lack of sanitary napkins.

Overall, women have felt the difficulties of daily life more harshly than men during this period. While women had achieved professional advancements, traditional roles in the home persisted with women shouldering the burden of the double day. Even though some women's jobs were geographically relocated closer to their homes due to transportation shortages, many were given the option of taking a 30 percent cut in salaries and reducing their work days by one-third. Women spent the majority of their time creating and "inventing" ways in which to obtain food. After about three years of the Special Period, the black market was in full force. The exchange rate plunged from 8 to 10 pesos per dollar in 1988 to 100 to 120 pesos for $1.00 in 1994. Those fortunate enough to access dollars either through relatives in Miami, jobs in tourism, or state jobs (where goods could be easily stolen and sold on the black market) did not always experience the general hunger that the majority of Cubans confronted. Transportation shortages led to bicycle use, thus contributing to exhaustion and tremendous weight loss among the Cuban population.

Women, in particular, began to devise ways in which to earn hard currency, illegally. Many women would bake, sew, clean, cook, create small craft items in exchange for pesos, which eventually were converted into dollars, or better yet, dollars plus a foreigner with access to shops to buy soap, cooking oil and detergent for them, as these items were not available on the ration nor in the black market. With electrical brown-outs, many food items for daily meals were acquired and consumed the same day in order to prevent spoilage. The daily preoccupation and challenge was to obtain food with dollars because dollars had greater purchasing power. However, the possession and use of dollars was considered counter-revolutionary and thus illegal.

People were expected to depend on a ration system that did not meet the daily nor monthly needs of the population, a black market which quite often was unattainable because of the extraordinary exchange rate (pesos and dollars), and to maintain hope that the tourist industry would bring about economic recovery, namely more food. The black market began to undermine the national economy, forcing

President Fidel Castro to legalize the use of dollars in July, 1993 (Figueros & Plasencia Vidal, 1994).

The stories that follow of three women and one unnamed fifteen year-old who decided to become involved in *jineterismo* provide us with a brief glimpse at women who resort to activities that the revolutionaries had proudly eliminated from Cuba in the early 1960s.

5. Women, Sex, and Tourism

Angeles agrees to meet with me late one summer evening in 1996. She appears nervous, embarrassed, but anxious to talk with someone about the anguish she experiences daily. She is a petite twenty-two-year-old university student anxious to leave Cuba. She lives with her parents who are unaware of her desires to marry a foreigner and leave the island. Angeles sadly states that the future of Cuba's youth is extremely unpredictable. She no longer feels secure as she did in her early teens. "I'm a university student, but I don't feel I'll benefit from my education. My parents work so hard to maintain our home. As you know, we lack everything, especially food. And without dollars, there's nothing for young people to do in this country. It's really hard to make sense of our lives during this time." Attending the university, worrying about her livelihood, and dealing with the lack of entertainment, Angeles desperately struggles to make sense of her life. Economic and social uncertainty led her to sex work in 1993. In September of 1997, Angeles married and now resides in Spain.

A pretty, fifteen-year-old bleached blond, personifies Havana's return to the decadence that Fidel Castro's revolution was supposed to eliminate four decades ago. She is barely five feet tall, weighs about 100 pounds, and is dressed in lemon hot pants and a black halter top. Her eyes are rimmed with thick mascara. "What country are you from?" she asks my colleague, blocking his way to the car door. Flirting in her childlike way, she tells my friend he is handsome, intelligent. She was not an aberration in the early phase of the Special Period. She was an important "hand-maiden" in the service of attracting desperately needed currency (Enloe, 1990, chapter 2). She is one of the many young Cuban girls and women who have turned Havana into an attractive "fleshpot" for foreign tourists. Every day, dozens of men arrive at Havana's José Marti International Airport to begin their vacations with young women like Ana. She had a carefree attitude about what she was doing. She was driven partly by the desire to obtain cash, and also a desire just to have fun in a country that offers little entertainment outside places that are closed to her unless she is on the arm of a foreigner.

Maria, a twenty-year-old University of Havana student, comes to the illicit arrangement with an astonishing air of practicality. One night, as the young woman awaits her "date"—a paunchy Spanish executive in his 60s who has promised to take her to the Havana Club disco—she calculates her advantages. "I can earn more in one night than my mother can in five months," she says, smoothing her sequined mini-dress that the Spanish executive paid for. "If it wasn't for the dollars I earn this way, I couldn't afford to continue my studies," she said. "I can make about $35 a night, eat a good meal and have a swell time." What does her Cuban boyfriend think? "He knows what I am doing. But we look upon this as an opportunity to get ahead, as a phase in our lives. It's no big deal."

These women are confronted with a choice between the glittery world of hard currency full of materialism and food against the difficult world of the average Cuban who has very little of either. The hard-currency world of cars, tourist shops, restaurants, discos and resorts is off-limits to the vast majority of the Cuban population—even though Article 42 of the Constitution specifically forbids such a segregated arrangement. But most Cuban women can break the barrier with a foreign tourist and briefly escape the harsh living conditions of most Cubans, who earn practically nothing and endure a monotonous diet of beans and rice. Practically anything worth buying—from jeans to shampoo—can be found only in stores once reserved for documented foreigners (who had to show passport, a visa or letter of affiliation, or invitation from some institution) but now open to anyone with dollars to spend.

With respect to the Cuban male's reaction, not all Cuban men are as tolerant as Maria's boyfriend. It is a source of resentment among Cuban males who cannot compete for attention without dollars, which were forbidden until 1993. Other men like Rosa's ex-husband will not tolerate the stigma of being associated with a *jinetera* either past or present. Rosa is a twenty-six year-old single mother living with her parents. I arrive at her two-bedroom apartment late one afternoon in the summer of 1996. She is mopping the floors preparing for my arrival, warmly greets me, and offers me a glass of water. Rosa states, "I became involved in *jineterismo* because of my family's economic situation and especially for my child. Without the dollars, I can barely clothe and feed my child." Rosa continues, saying that she was fortunate enough to meet a Cuban man and marry. However, once her husband learned she had worked as a *jinetera*, they divorced. Rosa showed me a set of beautiful wedding pictures; we both sobbed not so much over the dissolution of her marriage, but more so because of the contradictions and predicaments of life for so many Cuban women during the Special Period.

Later that evening, as I take another walk around the Hotel Riviera nightclub, the conflict is put into perspective. I notice a young couple dancing in front of a table of foreign tourists. Their rhythmic and synchronized moves are tantalizing and seductive. Shortly, they are invited by the foreign visitors to share a table. By the end of the evening, the young man is offering the sexual services of his female friend. During the ride home we asked the taxi driver, a young veteran of the Cuban forces who fought in Angola, about what we had just observed. He angrily stated that he did not fight in Angola to be banned from some lousy disco, so that Cubans could be treated like second-class citizens and Cuban women reduced to *prostitutas*.

In 1993, even though housing remained free or low-rent, food rations generally ran out by the middle of the month, forcing families to barter on the black market where stolen supplies and foodstuffs were sold. Educated Cubans scrambled for jobs they would have previously scorned: tending bar or waiting tables for dollar tips in luxury hotels, where most Cubans were barred from entering. At the Capri Hotel which is centrally located in downtown Havana, my friend tells a familiar story. "I was a professor for five years at the University of Havana. Now I work 12-14 hours a day as a hotel porter. I get good tips in dollars, of course. Here, this is called progress." Indeed, the inequity between the dollar and peso has created an inverted economy in which bellhops at resorts make more money in tips than doctors and college professors do in salary. Another friend who was an elementary school teacher left his job to work as a waiter in one of Havana's finest hotels. He tells me he can now walk with me comfortably and without embarrassment as he can afford to buy me a Coca-Cola. Another friend, one of Havana's pool of young and gifted medical specialists, apologizes for not being able to spend a Friday evening with me because she has no *divisa*, meaning dollars.

By 1994 more than 160,000 Cubans had applied for licenses to set up their own businesses. Many others are simply going it alone without bothering with the legalities. Lacking capital and resources, most businesses depend wholly on ingenuity. An older man who lives next door to my friend refills butane cigarette lighters that in most other countries would be disposable. He pays the government 50 pesos a month for his license, and another 24 pesos for every day he sets up shop in a nearby plaza with dozens of other artisans. Arts and crafts markets lined the streets of downtown Havana with artisans selling their works for dollars.

By 1995 food consumption had increased with the establishment of farmers markets, home restaurants (*paladares*), food stands (*particulares*), and the re-opening of a few state restaurants that accepted pesos. The famous Coppelia ice cream park now accepted both dollars and pesos. However, for many, especially young Cubans, tourists with dollars continued to provide the only access to certain goods and entertainment. In and around the clubs and hotels, particularly in Havana, cash exchanges for sex have become common practice. Additionally, women offer their company, their conversation, and their charm in return for an expensive meal, a night of drinks and dancing, or a chance to shop at the dollar stores. Beyond the hotels, on the streets and plazas, young men work in the underground economy, selling illegally obtained cigars and other goods and changing pesos for dollars at many times the official rate. Observations in 1996 and 1997 suggest that a small number of young men are also engaging in forms of sex work. (They are referred to as "*jineteros*" or the more vulgar street term, "*pingeros*").

Many now depend on the black market for goods that are virtually impossible to get otherwise, for instance, cigarettes. This inevitably affects the social conscience and consciousness of Cubans. The boom in black market activity has prompted police crackdowns. Cubans are being armed to protect "important economic sites" from burglary, and street thefts are rising. These developments could threaten to undercut Cuba's ability to offer tourists a safe and secure Caribbean vacation, one of the greatest advantages Cuba has over the other Caribbean islands.

The two-tiered system of currency created during the Special Period has contributed to a socially stratified Cuba and has also resulted in a "tourist apartheid." Many Cubans called for the elimination of the dual currencies to counter this trend. A single currency would allow Cubans to buy any goods or enter any establishment if they had enough money. To some extent, there would still be a division between foreign and domestic tourist activity, but it would be based on purchasing power and not on discrimination against Cuba's own people.

The government is uncomfortable with market mechanisms to curtail or increase domestic demands for foreign and luxury goods. Although it has taken a definitive stand on the currency issue, the government has essentially abdicated all other key tourist development questions to its semi-autonomous enterprises. These in turn proceed without any overall strategy. Yet the form of tourism that the government endorses—one that will benefit all Cubans by providing collective goods—presupposes a guiding political force and a plan. Yet, as the government loses its vanguard role in this now vital sector of the economy, it is relegated to acting as a kind of police force maintaining a favorable investment climate. Cubans thus enjoy neither the accumulative benefits of capitalism nor the input into the social process characteristic of the best aspects of Cuban socialism. By not permitting market activity within the domestic economy, while selling off access to chunks of the island to foreign investors, the government has taken a path that benefits those who least support the revolution. Everyone else suffers with the hope that the sacrifices will help them get through the crisis with health care, education, and other services kept intact for their families.

Despite the economic gains made by tourism and other economic strategies of the special period, many Cubans must struggle to obtain food. No doubt, overall food consumption has increased; however, monthly incomes remain insufficient for meeting the basic needs of the population. Thus *jineterismo* continues to flourish in the tourist areas. In addition to exchanging sex for food, clothes, entertainment and other necessities, women are now looking to various forms of *jineterismo* as a way of leaving Cuba; that is, to find potential foreign marriage partners.

6. The Politics of Sexuality and Cuba's Economic Crisis

The return of sex work has caught the attention of both the Cuban government and the Federation of Cuban Women (FMC). The official position on sex work argues that unlike women who worked to survive or were deceived into prostitution during the period of economic destitution before the Revolution, these modern-day sex workers are trading their bodies for consumer goods and recreational opportunities otherwise unavailable to them (Diaz, 1996, pp. 1-33). Because many of these young women are well-educated—some are even university graduates—their turning to sex work puzzles and dismays many Cubans, whether or not they support the policies of the revolutionary state. Researchers from the FMC and MAGIN (organization of prominent women from the National Women's Press Association) report that the circumstances for prostitution in today's Cuba are vastly changed from the period leading up to the Revolution in 1959.

A more critical gendered analysis brings new interpretations. *Jineteras* are seeking power in the new tourist marketplace, the power of access to consumer goods and otherwise unobtainable amusements and diversions that are associated with the privileges of tourists and foreign businessmen. Some of the important differences between present-day *jineterismo* and pre-revolutionary prostitution are in the type of clients, educational access, family and social reactions, and levels of self-esteem. These changes are linked to the rapid development of tourism and increased opportunity for contact with foreign men.

Prostitution's customers used to be primarily Cuban men; today's clients are tourists from all over the world. Most young women today have the benefit of extensive educational opportunity in Cuban society compared to opportunities for most women before the revolution. Based on research conducted by the FMC, many *jineteras* are not rejected by their families or by most of society. In fact, few have low self-esteem compared to women stigmatized prior to 1959 as putas or whores (Weisman, 1995, pp. 24-27). What has remained the same is in the social definition of illegality; yet, today's government prosecutes and offers treatment (especially in the case of related drug addiction) to *jineteras*.

Mirta Rodríquez Calderón, a leading journalist and co-founder of MAGIN, who has written and published extensively on gender and sexual politics in Cuba (including *Digame, Usted!*, a collection of thought-provoking columns in *Granma*), has interviewed women who have relations with tourists. She characterizes *jineteras* as young women who, with very few exceptions, do not have to practice commercial sexual relations to survive. Instead, she believes, what motivates most of these young, mainly dark-skinned, Afro-Cuban, women to practice *jineterismo* is the desire to go out, to enjoy themselves, go places where Cubans cannot afford to go and have fancy clothes. Other women, a minority, she estimates, may be engaging in *jineterismo* because they have families and truly need the money and goods. Rodríguez Calderón further describes the differences between modern-day *jineteras* and pre-revolutionary prostitutes in terms of power. Today's young women practice *jineterismo* for the "freedom" to go out—dancing, dining, to concerts, to visit Varadero Beach or other resorts, and to shop in dollar stores. Some of these young women are looking for potential spouses in foreign men in order to leave Cuba for a more stable and consumer-oriented life. Others look at current options in Cuba to earn a living and make money. A secretary, for example, currently earns 190 pesos a month (roughly $9.50—given the current exchange rate of roughly 20 pesos to $1), while a family doctor (the majority of whom are women) earns 250 pesos or about $12.50 practicing medicine, compared to $35 to $50 for one evening for a woman who is practicing *jineterismo*.

Calderón also theorizes the interaction of racism and prostitution. Many of the people who left Cuba since 1959 are light-skinned and living primarily in the United States; they are sending money to their relatives still living in Cuba to lessen the economic hardships. Young women without access to family resources in the U.S. have a greater need for the economic assistance of this kind of work, adding to increased racial segmentation in both class and gender status. Racism and the double sexual standard also create the market among European businessmen for the exotic/erotic "other." The combination of foreign men seeking sexual partners who are racially and culturally different, coupled with the sexual double standard's separation of women into "good" versus "bad" ones, reinforces the desirability of darker-skinned Cuban women as sex objects.

The government's inconsistent response to the rapid rise of sex work reflects the double gender standard. The major focus is on changing the behavior of women, not the behavior of male prostitutes (*jineteros*), foreign businessmen, or tourists. A number of feminists have called for a shift in emphasis. Instead of attacking the supply, attack the demand. What is most frightening about this unexpected result of tourism is the illusion of "freedom." Although *jineteras* do not appear trapped now, the practice of *jineterismo* may bring harm to young women in more serious and limiting ways. Celia Berger of the FMC states that if a young woman manages to marry and leave the country, she faces the possibility of being sold into sexual slavery (Weisman, 1995, pp. 24-27).

Therefore, the FMC is urging women in grassroots organizations to target schools through the leadership of the UJC (Union of Communist Youth) and encouraging the 50,000 social workers (mainly volunteers) associated with the FMC to conduct studies on the images of Cuban women portrayed abroad to promote tourism. The MAGIN is conducting the educational and training programs for tourism planners and economic decision-makers. The MAGIN further advocates a major shift in tourism's focus, emphasizing the wealth of health and medical, ecological, family/recreation and historic/cultural resources—instead of selling implied sexual adventure (Diaz, 1996).

While the current methods to reduce and ultimately to prevent the practice of prostitution are significant and timely, there is a need for fundamental economic, social, and political responses to *jineterismo*. Given the underlying cause of economic scarcity, the extreme difficulties of solving the economic crisis, and its further exacerbation by the U.S. government's foreign policy, can (or how can) the Cuban government overcome these structural barriers? The problem requires a gendered analysis of the construction of sexuality. For example, which women are *jineteras* and who decides what behavior is prostitution? Given the still unequal sexual division of labor in Cuban society and the relatively traditional socialization of men and women and their sexuality, how does "the Revolution" change the culture that creates the desire for prostitution by men and the perception of economic power by women who practice *jineterismo*? Only a social and political revolution of feminist values can provide a decisive analysis and vision for new constructions of gender, sexuality, and power relationships. Until women become more than a sector for development and accomplishments, power arrangements will continue to perpetuate models of domination. For many women inside and outside Cuba, it is a great shame that the Cuban Revolution can no longer claim to have eliminated both illiteracy and sex work.

7. Sexism, Tourism and International Politics

Further probing into the tourist industry from a critical, global, feminist perspective can shed light on international politics and long-standing political relationships between local residents and tourists. For example, Enloe (1990, chapter 2) argues that women in many countries are being drawn into unequal relationships with each other as a result of government sponsorship of the international tourist industry, some because they have no choice, but others because they are making their own decisions about how to improve their lives. Many women are playing active roles in expanding and shaping the tourist industry, as travel agents, travel writers, flight attendants, crafts women, maids, sex workers—even if they do not control it. Despite the good intentions of the feminist tourist/researcher, the relationship between the privileged tourist/researcher and *jinetera*, for example, falls short of any imagined international sisterhood (Enloe, 1990, p. 20).

Cuba, Tanzania, North Korea, Vietnam and Nicaragua are being governed today by officials who have adopted a friendlier attitude toward tourism. Indebted governments that have begun to rely on tourism include those that previously were most dubious about the tourism route to genuine development, especially if "development" is to include preservation and national sovereignty. Cuba and the other mentioned countries are being complimented and called "pragmatic" by mainstream international observers because they are putting the reduction of international debt and the earning of foreign currency at the top of their political agenda. Many of the advertisements luring travelers to sunny beaches and romantic encounters are designed and paid for by government tourist offices. Most of those bureaucratic agencies rely on femininity, masculinity, and heterosexuality to make their appeals and achieve their goals. Local men in police or military uniforms and local women in colorful dresses—or in the case of Cuba, very little dress at all—are the preferred images. The local men are militarized in their manliness; the local women are welcoming and available in their femininity.

Sex tourism is not an anomaly; it is one strand of the gendered tourism industry. While economists in industrialized societies presume that the "service economy," with its explosion of feminized job categories, follows a decline in manufacturing, policy-makers in many Third World countries have been encouraged by international advisers to develop service sectors before manufacturing industries have the chance to mature (Enloe, 1990, chapter 2).

To succeed, sex tourism requires Third World women to be economically desperate enough to enter prostitution; having done so, it is difficult to leave. The other side of the equation requires men from affluent societies to imagine certain women, usually women of color, to be more available and submissive than the women in their own countries. Finally, the industry depends on an alliance between local governments in search of foreign currency and local and foreign businessmen willing to purchase sexualized travel (Enloe, 1990, chapter 2).

The hushed and serious tones typically reserved for discussions of nuclear escalation or spiraling international debt are rarely used in discussions of tourism. Tourism does not fit neatly into public preoccupations with post-Cold War conflict and high finance. Although it is infused with masculine ideas about adventure, pleasure and the exotic, sexual relations are deemed "private" and thus kept off stage in debates about international politics. Yet, since World War II, planners, investors and workers in the tourist industry, and tourists themselves, have been weaving unequal patterns that are restructuring international politics. And they depend on women for their success (Enloe, 1990, chapter 2).

Cuban tourism might be providing much-needed liquidity, but it is not a solid foundation on which to build an economic recovery, especially as it relies on foreign investment to trickle down to the population. An alternative strategy would instead increase participation of the Cuban people in economic planning and implementation. Here the government could begin by engaging a public debate on how to develop a form of tourism that does not come at the expense and exclusion of Cubans. This debate could then extend to the larger issue of how to integrate market activity into a socialist country in a way that preserves the gains of the revolution. The absence of such an internal discussion will not forestall difficult choices, but it would mean simply that such choices will be made for Cuba by the more powerful forces of international capital.

8. Conclusion

On a global scale, government and corporate officials have come to depend on international tourist travel for pleasure in several ways. First, over the last decade they have come to see tourism as an industry that can help diversify local economies suffering from a reliance on one or two products for export. Tourism is embedded in the inequalities of international trade, but it is often tied to the politics of particular products, such as sugar, bananas, tea or copper. Second, officials have looked to tourism to provide them with foreign currency, a necessity in the increasingly unequal economic relations between poor and rich countries. Third, tourism has been looked upon as a spur to more general social development; the "trickle down" of modern skills, new technology, and improved public services is imagined to follow in the wake of foreign tourists. Fourth, many government officials have used the expansion of tourism to secure the political loyalty of local elites. Finally, many officials have hoped that tourism would raise their nations' international visibility and even prestige; tourism continues to be promoted by bankers and development planners, the majority of whom happen to be men, as a means of making the international system more financially sound and more politically stable.

Without ideas about masculinity and femininity—and the enforcement of both—in the societies of departure and the societies of destination, it would be impossible to sustain the tourism industry in its current form. It is not simply that ideas about pleasure, travel, escape, and sexuality have affected women in rich and poor countries. I am suggesting that the very structure of contemporary international tourism needs patriarchy to survive. Men's capacity to control women's sense of security and self-worth has been central to the continuation of tourism.

Feminist organizations concerned with *jineterismo*, both inside and outside Cuba, must seriously examine the larger question of patriarchy and international tourism in relation to Cuba's current economic crisis. Movements that upset any of the patterns in today's international tourist industry are likely to upset one of the principal pillars of contemporary world power. Such a realization allows us to take a more optimistic second look at the young women who seductively entice men along Cuba's Malecon for a fistful of dollars. They could have, with a certain combination of socio-economic conditions, the potential for reshaping the international political order, thus placing Cubans at the forefront of dismantling patriarchy and serving as a beacon of hope, justice, and democracy.

REFERENCES

Deere, Carmen Diana (1991) "Cuba's Struggle for Self-Sufficiency," *Monthly Review* (July-August), pp. 55-73.
Dello Buono, Richard (1995) "Rising Food Production Brings Relief to Cuban Consumers," *Caribbean Insight*, Volume 15, Number 4, p. 2.

_____(1992) "Race Against Time for Cuba's Socialism with Joint Ventures," *Caribbean Insight*, Volume 15, Number 6, pp. 4-5.

Diaz, Elena (1996) "Turismo y Prostitucion en Cuba," Working Paper Series, FLACSO, Havana, Cuba, pp. 1-33.

_____ (1996) "Cuban Socialism: Adjustments and Paradoxes," Working Paper Series, FLACSO, Havana, Cuba, pp. 1-20.

Eckstein, Susan (1994) *Back From the Future* (Princeton, New Jersey: Princeton University Press).

Enloe, C. (1990) *Making Feminist Sense of International Politics: Bananas,Beaches & Bases* (Berkeley: University of California Press).

Falk, Pamela (1996) *Conde Nast*, p. 40.

Ferguson, Ann (1991) *Sexual Democracy* (Boulder, Colorado: Westview Press).

Figueros, Miguel Alejandro and Sergio Plasencia Vidal (1994) "The Cuban Economy in the 1990s: Problems and Prospects," in Watson, Hilbourne A. (editor) *The Caribbean in the Global Political Economy* (Boulder, Colorado: Lynne Rienner Publishers).

Glazer, Jon and Kurt Hollander (1992) "Cuba's New Economy: Working for the Tourist Dollar," *Nation*, Volume 254, Number 23, pp. 820-824.

Kempadoo, K. (1996) "Prostitution, Marginality and Empowerment: Caribbean Women in the Sex Trade," *Beyond Law*, Volume 5, Number 14, pp. 69-84.

Lane, C. (1994) "The Long, Long Good-bye," *The New Republic* (October), pp. 15-18.

Lutjens, Sheryl (1995) "Reading Between the Lines: Women, the State, and Rectification in Cuba," *Latin American Perspectives*, Volume 22, Number 2, pp. 100-124.

Miranda, O. (1993) *La Mujer Cubana en los 90: Realidades y Desafios*, FMC document published in Havana, Cuba, (March), pp. 1-24.

Randall, Margaret (1992) *Gathering Rage* (New York: Monthly Review Press).

Rivery, J. (1991) "Ruedan en Cuba mas de 600,000 bicicletas chinas," *Granma* (DECEMBER) 14, p. 8.

Smith, Lois and Alfred Padula (1996) *Sex and Revolution: Women in Socialist Cuba* (New York: Oxford University Press).

Smith, Lois (1992) "Sexuality and Socialism in Cuba," in *Cuba in Transition* (Boulder, Colorado: Westview Press).

Strout, Jan (1995) "Women, the Politics of Sexuality and Cuba's Economic Crisis," *Cuba Update* (October), pp. 13-18.

Watson, Hilbourne A. (1994) "Global Restructuring and the Prospects for Caribbean

Competitiveness," in Watson H.A. (editor) *The Caribbean in the Global Political Economy*, (Boulder, Colorado: Lynne Rienner Publisher).
Weisman, Jean (1995) "From Maids to Companeras," *Cuba Update* (June), pp. 24-27.
Zimbalist, Andrew (1992) "Teetering on the Brink: Cuba's Current Economic and Political Crisis," *Journal of Latin American Studies*, Volume, 24, pp. 407-418.

5

What Color is Cuban? Complexities of Ethnic and Racial Identity

Christina Proenza

"Autoethnography" can illuminate contemporary examples of the negotiation of racial boundaries, the boundaries of whiteness in particular. By turning the ethnographic gaze inward, the author, a Cuban-American, deconstructs these qualifiers in order to bring to the forefront processes of identity construction, social location, and cultural politics. The history of United States immigration and naturalization laws, social network theory, and sociological approaches to ethnicity provide a theoretical foundation through which to examine the shifting meanings of the terms Anglo, Latin, American, white, and black. Through the filter of her own family history, the author traces the rise of Cuban cultural, economic, and political hegemony from segregated 1950s Miami to the present. Challenging sociology's paradigm of immigrant assimilation, the Cuban community generated a unique process of acculturation in reverse and profoundly influenced the identities of Miami's other ethnic groups. An examination of the transformation of Miami's ethnic groups brings into relief the micro and macro social forces that shape the negotiation of cultural meanings and social structure, the operations of race, and class.

Whiteness is a social construct, a legal artifact, a function of what people believe, a mutable category tied to particular moments. "White" is an idea, an evolving social group, an unstable identity subject to expansion and contraction, a trope for welcome immigrant groups, a mechanism for excluding those of unfamiliar origin, an artifice of social prejudice.[1]

-- Ian Haney Lopez, *White by Law*

Identities, goals, and aspirations are themselves fundamentally constructed phenomena....There is simply no such thing as a prestructured individual identity; both individuals and societies are the products and the contents...of interaction.[2]

-- Mustafa Emirbayer and Jeff Goodwin, "Network Analysis, Culture, and the Problem of Agency"

The notion that race is a social rather than a biological category has developed currency in academia, and yet the social sciences often continue to treat blackness as an apriori category and whiteness as racelessness, as a normative and natural quality. For example, upon telling a graduate sociology professor, one who embraced social constructivism, that I wanted to study race, he responded by saying, "go to Harlem." Since I did not mention any qualifiers, the professor immediately assumed that race signified black people. However, I am inclined to agree with Howard Winant that concepts of race remain deeply imbedded in every situation, every relationship, and every psyche. This is true not only of such large-scale macrosocial relationships as the distribution of wealth or income, or segregation in housing and education, but also of small-scale micro-level relationships.[3]

That race impacts all aspects of social life implies that racism affects not only the racial other, but also shapes the daily experiences and the individual and collective identities of whites. David Roediger began his ground-breaking study of what whiteness meant to nineteenth century American workers who defined themselves by it, with the autobiographical assertion: "Even in an all white town race was never absent."[4] Through this chapter, I hope to show that even in an all white family race was never absent. In an effort to investigate race I will not go to Harlem, but instead, I will go home.

My family was not part of the waves of more than one million Cubans who came north, en masse, as political exiles after the 1959 revolution. Arriving in 1947, they were "straight up" immigrants, seeking the American dream and broken off from their native land in the black and white, Protestant and Jewish sea of Miami when it was still a segregated southern town. In a heartbeat, a teacher at Citrus Grove Elementary School irrevocably turned my father "Mauricio" into "Morris." Over the course of months, another teacher taught him and his two older sisters English; all three were enrolled in first grade because of their inability to speak English. My grandparents, a dishwasher and a seamstress, would never learn more than few English words.

Coco Fusco, a Cuban-American self-described woman of color, made the brilliant observation that "to ignore white ethnicity is to redouble its hegemony by naturalizing it."[5] My family, fair-skinned, middle class, and Cuban, does not include itself in the category "people of color"; for they do not consider themselves to be non-white. At the same time, they do not describe themselves as whites. In American culture and in my family, the term white is tacitly synonymous with Anglo.

In his rise from lower-to-upper-middle class ranks, my father struggled between his cultural identity as a Latino and as a (white) American; but for him, his "racial" identity as white was never in question. For me, born into the middle-class status my father had secured, enjoying the benefits of being a white American and Latina—but never fitting squarely into either category—white ethnicity would become the central question. Coming of age in a new cultural climate that not only embraced diversity but actually idealized, idolized and glorified non-whiteness, I sought to renegotiate the whiteness my father had assumed.

America's racial boundaries are malleable. The American color line long relied on the "one drop" rule, where anyone with so much as a trace of African ancestry, visible or not, was classified as black. Those who could lay claim to whiteness, however, were not simply those who lacked any trace of African heritage. It has been documented that when Swedish, Irish, Italian, and Jewish immigrants came to the United States in the nineteenth century, they were often considered as belonging to an intermediate social category between white and black. Up until the beginning of the twentieth century, many European ethnic groups were considered to be outside of the white race. In the South some Italian children were forced to attend all-black schools. In 1914 a physician remarked that Slavs "are immune to certain kinds of dirt. They can stand what would kill a white man."[6] Immigrant assimilation or Americanization meant that succeeding generations of these groups would shed their distinctive ethnic identities and become whites. Since World War II, sociology's immigrant assimilation paradigm has been eclipsed by the notion of pluralism. Increasingly, ethnic groups consciously maintain rather than suppress a distinctive cultural identity. While the terms "people of color" and "mutliculturalism"and the ideologies that underlie them attempt to edge American society away from the polarity of black and white, a dichotomous and essentialized conception of race remains deeply entrenched.

Miami, Florida provides a unique context in which to examine racial identity and cultural boundaries. Built by the financial capital of northern whites and the labor of southern and Caribbean blacks, the city of Miami was incorporated in 1896. Ironically, the petition to charter the white supremacist municipal government was signed by black laborers, as Florida law required 300 signatures and Miami was home to fewer whites at the time. Like towns in the Deep South, early Miami was ruled by Jim Crow laws; status differences were enforced by the violence of authorities. While the Klu Klux Klan made some dramatic overtures, historical accounts reveal that the police physically enforced a degraded status for Miami's black population, their efforts always applauded by the media. When the first of the more than a million Cubans who would emigrate after the 1959 Cuban revolution began to arrive, black Miamians still paid their taxes at a separate courthouse window and were still excluded from Miami's beaches.[7]

The first waves of Cubans, mostly the privileged classes, in Miami, enjoyed the privileges of political exile status as well as the opportunities of emerging civil rights legislation. The anxiety of whites (Anglo) regarding the immense influx of Cubans would not reach its highest pitch until the infamous Mariel boat lift of 1980. But by 1986, the election of Cuban-born Mayor Xavier Saurez signalled the on-going escalation of Cuban political, economic, and cultural power which has since eclipsed the hegemony of whites. The triad of competing claims of native Blacks, Anglos, and Cubans in South Florida society is complicated by the influx of immigrants from various Latin American and Caribbean countries, most notably Nicaraguans and Haitians.

Miami's social structure has shifted dramatically over the last several decades and so have meanings given to terms of ethnic and cultural identification. This unique site of reverse acculturation, where Cubans have come to dominate the cultural, political and economic landscape, has in some contexts made the term Anglo a racial epithet, signifying cultural blandness. The Cuban population has become so threatening to the White Anglo Saxon Protestants (WASPs) that at Anglo social functions couched and pejorative references to "those people" no longer refer to the Blacks but to the Latinos. On the other hand, Miami's multicultural reality means that most Anglos find that their social and professional networks include Latinos. Furthermore, Latinos of a high-class standing and those who are "Americanized" are often treated by Anglos as honorary "whites."

The still surviving traditional Anglo prejudice against African-Americans was among the few Anglo customs to which many Cubans quickly assimilated. This is not to say that racism was absent in Cuba, but many regard dark-skinned Cubans as distinct from American blacks; blackness has different cultural connotations when it qualifies Cuban and when it qualifies American. Some have even argued that to a Cuban, a dark-skinned co-national is a Cuban while a dark-skinned American is a black.

Just as the meanings of black fluctuate in different cases, so too do the meanings of white. It is difficult to generalize the racial status attached to Cubans. Some regard Cubans as people of color, others see them as white. In many cases, particularly bureaucratic ones, the terms white and Hispanic are mutually exclusive, the latter conferring minority status and affirmative action opportunities. Despite the fact that Hispanic ethnicity confers minority status, in South Florida's Dade County Hispanics are the majority and the power elite; monolinguists who speak Spanish have more opportunities than those who speak English. Some Cuban-Americans in some instances are regarded as white particularly in relation to blacks, and in others as people of color, particularly in relation to Anglos.

Naturalization laws, until the 1950s, had only two racial categories, black or white, and it was not always clear how to consider immigrants in terms of America's definition of race. Originating in the U.S. Congress' 1790 provision limiting naturalization to "any alien, being a free white person who shall have resided within the limits and the jurisdiction of the U.S. for a term of two years,"[8] every naturalization act until 1952 included the "white person" prerequisite. In 1870 Congress extended the right to naturalize to "persons of African nativity or African descent'" setting in place a black and white dichotomy that would structure the legal boundaries of race in the U.S. This dichotomy was not based on skin color: blackness was defined by African descent regardless of appearance. The boundaries of whiteness were more fluid, brought into relief as the courts determined which persons, not of African descent, would be considered not-white. For example, Asian Indians, classified as Caucasian by anthropologists but regarded as non-white by several judges' estimations of "common-knowledge," were determined to be white by some courts and not in others. Exemplifying the shifting boundaries of whiteness, the federal government began a campaign to strip naturalized Asian Indians of their citizenship in 1923, denaturalizing at least 65 people.[9] These contradictory decisions are but one instance of the function of whiteness as an unstable, constructed legal category subject to contraction and expansion.

Further blurring definitions of race, Cubans, and Puerto Ricans are the only ethnic groups, historically, that had the ability, in some cases, to defy America's "one drop" rule, officially avoiding black status despite traces of African descent.[10] The Immigration and Naturalization Service (INS) has no official means of distinguishing between light and dark-skinned Cubans, and the ethnic categories black, Hispanic, and non-Hispanic white in the U.S. census do not distinguish skin color among Latinos. In practice, however, it is well-documented that dark-skinned Cubans often found themselves segregated from light-skinned co-nationals in cities like Jersey City and Tampa. As the nineteenth century Cuban settlement in Tampa was racially integrated, some have argued that ensuing segregation was a product of American polarization. In contemporary Miami, a geographer estimates that "black" Hispanics comprise 3-5 percent of the Hispanic population and are concentrated in neighborhoods between Little Havana (which is 99 percent "white" Hispanic) and the African-American enclave known as Liberty City.[11] How "mixed" Hispanics are classified is unclear.

With an extensive population of people who are visibly of African descent, Cuba has its own shifting racialized meaning system. Cuba was the last Spanish colony to abolish slavery in 1886 and the first nation in the hemisphere in which an independent black political party was organized. The war for independence was fought disproportionately by black Cubans, after which, despite their marginalization, "according to an elite-generated myth...there were no blacks and whites anymore, just Cubans."[12] The myth is supported by numerous instances of cross-racial alliances and mobilizations and challenged by events such as the government-led massacre of politically active black Cubans in 1912.

Cuba's nineteenth century and early twentieth century social construction of race was unique among the three-tier and multi-tier racial classification systems typical of most other Caribbean and Latin American nations, as Cuban mulattos were not differentiated from Cuban blacks. Like America, Cuban society enforced a single color line; unlike America, this line is not based on a "one drop" rule but the criterion of "visible" African descent.[13]   Spain's long history of miscegenation renders the Latin American conception of whiteness as being of "pure" Spanish ancestry as problematic as that of the U.S.[14]

Cuban society's notion of "whitening" was distinctive from those of other Latin American countries. The lack of distinction between mulattos and blacks meant that Cuba lacked Brazil's "mulatto escape hatch," where people of mixed ancestry could enjoy the political and economic advantages of whites. Peru's complex and fluid social hierarchy allowed some wealthy individuals of mixed ancestry to purchase certificates of "whiteness," and mixed children could be registered at birth in a higher social strata for a fee. Conversely, some physically recognizable whites sank in status as their fortunes declined.[15]   Generally, the process of "whitening" meant that some mestizos and mulattoes were allowed to inherit the social status of their European fathers. In Cuba, in addition to sexual union with a visibly lighter person, "whitening" included the notion of government subsidized European immigration and the marginalization of Afro-Cubans. Whiteness, however, was not always the preferred status in Cuba; Aline Helg notes that "several light mulatto leaders who could have claimed little African origin, if not whiteness, made it a point of honor to refer to themselves as black."[16]

Demographic shifts have rendered Cuba's current population largely black, with estimates ranging from over fifty to seventy percent.[17] While some argue that Cuban government propaganda touting U.S. racism prevented Afro-Cuban emigration, it has also been suggested that large numbers of dark-skinned Cubans came to the U.S., found the racism overwhelming, and returned to Cuba. Perhaps they faced an experience similar to that of the Bahamians who arrived at the beginning of the century.

Historical accounts reveal that unlike Miami's blacks from the Deep South, Bahamian immigrants arrived without a sense of social stigma associated with African descent: "In 1910, a Miami municipal court judge congratulated the Miami police for changing the attitudes of Nassau Negroes who upon their arrival considered themselves the social equal of white people."[18] The dark skin of the Bahamians, their recognizable African heritage, instantly transformed them from Bahamians to "Negroes" upon their arrival in Miami. Miami's all-white police force and segregated social structure were instrumental in "teaching" the Bahamians their new American status and identity conferred by their being considered black.

The Bahamians were "taught" their place in Miami's racial order as "blacks." How did fair-skinned Cubans learn and project their place in the racial order? Looking back over my own childhood, despite the explicit verbal suggestions that all people are equal, thousands of signs and symbols implied that black and brown were essentially different from, less than, white. My father participated in a bicultural world, yet he instilled in me the cultural tools for exploiting white middle-class cultural capital. Coco Fusco, to me, illuminates this situation:

> The socialization I and many other affirmative action babies received to identify racism as the property only of ignorant, reactionary people, preferably from the past, functioned to deflect our attention from how whiteness operated in the present. What bell hooks calls the liberal ideology of universal subjectivity (i.e., that we are all just people) made us partners in a silent pact that permitted "good" people of color to circulate among whites as long as racism was not mentioned as part of the immediate present.[19]

Unlike other members of my Cuban family, my father was able to become white. For a large part of his life, his social and professional networks were composed largely of Anglo Americans. He was well versed in the cultural codes of WASP society. His heroes, John F. Kennedy and Martin Luther King, signalled his "Americanness," considering that the Bay of Pigs and Civil Rights struggles held different meanings to many Cubans. But by the late 1980s, as Cuban political, economic, and cultural dominance began to crescendo, my father "rediscovered" his Cuban identity. His life began to include more Cuban people, music, and food. He increasingly embraced his "Cubanness" and distinguished himself from Anglo culture. My father's ability to renegotiate his ethnic identity revealed its socially determined rather than essential nature. His decision to do so paralleled the rise of Cuban cultural dominance in Miami and an emerging public discourse of cultural diversity in America.

My ancestry confers my status as Hispanic, while my socialization familiarized me with the cultural codes of whiteness. My access to the social networks of upper-middle-class Anglo society opened many doors for me, my status as Latina opened still others. My personal history bears out the knowledge I have gained as a sociologist of race—that whiteness is not a natural category but a cultural one. Whiteness is learned; it is a type of knowledge or consciousness that is culturally transmitted. Furthermore, whiteness is malleable; it changes with time, place, and social divisions of power. To recognize whiteness as an idea, rather than a fact, may help us rethink racial categories and help us to generate social categories more useful in a global community.

ENDNOTES

1. Ian Haney Lopez (1996) *White by Law: The Legal Construction of Race* (New York: New York University Press), p. 107.
2. Mustafa Emirbayer and Jeff Goodwin (1994) "Network Analysis, Culture, and the Problem of Agency," *American Journal of Sociology*, Volume 99, Number 6 (May), p. 1444.
3. Howard Winant (1994) *Racial Conditions* (Minneapolis: University of Minnesota Press), p. 2.
4. David Roediger (1991) *The Wages of Whiteness* (New York: Verso Books), introduction.
5. Richard Delgado (1996) "Uncolored People," *Lingua Franca*, Volume 6, Number 6 (September-October).
6. Mary C. Waters (1990) *Ethnic Options: Choosing Identities in America* (Berkeley: University of California Press), p. 2.
7. Alejandro Portes and Alex Stepick (1993) *City on the Edge: The Transformation of Miami* (Berkeley: University of California Press), p. 38.
8. Ian Haney Lopez (1996) op. cit., p. 43.
9. Ibid., p. 91.
10. F. James Davis (1991) *Who Is Black* (University Park: Pennsylvania State University Press), p. 158.
11. Navarro, Mireya (1997) "Black and Cuban-American: Bias in Two Worlds," *The New York Times*, September 13, p. 8.
12. Alejandro de la Fuente (1996) "Review of Our Rightful Share," *Hispanic American Historical Review*, Volume 6, Issue 6 (May), pp. 371-372.
13. Aline Helg (1995) *Our Rightful Share: The Afro-Cuban Struggle for Equality, 1886-1912*, (Chapel Hill: University of North Carolina Press), p. 3.
14. Pedro Perez Sarduy and Jean Stubbs(1993) (editors) *Afrocuba: An Anthology of Cuban Writing on Race, Politics, and Culture* (Australia: Ocean Press), p. 30.

15. Audrey Smedley (1993) *Race In North America: Origin and Evolution of a Worldview* (Boulder: Westview Press), p. 136.
16. Aline Helg (1995) op. cit., p. 14.
17. Navarro, Mireya estimates over fifty percent, "Black and Cuban-American: Bias in Two Worlds," *The New York Times,* September 13, 1997, p. 2. Mohl, Raymond. "Ethnic Transformations in Late Twentieth-Century Florida," *Journal of American Ethnic History,* Volume 15, Issue 2, 1996, p. 71., estimates seventy percent.
18. Dunn and Stepick (1992) "Blacks in Miami," in Grenier and Stepick (editors) *Miami Now: Immigration, Ethnicity, and Social Change* (Gainsville: University Press o f Florida), p. 42.
19. Coco Fusco (1995) *English Is Broken Here* (New York: The New Press), p. 76.

REFERENCES

David, James (1991) *Who Is Black?* (University Park: Pennsylvania State University Press).

Delgado, Richard (1996) "Uncolored People," *Lingua Franca,* Volume 6, Issue 6. (September-October).

Emirbayer, Mustafa and Jeff Goodwin (1994) "Network Analysis, Culture, and the Problem of Agency," *American Journal of Sociology,* Volume 99, Number 6 (May).

De La Fuente, Alejandro (1996) "Review" in *Hispanic American Historical Review,* Volume 6, Issue 6 (May).

Fusco, Coco (1995) *English Is Broken Here* (New York: The New Press).

Greenbaum, Susan (1985) "Afro-Cubans in Exile: Tampa, Florida, 1886-1984," *Cuban Studies,* Volume 15, Number 1.

Grenier, Guillermo and Alex Stepick (1992) (editors) *Miami Now! Immigration, Ethnicity, and Social Change* (Gainsville: University Press of Florida).

Haney Lopez, Ian (1996) *White By Law: The Legal Construction of Race* (New York: New York University Press).

Helg, Aline (1995) *Our Rightful Share: The Afro-Cuban Struggle for Equality, 1886-1912* (Chapel Hill: University of North Carolina Press).

Mohl, Raymond (1996) "Ethnic Tranformations in Late-Twentieth-Century Florida," *Journal of American Ethnic History,* Volume 15, Issue 2.

Navarro, Mireya (1997) "Black and Cuban-American: Bias in Two Worlds," The *New York Times,* September 13.

Perez Sarduy, Pedra and Jean Stubbs (1993) (editors) *Afrocuba: An Anthology of Cuban Writing on Race, Politics, and Culture* (Australia: Ocean Press).

Portez, Alejandro and Alex Stepick (1993) *City on the Edge: The Transformation of Miami* (Berkeley: University of California Press).

Roediger, David (1991) *The Wages of Whiteness* (New York: Verso Books).

Smedley, Audrey (1993) *Race in North America: Origin and Evolution of a Worldview* (Boulder: Westview Press).

Mary C. Waters (1990) *Ethnic Options: Choosing Identities in America* (Berkeley: University of California Press).

Winant, Howard (1994) *Racial Conditions* (Minneapolis: University of Minnesota Press).

6

From Black Cuban to Afro-Cuban:
Issues and Problems Researching Race
Consciousness and Identity in Cuban Race Relations

Clarence Lusane

Why and how to assess the nature and contours of race relations in Cuba is complicated by the problem of identifying exactly who belongs in what racial category and by the conscious decision on the part of the post-revolutionary Cuban government to not gather racially-oriented data. Furthermore, black Cubans appear to accept the official discourse that racism no longer functions with any power in Cuba. For these and other reasons, the author claims that the study of race must depend on narratives.   Constructed stories about (and by) Cubans of African descent—what is stated, what is omitted, and how the narratives change over time—are key to the study of race in Cuba, where racial inequality does exist even where racial discrimination has been eliminated. The chapter examines work by top Cuban scholars of race, Lourdes Casal and Alejandro de la Fuente, as well as established and newer writers from the United Sates about issues of race in Cuba.

I. Introduction

Racial identities and their boundaries have been shown to be untenable and illogical and, in the final analysis, a tangle of social constructions. Viewed through the lens of both biological and social sciences "race" muddles. Yet to leave the discussion at that level eviscerates the power of social categories, in this case that of race, to drive and shape society and the lives of people in it. This point is salient as we turn our discussion toward the issue of race relations in Cuba. In spite of the lack of a scientific or rational basis—in racially-stratified or differentiated societies such as the United States, Brazil, England, South Africa, and Cuba—race indeed matters.

The question that challenges scholars and researchers is how it matters and to whom. Assessing the nature and contours of race relations in Cuba is complicated by the problem of identifying exactly who belongs in what racial category and by the conscious decision on the part of the post-revolutionary government not to gather racially-oriented data. To a significant degree, this fundamental question of racial identification has been evaded by the present scholarship on race in Cuba.

It should be noted that to question the nature of racial categories in Cuba is not to obscure the very real history of racism that certainly existed. In Cuban history, slavery and racism were practiced despite the often nebulous nature of individual racial identification and categorization.

2. Current Scholarship on Race in Cuba

Numerous articles have been written about race in Cuba from the political Left and the political Right. On the left, those who have supported the revolution have generally agreed with the view, which is also held by Cuban political leaders, that racism has virtually disappeared from Cuban society. With the possible exception of individual racial prejudice, held onto by a portion of a disappearing elderly population, Cuban socialism eliminated the material basis for the reproduction of racism and racism effectively vanished within the first post-revolution generation, the argument goes. This theme is echoed in the fervent words of Marxist scholar Alexander Sukhostat who wrote that Cuba is "the one country in Latin America where all trace of four centuries of color discrimination has been erased finally and irrevocably."[1] In general, among leftists and socialists, there is agreement that the overthrow of capitalism and the establishment of socialism is the necessary basis for the eradication of oppressive social relations including racism, and that this necessary basis has occurred in Cuba.

On the political right, enemies of the Cuban revolution have contended that to the degree that racism continues to exist in Cuba, it is because the overwhelmingly white leadership has introduced a fictive conflict as a means to exploit and divide what had once been a racism-free society. This is the position held by Miami-based Omar Lopez Montenegro, who represents the Cuba-based opposition group the Association for Free Arts and the National Civic Union. Montenegro, in a theoretical slight-of-hand, wrote that "speaking of races always leads to racism," and then states disingenuously that in pre-Castro Cuba, "there were no segregated coffee shops or rest rooms."[2] Racism is configured as a discourse imposed from the top that has little historic, material, or social base and, by implication, will disappear when the current leadership does so.

In contrast to those who deny racism in Cuba, either pre-1959 or post-1959, are those who argue that racism has always existed in the country and continues today. Professor Carlos Moore, who is Afro-Cuban, contends that since the 1959 revolution, "Cuban Negroes played no greater part in Cuban politics than they did before 1958—if anything, less."[3] In his controversial book, *Castro, the Blacks and Africa*, Moore argues that "Fidel Castro began to resort to the 'Negro question' in order to discredit his enemies, both domestic and foreign, and to enhance his messianic hold over Black Cuba."[4] Moore, for the most part, engages in unsubstantiated speculations and generalizations, as in the aforementioned quote and, as scholars Lisa Brock and Otis Cunningham note, his "arguments are a-historical, convoluted, and contradictory."[5] While Moore somewhat moderated his criticisms in later years, he nevertheless viewed Cuba as recalcitrantly racist.

A more moderated position held by some progressives is that Cuba has eradicated institutional racism, but that racial prejudice and individual discrimination continue to occur at other levels. This position acknowledges the critical and positive role that socialism has played in addressing pre-revolutionary racial inequities, but it recognizes some shortcomings on the part of Cuban leaders in terms of being open and forthcoming about questions of continuing racial differences. As scholar Johnnetta Cole, who is a strong supporter of the Cuban revolution, states, "while there is ample evidence of the eradication of institutionalized forms of racism . . . there is also evidence that individual expressions of racism still exist in Cuba."[6]

While all of these studies are valuable in highlighting the contested discourses regarding race in Cuba, none of them interrogates the nature of the racial categories themselves. No exhaustive or extensive social science studies have been undertaken that earnestly and rigorously interrogate the construction and continuing evolution of racial categories in Cuba, nor how and why Cuban citizens self-define or place themselves into or out of particular racial groups. With the exception of researcher Alejandro de la Fuente and sociologist Lourdes Casal, both of whom have attempted to use available census data and other "official" information to assess the status of black Cubans, race-related hard data has been scarce in the literature on Cuba.[7] De la Fuente, using data from 1861 to 1981, attempts to extrapolate racial information by calculating percentages (see Table 1).

There are two major problems with the census data that can be implied from de la Fuente's work. First, the categories used in the early censuses were derived from models executed in the United States, that is, whites and non-whites. The

Table 1: Racial Population Distribution, Cuban Census

Year	Population	Whites	Blacks	Asians	Mulattos
1861	1,358,238	56.3	43.7	–	–
1899	1,572,797	66.9	14.9	0.9	17.2
1907	2,048,980	69.7	13.4	0.6	16.3
1919	2,889,004	72.3	11.2	0.6	16.0
1931	3,962,344	72.1	11.0	0.6	16.2
1943	4,778,583	74.4	9.7	0.4	15.5
1953	5,829,029	72.8	12.4	0.3	14.5
1981	9,723,605	66.0	12.0	0.1	21.9

Source: "Race and Inequality in Cuba, 1899-1981"[8]

second problem with the data, particularly the censuses of 1943, 1953 and 1981, is that it is not always clear whether it was the census-taker or the respondent who was providing information on the racial makeup of the household or even their own racial designation. Since race in Cuba was principally defined by the physical appearance of individuals, subjective decisions influenced significantly the outcome of the census. While de la Fuente questions the methodology of data collection, he never interrogates further the implications of how this data-gathering process affected the construction of the census or the notion of race in Cuba. Beyond the census, in the pre-revolutionary period, data on race is scarce. As Casal notes, "No formal studies of racial attitudes were conducted in pre-revolutionary society."[9]

Thus it becomes difficult to explain why in the 1981 census, for instance, about 66 percent of those surveyed claimed to be white, while only 12 percent said they were black. For any visitor to Cuba, this would not seem to correspond to the perceived reality that Cuba is primarily a dark-skinned and mulatto nation. This incongruity begs the question of how these racial categories are conceived at various levels including the state, the mass populace, and social institutions. Casal makes note of her frustration in attempting to accurately determine who is black and makes clear that her suppositions about the status of Afro-Cubans in housing and health care are conditional. She states that there is a "lack of reliable, serious studies of race relations in pre-1959 Cuba."[10]

3. Race in Cuba

"The normative system of values at the core of the definition of nationhood was egalitarian, and integrationist, but the practices were blatantly racist." —Sociologist Lourdes Casal[11]

As a consequence of these issues, studying race in Cuba presents a set of unique problems for researchers that can be summed up in two questions: (1) who is black and who is white in Cuba; that is, how do racial categories function in a socially-meaningful way? and (2) if distinct racial groups do exist in Cuba, could the relationship between them be characterized as racist? Our task as researchers and scholars is to determine the social force that race plays in Cuba—the formation, development, and nature of Cuba's particular racial categories—and how those categories have changed over time in a process of relationality.

Assessing the impact of the 1959 revolution on lessening or furthering racial inequality is predicated on how these categories function. As noted above, the theoretical and ideological position of the Cuban state and the Cuban revolution is that socialism eliminates the material and social basis for the production and perpetuation of racism. Racism is viewed as a capitalist-era phenomenon that, like class antagonisms, will whither away under socialism. This perspective reduces racism to the realm of market relations and ignores the social appropriation of whiteness—generally manifest in a Eurocentric social bias—as the core ideological and cultural engine of society. Also ignored are the political uses of racism as an historical engine of privilege and power accumulation and as a contemporary obstacle for full political achievement. This view also does not account for the socio-psychological factors that govern racial identity; that this is a constructed identity does not minimize its social power.

Until recently, with the rise of a regional Afro-Latino movement, the trope of racial democracy, common in a number of Latin American societies, facilitated the development of low race consciousness among the region's black population. This was done by attributing differences in social power to factors other than race, such as class, culture, region and, in many nations, by the creation of a "mulatto escape hatch" through which blackness or African-ness can be avoided.

In addition to the congruence with other Latin nations, Cuba illustrates the problem of race in several unique ways. First, Cuban socialism signals a different, though not unproblematic ideological approach on the part of the state to confronting issues of race. Bourgeois pluralist democracy, which fails to overthrow existing power relations, is seen for the sham it is. Ostensibly, under socialism, the state's anti-racist agenda is not simply the incorporation of a previously excluded racial group but rather the elimination of class and race inequities. As Cuban President Fidel Castro stated in 1966, "We believe that the problem of discrimination has an economic content and basis appropriate to a class society in which man is exploited by man.... Discrimination disappeared when class privileges disappeared."[12]

Second, the Cuban revolutionary leadership also sought to address specific dimensions of racial insecurity. One of the first declarations of the new regime was to specifically outlaw institutional racism. This policy cut both ways, however. Under the new law, any effort at expressed racial group consciousness, from black as well as white Cubans, could and would be determined to be racist, and would find legal and political resistance from the state whether its intended objectives were counter-revolutionary or not. The progressive content was to outlaw any overtly racist group or movement and, implicitly, individual acts of racism. This "color-blindness" in its conservative form, however, is a-historical in that it erroneously assumes that racial categories were constructed on balanced terms and, therefore, that black race consciousness emerges from the same historical and social processes as white race consciousness and with the same reactionary agenda. Here, a critical distinction needs to be made between identity politics, the political expression of an essentialized notion of race, and race consciousness—recognition of the social force that race may play under specific social circumstances. The former (the politics of essentialized identities), even when a response to the racist dictates of other social players is required, must be resisted as it merely reconstructs and perpetuates fixed categories of race that mirror those initially being struggled against.

Race in Cuba is further nuanced by the paradox of Cuba's broad acceptance of black cultural expressions directly tied to an African past in religion, dance, and music; yet it advocates a complete denial of race as a variable in social or political life. For this reason and others, the overwhelming number of black Cubans appear to accept the official view that racism no longer functions with any power in Cuba.

4. Theorizing Race in Cuba

Several theoretical frameworks offer suitable analytical tools for explaining and assessing Cuba's racial dynamics. One is the "racial formation" paradigm developed and employed by Michael Omi and Howard Winant in *Racial Formation* and elaborated further in Winant's *Racial Conditions*.[13] Their racial formation theory (RFT) argues that in all circumstances where racial groups exist, the relationship between them as well as the content of those particular categories cannot be reduced to or explained by ethnicity, class, or "color-blind" frameworks. Instead, they contend that racial categories have their own dynamics in which objective and subjective conflicts between racial groups emerge, are transformed, and constantly remapped; that is, race is "an unstable and (decentered) complex of social meanings constantly being transformed by political struggle". This is to say that while the particular social configurations of race relations will vary from society to society, one can still theorize and generalize about racial intercourse by noting and examining the ever-changing political construction and use of race, racial categories, and racial groups. Post-structuralists have emphasized the role of narrativity in identity construction including that of race. As researchers Margaret Somers and Gloria Gibson describe, "It is through narrativity that we come to know, understand, and make sense of the social world, and it is through narratives and narrativity that we constitute our social identities."[14] Racial identities, according to the paradigm, are constructed and mediated through political struggles that embody contending narratives across overlapping historic and social landscapes.

How do we operationalize these notions of racialization and narrativity in the Cuban context? Cuban history provides partial insight into these concerns. According to historian Aline Helg, the "mulatto escape hatch," prevalent in most of Latin America's racially-stratified societies, did not exist in Cuba for most of its history—thus creating a bifurcated system of racial division. She writes that "Such classification differs from the three-tier or multi-tier racial systems prevailing in many countries of the region."[15] Although a mulatto strata existed and some members enjoyed more privileges than blacks, for the most part, mulattos and blacks were sutured into a single racial caste. Racial identity and the preservation of caste were constructed along the lines of visibility rather than a formal set of guidelines as evolved in the United States—the "one-drop" rule—and in South Africa the codes and regulations of the Apartheid system. The social meaning of race was codified in physical features in a binary system with little room for mutability and racial conversion. The rigidity of this system affected even President Fulgencio Batista (1940-1944) who was denied membership in the racially-segregated Havana Yacht Club because he was not "white."[16]

Two other critical narratives shaped the complexity of race in Cuba. The centrality of black participation in the independence movement is critical in the national identity held so strongly by Afro-Cubans. It is impossible to relate a narrative about the freedom struggle against Spain that does not identify the critical, decisive role that Afro-Cuban leaders, such as Antonio Maceo, played. Maceo, who was mulatto, is viewed by all Cubans as a national hero virtually equal in stature to José Marti. An example of the reverence in which Maceo is held can be seen in the mammoth statute erected in his honor in Santiago, the largest in the country to any individual and perhaps the largest in the world. The strength of this narrative goes a long way in explaining the reluctance of Afro-Cubans to demarcate themselves from the rest of Cuban society. Yet, upon examination, even this narrative is problematic in terms of the racial history of Cuba. In 1900 a national commission examined Maceo's remains after he died and concluded that while his body was "black," his brain and, therefore, his military brilliance and acuity, was from his "white" side.[17]

The second narrative of note is the 1912 massacre of the leaders and followers of the Independent Party of Color (PIC). The all-black party emerged in the aftermath of the failure of the post-independence government to address concerns of Afro-Cubans and the resistance to black mobilization around those concerns. It is estimated that between 3,000 and 4,000 black Cubans, including the leaders of the PIC, were killed by white Cubans in the summer of 1912 in an effort to stop black protests in support of the party.[18] This bloody response to the black Cuban effort for equality had the long-term effect of quelling any and all attempts at race-based (black) organizing in Cuba. The trope of racial harmony was hegemonic, even as the massacres were occurring, as Cuban leaders of the period denied that the killings had anything to do with race. Even in the present era, Cubans remain reluctant to speak of the "little war of 1912." There is virtually no mention of the massacre in history books or museums, and many black Cubans have learned of the incident in whispered stories.[19] Thematically, a narrative duality of pride and apprehension has shaped and continues to influence the Afro-Cuban response to questions of race. For white Cubans, these same narratives may be read as texts of nation-building and deracialization resulting in one people (Cubans) whose racial legacy is best understood as mostly harmonious.

As is discussed below, although we now have a workable model by which to assess race relations, it is difficult to operationalize these categories in Cuba since data is not collected in a way that is broken down racially. In key areas, such as employment, housing, heath care, criminal justice and political participation, no current racial data exist. While there are some ways to compensate for these problems, such as comparing data collected at the neighborhood level where neighborhoods have traditionally been black, white, or mixed, this is obviously a serious methodological compromise.

5. Researching Race Relations in the Post-Revolution Period

The new government opened beaches, hotels, restaurants, clubs, recreational facilities, and other areas of Cuban society that had been previously closed to Afro-Cubans. In the aftermath of the 1959 revolution, strong language and legal statutes were used to address the issue of racism. No less a person than President Fidel Castro himself spoke to the issue. Early on after coming to power, he stated that "Of all forms of discrimination, the worst is that which limits the access of the Cuban black man to the work centers. Because it is a reality that in our country, in some sectors, there has existed a shameful procedure of exclusion of black people from work."[20]

In acknowledging Cuba's roots, he also stated that "African blood flows freely through our veins."[21]

Without a doubt, Afro-Cubans gained significantly from the revolution, although those benefits came indirectly in most cases. As McGarrity and Cardenas state, "The popular economic, social and political measures implemented benefitted mainly people of humble origin and thus most blacks and mulattos."[22]

Yet official social data before the 1959 revolutionary triumph and since the revolution offers little that is useful in scientifically assessing the impact of the revolution on Cuban race relations. As Casal states, the "paucity" of data makes it easy and problematic to distort the pre-revolutionary baseline of racial information. In other words, it is nearly impossible to scientifically measure with hard data what was the social status of blacks prior to 1959. So while it can be assumed with a great degree of accuracy that blacks generally suffered in relation to whites, exactly how is difficult to gauge. It is clear that certain occupations were closed to blacks until the revolution; for example, hotel desk clerks. It is unclear, however, exactly how the racial composition of those occupations was changed because no data is currently available.

What all this means is that the veracity of the claims by the post-1959 government that racism has been completely eradicated is tentative. As noted above, for the most part, the revolutionary regime has not kept racially-based data since it came to power. The revolution proposed no specific program of racial affirmative action similar to the programs and efforts to integrate women, youth, and the rural population into the new society. To implement an affirmative action-type program would have been "contrary to the egalitarian goals of the Revolution insofar as they tend to make the color of skin an issue."[23]

A number of points can be made about the actions and speeches regarding race relations. First, as the revolution came to power, racial discrimination was a factor significant enough in Cuban society to warrant state remediation. Second, the revolution's words and deeds were a powerful blow against the emergence of racism as a tool of the counter-revolution. Third, the fact that no special programs were initiated to address racial discrimination meant that the revolutionary leaders assumed that a rising tide would lift all boats, and that a broad distribution across all of Cuban society would necessarily benefit Afro-Cubans. This assumption was problematic on two fronts: first, it reduced racial discrimination to material relations. Political, social, and cultural-psychological dimensions as well as internal manifestations are simply dismissed and ignored; second, Cuba was and is an underdeveloped nation with limited resources and material capacities. Under normal circumstances, material shortages are to be expected, making it safe to speculate that those who are already marginalized will remain so.

Cuba's post-1959 struggle over the issue of race occurred in the context of unrelenting attacks from the United States to destroy the revolution. Internal sabotage, political assaults, an economic embargo, a military blockade, and a full-scale invasion necessitated survival strategies that shaped the capacity of the revolution to address race, gender, and other issues.

6. Contemporary Cuba

Life in Cuba remains qualitatively influenced by the still-existent U.S. economic embargo. Laws passed in the U.S. Congress in recent years, specifically the Torrecelli and Helms-Burton bills, have toughened the restrictions against Cuba. As a consequence of U.S. economic and political policies and the end of economic benefits lost in the dissolution of the Soviet and Eastern European communism, Cuba has entered what it terms a "Special Period" in which sacrifices of particular socialist goals and standards have occurred out of economic necessity. Every aspect of Cuban life is affected by the hardships.

Scholar Jorge Domínguez and other researchers argue that in the decades since the 1959 revolution racial inequality exists in Cuba even where racial discrimination has been eliminated. In areas of health and housing, for example, pre-revolutionary segregation gave way to post-revolutionary economic deprivation for all Cubans. However, in terms of health, for instance, Domínguez writes about the years after the change in power: "Cuban blacks and mulattos are demonstrably poorer; because they are poorer, they are more likely than whites to become sick. This was true before the Revolution, and it is still true in the 1970s."[24] Recent scholarship has also documented that in areas as diverse as criminal justice and views on interracial relationships, racist views and practices can be found.[25] With the coming of the "Special Period," unresolved economic inequalities that have a disproportionate racial consequence are likely to remain static or even become worse.

A critical decision in the "Special Period" was to have tourism become the economic locomotive. As McGarrity and Cardenas note, black Cubans appear to be excluded to a great degree from the tourism industry where access to foreign currency, including dollars, is critical for economic survival. This appears to be the case from our observations during a June 1997 visit. This means, first and foremost, that black Cubans are excluded from the lucrative tips in foreign currencies.

Race relations would also appear to be affected by remittance dollars from the United States, what one member of our delegation termed "racist dollars." It is suspected, though perhaps impossible to confirm, that most of the dollars sent home to Cuban family members and friends from the United States come from white Cubans and, in any case, are facilitating a growing class division between those who have foreign currency and those who do not. As scholar Walter Russell Mead notes, "Family remittances to Cubans from relatives in the United States have already created a privileged new group of Cubans in what had been a relatively egalitarian island economy."[26]

Every indication is that the "Special Period" will continue for some time to come. The United States shows little promise of softening its position of antagonism toward Cuba, and the global economy is also brutal. Cuban accommodation with multinational capital has begun in significant ways, and that too will likely change dramatically the nature of labor and labor struggles on the island. As these transformations unfold, their impact on race relations should be monitored and assessed. Whether this will happen or not depends on how strongly the Cuban leadership holds on to the notion that racism has disappeared (permanently) in Cuba.

7. From Black Cuban to Afro-Cuban: The Future of Race Relations in Cuba

In his autobiography, *Colored People*, scholar Henry Louis Gates notes that in completing his "personal statement" for graduate school at Yale, he used his family as metaphor to represent the evolution of race conscious identity designation among blacks of African descent in the United States. He wrote, "My grandfather was colored, my father was Negro, and I am black." At the beginning of the twenty-first century, Gates' children would undoubtedly claim that they are African American.

Gates' tale not only expresses the self-defining anxieties of African Americans, but also the transformation of black racial identity. For nearly 400 years, blacks in the United States have struggled with their nomenclature. Each transition in popular designation—from African to colored to Negro to black to African American—has been generated by political and social turning points. The most tangible lesson to be learned from this long history is that how blacks name themselves will continue to be contested both within and outside the black community.

In Cuba, the bulk of the population does not refer to themselves as either "black" or "white" Cubans, but simply as "Cuban." It is not uncommon, however, for the term "black Cuban" to be used as a descriptive by Cubans of all colors. In recent years, among a small but increasingly race conscious cohort of primarily exile black Cubans, the term "Afro-Cuban" has emerged, or rather, reemerged.[27] Does the development of a self-classification from black Cuban to Afro-Cuban indicate race consciousness? Yes. As noted above, race consciousness has generally been seen as inherently counter-revolutionary. For sure, if the revolution maintains a myopic view of race, there is a great potential that it could become so.

What if the Cuban government granted researchers carte blanche, how would one begin? First, one would have to note the impossibility of constructing an objective definition of race because the concept necessarily embodies ideological, political, and personal concerns. This has not been accomplished anywhere and it is not realistic to think it could happen in Cuba. Second, the Cuban people would have to be won to seeing the value of a social science intervention on the question of race. At this point, many Cubans feel that the mere discussion of race introduces racism into the environment. As much as possible, the citizenry must recognize the value to Cuban society to uncover the mask of color-blindness and, for the first time in Cuban history, conduct a study that informs and provides correctives for a problem that has plagued nearly every capitalist—and socialist—society.

ENDNOTES

* I would like to acknowledge and extend thanks to my research assistant, Jason Henry, for his assistance on this project.

1. Alexander Sukhostat (1983) "Nationality: Cuban," *World Marxist Review* (July), p. 57.

2. Omar Lopez Montenegro (1993) "Despite Cuba's History of Tolerance Castro is a Calculating Racist - Here's Why," *Miami Herald* (July).

3. Manning Marable (1984) "Race and Democracy in Cuba," *The Black Scholar* (May-June), p. 23.

4. Carlos Moore (1989) *Castro, the Blacks and Africa* (Los Angeles: California: University of California - Los Angeles Press), p. 57.

5. Lisa Brock and Otis Cunningham (1991) "Race and the Cuban Revolution: A Critique of Carlos Moore's Castro, the Blacks, and Africa," *Cuban Studies*, Volume 21, p. 173. See also, Cheryl Harris (1990) "House of Mirrors: Carlos Moore's Vision of Cuba, Race, and Africa," *Cuba Update* (summer), pp. 25-26.

6. Johnetta Cole (1980) "Race Toward Equality: The Impact of the Cuban Revolution on Racism," *Journal of Black Scholar* (November-December), p. 5.

7. Lourdes Casal (1989) "Race Relations in Contemporary Cuba," in Philip Brenner, William Leogrande, Donna Rich and Daniel Siegel (editors) *The Cuba Reader: The Making of a Revolutionary Society* (Emeryville, California: Grove Press); and Alejandro de la Fuente (1995) "Race and Inequality in Cuba, 1899-1981," *Journal of Contemporary History*, Volume 30.

8. Ibid., de la Fuente, p. 135.

9. Casal, op. cit., p. 476.

10. Ibid., pp. 471-472.

11. Ibid., p. 476.

12. de la Fuente, op. cit. p. 133.

13. See Michael Omi and Howard Winant (1986) *Racial Formation in the United States: from the 1960s to the 1980s* (New York: Routledge Press) and Howard Winant (1996) *Racial Conditions: Politics, Theory, Comparisons* (Minneapolis: University of Minnesota Press).

14. Margaret Somers and Gloria Gibson (1994) "Reclaiming the Epistemological `Other': Narrative and the Social Construction of Identity," in Craig Calhoun (editor) *Social Theory and the Politics of Identity* (Cambridge, Massachusetts: Blackwell Publications), p. 59.

15. Aline Helg (1995) *Our Rightful Share: The Afro-Cuban Struggle for Equality, 1886-1912* (Chapel Hill, North Carolina: The University of North Carolina Press), p. 3.

16. Casal, op. cit., p. 477.

17. Helg, op. cit., pp. 104-105.

18. Aline Helg (1990) "Race in Argentina and Cuba, 1880-1930: Theory, Policies, and Popular Reaction," in Richard Graham (editor) *The Idea of Race in Latin America, 1870-1940* (Austin, Texas: University of Texas Press), p. 55.

19. Casal, op. cit., pp. 427-473.

20. Cole, op cit., p. 10.

21. Marable, op. cit., p. 28.

22. Gayle McGarrity and Osvaldo Cardenas (1995) "Cuba," in Minority Rights Groups (edition) *No Longer Invisible: Afro-Latin Americans Today* (London: Minority Rights Publication), p. 96.

23. Casal, op. cit., p. 481.

24. Jorge Domínguez (1978) *Cuba: Order and Revolution* (Cambridge: Massachusetts: The Belknap Press), p. 256.

25. See Alejandro de la Fuente "Recreating Racism: Race and Discrimination in Cuba's `Special Period'," unpublished paper presented to Cuba Society Group forum, "The Role of Race in 1990s Cuba," Georgetown University, May 19, 1998; Alejandro de la Fuente (1998) "Race, National Discourse, and Politics in Cuba," *Latin American Perspectives* (May), pp. 43-69; and Nadine Fernandez (1996) "The Color of Love: Young Interracial Couples in Cuba," *Latin American Perspectives* (winter), pp. 99-117.

26. Walter Russell Mead (1995) "Rum and Coca Cola: The United States and the New Cuba," *World Policy Journal* (Fall), p. 40.

27. The term "Afro-Cuban" was first used in 1847. It has only been in recent years, however, that is has emerged in broad use, particularly by black Cubans outside of Cuba. Pedro Perez Sarduy and Jean Stubbs (editors) (1993) *AfroCuba: An Anthology of Cuban Writing on Race, Politics, and Culture* (Melbourne, Victoria, Australia: Ocean Press), p. 38.

REFERENCES

Brock, Lisa and Otis Cunningham (1991) "Race and the Cuban Revolution: A Critique of Carlos Moore's Castro, the Blacks, and Africa," *Cuban Studies*, Volume 21.

Casal, Lourdes (1989) "Race Relations in Contemporary Cuba," in Philip Brenner, William Leogrande, Donna Rich and Daniel Siegel (editors) *The Cuba Reader: The Making of a Revolutionary Society* (Emeryville, California: Grove Press).

Cole, Johnetta (1980) "Race Toward Equality: The Impact of the Cuban Revolution on Racism," *Journal of Black Scholar* (November-December).

De la Fuente, Alejandro (1998) "Race, National Discourse, and Politics in Cuba," *Latin American Perspectives* (May).

_____(1995) "Race and Inequality in Cuba, 1899-1981," *Journal of Contemporary History*, Volume 30.

Domínguez, Jorge (1978) *Cuba: Order and Revolution* (Cambridge: Massachusetts: The Belknap Press).

Fernandez, Nadine (1996) "The Color of Love: Young Interracial Couples in Cuba," *Latin American Perspectives* (Winter).

Helg, Aline (1995) Our Rightful Share: The Afro-Cuban Struggle for Equality, 1886-1912 (Chapel Hill, North Carolina: The University of North Carolina Press).

_____(1990) "Race in Argentina and Cuba, 1880-1930: Theory, Policies, and Popular Reaction," in Richard Graham (editor) *The Idea of Race in Latin America, 1870-1940* (Austin, Texas: University of Texas Press).

Marable, Manning (1984) "Race and Democracy in Cuba," *The Black Scholar* (May-June).

McGarrity, Gayle and Osvaldo Cardenas (1995) "Cuba," in Minority Rights Groups (editor) *No Longer Invisible: Afro-Latin Americans Today* (London: Minority Rights Publication).

Mead, Walter Russell (1995) "Rum and Coca Cola: The United States and the New Cuba," *World Policy Journal* (Fall), p. 40.

Montenegro, Omar Lopez (1993) "Despite Cuba's History of Tolerance Castro is a Calculating Racist - Here's Why," *Miami Herald* (July).

Moore, Carlos (1989) *Castro, the Blacks and Africa* (Los Angeles: California: University of California - Los Angeles Press).

Omi, Michael and Howard Winnart (1986) *Racial Formation in the United States: from the 1960s to the 1980s* (New York: Routledge Press).

Somers, Margaret and Gloria Gibson (1994) "Reclaiming the Epistemological 'Other': Narrative and the Social Construction of Identity," in Craig Calhoun (editor) *Social Theory and the Politics of Identity* (Cambridge, Massachusetts: Blackwell Publications).

Sukhostat, Alexander (1983) "Nationality: Cuban," *World Marxist Review* (July).

Winant, Howard (1996)*Racial Conditions: Politics, Theory, Comparisons* (Minneapolis: University of Minnesota Press).

7

Black Beans and MTV

Katia Perea

I am a Miami-born Cuban-American child of exiled Cuban parents. My generation grew up with families in "el exilio." Our impressions of Cuba come from memories and stories passed down to us. Given the diplomatic ties between Cuba and the United States, it is not easy to write about the cultural patterns in a country we can only visit illegally, or with a visa that is difficult to obtain. This chapter is both an exploration of Cuban identity in the United States and an ethnography of American-based Cuban solidarity groups. This ethnography explores the sentiments these groups carry towards Cubans in Cuba and in the U.S. It is primarily a critique on Cuban solidarity groups' lack of familiarity with Cuban-Americans and, therefore, their inadequacy to fulfill the needs of Cuban-Americans, the most important of those needs being a united Cuba.

1. Introduction: Los Cubanos - We are a House of Three[1]

(1) Los Cubanos en Cuba, the Cubans. Los que han nacido/vivido durante un gobierno socialista. Los sentimientos de estos Cubanos varían bastante. Hay de los que se consideran communistas fieles y tambien hay los que desean que Fidel caiga lo mas rápido posible.
(2) Los Cubanos emigrado para los Estados Unidos, the Cubans in America. Este grupo se puede dividir en tres emigraciones principal: (a) el exilio (1960); (b) el mariel (1980); y (c) los balseros (1994). Cada movimiento tiene su propia identidad. Los Cubanos del exilio trajeron los ideales de su sociedad. Los del Mariel, entroducidos a Cuba socialista, cambiaron la estructura social de la comunidad establecida aqui.[2] Y los Balseros llegaron con muchos de las costrumbres de la Cuba de hoy.
(3) Los Cubanos-Americanos, the Cuban-Americans. Aqui caigo yo. Escribiendo en español pero thinking in English.

"Cuando me fui de Cuba."

My mother, Yoyi, left Cuba thirty-five years ago when she was twenty years old. She had ten dollars sewn into the hem of her dress. When she disembarked from the plane there were Americans waiting to buy cigars at a reasonable price, like the box of cigars she carried in her hands which she sold for fifteen dollars. Yoyi slept on a couch in her aunt's living room under a window. She was frightened because the room faced a cemetery. At first she cried a lot, then felt she had to be strong because her family was relying on her. With monetary assistance received from the government, *el dinero del refugio*, sixty dollars a month, she gave twenty dollars to her aunt, twenty dollars for herself, and she would set aside twenty dollars in anticipation of her parents' arrival. She got a job as a secretary typing addresses onto envelopes. When her family arrived two years later, she had saved approximately seven hundred dollars. "Toma, Papa, para ayudarte," Here, Papa, to help you.

Her parents and young brother, Emilito, were having difficulties leaving Havana. Her brother eventually came over on the Peter Pan Airlift,[3] but her father had some difficulty leaving Cuba. His brother, my great-uncle, *tio-abuelo Bebito*, was a lawyer who happened to be the speech writer for Batista (the overthrown President) and was asked, ordered, by the president to give a speech explaining his departure. In the meantime, Batista had fled the island with a significant sum of money.

Bebito delivered this speech, after which he was placed under house arrest where he received daily death threats. Those suspicions from the revolutionary mob carried over to his brother—my grandfather Emilio. The revolutionary population was assuming power, and in that chaotic state anything could happen. Armed revolutionaries would storm into Emilio's house and threaten him at gunpoint. My mother got so scared at these raids that she often fainted. In one such raid, a truck load of revolutionaries pulled up to her house and started yelling. Yoyi knew surely that this would be her father's death. Before she could determine what they were yelling, she fainted. It turned out the maid's boyfriend was part of the revolutionary troops, and he had returned from the countryside to get her.

Emilio was a very honest man, a dentist by profession who kept his books clean and cheated no one, unlike the corrupt practices rampant in the Batista regime. His friends and colleagues were professionals in the community: doctors, lawyers, engineers, and all of them, honest or not, were suffering at the hands of the revolutionary mobs. These were the consequences of their association with the corrupt Cuban government.

Yoyi was finishing her bachelors degree in advertisement at *La Universidad de La Habana*, but in 1957 the university was shut down. She never got her degree. My mother had dated my father, Manuel, in Cuba, but they became separated due to the revolution. A year after her family arrived in Miami, she ran into her future mother-in-law and asked her about Manuel. It just so happened that Manuel would be arriving from Louisiana State University that very week.

My father had been living in Louisiana for some time before the revolution. When the revolutionary movement claimed the life of a neighbor, my dad's widowed mother, my grandmother, Abuela Marta, mother of three, took money from her husband's life insurance and sent my father away to college in Baton Rouge, Louisiana. Louisiana State University had a summer Spanish language intensive program at the University of Havana, and along with Cuba was one of the four universities in the world which taught *Quimica Azucarera*/Industrial Sugar Chemical Engineering. My father was pursuing a master's degree in Electrical Engineering.

In the early years of the struggle against Batista (1952-1959), almost everyone supported the badly needed social reforms. "Yo queria ayudar a mi pais, mejorarla," says Yoyi.[4] The social movement was a struggle for democracy, fueled by anti-Batista and anti-corruption sentiments. The extreme violence used by the Batista regime to suppress the movement for democracy transformed the mobilization for democratic freedom into a revolution. Most of the exiled Cubans in Miami were originally involved with the revolutionary movements. However, when Castro declared that Cuba would become a socialist state, many people changed sides.

My father took some of his university money and flew back home so that he could join the struggle. He changed the little dollars he had to Cuban pesos, rendering them worthless within the year. My father's side of the family had a much harder time emigrating to the U.S. due to their financial situation; yet somehow he managed to return to Louisiana to finish his engineering degree.

When he arrived in Miami in 1961 he met my mother. They began dating again and fell in love. In those early years of exile, most Cubans thought that they would soon be returning home. Reality sank in shortly. They clung to their memories. Memories were the lifelines to all they had lost and hoped to regain. They began to create their new lives in the United States as Cuban-Americans; they began to work and started having families.

Manuel and Yoyi got married and moved to New York City. My father got a job as an elevator operator, my mother as a doctor's secretary.[5] My *abuela* arrived the next year to help with the new baby, my older sister Ada. *Abuela* recalls when the social worker came over to the apartment for an interview. My grandmother requested a cradle for the new baby; the social worker told her, "Put a pillow inside the dresser drawer and lay the baby in there." One New York winter was all they could bear; they moved back to Miami and a year later I was born. It was March 23, 1968.[6]

2. October 2, 1996, The Cuba Place, New York City[7]

I was excited to go to The Cuba Place because many who met me in New York and found out that I was Cuban always asked if I had already been to The Place. I imagined I could receive some "Cuba nurturing" there, drink "cafesito" and hear Cuban stories. I arrived late one afternoon and rang the doorbell. The door buzzed and I climbed up a very slanted staircase. Like the interior of many non-profit organizations, the place was very drab. It was also very messy and painted in flat tones of beige-brown. It was almost as if political concerns blocked out all need for aesthetic pleasantries.

The hall by the door had three posters on the wall. I recognized the artist as the cartoonist who painted a political cartoon on a wall extending an entire block by the Malecon, the sea wall in Havana. The mural along the *Malecon* was a political cartoon mocking Jesse Helms. I was amazed at how much publicity he received in Cuba. I do not understand the logic nor logistics of making your nemesis a star. Standing at The Cuba Place's door, I knocked and went right in.

3. July 4, 1994, Habana, Cuba

I stood in front of the door with my palms all sweaty. It was actually a beautiful iron gate at the foot of a staircase that led to the house upstairs. I rang the doorbell. A woman I had never seen before leaned over the banister to look down. *Quien es?* (Who is it?), she called out. This question is the subject of this chapter. *Quien soy*? "Who am I?" Am I Cuban? Am I American? As I looked up the staircase I felt I was coming a little closer to my answer.

"Es Katia, la hija de Yoyi." I could hear the yells upstairs, *"Hay dios mio!"* *"Pero que es esto*!" *"No* me lo puedo creer!" My *tia-abuela* Margot,[8] the only family member who knew me, came downstairs with the rest of the family. We had not seen each other since I was twelve. There were many tears. I was home in a place I have never been. Family to people I have never met.

I had decided to go to Cuba on a whim while traveling through Mexico. I had to experience for myself the island paradise of which my grandparents had told me so many stories. I wanted to see the houses in which my parents grew up. I wanted to visit what might have been my home.

My family in Cuba was not expecting me. I had no way of contacting them since I did not have their telephone number. But I did have their address, so I just showed up. I had been very nervous at the airport, expecting customs officials to be wicked communists out to give me a hard time, as I had been warned by my Cuban community in Miami. Instead I received a warm welcome by the woman who stamped the card that goes in my passport.[9] "*Bienvenido a tu pais* (Welcome to your country)," she said and smiled.

My cousins, who are about my age, were as surprised as I was to find how much we had in common. They kept saying, "You are a Cuban, only born over there." The question "*Quien eres*?", who are you, was unraveling and complicating at the same time.

4. October 2, 1996, The Cuba Place: Entering the Office

"We actually expected you a few days ago." The first one to greet me was the man I had spoken to on the telephone when I called and said I wanted to volunteer. His name was Oscar. I guess that he was around 65 years old. White hair with a short white beard, very thin, very polite. Oscar had been working at The Cuba Place for over ten years. He is white, and very mild mannered. "Let me take your coat," he offered. He helped me take off my coat. I am not accustomed to old school chivalry and found it a bit awkward, although I did appreciate it. He hung my coat in the closet.

The main office was as drab as the hallway, with an overwhelming number of paper piles all over. There were five huge desks and the walls were lined with shelves filled with books, videos, and more stacks of paper. Attached to this room was a little room, more like a closet, with a photocopy machine and shelves of more books. I saw the words "Fidel" and "Che" on just about every other book. This room led to another little room, the "library." Another man of similar description, about 65 years old, was sitting by a computer.

This is Grover, the librarian. He is cataloguing, which is why the library will be closed for the next several months. This is one of The Cuba Place's main services. For $50 an hour Grover would assemble information on any aspect of Cuba. The research comes from newspaper clippings, news reports, and magazine articles. The Cuba Place also brings in all sorts of Cuban writings from Cuba, about Cuba, and always, as I would soon find out, "pro-Cuba". Their collection is primarily post-1959.

Susan, the director of The Cuba Place, returned from her lunch break and Oscar introduced us. She was in her late 50s. In a later telephone conversation she referred to herself as a communist. All the workers at The Place identified themselves as such. I introduced myself to her as a Cuban-American, "another hyphenated person in this country," I said. Some humor to break the ice; and boy, was she icy.

"We don't hyphenate it here." was Susan's curt response. I was enraged at this comment, although I kept my composure. I thought to myself that she was way out of line with that one. She could not say that I was only Cuban because I ate Doritos and ketchup. I drink Dr Pepper. I have been to Disney World over a dozen times. I have a blue passport. I was born in this country; and as far as being only American, my life is testimony to the contrary.

I did not speak a word of English until I was six. I feel that this consequently affected my ability to perform well on verbal skills in standardized testing. I grew up eating *picadillo con arroz y frijoles negros, yucca con mojo de ajo y aciete espanol, ropa vieja, malanga y mantequilla, vaca frita, arozz con pollo, malta con leche condensada, flan, coco rayado, boniatillo, cafe con leche*—and I am talking about real coffee, not brown water with milk. My grandparents only speak Spanish. My father has a heavy accent. In Miami, when I was young, there were bumper stickers that read ," Will The Last American To Leave Miami Please Bring The Flag."

I remember going to Publix, the local supermarket, with my mother; and when she would say something to me in Spanish some person walking by would make the remark, "Speak in English, you're in America!" My mother always responded with, "It's a free country, I can speak the way I choose." These attacks were frequent. My father, an engineer, says in order to get work he had to make his price lower than that of a white woman.[10] Although these prejudices were constant, I was too young to feel their alienating effects, or they carried no weight because they were from strangers, *los Americanos*, the U.S. Americans. Everyone I knew was Cuban.

My first experience as "the other" was in Louisiana. I was an undergraduate student and was baby-sitting two small children. When I said something in Spanish, the mother of the children asked me if I were Spanish. I told her I was Cuban. She did not seem to differentiate Cuban from Spanish. I am sure Puerto Ricans and Mexicans were "Spanish" as well. She said that she did not want me to speak "your language" in front of her kids because she did not want them to pick up any of it. I had always considered bilingualism a gift, a benefit, yet here was a woman who intentionally wanted to deny her children access to another language, or at least to Spanish.

Growing up, I never experienced what I have read as the typical scenarios that immigrant children go through: alienation in school and shame about family customs. Feelings of being an outsider, a minority, did not apply to me or to my peers. We, the Cuban children, constituted 90 percent of our classroom population, from kindergarten all through high school. Everyone I knew was like me. We had parents telling us stories about how "everything was better in Cuba." Sunday mass was given in Spanish, and we all learned to speak English from watching television shows like "Sesame Street" or "Captain Kangaroo." I grew up as an hyphenated American, a Cuban-American. I am from both worlds.

5. October 10, 1996, The Cuba Place

I walked in and Oscar was the only worker in the office. He told me stories about himself. He started working at The Cuba Place after he retired. The old location, in response to my inquiries, had been bombed twice.[11] Any questions about the structure or the history of The Cuba Place always received the answer, "Ask Susan."

Susan returned from lunch and she had a disgusted look on her face. I am not certain if it was from seeing me, but she made no effort to let me think otherwise. I felt that she did not want me to be there. She wanted to write me off. I imagined she had thought, "That little Cuban girl isn't coming back. She's offended by our posters of Ché and Fidel."[12] But there I was and now she had to deal with me. Right away she barked, "We expected you yesterday. You can help me upstairs."

We went upstairs to the room designated as the art gallery. It was very disorganized and messy with artworks piled up on the floor, on tables, covered in dust. She asked me to help her move a large object. "Can you pick it up Katia? I just had back surgery done in Cuba." Another one of my nerves was shot. I did not know why she threw that out, "surgery in Cuba," unless she wanted me to know that she had medical work done in Cuba. Perhaps she had an accident and had to receive emergency health care, I was not sure.

I attempted to place the large object on top of a bookshelf and I asked her to hand me some paper towels so that I could clean the surface first because it was quite dusty. "We have a cleaning woman. She's one of the Balseras; you'd be surprised how little she actually cleans." I was completely surprised. Was I supposed to think that she was generous in offering this woman a job as the cleaning lady? Not only was she being patronizing about it, but she was criticizing the woman's work!

"How do you bring this art from Cuba?" I asked her. "In my luggage, of course." This woman always responded to me on the defensive. She raised her voice to me when I mentioned that I had gone to Cuba without a visa. Apparently that was not the correct terminology. What I did was go to Cuba without a license.

While I was categorizing posters for the art show, she was on the telephone with someone who wanted to know the logistics of bringing Cuban cigars to the U.S. Off the top of her head this woman knew all the legalities to Cuban cigar importation.

The art posters were all kind of ugly and in bad shape, yet Susan made them quite costly. She was in the business of selling contemporary Cuban art. Being one of the very few who actually brought this art into the U.S., she determined its market value. I picked up a poster with the name Nicholas Guillen on it and I asked her if that was the artist. "No! That's Nicholas Guillen, the famous Cuban Poet!" She was rather indignant about it. I found this to be particularly disturbing for two reasons. First, aside from running The Cuba Place, she taught a course about Cuba at a community college in New York. A teacher should not be so impatient with those who did not know the information; that was why she was there—to teach it. Second, I felt that she was being contemptuous because I did not know as much about Cuba as she did. It was as if she had something to prove.

The ownership of information coupled with self-appointed leadership has been a problem with many leftist groups. In the Cuba solidarity groups, the ownership of information not only ensures your power within the group, it also positions you as more or less of a Cuba supporter. I think that these "supporters" of socialist Cuba have a "chip on their shoulders," when it comes to dealing with Cuban-Americans. Talking about Cuba and its problems has been a constant in my life. It is not a political choice. It is not a "cool thing to do." It is something that is a topic of constant concern for just about every Cuban family. It is not a bargaining tool that I can enhance or hold over another Cuban, "I'm more Cuban than you!" This is why I think Cuban-Americans are not welcome in the political Cuba solidarity groups,[13] unless you are "helpless and needy," the attitude taken relative to those in Cuba. The Cuban-American presence in these groups would require these non-Cubans to constantly question their position as supporters of socialist Cuba.

Cuban-Americans also have little interest in these groups because they do not fulfill our particular needs. In order for a Cuban-American to explore the conditions of contemporary Cuba, he or she would have to come to terms with the politics of his or her own family; identity issues with an unattainable homeland, torn and physically separated families, and legitimate issues for and against the revolution. These American-based Cuba-solidarity groups treat these needs as unimportant, or as symptoms of someone who does not support the Cuban government and therefore must be a bourgeois product of those who left the island.

6. Still at The Cuba Place

Susan asks me to remove a large painting off the wall. It is in "outsider" art style with words about a ghost bothering Madonna, and I don't mean the mother of

Jesus. "I want Madonna to buy it. It's about her, you know." Duh! "I told her about it at a party, I guess she's busy with the baby." Far too many Miami hipsters throw that line around to impress people. In fact, Junior Vasquez, notorious New York disc jockey, released a song called "If Madonna Calls—Tell her I'm not home," to mock the constant obsession people have with saying they know Madonna. I hardly expected the obsession from this fifty-odd-year old communist.

    "Why don't you call her?" I responded. If she knows her so well, give her a ring. Susan did not respond, but a few seconds later she mentioned out of the blue that she took Harry Belafonte to meet Fidel Castro. I finished my work for the day and ran screaming to the soothing calm of subway rush-hour traffic: "Please stand clear of the closing doors." My father has always told me that I inherited one of his habits. When I do not like someone they can always tell. She is severely trying my patience. I am not sure how much longer I can keep my cool. Yet I think this is an essential component in academic research which is better acquired early in one's professional advancement.

7. June 1996—Manhattan, New York

    After viewing the documentary "Gay Cuba" at the New York City Queer Film Festival, I went to the reception held afterwards for the filmmaker at the group meeting of the organization she had started, (name of group withheld). To my surprise, in a room of about thirty people, there was only one Latino other than myself. He was from El Salvador. I tried networking but as soon as I mentioned I was Cuban-American the conversation would die out. I left my telephone number and expressed interest in coming to future meetings, but no one ever called me.

8. July 1996—La Habana, Cuba
GALES Meeting (Cuban Gay and Lesbian youth group)

    I was late in arriving at the meeting. The group has about twenty members. There were only five members present. By listening to them talk I soon realized why the poor attendance. One by one they told their story. They had been harassed by the police for the past few weeks, ever since they marched in the "Celebration of the Revolution Parade" and carried the rainbow flag, a gift to them from a queer San Francisco based Cuba solidarity group. Each member told a similar story of being picked up at home by the police and taken down to the station for hours of interrogation. A black female member of the group said she was being questioned by a white officer and then they switched him with a black officer. Playing the good cop-bad cop routine, he tried to use race solidarity as a means of extracting information from her.

The police questioned them about their relations with U.S. groups. These U.S. political groups that strongly profess support for the revolution are not welcomed by the local Cuban authorities. Another source of conflict is that these U.S.-based leftist groups are assuming they can use the same tactics in Cuba that they use in the U.S. While these actions might be discouraged or ignored in our communities, in Cuba they are illegal! They could endanger the personal safety of the Cuban participants.

9. Appearance versus Reality:
Concluding Paradoxes in the Quest for Identity

The U.S.-based Cuba solidarity political groups are insensitive toward and deter membership of Cuban-Americans; yet they spend thousands of dollars in personal funds to retain relations with Cubans in Cuba.[14] Yet the Cuban authorities—by force of imprisonment or detainment— discourage Cubans from associating with American-based Cuban solidarity groups, despite their fervent support for the revolution.

The general Cuban-American population demands that U.S. politicians support the embargo, yet they routinely fill airplanes to visit their families in Cuba and deliver materials which are inaccessible in Cuba. In this context Cuban-Americans are being individual proponents acting against the embargo.[15]

More paradoxical is the reception of Cuban-Americans by Cubans in Cuba. By all accounts, it is warm and favorable. Like that song from the musical Grease, "Tell me more, tell me more..," they want you to fill them up with everything you know about popular American culture. Madonna, the Terminator, Cindy Crawford, MTV. My cousin Tomas told me that on Friday nights, Cuban movie night, if they do not broadcast a Hollywood film, the people are enraged. While in Cuba, I saw advertisements for "Twister," "Babe," and "Jurassic Park."

So, here is a socialist country whose population carries two wallets. One for Cuban pesos and one for U.S. dollars. There is even another Cuban currency (bills and change) that is printed as the U.S. dollar and coins equivalent. Cubans are obsessed with our pop culture, and they are dressed in our last year's fashion. The government proclaims socialism, yet capitalism is evident everywhere.

Political groups in the U.S. proclaiming to support the revolution are not allowed to meet with individual citizens, and Cuban-Americans who denounce Castro's regime are visiting Cuba daily. Where is a Cuban-American to turn when deciphering the complexities that face his or her community? The paradox of eating black beans and watching MTV.

ENDNOTES

1. Cubans—we are a house of three: (1) Cubans in Cuba, those who were born and lived during a socialist government. The sentiments of these Cubans vary. There are those who consider themselves faithful communists, and those who wish for Fidel's rapid demise; (2) the Cubans who emigrated to the United States can be divided into three principal movements: (a) the exile (beginning in 1960 and spanning nearly a decade); (b) the Mariel boatlift (1980); and (c) the most recent wave of immigrants—the Balseros/the Rafters (1994). Each movement has its own identity. The exiled Cubans brought their social ideology. The Marielitos, who had been introduced to socialism changed the social structure of the established Cuban community. The Balseros (Rafters) arrived with many of the customs and culture of present-day Cuba. (3) Cuban-Americans. Here I fall, writing in Spanish but thinking in English.

2. The media's portrayal of Cubans changed drastically in the 1980s. It went from Ricky Ricardo ("I Love Lucy") to Tony Montana ("Scarface"). This change in image came from the media's portrayal of these shifts in the social structure of Cubans in the United States.

3. The U.S. CIA distributed a document around Cuba claiming to be from the communist party stating: "All children will remain with their parents until they are three years old, after which they must be entrusted to the *Organizacion de Circulos Infantes*. Children from 3-10 years will sleep in government dormitories and will be permitted to visit their parents no less than two days a month" (Felix Masud-Piloto, *From Welcomed Exiles to Illegal Immigrants*). Fear of having their children taken away and put into communist care led parents to panic; the U.S. then responded to Cuban pleas with the Peter Pan Airlift. These planes were bringing in around 200 children a week and placing them in foster homes around the country. Cuban children were sent to Miami, New York, and remote locations like Nebraska and Montana.

4. "I wanted to help my country, make it better." A fact of the revolutionary movement that is usually overlooked is that most of the Cuban exiles were originally part of the mobilization against Cuba's corrupt government. The mobilization had strong support in the University and the intellectual community, as well as significant support from the professional community. This knowledge can be accessed through simple conversation with the Cuban exiles in the U.S.

5. Most of the first wave of Cubans were affluent people, generally middle and upper classes. Since they had been the upper-classes of Cuba, most of them were professionals and or college educated. Like many of the professionals from other countries, when they arrived, the language barrier did not permit them to have work according to their education and or preparation. Many lawyers, doctors, engineers (like my father), held labor jobs like driving trucks, operating elevators, or working in factories (like my grandfather, the dentist).

6 My younger sister, Carolina, was born in Miami on December 31, 1973. She insists on not being left out of my writings.

7. The names of the actual location and its workers have been changed to protect their privacy.

8. "It's Katia, Yoyi's daughter." ..."My God! What's this! I can't believe it!" My great-aunt Margot.

9. Since it is illegal for U. S. citizens to visit Cuba without authorization from the U. S. Treasury Department, the Cuban customs officials stamp a card to insert in the passport, or wallet or back pocket.

A visitor returns the card when leaving Cuba. This leaves the passport free of any proof of visit.

10. The contractors would hire a white man before a white woman, and a white woman before a Cuban man. I asked my father about the treatment of black Americans, but he did not know.

11. The violence displayed by certain Cuban militia groups has always been an embarrassment to the Cuban community. "From 1973-1976, the FBI and Miami police investigated 103 bombings and 6 assassinations. Luciano Nieves and Ramon Donestevez were killed for expressing a desire to coexist with Cuba, April 28, 1979. Eulalio Jose Negrin was ambushed and killed in Union City, New Jersey; Omega-7 claimed this one... they vowed violence for dignity and liberty..."(Masud-Piloto p. 77). Emilio Milan, a radio commentator, lost both his legs in a bombing. (Risech p. 66)

12. Ché Guevara and Fidel Castro, leaders of the Cuban revolution. Another white, self-identified communist, member of The Cuba Place asked me what my position was on Cuba. He said he wanted to "check" because many Cubans come to The Cuba Place and are offended by the Fidel and Ché posters. I was "offended" by his patronizing attitude, not the posters. However, I kept that to myself.

13. The names of these groups will be withheld. I would state that they all share some basic characteristics. They also have practically no Cuban-American membership. I would note, however, that religious and academic organizations supporting Cuba are very mixed with Americans, Cuban-Americans, and Cubans in Cuba; and they are also more diverse in their beliefs. Perhaps religion and academia base themselves on a more realistic position. Of course, these have their shortcomings as well.

14. The DHL shipping company charges $67 for a 1/2 lb. (8 ounces) package to Cuba. AT&T charges $6.54 for the first minute and $1.64 for each additional minute.

15. Although American Cubans in principle support the embargo, they continuously travel to Cuba with money and supplies. Yearly, an estimated $800,000,000 or more is sent by the Cubans in the U.S. to family and friends in Cuba. When the plane from Miami lands in Cancun, Mexico— where the connection is made to Havana—everyone in the airport takes notice. A flock of loud people shoving to be first in the boarding line, come barreling down the corridors. They continuously delay the flights to Havana due to the overbearing quantity of luggages they carry to their families. There is a weight restriction on the luggage, but not on individuals. Rather than pay the $20 per each extra pound, these Cubans have become very creative. They wear several shirts, three hats on their head, and put shoes in their coat pockets. Carmelita Tropicana, a New York performance artist, refers to what she calls the "Cuban Easter Bonnet," but instead of chocolate bunnies, they carry calculators, watches, bottles of aspirin. She says that on her trip to Cuba the woman sitting next to her on the plane had a pressure cooker on her head.

REFERENCES

Bengeldorf, Carolee (1994) *The Problem of Democracy in Cuba: Between Vision and Reality* (New York: Oxford University Press).

Lumsden, Ian (1996) *Machos, Maricones, and Gays: Cuba and Homosexuality* (Philadelphia: Temple University Press).

Masud-Piloto, Felix (1996) *From Welcomed Exiled to Illegal Immigrants: Cuban Migration to the U.S., 1959-1995* (New York: Rowman & Littlefield Publishers Inc.)

Risech, Flavio (1995) "Political and Cultural Cross-Dressing: Negotiating a Second Generation Cuban-American Identity", in Behar, Ruth, *Puentes A Cuba/Bridges To Cuba* (Ann Arbor, Michigan: University of Michigan Press).

Tate, Claudia (1989) *Black Women Writers at Work* (New York: Continuum).
Zigel, Leslie Jose (1994) "Constructing the Clave: The United States, Cuban Music, and New World Order," in *The University of Miami Inter-American Law Review* Volume 26, Number 1, (Fall).

8

Nation, Cinema and Women:
Discourses, Realities and Cuban Utopia[1]

José B. Alvarez IV

Cuban cinema has been in the forefront of Latin American cultural production since the creation of the state-sponsored Cuban Institute of the Arts and Cinematographic Industries (ICAIC) in March 1959. Cuban cinematography has produced an ideologically complex body of films that provide constructions of a gendered national subject that often differ from the revolutionary discourse espoused by the state. However, despite the long tradition of filmic portrayal of women and its contribution to the national image, there exists an incongruent and obvious lack of self-representation by women in Cuban film. Only one woman, Sarah Gómez, has directed a full-length film, *One Way or Another* (1994), while two female directors, Ana Rodríguez and Mayra Vilasís, participated in the production of five short films that comprised *Mujer Transparente* (Transparent Woman), under the overall direction of Humberto Solas. Cuban directors have placed women in the protagonistic plane in order to narrate history; thus producing a cinematic discourse that is limited with subjectivization, what Teresa de Lauretis calls "en-gendered" discourse. Moreover, in the Cuban cinema, there is a disjunction between the hegemonic patriarchal discourse and that which has been represented in a number of contestatory films. This chapter examines three films: Daniel Díaz Torres' *Alicia en el pueblo de maravillas* (Alice in Wonderland) (1990), Julio García Espinoza's *Reina y rey* (Queen and King) (1994), and the five short films that comprise *Mujer Transparente* (1990). The discussion is based on an ongoing research project on Cuban filmmaking during the Revolution and its contribution to the reconstruction of national history.

If it is true that Cuban cinema of the Revolution (1959-present) has neglected to represent the participation of black and gay figures in the process of social change initiated on the island, one cannot say the same about the representation of women and their contribution, integration, and dialogue with the Cuban Revolution. In this chapter, which is part of an extensive study on Cuban cinema, I would like to create a dialogue about the representation of women as allegorical figures within Cuban cinematography and how this portrayal is inscribed into what has been coined the Discourse of the Nation. In referring to the novel *Paradiso* (1966), the Argentine writer Julio Cortázar stated that the characters of Lezama Lima's masterpiece are constituted in essence and not in presence. In the case of the female characters that abound in protagonistic roles in revolutionary cinematography, we are presented with the opposite situation. In the forty-odd years since the foundation of the Cuban Institute of Art and Cinematography (ICAIC), there exists an ample range of movies that posit women as the central character of the narration.

It needs to be made clear that, just as with other Latin American productions, the female protagonist in Cuban celluloid is not a phenomenon initiated in the decade of the 1960s. In an informative article, José A. Lezcano (1990) delineates five categories in which Latin American cinema typecasted women's roles between the decades of the 1930s and the 1950s: (1) the femme fatale; (2) the romantic heroine; (3) the middle class woman in conflict; (4) the Indian; and (5) the suffering mother. "Women were simply the central figures of the mushy movie that never gave answers to the implicit questions in their social text...[their] two basic functions [were those of] sex object and one vertex of a love triangle" (pp. 45-47). In the Cuban case, one must include the variant of the cabaret dancer with her exuberant exotic corporeality. Some examples that support our assertion include the films *El Romance del palmar* (The Romance of the Palm Grove) directed by Ramón Peyón in 1938, or Juan Sariol's *Sandra la mujer del fuego* (Sandra, the Woman of Fire) of 1953. The structural theme of the latter film, for example, establishes itself from the first sequence. The viewer is situated face-to-face with a musical spectacle in the crowded cabaret of the Hotel Comodoro. There we see the protagonist, Sandra, wearing a revealing satin dress, moving to the rhythm of the bolero mesmerizing the crowd as she sings: "Sueño que sueño contigo. Sueño que dices 'te quiero.' Solo tu amor es mío y sigo soñando que sueño ... quiero volver a soñar que sueño con tenerte." (I dream that I dream with you. I dream that you say 'I love you.' Only your love is mine and I continue dreaming that I dream [...] I want to return to dream that I dream of having you). The discourse evoked by the protagonist, in this case, the woman-object who is as desired by the men as admired by the few women present who confess yearning to be like her, reaffirms for the Latin American spectator in general the notion that women are lineal subject, marked only by the desire to dream of male recognition. This theme is recurrent throughout the film which concludes with the woman still passive—at the margin of the construction of her own story—observing two men that in a duel with machetes dispute the right to decide and therefore appropriate her future; a scene that is reminiscent of the final moments of Federico García Lorca's *Bodas de sangre* (Blood Wedding), in its Cuban reinterpretation.

As a possible reaction against the previous lineal characterization of women, beginning in 1959, much more diverse female protagonist roles abound within Cuban cinematography. In place of the categories already mentioned, the Cuban screen initiates a change in its representation of women, they are now complex and heterogeneous subjects that are participants in the social history of the country. The exotic cabaret dancers are replaced by the guerrilla fighters in *Manuela* (1966); textile workers in *Retrato de Teresa* (1979) (Portrait of Teresa); dock workers in *Hasta cierto punto* (1983) (Up to Certain Point); tobacco farmers in *Lucía*; students in *Una novia para David* (1985) (A Girlfriend for David); teachers in *Madagascar* (1994); lawyers in *Techo de vidrio* (1977) (Glass Ceiling); journalists in *En el aire* (1988) (On the Air); artists in *Zoé*, the fourth short film from *Mujer transparente* (1990) (Transparent Woman); housewives and former servants in *Reina y rey* (1994) (Queen and King); and scientists in *Plaff* (1988).

In 1966 a long list of movies that would attempt to focus their themes on the role that women played in the historic process of Cuban nation-building began. *Manuela* is a half-length film by Humberto Solás, and the first reel where the figure of the Cuban woman, in this case a mulatto whose family is assassinated by Batista's army, is motivated to join the rebel army in the Sierra Maestra mountains. *Manuela* is not presented under reductionist precepts but rather as exploring her possibilities in Cuba's history. In this movie the Cuban female spectator of low economic means for the first time can see herself genuinely represented and insert her own experiences and conflicts in the film's narrative, establishing a dialogue that allows her to relate to the complexities of the protagonist and the challenges she confronts. Furthermore, *Manuela* portrays on the screen the dichotomy of the housewife that also functions as an active participant in social change; that is, *Manuela* embodies and promotes the reality of the woman's double workday, a fundamental staple of the economy of the era.

With Solás' effort, the Cuban cinema of the revolution attempts to leave behind the representations of women as objects limited to the cabarets or the domestic life in the kitchen, allowing them to represent the shaping of another course of history—both public and private—by positing them in the construction of the nation as subject participant and no longer as an object at the margin of discourse. Within this collective effort and by way of the revolutionary cinema, Cuban official culture tries to go beyond the double phenomenon of the violence in the rhetoric and the rhetoric of the violence. Teresa de Lauretis argues that this is an inseparable fact of the notion of gender and, therefore, in the traditionally capitalist cinema, "violence is engendered in representation" (pp. 32-33). As Jacqueline Rose states:

> What classical cinema performs or "puts on stage" is this image of woman as other, dark continent, and from there what escapes or is lost to the system; at the same time that sexuality is frozen into her body as spectacle, the object of phallic desire and/or identification (cited in Stam, 1992, p. 172).

The productions to follow in the development of this theme will be multiple and diverse. Solás, two years after *Manuela*, directs *Lucía* (1968), his first full-length film, which is followed by *Cecilia* (1982), *Amada* (1984) (Beloved), and the coordination of *Mujer transparente* (1990) (Transparent Woman), a film composed of five short films that are directed by young Cuban directors—two of whom are Mayra Vilasis (Julia) and Ana Rodríguez (Laura), two women challenging the male monopoly in Cuban movie-making. Complementing Solás' movies, there are others: *De cierta manera* (1974) (In a Certain Way) by Sara Gómez, *Retrato de Teresa* (1979) (Portrait of Teresa) by Pastor Vega, Tomás Gutiérrez Alea's *Hasta cierto punto* (1983) (Up to a Certain Point), *Una novia para David* (1985) (A Girlfriend for David) by Orlando Rojas, *Lejanía* (1985) (Distance) by Daniel Díaz Torres, *Reina y rey* (1994) (Queen and King) by Julio García Espinoza, Fernando Pérez's *Madagascar* (1994) among others.

Clearly, Cuban cinema after 1959 places on the big screen the protagonist figure of women. This depiction is immersed in diverse complexities that reflect images of easily identifiable Cuban spectators of both sexes. It is enough to remember the conflicts of Teresa, Ofelia, Alicia, Isabel, Zoé, or Concha in the films. To a certain degree, these movies comply with Law 169 by which ICAIC was created: "Cinema should... dramatically posit in a contemporary fashion the great conflicts of man [sic] and of humanity... Cinema constitutes... an instrument of opinion and formation of the individual and collective conscious" (cited in *Diez años de cine cubano*, p. 8). Likewise, revolutionary cinema strives to reflect the participation of women in the revolutionary process that Fidel Castro asks for in the closing ceremony of the Second Congress of the Federation of Cuban Women: "The day must come that we have a party of men and women, and a leadership of men and women, and a state of men and women, and a government of men and women [...] that is the need of the Revolution, of society, and of history".

In studying Cuban cinema of the Revolution, it is essential to bear in mind a remark by Solás ten years after the filming of his first full length film: "Lucía is not a film about women, it is a film about society. But within that society I have chosen the most vulnerable character, she who is most affected in every moment by contradictions and changes" (Alvear, 1978, p. 29).

I propose that Solás' evaluation does not limit itself to *Lucía* but rather Cuban film production in general from *Historias de la revolución* (1960) (Histories of the Revolution) to the filming of *Alicia en el pueblo de Maravillas* (1990) (Alice in Wonderland) and *Mujer transparente* (1990) (Transparent Woman). Even when some narrative traits of Cuban cinematography can be associated with female subjectivity, under no circumstance can it be maintained that Cuba has a tradition, neither in form nor content, of a cinema of women. In the forty-plus years since the foundation of ICAIC, Sarah Gómez has been the only woman to direct a full-length film. Moreover, the case of cinema encounters its mimesis in other spheres of cultural production. Suffice to mention here, that it is not until 1996 with the publication of *Estatuas de sal* (Statues of Salt) that a collection of short stories written exclusively by Cuban women is anthologized.

Solás argues that in *Lucía* he uses the most vulnerable individual to represent the contradictions in society. Using his evaluation as a point of departure, I assume the discourse of Cuban film in the already mentioned movies to be a political allegory of Cuban society as a whole, marginalized by the patriarchal hegemony and authority that binds the entire population to restrict itself to a code of assigned identity and in the face of this obligation, all its constituents become vulnerable beings. *Retrato de Teresa* (Portrait of Teresa) is a movie that motivated strong controversy in Cuba towards the end of the 1970s, a time when by official decree—in passing the Family Code in the middle of the decade—the regime strove to terminate the double work day historically assigned to women.

Teresa is a character with whom Cuban women can easily identify: worker and wife, laborer and mother, public woman and private woman, who tries to please the demands of both spaces. She is a transparent and vulnerable individual, capable of establishing direct communication with the majority of spectators. The discursive order of the film is established from the first take: the camera pans the Havana Malecón, that space of daily encounter, of confluences, where adults walk while enjoying casual conversations, children play, sweethearts share moments of passionate vertical love. From this public survey, the camera passes to center itself on a concrete object that before was nothing more than part of the background: a fortress with a white tower, erect, that initially appears to be on top of the population and later is situated directly above the figure of the protagonist. This symbol is semiotically interpretable as a phallic marker that permeates cultural thought and oppresses female subjectivity, and throughout the filmic discourse will be a recurrent motif.

In 1990, the year that *Mujer transparente* (Transparent Women) premieres in Havana's cinema houses, the homogeneous construction of socialist Cuba is already a proven impossibility. Since then, the historic changes and fragmentation are being represented gradually in Cuban cinema. However, we still see the anachronism in the portrayal of women's roles historically in society as is the case of the protagonist of *Isabel*. In this short film, we see a woman subjected to a symbolic repression, engaged in a constant fight to obtain a legitimate space as a subject of society. *Isabel* is that individual in search of an autonomous social sphere, yet who cannot escape dependence upon the look of recognition from the dominant ideological apparatus. It is she who embodies the frustration of society as a whole, one which is crippled and thus prevented from expressing freely, a paradox evident in Isabel's confession: "because I always do the opposite of what I think." Captured within *Isabel* are contradictions already present in *Portrait of Teresa* and the dichotomies expressed in *Up to a Certain Point* more than a decade earlier. *Isabel* is enmeshed in an individual search that wavers between the desire for social recognition, for personal contentment, and for public and private belonging. In making it impossible for her to reach a resolution, she is forced to abandon the space of conflict and sit passively to dream. We must remember that this is what Tomás Gutiérrez Alea and Juan Carlos Tabío propose on a highly dramatic level in the internationally acclaimed *Fresa y chocolate* (Strawberry and Chocolate) (1993). In an allegorical reading, Diego is Teresa, Isabel or the Clarita of *Plaff*, that is to say, a contestatory subject that, relegated to the social margin, is forced to abandon the plane of social action that only authorizes cultural homogeneity. In the case of the penultimate movie by Gutiérrez Alea, the exile of Diego is the only possible ending; his symbolic death perpetuates the cycle of alienation for the marginalized individual.

In a different vein and going back to our discussion of *Transparent Woman*, the fourth short of this film presents us with another marginalized individual in the person of Zoé, a punk girl, painter, that unlike the above examples is in control of her living space: the garage of her mother's house. *Zoé* is filmed entirely in this postmodern transgressive space, where dissonant figures converge with the utopias of a socialist Cuba. The visual space is accentuated by a recorder that emits a sound that she calls "noise." Unlike the earlier mentioned films, the protagonist of this short film is not subdued to cultural homogenization. Her discourse is supported by actions that do not vary even when the State—represented by a militant of the Communist Youth Union who visits her, and whom she baptizes, "The Battleship Potemkin"—invades her space. *Zoé* is up to this point the most daring film of Cuban cinematography, not only for deconstructing the relationships of power, but also for presenting a marginalized individual in control of her social space. On an allegorical level, in which we have proposed to read the movies commented on here, *Zoé* exalts heterogeneity, and in doing so destabilizes the cultural paradigms of the revolutionary establishment. The film discourse of Mario Crespo's *Zoé* approximates more closely than any other in the history of Cuban cinematography the assertion by Homi Bhabha (1990) that:

> Once the liminality of the nation-space is established and its "difference" is turned from the boundary "outside" to its finitude "within", the threat of cultural difference is no longer a problem of "other" people. It becomes a question of the otherness of the people-as-one [....] They no longer need to address their strategies of opposition to a horizon of "hegemony" that is envisaged as horizontal and homogeneous (p. 301).

Cuban revolutionary politics have repeatedly questioned the validity of a person's individuality and difference, a policy that has permeated the arts since the adherence to a Marxist-Leninist political system in the early 1960s. After the creation of the Ministry of Culture in 1976 a more tolerant approach was initiated, insisting on the decentralization of cultural production. More than thirty years since the filming of *Manuela* and with the emergence since the end of the 1980s of an alternative cinema, coincident with other cultural expressions that will give much to talk about in the years ahead, the Cuban film industry is entering a phase that will allow a process of cultural (re)construction, embracing controversial sectors of society that have been hitherto silenced.

ENDNOTE

1. A version of this paper was presented in Spanish at the Hispanic Cultural Locations: An Interdisciplinary Conference, University of San Francisco, October 10-17, 1997. I am in debt to Rosalind Sylvester for the translation of the original manuscript and to Christina Buckley who gave me invaluable suggestions.

REFERENCES

Alvear, Marta (1978) "An Interview with Humberto Solas" Translated by Julianne Burton, *Jump Cut*, 19, pp. 27-33.
Bhabha, Homi K. (1990) "DissemiNation: Time, Narrative, and the Margins of the Modern Nation," in Homi K. Bhabha (editor) *Nation and Narration* (London: Routledge), pp. 291-322).
Castro, Fidel, "Discurso pronunciado en la clausura del Segundo Congreso de la FMC," *Boletín de la FMC* (no publisher, no date listed).
De Lauretis, Teresa (1987) *Technologies of Gender* (Bloomington: Indiana University Press).
Marcha (1969) *Diez años de cine cubano* (Montevideo: Marcha).
Lezcano, José A. (1990) "La mujer en los tiempos del cine," *Cine cubano*, 132, pp. 45-49.
Mujer transparente (1990) Directors Leonor Arocha, et al. (ICAIC).
Retrato de Teresa (1979) Director Pastor Vega (ICAIC).
Rose, Jacqueline (1986) *Sexuality and the Field of Vision* (London: Verso Books).
Stam, Robert, Robert Burgoyne, and Sandy Flitt (1992) *New Vocabularies in Film Semiotics: Structuralism, Post-Structuralism, and Beyond* (London: Routledge).

9

The Cuban Film Industry
Between A Rock and a Hard Place

Diane Soles

Cuban filmmakers must finally contend with both the art and industry of film production, after decades of being insulated by state subsidy . Since then, the Cuban film institute—*Instituto Cubano del Arte e Industria Cinematográficos*—(ICAIC) has moved to self-financing, exposing the Cuban film industry to the logic and vicissitudes of the market for the first time. They now have to contend with familiar political constraints and new economic constraints as they struggle to keep the industry alive. In addition to ICAIC's institutional efforts, individual Cuban filmmakers have had to employ a variety of discursive strategies about national identity to navigate this unfamiliar terrain. This chapter examines the emergence of Afro-Cuban musical traditions as an example of one discursive strategy used by Cuban filmmakers to negotiate between a rock—political constraints tied to Communism of the past—and a hard place—international market imperatives.

1. Introduction

> Now we are ready to have to reconcile art and industry, like they do everywhere or just about everywhere else in the world.[1] — Manolo Pérez, Cuban filmmaker

The seismic political upheaval in Europe and elsewhere during the late 1980s and early 1990s has given way to continued political and economic restructuring across the globe. These events have produced devastating consequences for life in Cuba and have required, as quoted above, that Cuban filmmakers must finally contend with both the art and industry of film production. While filmmakers in the rest of Latin America have had to confront this challenge all along, those in Cuba were insulated by state subsidy until the early 1990s. Since then the Cuban film institute—*Instituto*

Cubano del Arte e Industria Cinematográficos (ICAIC)—has moved to self-financing, exposing the Cuban film industry to the logic and vicissitudes of the market for the first time. While the 1990s have seen some ideological aperture in Cuba, the political parameters of the communist Revolution remain intact.[2] Thus filmmakers have to contend with familiar political constraints and new economic ones as they struggle to keep the industry alive. In addition to ICAIC's institutional efforts, individual Cuban directors have had to employ a variety of discursive strategies about national identity to navigate this unfamiliar terrain. This chapter will examine the emergence of Afro-Cuban musical traditions as an example of one discursive strategy used by Cuban filmmakers to negotiate between a rock—political constraints tied to Communism of the past—and a hard place—international market imperatives.[3]

To understand the conditions that have given rise to this strategy, and moreover the very survival of the Cuban film industry, it is indispensable to look beyond the simple economic explanations of globalization. The industry defies economic wisdom, given the impossibility of amortizing films on the island and the depth and breadth of the economic crisis that has engulfed it in the 1990s. What is interesting here is not so much the outcome—ICAIC's survival—but rather the process that has allowed it to continue to exist. Theories on globalization need to look beyond economic forces with a particular eye on how national actors negotiate between competing demands and constraints. By examining aspects of this process, this chapter will identify some of the conditions in which heterogeneity may arise or remain, despite economic and other pressures towards homogeneity of the market.

The following section outlines the split in globalization theories over homogeneity and heterogeneity, provides background about ICAIC's institutional responses to political and economic restructuring and considers the impact of these changes on Cuban directors. The interviews with filmmakers about their use of Afro-Cuban musical traditions reveal a strategic discourse on national identity and film. Finally, the concluding section will examine the conditions that gave rise to this discourse and the implications of those findings for globalization theory and future research.

2. Theory and Background

Arguments about the effects of globalization and what globalization is can be loosely grouped into two opposing camps: those who claim that homogenizing forces outweigh the maintenance and creation of differences across the globe, and those who stress the proliferation of hybridity, diversity and heterogeneity.[4] This issue seems central in developing a critical theory capable of posing alternatives to the increasing encroachment of the marketplace on all aspects of life. Yet few theorists have attempted a critical engagement that questions the merits of the terms of the debate over who is "winning"—the forces of homogeneity or those of hybridity.[5]

The Cuban film industry provides an intriguing case study on several counts. Cultural production, and particularly film, straddles economic and artistic fields thus answering to both economic and aesthetic imperatives. The question of how to address both national and international imperatives is one that has confronted new Latin American filmmakers since the 1960s. However, the Cuban film industry is especially intriguing since it only recently entered the international capitalist market and still forms part of a political system resistant to market imperatives. Cuban film makers must still contend with the political constraints of working within the parameters of the Cuban Revolution, which resist market imperatives, and at the same time address the logic of the international market in order to secure co-productions. Thus contradictory forces are at work on both the national and international levels that limit the discursive space in which heterogeneity may arise or be maintained.

On the national level the struggle pivots on balancing the need to work within the political boundaries of the Cuban Revolution, predicated on protecting a certain image of the state and society, versus the cinema's tradition of social critique and commitment to engagement with the changing social context. Here, the problem is the growing distance between the state/party line and the realities of Cuban daily life captured on film (Quiros, 1996). These contradictory national trajectories mitigate against pressures from the international market to produce saleable formulas and tropes to the detriment of the quest for a distinct national identity. Yet Cuban filmmakers must temper their traditions and national dialogue in cinematic form with the omnipresent need to obtain hard currency to support film production. It is precisely in this context that the Cuban film industry finds itself between a rock and a hard place.

Since moving to self-financing several years ago, ICAIC has intensified three pre-existing strategies for generating hard currency from abroad: service fees; international distribution and sale of Cuban films; and international co-productions. In the midst of Cuba's deep and prolonged economic crisis, film production has dropped dramatically. Previously ICAIC annually produced on average 40 documentaries, fifty-two weekly news shorts, and eight full-length feature films. As of the mid-1990s the news service had disappeared and ICAIC managed to squeeze out an average of half a dozen documentaries and two full-length features per year (personal interview, Manolo Pérez, 1996). After reaching the apparent nadir of production in 1996,[6] when ICAIC did not release any full-length feature films, prospects for the Cuban film industry became more optimistic. Three new films were premiered in 1997, and there were several projects anticipated for 1998 (ICAIC Press Conference, December 10, 1997).

With the overall decline in production, fees from services, equipment, and facilities have taken on new importance. The ICAIC offers to foreign producers a variety of services including: natural locations (tropical settings); film studios (including animation); film production and post-production facilities and equipment; script writers; qualified technical staff; actors and actresses; make-up, sound, editing and other specially trained personnel (Cicero Sancristóbal, 1997, p. 1). For 1993 ICAIC reported service fee revenues of US$454,400, an amount equal to that earned in international sales and distribution of films. These figures are significant on two counts, both related to the decline in production. First, parity between service fees and film distribution/sales revenues directly reflects the impact of low production and indicates a restructuring of ICAIC's economic base.[7] In the nine years prior to the economic crisis, film distribution and sales abroad accounted for more than 75 percent of revenues, with service fees comprising the remaining portion[8] (Pollo, 1994). Second, even with the increased funds from service fees, the amounts generated by these two strategies were insufficient to sustain the film industry. Camilo Vives, head of the Production Unit, estimated that by the mid-1990s it cost an average of US$600,000-700,000 to produce a full-length Cuban feature film (personal interview, 1996). Given the gap in resources and needs, the search for international co-productions has come to occupy center stage. Of ICAIC's efforts to secure hard currency, international co-productions have had the most significant impact on shaping the creative process.

Although co-productions had begun on a small scale before the shift to self-financing, in the 1990s they have become critical to all feature film projects.[9] In addition, directly or indirectly, the funds from co-productions also support financing of other Cuban film projects, purchasing new equipment, and updating facilities. The centrality of international co-productions has led to significant changes within the Cuban film industry ranging from the new importance of the producers and the increased power of the Production Unit[10] to the atomization of the creation process and an epistemological shift giving new priority to international audiences and producers.

This new orientation is evident in comments from directors and producers alike. For example, Camilo Vives has described this transition as that of a group of animals raised in the zoo, who are suddenly released into the jungle. Though movement was restricted in the zoo, the animals' basic needs were all met. The jungle, on the other hand, promises more freedom of movement but places a very high price on survival. In the transition to the jungle, directors have increasingly turned to individual strategies.[11] The ICAIC directors, formerly a more collective group, have become more dispersed,[12] devoting more and more time to activities off-island in order to supplement their incomes, maintain international visibility, and seek out funding for projects in development (personal interviews with Pastor Vega, Daniel Díaz Torres, Orlando Rojas, 1996; Arturo Sotto, 1997). For the first time many have had to worry about "the bottom-line," their film's salability on an international market, and the tastes and preferences of international producers. This new orientation has led to an epistemological shift from asking the question, "What do I want to say about Cuban society to Cubans?" to "What do I want to say about Cuban society to the rest of the world?"

When I asked the director Pastor Vega if he had been pressured by economics to adjust his work style during the long period of crisis, he replied:

> Have I changed how I conceive of my work? Absolutely. Before, one worked only thinking about the Cuban people. Now, you have to think about "marketing," "profits," all of that. For that reason, the two projects come out of here, from this type of thinking, about what could be interesting —before I always said, "What would be interesting to Cuba?" ... and because of this [the crisis] one has to change.[13]

This epistemological shift, at least initially, has involved re-conceptualizing the audience more than abandoning specific aesthetic or personal stylistic considerations. As another director, Orlando Rojas, described it,

> Up to now no one has bet on commercial success. I believe that now, people are beginning to think about it and they will do so according to their own aesthetic orientations. I believe that in any event there are not a lot of mercenaries as of yet; but I would say that there are a lot of realistic people and from [them] there will come another type of film.[14]

This realism requires that Cuban filmmakers develop strategies that will address both the need for a critical engagement with national identity and be attractive to foreigners. Interestingly, despite the decline in collectivism among directors and their associated atomization, some common strategies have emerged among the ICAIC directors. The following section outlines the rise of Afro-Cuban musical traditions as an example of one emerging discursive strategy. Examining how this discourse fits into larger context of challenges facing Cuba will help to explain some of the recent developments in the Cuban film industry that extend beyond the reach of economic theories.

3. Afro-Cuban Music and National Identity: Yo soy del son a la salsa[15]

Interviews with several Cuban directors in July 1996 revealed a common turn toward drawing inspiration from Cuban musical traditions, particularly Afro-Cuban. It is beyond the scope of this chapter to determine if this strategy has been successful in resisting the siren song of the international market which threatens to replace the critical edge of Cuban cinema with formulas and stereotypes for international consumption. Nonetheless, as will become clear, this strategy makes sense in this historic juncture when viewed as part of a larger discourse in which Afro-Cuban music is both "essentially Cuban" and internationally appealing. This balancing act allows film makers to assert a sense of national identity consistent with locally resonant themes while at the same time attracting needed international support.

The projects that constitute the findings refer to films that feature dance, venues, songs, rhythms, musicians' milieu, and spectacles related to Afro-Cuban music, all with their highly coded meanings. Of the six directors I interviewed in 1996, four described projects in various stages of realization that drew from Afro-Cuban musical traditions.

Mayra Vilasís, for example, was just completing a documentary about the female acapella group, Jema 4. She explained to me that the project highlighted several themes that were important to her, including women and music.[16] Part of the appeal of this group was that the members were very conscious of their links to earlier traditions of female quartets. One of the singers described to me how they were reclaiming and resurrecting Cuban traditions, modernizing them to make them more attractive to the international market. Vilasís planned to convert the film to video and package it for sale along with the group's two compact discs. In this context she was both reaffirming Cuban identity and projecting her work into the international market.

Another director, Pastor Vega, was searching for financing for a completed script. The film project would be a full-scale musical, centering on an outdoor market with an adjoining building where a group of *rumberos* practices music. His inclusion of musical traditions as the centerpiece was deliberate. In an effort to modify his work in keeping with the new economic context, Vega added: "I thought ok, Cuban music is extraordinary, loved everywhere, and so we said to ourselves that the musical part was... the most interesting."[17] Clearly, Vega sought to balance two elements in this strategy: highlighting that which is "essentially Cuban" with that which will attract an international audience.

Filmmakers are not the only ones who speak about and conceive of Afro-Cuban music in this way, nor is this theme appearing for the first time. In fact such comments form part of a broader discourse on racial and ethnic mixing as the "essence of Cuban identity" and the key to Cuba's international appeal. Moore (1995) specifically links the distinctiveness of Afro-Cuban musical traditions to discourse about national identity. He argues that these two themes came together[18] in the "critical decade" between the early 1920s and mid-1930s, ending with the revolution against Gerardo Machado. That period was marked by social and political turmoil, significant aesthetic changes, including a "recentering" of Afro-Cuban expressions "so that they can play a much more important role—ideologically, and in many instances stylistically as well—in contemporary conceptions of *cubanidad* (Cubanness) and national culture" (Moore, 1996, p. 166).

Over time Afro-Cuban music has become one of the centerpieces in discussions about Cuba's contribution to and influence on the rest of the world. Evidence of this abounds in popular sources, such as music lyrics themselves. The following excerpt from a rumba written by the famous Tío Tom (Gonzalo Asencio Hernández) illustrates music's multiple importance: its essentially Cuban quality and attractiveness to foreigners.

Los cubanos son rareza (The Cubans are unique)/The Cubans are unique, with drums in their hands/they make the earth shake, and the Mexicans say/when they feel the drums, "I'm off to Cuba to have a good time"/(Refrain). If you want to have fun, listen to this good rumba[19] (Acosta, 1991, p. 65, translation by Peter Manuel).

Although many musical genres contain lyrics declaring their own importance, it is interesting here that those who cannot resist Cuban music do not reside on the island, but rather in Mexico. Moreover, the influence of Afro-Cuban music is often described as not merely regional, say in Latin America, but as worldwide.

This belief is also reflected in a 1996 editorial in the Cuban newspaper, *Juventud Rebelde*. Journalist Enrique Núñez Rodríguez asks himself the following question: "What makes tourists want to return to Cuba?" His reply is, "The people, that is to say, their way of life, customs, culture." For him the people are mestizos, descendants of Spaniards and African slaves. Like the people, Cuban music also sprang from this union "...the concubine of the feminine, sweet Spanish guitar and the rough and virile African drum gave birth to our music."[20]

Not only is Afro-Cuban music essentially Cuban, but it also attracts tourists—foreigners to Cuba. Núñez Rodríguez highlights the power of this lure by citing the universal popularity of Cuban music: "The son, rumba, conga, cha cha chá, bolero, mambo and the salsa have traveled the world." Although the author cites other arts in addition to music, such as literature, ballet and film, music receives the most attention and its intimate links to the birth of the Cuban population set it apart from other forms of cultural production and expression. Afro-Cuban music thus occupies at once an "essential" place in national identity and leading position in attracting foreigners to the island.

The discussion would be incomplete without addressing the textual treatment of these traditions, especially in recent Cuban cinema. Of the three feature films premiered by ICAIC in 1997—*Los Zafiros Locura Azul*, Manuel Herrera; *Kleines Tropikana*, Daniel Díaz Torres; and *Amor Vertical*, Arturo Sotto—all included scenes of Afro-Cuban music and dance. In fact, these tropes are central to the stories in the first two films. Moreover, both films present Afro-Cuban music and dance as attractive to foreigners. While space limitations do not permit a more detailed analysis of these films, it is possible to highlight a series of key questions that must be addressed to evaluate if these representations of Afro-Cuban traditions constitute an instance of heterogeneity in the context of globalization. The heterogeneity of interest here is one that operates relative to both hegemonic national and international discourses. In the case of Cuban cinema, it refers to a critical discourse on national identity that neither mimics the official state/party line nor succumbs to the lowest common denominator of market dictates.

Such a textual analysis must also include, among other questions, which issues are treated critically and which are not in these films? How are these themes and their treatments embedded in broader economic and cultural discourses and policies? In Cuba, these questions must be asked particularly with reference to tourism, which not only has replaced sugar as the leading source of hard currency, but also has become the main source of contact between Cubans and foreigners.[21]

4. Rock Hard? Questioning the Conditions of Heterogeneity

Thus far, the discussion has traced the rise of Afro-Cuban musical traditions as a discursive strategy for asserting national identity and soliciting international co-productions.   However, this discourse is only one of many possible strategies employed by Cuban filmmakers in the 1990s. According to many Cuban film critics, social critique is the unifying theme in Cuban cinema of the 1990s. Arsenio Cicero Sancristóbal predicted in 1993 that Cuban cinema in the 1990s would "not fear words, images or ideas. It would be a cinema that deals with thorny themes, that cut to the quick but make us who we are." In this category Cicero includes a variety of controversial issues, such as disintegration of the family, exile, the loss of values, institutionalized double morality, and repressed religions, among others[22] (1994, p. 37).

These issues must be packaged in a manner both tolerable by the current regime and attractive to the international market. Though Cuban filmmakers are long accustomed to dealing with the first set of constraints, they are still adjusting to the pressures of the market. It is not surprising then that the theme of social critique has not come to occupy a pivotal place in the discourse among the ICAIC directors. Though social critique may be central to Cuban cinema, it is not necessarily part of what makes it attractive internationally. Undoubtedly, negotiations between national directors and international producers are critical in determining which features of Cuban life, tropes, and themes are promoted in a national cinema based on international co-productions.

Finally, a thorough analysis of the Cuban film industry would have to ask what conditions and which players frame the terms of any particular discourse and how? Only by examining over time the interplay of all of these factors—political, cultural, economic, national and transnational—will it be possible to fully assess under which conditions heterogeneity can emerge from between the rock of old political constraints and the very hard marketplace of international sales and distribution.

ENDNOTES

1. "Ahora estamos dispuestos a tener que conciliar arte e industria como se hace en todo el mundo o en casi todo el mundo..." (personal interview, 1996). All translations are mine unless otherwise indicated.

2. Throughout the early 1990s there were a series of policy changes that signaled this opening, such as elimination of the term Leninist in the description of the state and a shift from an atheist to a secular state in the Constitution. Religious affiliation is no longer prohibited for members of the Communist Party. Films such as *Fresa y Chocolate*/Strawberry and Chocolate (Gutierrez Alea and Tabío, 1993) have been tolerated. Nonetheless, the enormous political scandal over the film *Alicia en el pueblo de Maravillas*/Alice in Wondertown (Díaz Torres, 1991), the cancellation of the *Cerrado por Reforma*/Closed for Reform (Rojas, 1996), indicate that censorship remains.

3. Data for this chapter were gathered during two trips to Cuba as part of my on-going research as a Ph.D. candidate in Sociology at the University of Wisconsin, Madison: May-July, 1996, and December 1997. The Tinker Foundation provided funds for the initial trip during which I interviewed more than 20 members of the Cuban film industry including producers and directors, critics, actors and make-up artists, among others. In addition, I want to thank Jane Collins, Julie D'Acci, Wilfredo Cancio Isla, Jutta Joachim, and Arsenio Cicero Sancristóbal for their comments and support. The views presented here are strictly my own and do not represent those of the Tinker Foundation, the University of Wisconsin or other individuals.

4. See Stuart Hall (1991) on this divide with reference to ethnicity and Britain.

5. This article begs for a longer, more in-depth review of current globalization theories than space allows here. It would be especially useful to explore the gray terrain between the two camps described here. For a provocative and comprehensive treatment see, Boaventura de Sousa Santos (1995).

6. The worst year of the general economic crisis was 1993. However it was not until 1996 that ICAIC failed to complete a full-length feature film. In addition to economic and political factors, initial research suggests that the shift to self-financing may have contributed to this situation. For example, several filmmakers described both a decline in creative output (fewer and less interesting scripts) and a more extended and prolonged pre-production cycle (Rojas, Díaz Torres, Vilasís, 1996).

7. More recent figures might reveal that sales and distribution of Cuban films account for a greater portion of total revenue, especially in light of the phenomenal international success of "Strawberry and Chocolate" (*Fresa y Chocolate*, Gutierrez Alea and Tabío, 1993). Since production levels continue to be lower than they were in the 1980s and 1970s, it seems unlikely that sales can continue to yield their former proportion of annual earnings.

8. Between 1981 and 1990, ICAIC earned a total of approximately USD$7.7 million, with $5.9 million from film sale/distribution, primarily in Western Europe, and $1.8 million in service fees (Pollo, 1994).

9. By the late 1980s ICAIC had signed agreements of cooperation with several countries, including Venezuela and Spain. ICAIC had also co-produced documentaries and feature films off-island in places such as Nicaragua, Peru, Mexico, and Bolivia, among others (Getino, 1988, p. 49). During the XIX Havana Festival of New Latin American Film, Camilo Vives announced the 1998 launching of a new regional initiative, Ibermedia. This entity, intended to increase co-productions within Latin America and with Spain, is modeled after the European Community's *Eurimage*. It will be a revolving fund to support costs of production, distribution and script writing. Part of the founding agreement is that each government donate funds in addition to their regular budget for national film production, so as not to undermine national cinemas. Whether this initiative generates films that have regional, and ideally international appeal remains to be seen, as does its impact on already struggling national cinemas. The countries that have agreed to participate are Argentina, Bolivia, Brazil, Colombia, Chile, Cuba, Mexico and Spain. So far, Spain has

agreed to contribute $2 million, Argentina $1 million and Mexico $500,000. Brazil has yet to set the amount of its contribution and the other countries are each expected to contribute between $100,000-$200,000.

10. Although co-productions began in Cuba in the 1980s, prior to the crisis, Cuban producers played a relatively minor part in each production. Now that movies must appeal to a broader, international audience and film makers must rely almost completely on foreign sources for financing their productions, the Production Unit headed by Camilo Vives has acquired new significance. Approval and support from the Production Unit is now necessary for the completion of any project. This point was made clear in 1996 when budget considerations were given as the reason for abruptly terminating the filming of *Cerrado por Reforma*/Closed for Reform (Rojas) (Rojas, Pérez, personal interviews, 1996). The fact that the financial bottom-line was offered as the official explanation for canceling a project is new in the Cuban industry and signals increased power for the Production Unit.

11. This atomization contrasts sharply with the collectivist structure of ICAIC in the late 1980s which featured the Creation Groups (Grupos de Creación). During the ICAIC Presidency of Julio García Espinosa, 1982-1991, and under his initiative, directors formed three groups based on personal and aesthetic affinities. Members discussed projects and decided which ones to revise further and which ones were ready for implementation. In addition, one group headed by Humberto Solás, produced a collective film project, *Mujer Transparente*/Transparent Woman, 1991. Following the chaotic events of 1991, including the scandal over the film *Alicia en el pueblos de las Maravillas*/Alice in Wondertown (Díaz Torres), the successful resistance to governmental efforts to dismantle ICAIC, and the replacement of Julio García Espinosa as President, with the return of founding President, Alfredo Guevara, the Creation Groups have ceased to function.

12. In addition, the bleak economic panorama and precipitous drop in creative options on the island led many artistic and technical staff to leave the island, further tearing at the communal fabric that was ICAIC (Cancio Isla, 1996, p. 2).

13. "Si modifico algo en como concibo mi trabajo? Absolutamente. Antes uno trabajando sólo pensando en el pueblo cubano. Ahora nó, hay que pensar en "marketing", "profits", todo eso. Justamente por eso, los dos proyectos salen de aquí, de eso tipo de pensamiento, de que puede interesar—antes yo decía "Qué puede interesar en Cuba?...y por eso uno se cambia."

14. "Hasta ahora nadie aquí apostaba el éxito comercial. Yo creo que ahora, la gente empieza a pensar en eso. Y cada uno pensará de acuerdo su presupuesto aestético. Yo creo que de todos modos muchos mercenarios no hay en estos momentos todavía. Pero, lo que sí hay es mucha más gente realista y allí van a subir otro tipo de película. "

15. This line refers to the title of a 1996 Cuban musical documentary by Rigoberto López. Loosely translated it means "I am from the son to the salsa," with both son and salsa referring to types of Afro-Cuban music.

16. Mayra Vilasís has given priority to female subjects in her literary and cinematographic work. Prior to her documentary on Jema 4, she had completed another one about an all female Cuban chamber music ensemble.

17. "Pensé bueno, la música Cubana es extraordinaria, gusta en todas partes. Y nosotros nos deciamos que la parte musical ...más interesante."

18. At other moments throughout Cuban history African based traditions, musical and otherwise, have been more or less violently repressed, banned or celebrated. A review of that literature lies well beyond the scope of this study. However, for an introduction to these vagaries, see Lisa Waxer (1994).

19. "Los cubanos son rareza, con un tambor en la mano/hacen la tierra temblar, y dicen los mexicanos/cuando sienten los tambores, a Cuba voy a gozar/(Refrán) Si tú quieres divertir, escucha esta rumba buena."

20. "Qué es lo que le hace desear volver a Cuba? Su gente, suelen contestar. Su gente; es decir, su vida, sus costumbres, su cultura....La mezcla de sangre produjo una nación mestiza. Y del concubinato de la femenina y dulce guitarra española con el bronco y virile tambor africano nos nació la música nuestra. El son, la rumba, la conga, el cha cha chá, el bolero, el mambo y las salsa han recorrido el mundo." (Núñez Rodríguez in *Juventud Rebelde*, 1996). Interracial couplings during the colonial period more likely and more frequently involved Spanish men raping African women. Núñez Rodriguez, however, has purged history of its violence and reassigned ethnic and racial identity to coincide with essentialized notions of sexual difference. The complex interplay between race and sexuality over time in Cuba begs for further examination.

21. "que no teme a las palabras, a las imágenes o a las ideas. Un cine que trata con temas espinosos, que nos laceran per nos componen: la desintegración familiar, el exilio...la pérdida de valores...la doble moral institucionalizada, las religiones reprimidas" Also see Frank Padrón Nodarse, 1994, for a discussion of other critical issues such as sexuality in film.

22. Sex tourism and its relationship to the stereotype of the hyper-sexual and irresistible Cuban mulata (often portrayed dancing) may also be relevant here.

REFERENCES

Acosta, Leonardo (1991) "The Rumba, The Guaguancó, and Tío Tom," in Peter Manuel (editor) *Essays on Cuban Music: North American and Cuban Perspectives* (Lanham, Maryland: University Press of America: Maryland), pp. 51-73.

Cancio Isla, Wilfredo (1996) "El encanto perdido de la fidelidad: revelaciones de un cine en trance" presented at Fifth Studies in Latin American Popular Culture Conference, Tulane University, New Orleans in October.

Cicero Sancristóbal, Arsenio (1997) "El cine cubando hoy: una mirada," unpublished manuscript.

_____(1994) "En torno a la sana virulencia," in *Memorias del 2ᵈᵒ Taller Nacional de Crítica Cinematográfica*, Camagüey (La Habana: Centro de Informacion del ICAIC), pp. 30-39.

Getino, Octavio (1988) *Cine Latinoamericano economía y nuevas tecnologías audiovisuales* (Editorial Legasa: Buenos Aires).

Hall, Stuart (1991) "The Local and the Global: Globalization and Ethnicity," in Tony King (editor) *Contemporary Conditions for the Representation of Identity* (London: Macmillian Education Ltd), pp. 19-39.

Moore, Robin (1995) "The Commerical Rumba: Afrocuban Arts as International Popular Culture," *Latin American Music Review*, Volume 16, Number 2 (Fall-Winter), pp. 165-198.

Núñez Rodríguez, Enrique "La más hermosa" in Juventud Rebelde. No page number or date.

Padón Nodarse, Frank (1994) "La realidad en el cine cubano de los noventa: las eternas luchas del espejo y la imagen," in *Dicine* (Mexico D.F.) No. 57 (September), pp. 19-23.

Pollo, Roxana (1994) "Puede ser este un año favorable para la economía del cine cubano," *Granma* (May), No page number.

Quiros, Oscar (1996) "Critical Mass of Cuban Cinema: Art as the Vanguard of Society," *Screen*, No. 37, Volume, Number 3 (Autumn), pp. 279-293.

Santos, Boaventura de Sousa (1995) *Towards a New Common Sense: Law, Science and Politics in Paradigmatic Transition* (New York: Routledge).

Waxer, Lisa (1994) "Of Mambo Kings and Songs of Love: Dance Music in Havana and New York from the 1930s to the 1950s," *Latin American Music Review*, Volume. 15, Number 2 (Fall-Winter), pp. 139-176.

10

Literary Critique: Blindness and Possibility

Victor Fowler Calsada

The case is made succinctly that Cuban literature, since the middle of the 1990s, has been emerging from a period of severe damage to Cuban social thought. One result of the damage arising from the ideological or cultural Cold War is a "blindness" exhibited by those who normally have first access to and evaluate contemporary Cuban literature. Established writers of literary criticism have responded to the new plurality of literary production— for example, women/feminist, gay and lesbian, marginalized youth, and anti-hero writings—either with a knee-jerk reaction, seeing these diverse works as evidence of hostile, "outside" influences or with "blindness" to their existence, simply ignoring the newer trends. Some examples are suggested for further reading.

When I was invited to participate in a round table discussion about the "state of literary critique in Cuba today," I thought that the words, that is, the subtleties of their management, could have some meaning, so I decided to call my intervention "blindness and possibility." In our tradition, the title plays with the words of an article by José Lezama Lima, "July 26: Image and possibility," and moreover, those from another text, "Blindness and Insight" by Paul de Man. In addition to the private homage paid to the authors that I read with pleasure, and for whom the relation between subtext and surface is basic, I was interested in proposing a shift in emphasis.

In general terms, literary critique written in Cuba today can be characterized by its inability to locate the literature in the next century. I am suggesting that beyond mere descriptions, to the detachment between the fragmentary treatments of what happens in the terrain of literary production and the totality of the social body, we must add: its blindness. There is no doubt that in Cuba, an island—multiply isolated if we consider its double cultural estrangement, a blockade from outside and a self-blockade—there is a special case of temporality.

We live the celerity of our internal social and cultural processes, its great and often rapid changes, its waves of upheaval, in the midst of a permanent and organized disconnection with the reality of the events that occur "there" and "outside." This disconnection is achieved by the merging of two constraining efforts. First, we receive an "outside" that intervenes in the cultural production of the island, closing the paths for the promotion of what is done here, or establishing, for that matter, debilitating forms of devaluating classifications. The second effort, from "inside," is characterized by the gigantic possibilities for control, which works in the manner of an enormous filter for the inhabitants of the country, delivering to them primarily the "purified" thought of the "other," that comes from the "outside."

It is clear that I am speaking in harmony with the metaphors of a Cold War, although the disappearance of the old socialist bloc has made such cultural filtration obsolete. To imagine that in Cuba it has ended, however, is a mixture of ignorance with political ingenuity—and perhaps a little bit of ill intention. We speak about an organization in the field of cultural production that remains obligated to subordinate itself to the events of that greater stage of politics and ideology signed by the fathers of a war.

For this reason, it is singularly important to verify that there has been a change in the nation's literary production. This is so visibly marked by the proliferation of manuscripts that it destroys the idea of a unitary subject from that universal system that was considered revolutionary until the beginning of the 1980s. Today, any reading of the multiple layers of cultural production that interprets the variation and magnitude of literary production in an automatic, knee-jerk reaction as rebelliousness in the ideological and political sense, or with theoretical or activist anti-socialism, is simply grotesquely diminishing it. The fact is, we cannot separate the coincidence of the global changes from the multiplication of writing stances (diverse themes, focus, currents, groups, poetics) that we have been experiencing since the middle of the 1980s, the years of socialist crisis in the world and in Cuba.

From the break-up of that spherical and perfect individual, always recovered at the end (no matter how smoothened its critical distance was) for the Socialist Project of the Future, new voices are being born and more than a few of them emphatically position themselves in the place of those who have been traditionally the socially marginalized. What I am trying to say is that the "narrowing" of the future and its possibilities has generated an explosion of literature in which certain topics become common and not the exception. We see boredom, the tendency toward self-destruction of the characters, revisions of history, the insignificance of language; and to this we add the niche literature, feminine/feminist, gay and lesbian, others marginalized, even those who use escaping as a theme. The newer themes are too broad to be exhausted in a discussion of only few pages.

We do not have to be great connoisseurs of Cuban literature to admit that none of this would have happened in the country twenty years ago, when the judgements of an implacable code of morals simplified and ruled the action and destiny of the characters and literary models. I will stop and take note of the most recent Cuban literature, and deliver names that will allow you to continue following the paths of our literary development in the future. Although the voices here usually intertwine, nevertheless, as a provisional placement and first glimpse to a collection this list may be useful for those who are not informed about today's panorama.

(1) A gay and lesbian voice has secured a position with the work of authors such as Pedro de Jesus López, Juan Carlos Valls, Norge Espinosa, Ena Lucia Portela, Alberto Acosta, Antón Arrufat.

(2) A feminist voice has secured its presence with Reina Maria Rodríguez, Caridad Atencia, Marilin Bobes, Elvira Rodríguez.

(3) In the last decade, a marginal literature arose with a new voice and secured its presence. A great deal of it moves towards the youthful universe of writers, such as Raul Aguilar, Ronaldo Menéndez, Recardo Arrieta, Daniel Díaz Mantilla, Ismael Gonzalez Castaner, José Miguel Sánchez, Alberto Abreu, Felix Luís Viera, Karla Suárez, Ana Luz García Calzada, Ena Lucia Portela.

(4) The emergence and deepening of the literature of the anti-hero continues, and becomes more radical, in the work of the "narrative of violence" of the Cuban 1960s. Several of these writers have taken as the setting Cuba's participation in wars during the decades of the 1970s and 1980s in Africa, especially Angola, among them Angel Lázaro Santiesteban, Alberto Garrido, Roberto Luís Rodríguez Lastre, Alberto Rodríguez Tosca.

(5) Emergence and extension of a meta-textual and self-reflecting literature that appeals to the philosophical postulates of post-modernism is clearly visible in the works of the Diaspora group, although not limited to cultural production outside the island. I refer to Rolando Sánchez Mejias, Rogelio Saunders, Carlos Aguilera, Pablo Herrera Veitia, Alberto Garrandes, Ricardo Alberto Pérez, Rito Ramón Aroche.

What I have called "critical blindness" at this point is the absence of recognition and an enormous debate about the place and significance of this new cultural production at this present moment of our national literary heritage. With so many names and tendencies, it is pitiful to be waiting for some larger public discussion about its relation to the past, to the trajectory of the whole society, or about the future place of these writings. Yet there is hardly any sign of that debate.

The greater part of the works that refer to these writers do very little to supersede the state's descriptions. In my opinion, there are at least two reasons, and both derive from the framework of the Cold War mentioned above. The space for a public debate is as narrow and provisional as it is scarce; the theoretical instrument of what has been called "Marxist thought" does not talk with other contemporary thought tendencies. "Cultural studies," "subaltern studies," "postcolonialism," "postmodern anthropology," "gay and lesbian studies," are words that barely touch upon the critical production in Cuba today. But the same thing also happened with previous forms of knowledge such as feminist theory, Lacanian psychoanalysis, hermeneutics, semiotic and structuralist thought.

The rejection of a dialogue of ideas during the Cuban 1970s, when we received a Marxism devoid of conflict as the sole possible way of thinking, allows us to say that during those years Cuban social thought suffered complete damage. That decade represents the era of least cultural density in the history of the revolutionary period, and maybe of the century. The cultural consequences of that period are still seen in the poverty of the conceptual instruments with which critique confronts the new literary projects.

One could have hoped in recent years to see more from the production and distribution of the cultural institutions (in this case, those that deal with the study of the literary text). These are the times when a revision and the refilling of voids are supposed to be in place. But the two sudden pivotal points in our recent life, the "opening to the outside" [the Soviet outside – editors' note] in the 1970s and the loss of those points of reference with the fall of the socialist bloc in the late 1980s, were truly fascinating experiences. Around each of them, our institutional life remained paralyzed in an ecstasy of astonishment. However, it is exactly thanks to these great turning points that the recent years are also full of awakenings and desires, because a world without references compels the reconstruction of the coordinates and the horizon.

Thus it is not coincidental that there began to emerge elaborate reviews that seek new forms to capture the subject of the text. The feminist studies carried out by Nara Araujo, Luísa Campuzano, Susana Montero y Sayda Capote, the reception of the Lacanian psychoanalysis in Pedro Marquez de Armas, the reading parting from the postmodernism of Maggie Mateo, the alternative of minor philosophy proposed by Emilio Ichikawa, the studies about gay and lesbian literature of Pedro Pérez and, perhaps, my own open up an expectation for Cuban critique, and perhaps a renunciation of its blindness.

11

The Non-Modern Condition:
Societies Without Sociology?

Emilio Ichikawa Morin

This chapter makes a theoretical claim that modern social theory, which originated in Europe and grew out of the Enlightenment project, is not relevant to explain the condition of social life in most of Latin America. Because Durkheim, Weber, and Marx theorized transitions to modernity, primarily in Europe, their contributions have only limited explanatory value in large parts of the world. Sociology as the "science of modernity," especially its critical theoretical applicability, is better seen as an instrument of liberation from both traditional illiteracy and the neo-illiteracy of the Hemisphere (not merely the southern half of the hemisphere) today.

1. Introduction

It has always been said (accurately) that thought is limited by definitions. It is not necessary to be a specialist to conclude that many recurring terms in narrative knowledge like "modernity," "postmodernity," "ideology," "power," or "democracy" do not have a precise logical configuration. No consensus has been established around them. This poetic dimension of social thought has penetrated even the exact natural sciences, which underwrites the decision of an academy of literature and languages in Germany to nominate annually an award for scientific prose.[1]

When I speak of sociology, I do not use capital letters; I mean sociology in its broadest sense, as a social knowledge, as a discursivity on problems constituted from "social facts"—as Durkheim said in establishing the "rules of sociological method."[2] Sociology, here, refers to a knowledge that explicates its objectives starting from Spencer and Marx.

Generally, this type of knowledge has focussed on explaining a *condition*, while we propose to assume it here as a possibility. From this perspective, it is possible to note that ontological and epistemological preconditions exist that make sociology appear in some contexts and not in others. Thus there would be "societies with sociology" and "societies without sociology." That is to say, societies where the preconditions for a sociological emergence, the conditions of modernity, do not exist, or exist in a partial metamorphosed form. It is in this context that I locate Latin American societies in general, and Cuban society in particular.

Of course, it is not correct to deny (or even question) the existence of a regional sociology, because in Latin American societies there are real conditions (though in enclaves sometimes) for its flourishing, and also because one can document an entire sociological tradition that spans more than a century.[3] Yet, when talking about "societies without sociology," I would like to call attention to the fact that the development of sociological thought in the region owes its peculiarity not only to the subjective process of innovation, but also to a singular historical and cultural condition. To say it precisely, they are *Latin American* "societies without sociology," in the traditional sense of the term.

For a long time our intellectual and political elites—at times coinciding, not at others—believed that the most sound alternative for the material and spiritual prosperity of the region depended on an optimal "metropolitan paradigm." Thus they resolved to copy the most diverse models: the French, the Anglo-Canadian, the North American, the Swiss, even the Spanish, and, of course, the German. It is not a secret either that in recent times they have been (and are) looking at the Soviet-Russian, Japanese, and Chinese paradigms. Nevertheless, it did not take long to understand, and what is worse, to confirm, that imitation is not the correct path to configuring successful projects.

Regarding thought, the option has been to substitute what has been called "creative assimilation" for the cruder term "imitation." This formula, in spite of its appeal, falls progressively under suspicion. Everything indicates that it is not enough to assume creatively North American or European thought, but that it is necessary to generate one's own theory.

The historical and social Latin American constitution, its very facts, are penetrated by a different rationality, as Latin American art, especially the novel, has shown sufficiently. But sociological thought has not. The license with which scholars treat original categories of European and North American thought contains a very curious duality: on one hand, explicit obedience of authority; on the other, real irreverence in scientific practice. In Latin American circumstances it is not only the sociological contents that are modified, but also the scientific attitudes and expectations themselves. The diagnosis, forecast, interpretation, and measurement have, here, very different possibilities (or lack thereof). The explanatory insufficiency of some zones of classical sociology in their confrontation with the American facts can be shown with several examples.[4]

2. Sociology and Modernity

If sociology is a science of social institutions, it is also, consequently, a science of modernity. Modernity refers to the historical state in which society is institutionalized globally. The thesis that sociology is a science of modernity is in fact redundant because, if it is a science, it cannot be but from the modern epoch; furthermore, from the modern West. Even though there is talk of oriental science, of ancient and medieval science, an economic perspective of thought suggests limiting science to the modern West. Just as we should not speak of a pre-modern science, we should not qualify as strictly sociological the ancient and medieval reflections about society.

In our academic milieu, Professor V. C. Bobes has radicalized the previous thesis; she has gone to the extent of saying that sociology is *the* science of modernity. If it is true that this formulation is drastic and even harsh, it must be acknowledged that there are elements in its favor. Speaking of modernity usually fuels at times the unfounded phrase "moderns *versus* ancients." This polemic was entertained by only one of the contenders, the moderns, for which reason the partiality of the confrontation is presumed. As Harold Laski well pointed out, not everything that the "moderns" criticized in preceding societies qualified as "ancient" by their convention, was expendable.[5] It is worth noting that even though the controversy was very visible in the sixteenth and seventeenth centuries, it paled afterwards. No longer was the contrast with the past that which mattered, but the validation of the present.

In Habermas' text, *The Philosophical Discourse of Modernity*, modernity appears as a "self-verifying" historical state of the West. He writes that:

> Modernity no longer can or wants to take its criteria of orientation from other epochs, it has to extract its normativity from itself. Modernity has no other way out, nor any other remedy than to use itself. This explains the irritability of its self-awareness, the dynamic of the attempts carried out incessantly until now to "fixate itself," to "corroborate itself."[6]

Modernity, in taking distance from "the ancients," discards the possibility of using the past as a justificatory historical argument. It makes itself elaborate a legitimating auto-discourse, an "ontology of the present"—as Foucault would say at a conference in the College of France in 1983— within a cultural frame of self-praise. According to Foucault, this is precisely what Kant inaugurated in his work, "Was is Aufklaërung?": an ontology of ourselves.

If it were true, as we think, that institutional functionality is the specific difference of modern from traditional society, and that this functionality is the fundamental object of sociological knowledge, then it would be possible to conclude that from the point of view of the "self-verification" of modernity, sociology would rise as the science par excellence.

When philosophy inquires about the real motives of its existence, when it tries to explain its social space, its functionality, it walks towards its demise. Rigorously speaking, philosophy does not die; it becomes extinct, weaving from itself a progressive process of sociologization. Philosophy becomes trapped in the logic of sociology and not even the apparent firmness of its apologists can hide its agony. With its death philosophy fertilizes the consecration of sociology as a science of modernity. Now it is the latter that lords over narrative knowledge and decodifies even the most intimate spheres of modern life; a sociologization of the hidden appears, even knowledge of the signification of silence and of blank space: sociology of the ordinary, of the everyday, of myth, of sex; the sociology of the human-absolute.

Nevertheless, this victory parade is curtailed in a surprising manner. Progressively, sociology itself becomes self-reflexive, it inquires about its limits, about its epistemological condition, about its possibilities of truthfulness and the efficacy of its techniques. It generates a meta-sociological level that drives it to a zone of "speculation on the limits of sociological knowledge." Sociology begins to "philosophize itself," and with that it nears its own suicide.

Out of the double extinction of philosophy and sociology, a multi-disciplinary space arises from where the most brilliant social thought is erected today. If the interdisciplinary incursions of classical sociologists had their explication in personal genius and erudition, today they have it in the appearance of a field of heteronomous knowledge. In this zone, celebrity has been gained by names like Foucault, Bordieu, Habermas, Harris, etc. What are they really? Sociologists, philosophers, anthropologists, linguists, communicationalists? Their differentiated institutional location shows the complexity of the classification. The same uncertainty is present when classifying their works. The *Theory of Communicative Action* (Jurgen Habermas), for example, partakes of sociological theory as much as of the history of philosophy, the study of communication, the analysis of language, the dimensions of political reform, and the utopian project.

Sociology, then, arises in modernity and there it gains its own fissures; but all of this it bears *for* modernity, to account for its institutional functionality. Those institutions are assumed as constituting and constituted by a system that, following Luchmann, has received or could come to constitute itself as "autopoetic." There are no medieval studies about the institutional functionality of the church in the European feudal order, as there are no Athenian studies of the political signification of sophistry education. We rely only on modern studies of those happenings; that is, only modern sociological thought has been interested in the functionality of an event.

Our presupposition is that sociology and modernity coexist in a relation of genetic complicity. This nexus has been acknowledged and about it several theoretical proposals have been made, among them Agnes Heller's sociological project on the *defetishing of modernity*. As can be supposed, "to defetish" goes beyond "impartial" description or diagnostic; it implies also to denounce, to disrobe, to protest. To "defetish" modernity is to rebel against its illusory dimension.

The author understands "defetishing" as a whole strategy of sociological action, as the comprehension of the endemic truth of modernity. A change in the sociological paradigm allows us to deconstruct (in the real action of modern life) categories such as *state*, *class*, *power*, which have become disguising fetishes of the authentic actors in social functioning. It proposes, alas, to come closer to "method-ological individualism."

3. Sociology, anti-modernity and a-modernity

It will not be a problem for anyone to accept the link between modernity and sociology, nor the definitions of that knowledge in an institutionalized context. But, what happens in those societies that know only a marginal, distorted, enclaved modernity? Are they marked by a likewise marginal, distorted, enclaved sociology? Rigorously speaking, does *sociology* exist there?

In an essay on the theoretical dimension of sociological knowledge, Agnes Heller herself asserts: "When research is done in a pre-modern social frame or in a pre-modern enclave of a modern society, we are talking about anthropology or ethnology and this is not only a problem of vocabulary."[7] If a general agreement is possible with the previous thesis, there should be additional inquiry (also not a matter of words) into the epistemological quality when the general context is pre-modern with resonant modern enclaves. This is, as I understand it, the situation of Latin American societies today.

It should be emphasized that the objective of this exposition is to critique the same modernity-sociology relation that, even if it were unquestionable for the European West, is severely lacking for our region. The fragility of the modernity-sociology axis in the Latin American context embarrasses the theoretical legitimacy of sociology, understood as "science of modernity." This can be better understood when illustrated with the behavior of some basic terms.

(a) The actors

In the foundations of classical sociology there is an invariant about the rationality of social actors. Karl Marx already assumed that by adding "the consciousness of oppression" to oppression the working class could be induced to revolution. This shows that he was convinced that even the proletariat, the least enlightened class of nineteenth-century urban Europe, could understand and change the mechanisms of its own oppression. It was necessary only that along with the convergence of some objective conditions, the class would provide a political, scientific, and pedagogical avant-garde capable of leading it through (history-making) the events of social change.

In this analysis by Karl Marx, the rationality of the working class is also presupposed in terms of goals and morality: the working class has an "interest" in anti-capitalist revolution ("it has nothing to lose but its chains") and the very capitalism to be destroyed is unfair and amoral or immoral ("man is to other men like a wolf"). At the climax of that conviction, Lenin recommended the study of Hegelian and Kantian philosophy to Russian workers, as well as the texts of the scientific and economic avant-garde of the time, as a way of strengthening political consciousness. I am referring to "books that cannot be missing from the library of any conscious worker," and among which was included no less than *Das Kapital*. As is evident, even Lenin did not doubt the rationality of the central actor of the new era.

In the evolutionist Durkheimian scheme there is a similar belief. As Durkheim postulated, the change in forms of solidarity implied a transformation in the type of penalty (Foucault will follow his path talking about "punishment") in the sense of a change in the direction of the loss of (explicit) intensity. That is, the penalty is notably less harsh, more moral, and less physical. From a critical point of view it can be affirmed as possibly due to a growing consolidation of order. The society that is formed *evolutionarily* would have a less coercive character, unifying itself increasingly through ties of solidarity. The rational interest of actors would be the base of that ordering, and at the same time, the substance of social rationality.

Weberian sociology places great faith in the rationality of modern society, a faith placed perhaps more emphatically in its functioning than in its tendencies. At its base lies the same assumption as in the reflections of Marx and Durkheim: social actors arrange their actions around goals that they differentiate, and become aware of, according to their economic and moral-spiritual interests. Weber's comprehensive study about the origin of capitalism, his detailed analysis of modern society, his study of the basic bourgeois institutions (the capitalist enterprise and bureaucracy), as well as his diagnosis of the present and future of capitalist society presuppose the rationality of the actors and institutions that it evaluates.

From the Weberian scheme, the category of "modernization" enters sociology in the mid-twentieth century, and this occurs in the shelter of the functionalist theoretical paradigm. The belief is established that access to modernity is possible through a non-western path, that is, appealing to "exogenous" props in the "generation of modernity" and to an intellectual tradition divergent from the one that was orchestrated around European rationalism. This thesis seemed to be verified by the process of modern "leaps" by Japan and other Asian countries' paths to modernity.

Most interesting from the point of view of what we seek here is that all those processes, independently of the props used in the race towards the model of Occidentality, make evident a global systematization of roles. That is to say that they achieve, as in previous cases, a rational structure and functionality. Even the individualist methodological alternatives proposed by Anglo-Saxon sociological thought (Rational Choice) are undoubtedly more dynamic for the theoretical elements they incorporate— game-theory, paradox of decisions, etc.—and for the social subjects on which they focus. The same premise prevails: the belief in the rationality of the social self, subjective as well as objective.

Occidental sociology does not in anyway foresee the topological existence—although accepting it sometimes as a negligible exceptionality—of societies where the behavior of social actors is ordinarily divergent from what would be expected in terms of teleological and moral rationality. If we hold to classical standards, it would be more appropriate to describe these social behaviors in terms of irrationality or a-rationality. How, for example, do we explain agreements that go against one's own interests: as irrational consensus? What about solidarities taken beyond the minimum moral normativity? This "irrationality" could be no more than a proto-enlightened "pre-rationality," more complex now due to the uncontainable irruption of "post-enlightened" technological media.

Latin American societies still conform to criteria of affectivity that take primacy even over the individualist disposition of modern personality. Sometimes there is talk about the end of the individual; there could also be discussion about the non-emergence of the individual. The different levels of social orders color even more the maintenance of precarious solidarities. The sociological implications vary so widely, from the local indigenous chief to the national president, that a general theoretical design of what is desirable is hard to make.

Totalitarianism, for example, which annuls initiative and is undesirable from a micro optic, is an unequivocal guarantor of order at a macro level. A democracy that stimulates initiative on a small scale is incapable of coherence at a generalized level. This explains the proliferation of autonomous powers in the region—death squads, cartels, cultural and sports mafias, etc.—that would be unthinkable within totalitarian functioning.

Occidental sociology (even Marxism) has no explanatory answer for groups that avalanche their own interests, or for centenary moral patterns, neither for theorizing what can be called "irrational actions aimed at goals." They are phenomena that classical sociologists did not foresee, or when they did, they did not heed sufficiently.

The preceding suggests strongly that if rationality is a decisive characteristic of modernity, and the latter is itself an ontological support of sociology (sociology is a science of modernity), we can question once more, now from the perspective of the social actors, the very possibility of this knowledge to explain the conditions of our region.

(b) Problems of legitimation

"Legitimation" appears as one of the most visible chapters of the political history of modern states. Even though we can find in *Pipino* an explicit justification of God, and in *Justiniano* support of the juridical normativity of the *Digest*, it is not until modern times that we find the political necessity to argue the maintenance and exercise of sovereignty. In the *Second Essay on Civil Government*, John Locke inquires about the sources of power. Taking his analysis back to the garden of Eden where Adam was "king," Locke shows that power still does not have an explicit justification; and then the search for justification appears as a problem.

If it is true that earlier social thought deals with this issue, it is Max Weber in the early twentieth century who places it as one of the main and almost requisite themes of the sociological tradition. Not even the irreverent proposals of postmodern thought have turned their backs on the issue, though they seem to have turned the problem of the legitimation of order into that of the legitimation of knowledge (the treatment by Lyotard of legitimation by "*paralofia*" is the most notorious case).

Sociological currents today recognize that modern governments are forced, or at least compelled, to legitimize their power. After G. Levski analysis in *Power and Privilege*, 1966, Habermas asserts that all class societies, in particular the beneficiaries, have to deal with a dilemma: distributing the social output unequally; and nevertheless, legitimately.[8]

If we review the outcome of occidental revolutions, we would ascertain that in fact none was made to establish equality, but to rectify inequality. That is, political leaders sought to trade an illegitimate inequality for a legitimate inequality: the opulence of the nobility for the opulence of the bourgeoisie. The justificatory argumentation of inequality is the axis of modern ideologies; from that perspective nineteenth-century socialism appears, in its non-operationalized theoretical purity, as an anti-ideology. The need for this "machinery of ideas" is another of the unquestioned (not unquestionable) presuppositions of classical sociology.

When Max Weber analyzes different types of domination, he is concerned with how and in what conditions this legitimation is constituted as effectively legitimate. He enumerates three abstracts forms of legitimation, making all the factual qualifiers corresponding to the construction of a general theory. Almost as an exception, and only when he studies the formation of certain classes of cities, does Weber use the term "not legitimate"; but the sense is very different from what one would at first expect.[9] That expression, perhaps casual, is very far from meaning a dominating order without justificatory alibi. Actually, he never paused to analyze what has later been termed "illegitimate domination."

For Max Weber the legitimacy of domination was an unavoidable chapter of modern governments, an epiphenomenon of their political statement. In fact, domination seems to be the general situation: fascism, liberalism, the dictatorship of the proletariat, post-modern monarchies, fundamentalism—they all have a justification, a system of legitimizing arguments. In the realm of modernity legitimation is also an answer to a demand of legitimation from (presumably rational) social actors that, supposedly, must give their approval to a relation of domination. That is, making a contract version of the Weberian postulate, social actors establish a mutually favorable transaction (agreement) with power for the sake of order. In periods of crisis of legitimacy we could expect demands of legitimation; and the center of power would be forced to offer new legitimating arguments—or to reformulate the old ones—in order to satisfy that characteristic of modern political logic.

An examination of Latin American societies shows that large masses of the population stay at the margins of political activity, even at the margins of political interest itself. They seem to suggest that Alan Tourraine is right:

> In each of the countries the absence of political mobilization appears as the most striking fact. During the eighties, most countries of the region have lost from 20 to 40% of their living standards .... And nevertheless (...) social movements cannot be seen.[10]

Regional social actors, for many reasons, which cannot be addressed in this chapter, do not behave actively, do not demand rights nor raise arguments about the political crisis of legitimacy, which would put in disrepute the rational character of their constitutions. In the Latin American social and historical circumstance, the concept of legitimacy does not have enough explanatory capacity, much less when it is prescribed as a requisite of political functioning.

I think that along with the previous terms we should put to work a-legitimacy, which would call attention to the political stillness that characterizes a vast social sector in conditions of cultural marginality, and very distant from that condition we call rational. This condition has nothing to do with occidental political absentee-ism (which is modern and active in its rational dimension). A-legitimacy does not point to de facto governments without argumentative justifications, nor to a political centrality that has achieved contract obedience. This term points to the fact that there exist in Latin America governments that, even though they have not been legitimized through recognized formulas, it would not occur to anyone to call them "illegitimate" governments. In an ironic sense, we could say that they are governments legitimized by the indifference of the great masses.

It is necessary to add another facet concerning the globalization of political relations. In the United Nations, governments demand of each other an "ostentation of legitimacy." To justify their power, they even have to present their own "opposition," which alters them from elements of contestation to elements of support. As part of that international ritualistic pressure, some regional governments are forced to celebrate elections (procedural legitimation), decree amnesties, convoke referenda, etc. Because these decisions respond more to world reordering than to internal political dynamics, this phenomenon also escapes the frame foreseen by classical sociology, which saw in the justificatory process an answer to the activity of demand of the "subjects."

The concept (better the notion) of a-legitimacy has, for all this recurrence of circumstances, a not-too-shabby explanatory capacity; it can at least function temporarily as a working hypothesis. On certain occasion , Habermas spoke of "pseudo-legitimacy,"[11] but I think that with it he signaled the need for another issue: the truthful, or not, character of the legitimating rhetoric and grammar.

Legitimation continues to be a central theme of contemporary sociological theory; it is an axis of any political praxis. We do not know what to expect in the future, perhaps an ecstasy of legitimating supply and demand, perhaps a generalized skepticism that leads to a loss of political will and with it the disappearance of the problem. Lastly, to appeal once again to the utopian ideal, a consensus could be established around power, based on rational precedence and subordination; with this, it might be possible to resolve the basic problem.

(c) Reality

The assertion of exceptional conditions in Latin America is not new in the intellectual fruits of the region. Early designations such as "New World," "Fourth Land," and "New Spain" show a whole vocation for difference. This tendency (or temptation) has been qualified by Jorge Ferrer as Latin American discourses of exceptionality, especially notable in social and political Cuban literature. To incorporate into sociology this claim of difference is to tighten the tension of the tightrope of identity, now from the point of view of theoretical identity. At any rate, it remains to be settled whether that exceptionality is illusory or real; if it can be located only at the level of discourse, or if it also can be found in the realm of reality.

Regarding the ordinariness or exceptionality of the Latin American circumstance there are not many margins of response. Regional thought has accepted it as different, has denied it as such, or has doubted the whole thing. Even though all these variations are legitimate in the cultural drama of our region, it is fair to affirm that the greatest regionalist vocation is the assertion of the exceptionality of Latin America. It could be wrong scientifically, but not ethically and politically. If our region of America constitutes a different level of reality, the trust in European and North American explanatory schemes that have dominated our regional thought would not be justified.

When in his *Lessons on the History of Philosophy* Hegel introduces Christian thought, he makes an interesting digression on miracles. According to him, the belief in miracles is testimony of a dissatisfaction with nature; the miracle appears here as an accident of nature. However, José Martí planned to make a whole book about miracles; "... for my book about miracles in America," he notes in one of his journals.[12] From his perspective, the miraculous was not something accidental in the history of Latin America, but constitutive. Now it was not so much the logic of miracle, but the miracle of logic.

This reference suggests the possibility of an American ontological personality. It is something that Latin American art captures constantly, but that social thought cannot accept. If this were so, the sociological approach to the American self would also have to be specific. The determination of the Latin American historical condition is the axis through which traverses the definition of its sociology, the premise of its social science.

If we accept that sociology must defetishize modernity, we have to take into account the particularity of "American modernity." "The main characteristic of Latin America"—Touraine diagnoses—"is that the classical image of the functional differentiation of social classes, labor unions separated from parties, themselves separated from the state, with a bureaucratized public administration, has never existed."[13]

The wave of literature about modernity and post-modernity that flowed through Latin America during the 1980s intensified to the point of irritation one of the crucial points of the sociological polemic: the pertinence of the modern project and its enlightened chapter. This issue, of course, contained the characterization of the historical status that the region had ultimately reached. Though not unanimously accepted, the thesis was diffused throughout wide circles that for Latin America, modernity was a pending project, an echo of the posture of Habermas in the debate, presented by the German sociologist when he received the Theodor Adorno Award in 1980.

Personally, I am not only convinced theoretically that modernity is a pending passage of our history, but I also believe that it is necessary to operationalize a neo-enlightening praxis that contributes to a libertarian rationalization of the regional social subject. Along with the traditional illiteracy, there is in place today a neo-illiteracy. These problems are made more acute not only by the lack of technologies and financing but also, what is worse, by lack of time. As was suspected by Sarmiento in his time, Latin America today does not have time; it has to turn into a high-velocity lens of historical resolution if it does not want to keep feeding the utopia of redemption in future generations.

A neo-enlightening educational project, as a part of Latin American modernization, is an essential ingredient to reform the regional political a-legitimacy. Critical-sociological thought must be a part of the contents and the agent of that reform. With this, sociology suffers a metamorphosis: it does not diagnose or defetishize a modernity that in fact does not exist. If sociology, as daughter of "enlightened reason," operationalizes itself once it is born as theory, in Latin America it is *born as instrument.* It is not an emergent sociology; it is an induced sociology. It seems that we are not in the presence of societies without sociology, but in societies now exposed to a radical redefinition.

4. Conclusion: Societies without Sociology?

I have sought to demonstrate that the self-understanding of social theory in the region is problematic, especially when its assumption is attempted from the characterization that European-North American sociology has made of it. I am not, of course, pandering to the thirst for exoticism left by an excessively homogeneous world; I would only like to highlight that the Latin American historical specificity—imaginary or factual, always *real*—forces the reconsideration of the signposts on which we have erected our definition. I confirm the need; the task remains pending.

ENDNOTES

1. Jurgen Habermas (1990) *Pensamiento postmetafisico* [Postmetaphysical thought], ((Barcelona: Taurus), p. 240.
2. Editor's note: Other broad definitions would include "the study of social life" and "the study of social relations."
3. Velia Cecilia Bobes (1990) *Para una periodización de la sociología en América Latina* [Towards a periodization of sociology in Latin America], (La Habana: Editorial de Ciencias Sociales).
4. Editor's note: Ichikawa uses "America" to refer to the hemisphere, not to the United States as the majority of the U.S. population has been culturally conditioned to assume.
5. It is not indolent to stress that Marx himself felt special attraction for the medieval model of artisan production where the producer had a direct relationship with the means of production. Laski, as well, valued highly the clear-cut hierarchic definition of medieval Europe and its chivalric ideal.
6. Jurgen Habermas (1989) *El discurso filosófico de la modernidad* [The Philosophical Discourse of Modernity] (Barcelona: Taurus), p. 18.
7. See H. Albrow (1990) (editor) *Globalization, Knowledge and Society, readings from international sociology* (London: Sage Publications).

8. Jurgen Habermas, op. cit., p. 118.

9. Max Weber (1971) *Economía y sociedad* [Economy and Society], (La Habana: Editorial de Ciencias Sociales).

10. A. Touraine, "Interview," in *El Nacional*, Mexico, 7 January 1993.

11. Jurgen Habermas, op. cit., p. 137.

12. José Martí, *Obras completas* [Complete Works] (La Habana: Consejo Nacional de Cultura), 1965, Volume 21, p. 195.

13. A. Touraine, op. cit.

12

Thinking in Cuban-A Conversation with Monsignor Carlos Manuel De Cespedes about Religion and Culture

Marisel Caraballo Sánchez

Carlos Manuel de Cespedes Garcia-Menocal, great-grandchild of the Father of the Nation, likes to define himself as part of the phenomenon that is called the Cuban nationality. This priest is an illustrious and intellectual part of the Cuban-Catholic mind. He was instrumental during the renovation of the Catholic Church that was brought about by the Second Vatican Conference in the first half of the 1960s. In his pastoral letters from 1969, he stated his position against the embargo and his desire to reconcile Catholics and Marxists. Knowing that the Cuban people are religious, although not devout Catholics, Monsignor de Cespedes is partly responsible for the Church's acceptance of a growing mixed-race congregation and its religious repercussions. His personal gift for charming people has not diminished through the years. He enjoys a lot of respect, especially among the young people who go to his church to watch a good movie, listen to an opera, or simply to hear him speak, with equal passion, about Cuba or religious faith.

Marisel Caraballo Sánchez: Carlos Manuel de Cespedes, don't you think that you have given up a lot of things to be a priest?

Carlos Manuel de Cespedes: Yes, I gave up a more active and direct participation in some areas of life, but I was able to participate in other extremely enriching realities as a priest. I renounced the family, marriage, and children for religious celibacy; but that has given me enormous freedom with my dealings with others. Yes, I have no biological children or a wife, but I am a father for many people and a brother to many more.

Any selection implies a renunciation in life. There are too many things in life that interest me. I have lived out my priesthood for thirty-six years without having renounced other political, cultural and economic realities around me. I deal with people who agree with my Catholic faith, some who believe in other faiths and some who have no religious beliefs. I have tried to get along with everyone and to maintain an open mind, ear and understanding. Being a priest has not signified a rupture with the cultural and political tradition of my family, it has just changed the way that I have realized my goals in those areas.

In the end, I always think as a Catholic. Some of us are priests because it is God's will, and this has given us the motivation to follow that direction unconsciously.

Marisel Caraballo Sánchez: Talk to me about the role that the Catholic Church played in the formation of our national identity.

Carlos Manuel de Cespedes: Catholics were a principal part of the colonizing process, despite all the contradictions implied by that process. We are partly descended from the Spanish men and women who came to Cuba. Some were sincere and some were brutal; however, they were Catholics and their influence permeated our culture during the centuries of Spanish rule.

When the inhabitants of this island began "thinking in Cuban," there were persons and institutions within the Catholic Church that had very decisive roles in the formation of the national identity of this country. For example, I can think of the San Carlos and San Ambrosio Seminary, the San Basilio el Magno Seminary in Santiago de Cuba, and the Real Pontifica Universidad de San Jeronimo in Havana. From the end of the eighteenth century until the end of the nineteenth century, "intellectual" studies were only offered in those three institutions of higher education. We should reflect on the decisive role that Father Felix Varela, Catholic priest and professor in the seminaries, exerted on *criollo* thought.

I think this current of Catholic thought has been present after the formation of Cuban intellectualism, even in persons who distanced themselves from the Church but whose ethics and philosophies still maintained Christian, specifically Spanish Catholic, connotations. I cannot help but think of José Marti, the greatest of all Cubans, practicing Catholicism in his youth. He later distanced himself from religious practice but maintained his Catholic ethics and values at the heart of his philosophy. He considered himself a remote disciple of Father Felix Varela, whose philosophy he appropriated and utilized to enlighten his new realities.

Later, during the Republic, things became more diversified. After 1902, we witnessed Catholicism, Protestantism—Christian but different—Liberalism and Marxism, and other currents of thought distant from those of the Catholic Church. In the end, the foundational Catholic element has remained present in Cuban identity.

Marisel Caraballo Sánchez: Monsignor, can you validate the notion that symbols like the Virgin of Caridad del Cobre represent expressions of national identity?

Carlos Manuel de Cespedes: I think so, although I would not overdo it. There is a very recent book by Olga Portuondo, historian and professor in Santiago de Cuba, precisely titled, *Our Lady of the Caridad del Cobre and National Cuban Identity.* This is the most comprehensive work that exists about the history of the image of Our Lady of the *Caridad del Cobre*, and it supports the notion that this is the universal symbol of Cuban nationality. This point of view coincides with Hemingway's point, who by the way, was not Catholic. He had a special sensitivity toward our patron lady-saint. When he won the Nobel Peace Prize, he donated his medal to Cuba and sent it to the Sanctuary of *El Cobre*, where it is still located. Personally, I think that the Virgin of *Caridad del Cobre* is a symbol of Cuban nationality in many respects because it was present since the beginning of the seventeenth century, perhaps with more devotion in *Oriente* (eastern region of the island). In the west, it became more pronounced at the end of the eighteenth century and, of course, in the nineteenth century, it was very latent during the independence wars. Carlos Manuel de Cespedes, my great-grandfather, was a devout believer of Our Lady of *Caridad del Cobre*, and during the Ten Years War, when he liberated the region of *El Cobre*, he went to the sanctuary to pray before he went to the public acknowledgement of liberation. He always carried a chain with the image of Our Lady that his wife, Ana de Quesada, had given to him. Many patriots shared the same devotion. We should remember that the veterans of the war had asked Pope Benedict XV to name Our Lady of *Caridad del Cobre*, the patron saint of Cuba.

I think it is a symbol of nationality, agreed upon by even non-Catholic persons. But we must reduce her to that. It may be that she is the universal symbol that unites all Cubans. However, there are Cubans who do not believe that the Virgin is symbolic of their nationality.

Marisel Caraballo Sánchez: Even so, non-believers invoke her name. What does that mean to you?

Carlos Manuel de Cespedes: Yes, there is that tendency. There is a small Spanish saying that goes: "Everybody remembers Santa Barbara when there is thunder." In Cuba, the most common invocation of the Virgin is that of Our Lady of the *Caridad del Cobre*. I want to stress that I do not intend to diminish her importance as a symbol of nationality; however, I would like to remain partial to those non-believers who are as Cuban as I am, and who would rather assign other "more human" symbols to Cuban nationality. There is no doubt that the symbol of *Caridad del Cobre* is like "the great house of the people."

Marisel Caraballo Sánchez: How do you value the relations between the Catholic faith, the popular religion, and other religions that span from other cultural origins, in Cuba?

Carlos Manuel de Cespedes: I would like to start with popular religion. Popular religion belongs to the people and, in the case of Cuba, it is very diverse in its manifestations. First, we have the "eminent" Catholics. We call them as such because they are not culturally diverse and they do not know the full meaning of the Catholic faith. They do not exhibit any influence from other religions and they practice the simplest form of Catholicism. They feel completely Catholic by just praying at home, not organizing into churches and being generous to others.

There also exists another popular religion, one that is more syncretic, more diverse, with Catholic and African ingredients. A lot of the people who practice it often come to the church, participate in mass, come to Saint's Day festivities like those of San Lazaro or Santa Barbara, they come at Christmas or during Easter. Here Catholicism is fused with Afro-Cuban elements. They are considered popular religions because they are not endorsed by any institutions.

There are also other currents of Christian religion, Protestantism in all its forms, and new religious movements that are considered "sects," although I do not like to use that word because it connotes pejorative tones. I am not sure if they can be incorporated under the term "popular" because they are a minority. However, certain respected and significant sectors of society practice these types of religion. There are also new Protestant movements and Jehovah Witnesses. We also find very small groups of Buddhism.

Marisel Caraballo Sánchez: In what way do Cuban Catholics practice a different type of Catholicism from other countries?

Carlos Manuel de Cespedes: I don't think that Catholics practice a different Catholicism in different countries. It is a common religion, historically supported by an institution; in addition to being universal and having millions of followers. Catholicism in Cuba is the same as in other countries. Catholic Cubans, Germans, Italians, and Japanese identify with the same static cult, the same church structure, the same commandments, the same creed, and the same prayers. In other words, the Catholic Church is the same in other parts of the world.

Religious believers are another issue. Many of them can make reference to the Catholic religion for what it has represented in the formation of the Cuban national identity. However, they have become "believers in their own faith", which might mean that they are not "real" Catholic believers. The syncretics, as they are called, tend to have a certain degree of indifference to the Catholic faith and tolerance toward a different form of religious life, which makes it easier to be a "believer". This is a problem in other parts of the world, and it varies according to cultural roots and other religious phenomena.

It is very common that these believers in their own faith, or syncretics, practice Catholicism mixed with African religions, *santeria* or other beliefs. If we were in Mexico, Guatemala, Peru or Ecuador, we would find Catholics who practice Catholicism in that periphery, blending it with their own aboriginal religions, where there is an abundant indigenous population. The phenomenon of mixing races in the Caribbean is common, whether it is the Spanish and Latin Caribbean—like Haiti, Puerto Rico, Dominican Republic, Cuba, or the others. Jamaica and other small islands in the Anglo-Saxon Caribbean follow similar practices. Brazil and Africa also have mixed races. Africa has many well-established Catholic religions, for example, in Angola and Mozambique. These are ex-colonies of Catholic countries, where there is also syncretism. In other words, this phenomenon is present everywhere.

We must bear in mind that there is a difference between these syncretic Catholics who "practice" within the periphery of the Catholic Church and the "pure" ones. Some of the syncretic Catholics are cultured and educated, some of them are baptized and also often go to church. Even so, they syncretize Catholicism with other practices and they follow a lifestyle that has little to do with Catholicism.

Marisel Caraballo Sánchez: If there is syncretism in religious practices in Cuba and other Latin American countries, do you think that the Church has opened a window of tolerance toward it?

Carlos Manuel de Cespedes: We can talk about tolerance and respect, or rather of respect and reality. Religion cannot be imposed. In the Middle Ages the Church tried to impose itself upon the origins of Christianity, when it became the center of the Roman Empire. But we know that if religion is imposed, it gets shunned. These days we have a better understanding of these situations, we are more knowledgeable of human nature, and through psychology we know that the Church must offer its religious message to people and that people will take whatever suits them. Some might change their way of life, some might convert to Catholicism and others might stay the same or syncretize their religious beliefs. This is a serious issue. We can talk about tolerance, but I would much rather speak of respect and reality when speaking about non-Catholic religious phenomena in different cultural contexts.

Marisel Caraballo Sánchez: Has there been an increase in religious practices in Cuba?

Carlos Manuel de Cespedes: We can verify the growth in Catholicism through the statistical reporting we undertake to send to Rome every year. We report on baptisms, church attendance, Holy Communions, weddings, etc. The increase began in 1979. From the 1960s to 1978 the statistics were declining. Since 1979 they started increasing until 1990 and 1991. After that the figures stabilized at a higher level than in 1979, but lower than during the pre-revolutionary period. Through conversations with Protestant pastors, I have confirmed that there has been an increase in Protestant religions as well. It is also evident that syncretism has also grown, from what I see in the streets. The increase might not be in faith per se, but in religious practice and belief. I have a feeling that in the last two or three years we have hit the ceiling.

Marisel Caraballo Sánchez: Do you believe that we have embraced Catholicism influenced by the Spanish model rather than by the Church as an institution?

Carlos Manuel de Cespedes: Religious practice in Spain in the past was stronger than at the present time. We would need to explore if this was due to stronger morals or favorable social environment. From monarchial times to Franco's time, the Church was a state apparatus. Afterwards, the country entered into modernity and the Church's status declined. The social environment changed and people began enjoying more liberties. People stop wearing masks when there are new truths.

I don't know if the decrease in religious practices is equal to a decrease in religious beliefs, or simply an abandonment of people's masks. Perhaps we have reached the truth of the situation. This is a complex phenomenon, for which I don't have a definite opinion. In the case of Spain, which is close to us because we are Cubans, there was an immediate decline in religious beliefs after Franco's regime fell. We have to ask ourselves if it is actually a decline in religious beliefs or a decline in formal religious beliefs which corresponded to a time when going to church was viewed favorably.

When this ceased to be viewed favorably and became an everyday activity, those who considered it a formal activity ceased to go. Were those people genuinely Catholic? I think not. Perhaps they had a certain "religiousness" in them, and although they continued to go to church, there was never a real commitment.

Marisel Caraballo Sánchez: Could it be that in modern times the Church has remained a bit archaic with respect to social precepts and people don't identify with it anymore?

Carlos Manuel de Cespedes: No, the precepts do not change. The Church began predicating them during the first century, while being opposed to the laws and customs of the Roman Empire. It will never abandon the precepts that constitute its essence.

The Pope asks all young people to swim against the norm. Without any pressures they will find God, and I believe there are some that do and they become convinced that the "real" values lie in Him. Just as it happened in the first century, now we find an extremely corrupted society at all levels. Christians arrived without having any power or resources; immigrants, persecuted, while preaching against the way people lived. That's how they started spreading the Word. After four or five centuries, half of the Roman Empire had converted to Christianity. It is not a question of being archaic or being modern, but of faithfulness to Jesus and his teachings. Of course, as the knowledge of science keeps growing, the Church can embrace a broader array of lifestyles because it recognizes change. However, the basic precepts—what constitutes the Faith and Christian morality—are the same now as they were twenty centuries ago. They are the same in Cuba, Africa or Japan. You can either embrace it or not.

Marisel Caraballo Sánchez: During the last decades in Latin America, the Church advocated a theory named *Teologia de la Liberacion* (Liberation Theology). Why did the Cuban Catholic Church stay out of this trend?

Carlos Manuel de Cespedes: The Protestants in Cuba discussed it more than the Catholics. We studied it in the seminary as an incorporated discipline, but this was a Latin American current that did not prosper for many reasons: one of them being the economic, social and political conditions specific to certain countries. The father and writer of the first book of the theory is the Peruvian priest Gustavo Gutierrez, my study partner in Rome. The theory developed in Peru and was adopted in Brazil by the brothers Boff.

I think that the conditions in those countries, the military regimes they had and their economic conditions, gave way to the boom of that theory. When I travel through Latin America, I get the feeling that it was an historic phenomenon. The old Liberation Theologians are still alive; some have abandoned their previous positions, some still have them but they are isolated. There are no young priests who cultivate the theory. It is still studied as a religious current in the 1970s and 1980s, but it never really transcended into anything major.

Under the influence of Liberation Theory, many base communities surfaced. Today, those communities are extinguished and in other places, they are only remnants of what they were. For better or worse, more and more, it is becoming a thing of the past. For better, because it was a poor theory; for worse, because it carried a set of values that called for more sensibility towards social problems. I hope that theology and the Church can assimilate those values.

Marisel Caraballo Sánchez: Many communities in Latin America felt protected and sheltered by this theory. Do you agree that it gives people strength to go on living?
Carlos Manuel de Cespedes: Those needs still exist. For example, one of the places where the theory was promoted was in Nicaragua, during the time of the Sandinistas. Curiously, it started during the Somoza dictatorship, it became stronger during the time of the Sandinistas, and then it disappeared. Today nobody speaks about Liberation Theory in Nicaragua. However, the economic conditions there are worse now than they were 20 years ago. Perhaps there remained a better sensibility toward the economic and social problems, and people have adapted to its values.

Marisel Caraballo Sánchez: John Paul II, like Ché Guevara, spoke of the "new man." What is the meaning of the "new man" for the Catholic Church, keeping in mind the realities we live in today?
Carlos Manuel de Cespedes: For the Catholic Church and for Christians in general, when one speaks of the "new man," it is understood as what St. Paul spoke about in the New Testament. It is the "new man" incarnate in Christ, the one that abandons his previous life—in this case, pagan life and Jewish life—and who assumes a different existence because he joins Jesus by going through with baptism and following the sacraments. He tries to ground his existence in the spiritual order, and projects it in his life, living like Jesus Christ, following the Word. That is the new man for St. Paul and that is the way the Church speaks of him: the man who lives with

Christ and who tries to incorporate in his life the values that the Church stands for, the Word and the teachings of Christ.

Of course, that happens all year long, in the whole world, in all the cultures, because there are always values that go against human beings. The "new man," among other things, is the man who deals with the truth, with generosity, with fraternal love. These are universal values that we always have to preach and renew in the contemporary world. During the Middle Ages and in the next thousand years, we will still be preaching about the "new man" incarnate in Christ, capable of living in simplicity, austerity, truth, and generosity.

Marisel Caraballo Sánchez: Monsignor, how can the concept of the "new man" actually be accomplished?

Carlos Manuel de Cespedes: The problem is that to assume the lifestyle that the Church preaches, one must assume that everyone has Christian faith, which is not true. Under what pretense can we ask a person to have faith, to look at Christ as the complete model of human existence and as the correct path for human fulfillment? For us Christians, this is very clear; and we try to maintain our commitment to him, although we are limited and therefore we are sinners. We know the way to God and we know that the goal is to preach the Word. But not everyone shares in the faith, and others might have other goals or other ideas about life. For others the "new man" might mean something different and they might have other ideas about, say, war. In Islam, a religion I respect deeply, it is thought that war and violence are necessary parts of human beings, to defend their ideals. The Catholic Church held a similar view in the past, the concept of Holy War, but it has renounced it. Muslims, who are very coherent in their faith, might think that violence is a way to conquer their ideals to realize their Muslim truths. We think that today, truths are given and not imposed, and even less through arms. We could speak of other theories in the Far East, Japan, China and even here in the West with Marxism, where the "new man" might mean something different. It depends on the ideological and philosophical position of a person. The Catholic Church proclaims its ideals, proposes them and tries to live them. To accept it or not depends on human freedom and the grace of God.

Marisel Caraballo Sánchez: You spoke of the goals of the Church in the past. It would be timely if people reached those goals; however, it seems that the contemporary world is more distant to those goals. Considering the problems of the present, do you think arms might be the only way to go?

Carlos Manuel de Cespedes: Unfortunately that is the situation. But one has to get tired. There are non-Christian people who have shown to us that the tenacity of a proposition is sometimes more effective than arms. A man like Mahatma Gandhi in India achieved independence without violence by preaching his ideals, opening the dialogue with the rest of the world and died a victim of his active pacifism. Let's think of Nelson Mandela in South Africa and the value of his life; about Martin Luther King and the fights for racial equality in the United States. These men were martyrized for their ideas but never resorted to violence, although that does not mean that they were passive pacifists. On the contrary, they were very active and involved with the truths they proclaimed, but they were not violent. Some achieved their goals in the long run. Thirty or forty years ago, who would have thought that blacks in South Africa were going to share the same seats in government with the same Whites who discriminated against them? That has all been possible because of a man named Mandela. It is a very long and treacherous road, but it is the only constructive one.

Marisel Caraballo Sánchez: Do you think that the presence of the Pope in Cuba will increase the level of dialogue between the Church and the government?
Carlos Manuel de Cespedes: I don't think it will increase it in the future, if it did not do so while we were preparing for his visit. But, of course, the Church's message has gone out to more people because of the Pope's visit. I suppose that did not stop when he got on the plane back to Rome on January 25, 1998. Those conversations, dialogues, trust and relations that have been established will continue. I don't have a crystal ball to see the future but I think it would be normal if there was a before and after effect of the Pope's visit.

Marisel Caraballo Sánchez: What are the expectations in Cuba stemming from the Pope's visit?
Carlos Manuel de Cespedes: His visit was a pastoral visit, just like all his visits to other nations. It has tried to re-animate the faith of Christians, to show his pastoral interest toward them, to show his closeness to the Cuban Church, and this could mean a renewed interest in the Catholic faith for those who already had it.

Also, there are the non-Catholic people who respect the figure of the Pope. They sympathize with him, because he is a man who embodies contemporary values. His presence in Cuba could also signify an incentive for a better life or at least the cultivation of ethical values that were always here but were forgotten. Only time will tell if the Pope's visit will change people's lives.

PART 2

ECONOMIC AND ENVIRONMENTAL ISSUES

13

The Cuban Economy has Turned the Corner:
The Question now is Where is it Going?

Al Campbell

The 38 percent drop in the gross domestic product (GDP) during the early 1990s ended by late 1994. Following the impressive growth rate of 7.8 percent in 1996, few but the blindest opponents of the Cuban revolutionary process were still talking about economic collapse. Some of the more perspicacious opponents of the revolution—for example, Mesa-Lago (1994)—and a number of sympathizers of the revolution have begun to put forward the possibility that the present market reforms, and especially those that might follow, could result in the restoration of capitalism in Cuba. The central question now to be addressed is where are the Cuban economy and social structure going? This chapter addresses several issues relating to this question by: (1) reviewing the extent of the economic downturn and the beginning of a recovery; (2) looking at some of the economic experiments that began during the five years before the special period and had mixed results in the 1990s; and (3) comparing specific changes that occurred in the early 1990s to some changes after 1994.

1. Introduction

In 1989 Cuba conducted 64.8 percent of its foreign trade with a single country, the Union of Soviet Socialist Republics (USSR), and an additional 14.4 percent with East European countries.[1] Following delays and some import reductions in 1990, Cuba's trade with the East European countries dropped to almost zero in 1991, and its trade with the USSR began a sharp three-year decline. With roughly 35 percent of its GDP generated by foreign trade, such trade disruptions would be expected to have devastating effects.[2] Beginning in 1990, the Cuban GDP declined for four consecutive years, first slowly and then precipitously.

This chapter will present several quantitative indicators of both the decline in the Cuban economy after 1989 and the partial recovery that began in 1994. A number of important structural changes introduced in the Cuban economy in the 1990s will then be discussed. In the final section, I will consider several of the issues under discussion in Cuba relative to the course of the Cuban economy.

An explanation is in order about the extensive notes at the end of the chapter. The scattered nature of much of the information on the Cuban economy from 1990 to the present (often given publicly only in speeches during the early 1990s), and the lack of citation of sources in much of the writing in the United States about the Cuban economy, motivate extensive citation of sources in this chapter. Additionally, some of the assertions I make rest on detailed considerations concerning the Cuban economy. The assertions necessitate the details, but to put so many details in the chapter would confuse the general presentation. For this reason, a few lengthy discussions are included as endnotes. In addition, I have cited fairly accessible and reputable English language sources that in turn cite Cuban sources, which will assist the interested reader in validating the references.

2. The Decline and Partial Recovery of the Cuban Economy

Cuba suffered a major economic downturn in the early 1990s, but it was much less precipitous than is commonly presented by the U.S. media and government. Contrary to frequent assertions in the U.S., it was not comparable to the "collapse" or "free fall" that one gets in war situations such as in parts of the former Yugoslavia. Furthermore, it was less than both the recent downturns in Russia, and the U.S. depression at the beginning of the 1930s. The recovery began in late 1994, and by the end of 1997 between a quarter and a third of the economic decline had been regained.

On September 26, 1990, it was officially declared that the economic problems that had been developing in late 1989 and in early 1990, and the responses that were necessary to address them, constituted a "special period in peacetime" in Cuba. The period from 1990 to the present has been labeled "the special period" in Cuba.[3]

2. 1. The Decline of the Cuban Economy in the Early 1990s: GDP

From 1989, the Cuban GDP (constant 1981 prices) is given in Cuban pesos, and there are no carefully worked out purchasing power parity calculations for the value of a peso in U.S. dollars. However, the official rate of 1-to-1 seems as good as any other for rough considerations.[4] The Cuban GDP declined as indicated in Table 1.

Table 1: Decline in GDP (at constant 1981 prices)[5]

Year	GDP (billions of pesos)	Percentage decline from previous year
1989	19,585	n/a
1990	19,008	-2.9
1991	16,980	-10.7
1992	15,010	-11.6
1993	12,780	-14.9
Cumulative 3 year drop		33 Percent
Cumulative 4 year drop		Almost 35 Percent

This means a three-year drop of 33 percent (1990-1993) and a four-year drop of almost 35 percent (1989-1993).

In the early and mid-1990s, much of the U.S. media created an image of Cuba going through an economic collapse. While it was a serious crisis, the image of economic collapse was inaccurate. The extent of the drop in output can be compared to that of the U.S. Great Depression. In his seminal work on the topic, *National Income, 1929-1932*, Kuznets calculated the U.S. drop to be from $89 billion in 1929 to $49 billion in 1932, a 45 percent drop over three years. In addition, distribution in Cuba is much more equitable than it was in the U.S. in 1929, so the suffering of the poorest layers of society has been less in Cuba than in the U.S. Great Depression, notwithstanding that the Cuban crisis is severe and the population has suffered greatly.

It is interesting to compare the drop in the Cuban economy to the drop in the Russian economy, noting that the leadership in Russia, backed by financial assistance from the West, is attempting to convert the Russian economy to a standard capitalist economy. Under the neo-liberal conversion programs, the Russian economy had a four-year decline of 42 percent, 1991-1995. It continued to drop the following year, though at the diminished rate of 6 percent, bringing the five-year decline to 45.5 percent.[6]

2. 2. Capacity Utilization

The rate of industrial capacity utilization generally indicates economic booms or downturns. The data on Cuba for this period clearly reflects the latter. Using 1989 as the base year with an index of 100, Table 2, below, presents the decline in utilization of productive capacities for the non-sugar industry[7]

Table 2: Decline in Use of Productive Capacity for the Non-Sugar Industry

Year	Level of Capacity
1989	100 percent
1990	70 percent
1991	50 percent
1992	25 percent
1993	10-15 percent

2. 3. Overall Imports and Exports

The precipitating and primary (but not exclusive) cause for the reduction in output from 1989 to 1993 was external. Beginning in 1990 and 1991, imports were delayed or simply not delivered, causing serious disruption in domestic production. The abruptness of the diminution was particularly problematic.

The figures for exports and imports during the decline are illustrated in Figure 1, compared to 1988 figures. Thus there was a 75 percent reduction in imports over the four years 1989-1993.

2. 4. Oil

The delays and then reductions in petroleum imports stand out as the single most important import problem. In 1989 Cuba had imported about thirteen million tons of petroleum products, in line with its imports for the several preceding years, while Cuba's domestic oil production was under one million tons.[8] Imported oil was Cuba's main energy source for both industrial and agricultural production. In 1990 Cuba contracted for the same 13 million tons, but only ten million tons were delivered, a drastic 23 percent reduction in one year. In 1991 the reduced quantity of ten million tons was contracted for, but only 8.6 million tons were delivered, an

Figure 1. Changes in Exports and Imports over six years 1988-1993 (in billions of dollars)

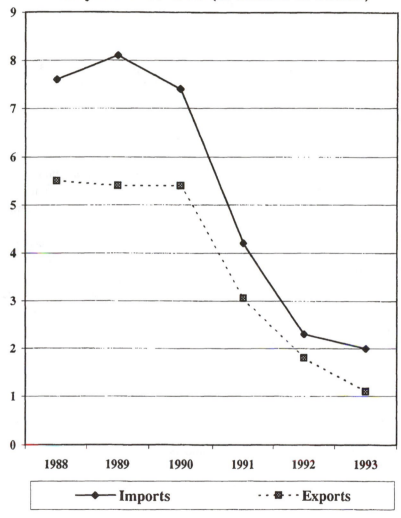

Figure 1 was calculated by the author based on Cuban sources and data from the Economic Intelligence Unit (EIU). Data for 1992 and 1993 have been updated by the editors according to the Cuba Country Profile 1998/1999, which had used data supplied by the Banco Nacional de Cuba (BNC).

additional 14 percent reduction. In 1992 oil product imports dropped another 24 percent to 6.5 million tons.[9] In three years, Cuba's main energy source had been reduced by 50 percent.

2. 5. Food

In 1986 Cubans consumed a daily average of 2,948 calories and 79.7 grams of protein per capita.[10] Figure 2 shows the slide, then precipitous fall in daily caloric intake.[11] To interpret the changes in the 1990s, it is helpful to compare Cuban food consumption to that of its neighbors, some higher income countries, and to its own internal changes.

In 1992 Alfredo Jam reported that by the end of 1991 average per capita caloric intake had dropped to 2,700 calories and a little more than sixty grams of protein. By 1993 daily caloric intake was down to 1,863 and protein to forty-six grams.[12] The figures for calories consumed in Cuba's neighboring countries and a few higher income countries shown in Figure 2, help put both the 1989 and 1993 numbers in some perspective.

When Cuba began its food rationing in 1962, it could only guarantee 2,000-2,100 calories per day.[13] At that time, although the national average may have been higher, there must have been a significant portion of the population that was getting far less than that, or there would have been little reason to introduce the guarantee program. In 1965 the daily averages had risen to 2,552 calories and 66.4 grams of protein, significant improvements in three years.[14] The late 1991 figures reveal a few more calories but less protein intake than in 1965.

Given Cuba's relatively equitable distribution of goods including food, compared to most other countries, the country was able to prevent the drastic drop in available food from resulting in starvation or even clinical hunger. It must be noted, though, that malnutrition certainly increased in the 1990s.[15] This is contrary to the image portrayed by much of the U.S. media. It is also contrary to the effects of economic downturns in most poor or middle income (and some rich) countries, and an important point to consider in understanding the Cuban economy, how it works, what its goals are, and what Cubans think about their economic system.

2. 6. The Value of the Peso

As the crisis unfolded output dropped sharply, as we saw above. In an economy where the state runs most production, this meant that state revenue from

Figure 2. Food consumption in daily caloric intake per capita - Cuba over time (1962-1993) and intake compared to others in Western Hemisphere in 1993

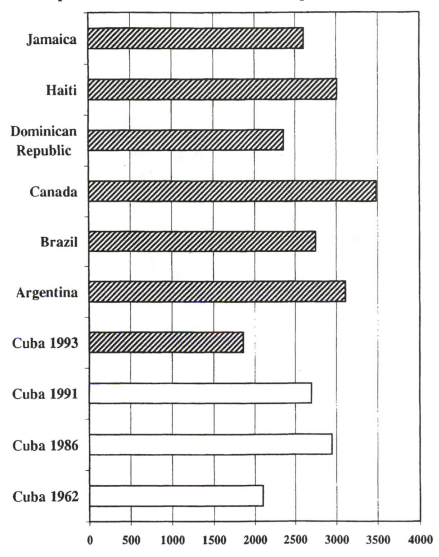

production plummeted. To protect the living standards of the population, the state maintained salary payments (sometimes to people who had not worked for years). To replace the drop in revenue from sales, the state printed more pesos. Those increases are shown in Table 3.

Table 3: Pesos in Circulation (end of year in billions)

Year	Billions of Pesos in Circulation
1990	5.9
1991	7.0
1992	8.4
1993	11.4
May 1994 (high point)	11.9

Prices on officially distributed goods were maintained at their previous low levels even as the quantity of such goods dropped sharply. People were left with large quantities of pesos after they had bought everything they could find through official channels. Too many pesos were chasing too few goods, which led to the illegal black market. The black market exchange rate of the dollar for pesos rose sharply from 6 or 7 per dollar in 1989 to 12-13 per dollar in 1990, to a peak of around 130 or 135 per dollar in spring 1994.[16] This depreciation of the peso was not just a reflection of a lack of international confidence in a given government or international lending practices, as changes in exchange rates often are. Rather, this depreciation was a reflection (in part) of the problems of the Cuban economy.

3. The Partial Recovery of the Cuban Economy, 1994-1997

3. 1. Gross Domestic Product

The Cuban economy bottomed-out in 1993, and it began recovering in late 1994. The official growth figures are shown in Table 4 (again, in constant 1981 prices).

Table 4: Growth in GDP, 1997[17]

Year	GDP, Billions of Pesos	Percentage Growth
1994	12,870	0.7
1995	13,900	2.5
1996	14,220	7.8
1997	14,575	2.5

Using figures given earlier (Table 1) for GDP decline, the 1990s turn-around brings the 1997 GDP to 74.4 percent of the 1989 level.

3. 2. Capacity Utilization

Non-sugar capacity utilization returned to 20-25 percent in 1994 and 35 percent in 1995.[18]

3. 3. Overall Imports and Exports

From the low in 1993, given in Figure 1, imports and exports expanded as shown in Table 5. Imports were thus back up to 43 percent of their 1989 level by 1997.[19]

Table 5: Changes in Imports and Exports (billions of dollars)[20]

Year	Imports	Exports
1992	2.32	1.78
1993	1.98	1.14
1994	2.02	1.38
1995	2.88	1.51
1996	3.48	1.87
1997	4.09	1.82
1998	4.23	1.44

3. 4. Oil

Oil imports in 1995 were up to six million tons, and 1997 imports were seven million tons. With domestic production, 1996 fuel consumption was back to 8.2 million tons.[21] Oil as a percentage of total imports rose steadily from 27 percent in 1990 to 39 percent in 1994, and dropped to 29 percent in 1996.[22]

3. 5. Food

While there is widespread agreement by commentators on Cuba that the food situation has improved dramatically from the low point of the downturn in 1993, I have seen no figures on caloric or protein levels since 1993.[23] Anecdotal data about some important basic staples indicate that Cuba still needs to advance the pace of economic recovery. In 1987 Cuban farms had produced 1,000 million liters of milk; three years into the recovery in 1996 they produced only about 400 million liters. Egg production in 1995 —after two years of recovery—was 45 percent of its 1991 level, and poultry meat was 46 percent.[24] Nevertheless, it is widely held by Cubans that their food situation has markedly improved from its worst situation in 1993.

3. 6. The Value of the Peso

From its low of 130 or 135 to one US dollar in May 1994, the peso recovered to around 35:1 in June 1995; and settled, with mild fluctuations, at about 20:1 during 1996 to mid-1998. Several government actions gave rise to this recovery.

4. Structural Changes in the Cuban Economy in the 1990s

The least one can say about the structural changes in the Cuban economy in the 1990s is that there is not a single economic organization, institution, or relation in Cuba that has not been significantly changed. As of this writing, the process seems far from over.

There are at least three fundamental issues to consider in the economic changes now occurring in Cuba: (1) the nature and role of the government as an economic actor; (2) the nature and role of enterprises as economic actors (and there will be somewhat different roles for the different types of enterprises that are developing); and (3) the nature and role of markets and market-like mechanisms in determining the functioning of the economy.[25]

Concrete changes cannot be placed exclusively into one category but rather have an impact on all three. Consider, for example, the reduction of subsidies to enterprises. It reduces the government's deficit and strengthens the peso, and it also likely led to salary cuts for some workers. The working capital previously used for subsidies must now go to some other institution, in Cuba's case, to the new banking system. However, banks will push enterprises to change their behavior. Since loans will be made on a profit/loss basis, the borrowing process will reinforce government efforts to switch the central state enterprise goal from meeting a material plan to making a profit.[26] Hence, this change reinforces the role of market-like mechanisms in enterprise decisions on what to produce, what to invest, and so on.

It is helpful to focus on ten concrete changes in the Cuban economy over the course of the 1990s. They will be introduced more or less according to when they first arose, thus highlighting the overall process of change in which each change was affected by the previous ones. The three issues of the economic role and nature of the government, the enterprises, and markets will be given careful consideration.

4. 1. Foreign Tourism

Cuba decided to open up to foreign tourism well before the beginning of the special period, but it was only then that tourism took off.[27] The dramatic increase in international tourists (in thousands) and gross revenue (in millions of dollars) is illustrated in Figure 3. Compare the $1.3 billion earned in 1996 to the total earnings from all merchandise exports that same year, $1.8 billion.

Tourism currently plays an important role in the Cuban economy, unlike the period before 1990. This is particularly the case in generating hard currency that is needed for food imports, medicine, machinery, and much more. However, it is unlikely that more than 40 percent of gross revenues remain on the island.[28] Salaries for joint venture workers (and those working in state hotels that charge in dollars) are paid to the state in dollars, and the state pays the equivalent value in pesos to the workers.[29] The workers do get a part of the dollar flow directly through bonuses and tips.

The economic success of the tourist sector, the life-style of the tourists from capitalist countries, and the weakness of the peso, especially in the early 1990s, sent a message to some Cubans that markets and capitalism were the only salvation for the troubled Cuban economy. That message is not as strong now following the beginning of the economic recovery, but the tourist sector is still seen by some Cubans as a model that should be reproduced throughout the economy. On the other hand, as

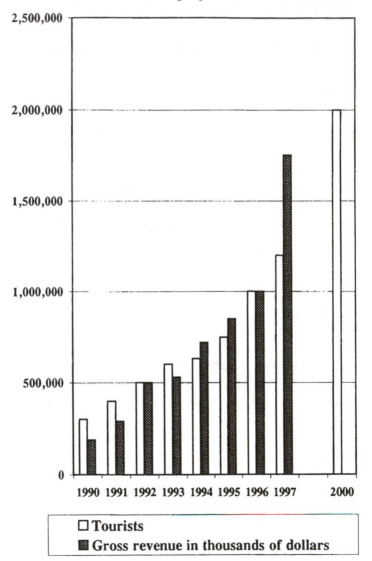

Figure 3. Trends in growth of revenue from tourism
over 8 years (shaded bars) relative to number of
tourists (white bars) & projected tourists in 2000

witnessed by many discussions in meetings of trade unions, the women's organization and other social meetings, Cubans see tourism as socially corrupting and debasing, and aside from its generation of much needed hard currency, something that should be rejected as central to the long-term restructuring of the Cuban economy.

4. 2. Joint Ventures

While tourism dominated the earliest joint ventures at the beginning of the 1990s, joint ventures have since then moved into almost all sectors of the economy. Figures on the number of joint ventures have been provided by the government over the years: (cumulative) 1989, 1; 1990, 2; 1991, 14; 1992, 47; 1993, 107; 1994, 181; 1995, 212; 1996, 260.[30] In early 1996, the government put forward the figure of $2.1 billion as the amount of capital these joint ventures represented; but that appears to be the sum of agreed future investment, while actual disbursed investment at the time was not likely to exceed $750 million.[31]

Cuban officials have constantly stressed that foreign investment could help in the economic recovery, but that it is far from central. The capital investment figures cited above support that claim. Furthermore, only 3 percent of the national income in those years came from associations with foreign capital; and roughly half the capital involved in them was Cuban.[32] A slightly larger measure of the impact of foreign investment is its role in operating 8.5 percent of the non-sugar industrial capacity. Thus it is an ancillary but quite important factor.[33] At the end of 1995 there were only 105,953 workers in the joint ventures, out of an official total civilian workforce of 3.8 million.[34] As tourism increases, that number can be expected to grow.

Some of the structural changes underway in the Cuban economy were related to the needs of the joint venture sector. In July 1992 the National Assembly acted on the proposals from the Fourth Congress of the Cuban Communist Party (October 1991) and amended the Cuban constitution. Not only were changes made specifically to protect foreign investment, but they were also designed to end the state's monopoly in foreign trade, among other changes in the state's economic role in property, and private enterprise regulations.[35] The very important Foreign Investment Act, Law 77, passed in September 5, 1995, came directly from the needs and concerns of potential joint venture investors and extended the ability of foreign capital to operate in Cuba. For example, the provision for "companies with totally foreign capital" and the provision for free trade zones.[36] How much influence these capitalist companies and their operational rules and procedures will have on the state enterprises and their management is an important issue for the type of economy that Cuba will develop.

4. 3. Legalizing the Possession and Use of Dollars

Following discussions since late June 1993, Fidel Castro announced that possession of dollars and their free circulation would become legal. This decision was enacted in August 1993 with Decree Law 140.[37] One effect was to increase the attraction of professionals, including doctors and professors, to seek work as drivers for embassies or in various jobs for the tourist sector where they could obtain dollars. This mis-allocation of human resources and waste of training will be detrimental to the Cuban economy in the long-term. A second effect of "dollarization" was to increase the political and social weight of those Cubans who receive dollars from abroad.[38] An important third effect—the reason the government instituted this policy—was to increase access to hard currency in order to pay for imports of food and intermediate capital inputs.[39]

4. 4. Legalizing Self-employment

On September 8, 1993, a law was passed listing over one hundred occupations as open to self-employment. Subsequently, many additional occupations were declared acceptable. This was to be a private market. In particular, prices for these services would not be set by the state but in accordance with market forces.

At the end of 1995 the number appears not to have changed dramatically over the previous two years; there were 200,727 registered self-employed workers, 5.3 percent of the total civilian workforce of 3,788,587.[40] However, Cuban economists have estimated that there are three to four times as many unregistered back-up producers or ancillary staff who are being paid by the registered self-employed workers. If this is the case, this would significantly alter the estimates of the weight of private employment and production in the Cuban economy.[41]

4. 5. Breaking Up the State Farms into UBPCs

On September 10, 1993, a law was passed to break up the state farms and turn the land over to new organizations called UBPCs (*Unidades Basicas de Producción Cooperativa*). Significantly, these units would own the crops they produced. What this meant became clear only when the state organized an alternative means for marketing agricultural products to the population (see section 4. 7.). After selling a required quantity to the state, the UBPCs can sell whatever else they produce in markets where prices are determined solely by supply and demand.[42] By summer 1996, the UBPCs cultivated 42 percent of Cuban farmland. For comparison, state farms cultivated 33 percent, "old" cooperatives 10 percent, and private farmers 15 percent. They employed about 300,000, or 8 percent of the labor force, at the end of 1995.[43]

The motivation for converting state farms to UBPCs was to raise agricultural productivity and agricultural output. By setting up units aimed at making profits, with the workers entitled to share the profits, agricultural production measured in output per worker would increase, it was hoped. Of course, higher profits could also be achieved by price increases, but the state controlled the prices of all the output to which it was entitled by law, including all the output from the sugar cane cooperatives. Prices were allowed to rise in the free markets, but only on the surplus above that produced to meet state contracts. The Cuban government hoped that with prices only partially fixed, workers would increase food output—the basis for a national improvement in the standard of living—in order to reap the profits. As of 1997, productivity gains have been much less than anticipated. About 70 percent of the UBPCs are running at a loss, and the government is giving high priority to improve this aspect of the economy.[44]

4. 6. Reducing the Budget Deficit and Pesos in Circulation, and Restoring Value to the Peso

Three steps were central to the recovery of the peso. The first two were aimed at reducing the state budget deficit: raising prices and taxes and reducing subsidies to enterprises. Prior to 1989 the budget deficit had been financed largely by borrowing; after 1989 it was financed largely by printing more pesos. The third component involved increasing the goods that could be bought with pesos. Reducing the budget deficit and subsidies to enterprises and raising prices and taxes represent a huge shift in the roles of the state and enterprises in the production process.

In December 1993, Finance Minister José Luis Rodríguez proposed to the National Assembly a series of measures to address the developing financial and budget crises, including price increases, taxes, and cuts in enterprise subsidies and other government spending. While it was generally accepted that something drastic had to be done and no viable alternatives were available, his suggestions, nevertheless, generated an unusual level of discussion and expressions of concern in the

National Assembly over the problems that could ensue.[45] The proposals were put on hold until Cuba could conduct a public discussion on these and other current economic issues, such as how to raise enterprise efficiency and how to deal with economic theft. From January to March 1994, three million workers, about 80 percent of the workforce, participated in "Workers' parliaments" in 80,000 workplaces, offering suggestions on how to address the various problems.

Summaries of these proposals were central to the proceedings of the May 1-2, 1994 special session of the National Assembly. Several decisions followed the suggestions from the workers' parliaments.[46] Decree 149 on May 4, 1994 cracked down on the much resented theft of state property as a source for private income. Next, the Executive Committee of the Council of Ministers instituted price increases on a broad group of goods and services. On July 7, 1994, the Executive Committee eliminated subsidies and instituted or raised prices for a number of goods and services formally provided at no cost by the state, including a special provision to help low-income families adversely affected by the price increases.[47] In August 1994 a new tax law was instituted. Sales taxes continued to be the most important source of tax revenue, and they rose from 3.3 billion pesos in 1993 to 5.8 billion in 1995.[48] These were aimed primarily at "luxuries," such as tobacco and alcohol. The tobacco tax alone brought in 1.6 billion pesos in 1994.[49]

The drive to reduce enterprise subsidies began seriously in 1994. In 1993 enterprise subsidies had reached 6.17 billion pesos, over 43 percent of the total budget expenditures of 14.57 billion pesos. In 1994 that was sharply reduced to 3.97 billion, 30 percent of the total of 13.30 billion pesos. Enterprise subsidies were further reduced to 3.19 billion pesos in 1995, 25 percent of the total of 12.68.[50]

The soaring subsidies, caused above all by the continuation of payrolls even as production dropped precipitously, had led to a mounting budget deficit. The 1994 measures were designed to reduce the deficit dramatically. The degree of the financial crisis that was developing, the unsustainable nature of budget policies in the early 1990s, and the rapid turn-around can be seen from the change in budget deficits as a percentage of GDP. Figure 4 shows (in billions of pesos) both the deficit trends and the deficit as a percentage of GDP.

Clearly, the fiscal reforms sharply reduced the number of pesos in circulation: from the high of 11.9 billion pesos in May 1994 when the peso reached its weakest level, to 9.7 billion pesos by the year's end, to 9.3 billion pesos at the end of 1995.[51] Together with the sharp increase in goods available for pesos (see the next two sections), this was the key to the restoration of the value of the peso.

Figure 4. 1991-1996 budget deficits in millions of pesos (broken line) and as percentage of Gross Domestic Product (solid line)

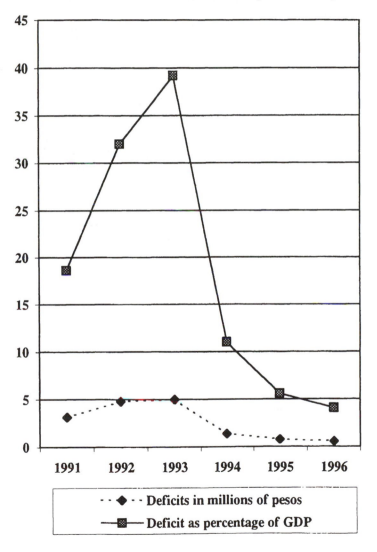

4. 7. Agricultural Products Markets

On October 1, 1994, approximately 120 Agricultural Products Markets were opened.[52] Private, cooperative, or state producers can sell in these markets anything beyond the quantity they are required to sell to the state. Prices in the markets are determined strictly by supply and demand, and they have been well above the prices of rationed goods but well below the black market prices that existed prior to the opening of these markets. Food prices have dropped continuously since 1995, reflecting the increased supply of food passing through these markets.[53] These product markets were now generally viewed in Cuba as one important contributor to the increased food supply that has been reaching the population since the markets were opened.[54] Despite widespread complaints that the market prices are too high, the markets are nevertheless broadly supported by the Cuban people.

The Cuban leadership hopes that these markets will go beyond improving food distribution to actually improving agricultural productivity. Beyond that, the markets are key to the change in the concept of agricultural enterprise represented by the UBPCs.

4. 8. Other Market Extensions, Fall 1994

While the bulk of the commentary on the growth of domestic markets focused on the agricultural products markets for this period, several other changes from 1994—especially Decree Law 192, October 21—may in the long run prove equally or more important. Here I will note just two. First, the previous strategy of keeping foreign investment constrained to only certain sectors of the economy was abandoned. Carlos Lage announced that henceforth "no productive sector will be excluded from foreign capital investments."[55]   Second, the 1993 law on self-employment was extended in three important ways: (a) more markets, shops and bazaars were opened; (b) the 1993 law, which was directed largely at people who provided services or artisans/craftsmen—for example, makers of sandals, cutlery, pots and pans—was expanded in 1994 to a significant focus on manufacturers; and perhaps most important, (c) in addition to individual manufacturers, the law also allowed factories or work sites run by local authorities, the Ministry of the Interior, and state enterprises to produce for the supply-and-demand-priced markets,[56] if they receive permission.[57]

4. 9. Banking Reforms

Prior to the recent reforms, the Banco Nacional de Cuba performed almost all of Cuba's banking functions, including those of a central bank.[58] There were two others, *the Banco Popular de Ahorro* for savings by the population and the *Banco Financiero Internacional* (BFI) set up in 1984 for banking by foreign companies or joint ventures.[59]

Two main waves of reforms have followed directly from the new requirements of the Cuban economy. The first was spurred by the need for hard currency. With the growth of both hard currency trade and interest in joint venture investment in the early 1990s, Cuban capital available for financing these types of activity through the BFI became entirely inadequate. In March 1994, a license was granted to The Netherlands Caribbean Bank to open a representative office in Cuba, the first foreign involvement in banking in Cuba since the banking nationalizations in 1960-1961. By late 1996, there were twelve foreign banks operating in Cuba.[60] With the legalization of financial transactions in dollars in the summer of 1993, there arose a need for exchange centers. The CADECA (the state bureau of exchange) set up pilot *Casas de Cambio* in Havana and Veradero in mid-1995. Since then, the public booths for money exchange have been extended throughout the country.[61]

A second wave of reforms stemmed from the increased need for credit by Cuban enterprises. An holding company, *Grupo Nueva Banca*, or GNB, now oversees the following Cuban banks: *Banco Internacional de Comercio SA* (BICSA), established in 1994, a merchant bank that arranges foreign financing and provides trade financing for Cuban enterprises; *Financeria Nacional SA* (FINSA) that provides short term finance for Cuban enterprises; Banco de Inversiones, which provides medium and long term development finance for Cuban enterprises; and the Banco Metropolitano, established in June 1996, that provides banking services including foreign currency, investment, and deposit accounts for foreign diplomats and others. In addition, the *Banco Agro-Industrial y Comercial* has been set up outside the GNB, taking over 200 branches from the BNC to offer commercial banking services to farmers and the UPBCs.[62] The banking reforms are being driven by and are facilitating the further development of both market-like relations and markets in Cuba, and they are one of the most important structural changes.

4. 10. Free Trade Zones

Chapter XV of Law 77 established the right of the Executive Committee of the Council of Ministers to establish duty-free zones and industrial parks, and Article 53 called for special legislation to establish their norms of operation. Decree Law 165, Free Zones and Industrial Parks, was issued in June 3, 1996.[63] How important a role these will play in the restructured Cuban economy has not been established. They have the potential to become a major form for foreign investment, or they could end up being merely an aside to that process. In May 1997, two of the four originally planned zones officially opened: Berroa and Wajay.[64] Two more at Mariel and Cienfuegos were scheduled to open later.

The laws for these commercial and industrial zones are particularly interesting. The Cuban authorities specifically included the possibility that enterprises operating in the free trade zones can, by request, establish relations with enterprises operating in the domestic economy. This is interesting because free trade zones throughout the world have generated less linkages than were hoped for by their proponents, and hence have done less to help stimulate the domestic economies. Cuba has taken note of that and is considering ways to avoid a similar problem. The zones represent a further step away from the early 1990s Cuban strategy of trying to keep foreign capital somewhat isolated from the domestic economy. Another major point of interest is that, contrary to early rumors, the Cuban government did not, up until the time of this writing, allow foreign enterprises in these zones to hire Cuban labor directly, a reform that foreign capital hoped would be a first step in establishing a "normal" labor market throughout Cuba.[65]

5. Where is the Cuban Economy Headed?

There are two central questions being discussed both in and outside Cuba on the future of the Cuban economy: will capitalism be restored, and if not, what will the new non-capitalist economy look like? If the answer to the first question is yes, the future is more or less clearly determined. While there are certainly some differences between Chilean and Costa Rican and Guatemalan capitalism, Cuba's future, then, would be some sort of third world capitalism. The productive base of the Cuban economy is not high enough to generate the welfare capitalism that is prevalent in Northern Europe. Furthermore, the extensive health, education, and welfare systems in Cuba would have to be dismantled. If the answer to the first question is no, then some sort of socialism would be maintained and developed, and the question is then what that socialism would look like. It certainly would not look like the Cuban system before 1989.

5. 1. The Case That Cuba Will Return to Capitalism

Simply put, the case that Cuba will return to capitalism is influenced by (1) the fact that the market reforms which have been introduced have a logic of their own, and that the reforms enacted required additional market reforms to guarantee their efficiency. This process is expected to continue until capitalism has been established; (2) what is going on in Cuba is a repetition of what occurred in Eastern Europe, only at a slightly slower pace; (3) the political pronouncements that socialism will be achieved either reflect a lack of understanding by the Cuban authorities of the nature of the process they have unleashed, or are knowing deceptions of the Cuban people to keep them pacified and in support of the transformation in the face of the economic and social difficulties that such a transformation inevitably brings.

Mesa-Lago, a well known U.S. academic Cuba specialist and long-time proponent of the restoration of capitalism in Cuba, clearly presented the first two of these positions in his hopeful monograph, *Are Economic Reforms Propelling Cuba to the Market?*, following the introduction of the wave of reforms discussed above in 1993:

> But the dynamics of the reform call for further change. The government legalizes some of the economic activities that are taking place, although it tightly regulates them, and such a step is seen as a green light to expand those activities. Restrictions are ignored, and there is a move to new illegal operations. This, in turn, puts pressure on the government to grant another concession, which is followed by a further push toward the market. In his speeches at the beginning of the 1990s, Castro warned against the danger of a chain reaction or the snowballing effect of the economic reforms in the USSR and Eastern Europe that ... led to a market economy, but he felt confident that such a process would not take place in Cuba. Yet recent events suggest that history is repeating itself in the Caribbean.[66]

The key changes that advocates of a restoration of capitalism see as positive are the switch to profits as an enterprise goal and the increased enterprise autonomy. They view the latter as constituting or approximating privatization, and by its nature in time should lead to actual privatization. The Caribbean Trade Advisory Group to the British Overseas Trade Board, following an early 1990s mission to Havana by British businessmen, envisioned the emergence of a "broadly socialist" model. Its retention of social welfare benefits would be characterized by firms increasingly owned by private capital and by inter-firm competition for profits:

> It is a structure that ... encourages competition between autono-
> mous and older state enterprises, profit (referred to in Cuba as
> benefits), and the retention of hard currency earnings by each
> enterprise through an independent banking system. It ... might
> be described as creeping privatization, except in respect to land
> ownership, and ... in many respects is more advanced and
> flexible than the process taking place in Russia and Poland.

According to these advocates, the two biggest barriers to date to the restoration of capitalism are the refusal to free prices and the refusal to create a normal labor market:

> The central control of prices continues to restrict the scope for
> the allocation of goods, services and capital through the market
> mechanism.[67] Enterprise reform has progressed steadily but
> remains hampered by price and labor controls.[68]

On the latter point, they are clear that if Cuba is to have a competitive third world capitalism, it would have to eliminate the system of extensive benefits that Cuban labor has enjoyed. In November 1993 a delegation from the International Monetary Fund (IMF) visited Cuba. In addition to urging Cuba to be less hesitant "over the basic issue of allowing more private property and individual decision-making in the economy," the delegation stressed the importance of "a rethinking of Cuba's extensive social transfers." The IMF delegation argued that the market forces "will prove irreversible and much stronger than the current perception of the Cuban authorities."[69] When the former Spanish Economy Minister Carlos Solchega visited Cuba in 1995, after stating that things were much improved in the way enterprises did business, he stressed the need to form more private companies (foreign, mixed, and national capital), and their need to hire labor directly. He also called for further changes in unemployment benefits.[70]

Throughout the economic reform process of the 1990s, Cuban officials have indicated that they intended to maintain socialism, and they have stressed that message since the spring of 1996. Advocates of a return to capitalism such as the *Economist Intelligence Unit* dismiss such statements as predominantly cynical posturing, which in any case is not something that will impede the conversion to markets that the government is conducting:

> ... hardline speeches will deflect attention from a shifting ideology and a deepening of economic reform and social transformation. There are indications that the PCC congress [the fifth party congress of the Partido Comunista de Cuba in October 1997- A.C.] will include efforts by party ideologues to link the market reforms so far introduced to the idealistic socialism identified with the national hero, Ernesto "Che" Guevara.[71] ... [the congress] could yet herald a new phase in the economic reform process behind a cloud of rhetoric.[72]

These groups hold that just as surely as capitalism is being restored in Eastern Europe, it will also be restored in Cuba and that only the pace of the restoration is undetermined. "However, the Cuban transition to a market economy will be more gradual than the transition of other formally planned economies.[73] When Cuba turns capitalist, the cold war will be over."[74]

5. 2. The Case That Cuba Will Not Return To Capitalism

Given that the reforms in the 1990s generated various pressures for a restoration of capitalism, what would prevent such a restoration? There are two groups in Cuba that could be important in preventing the restoration of capitalism: directly, the political leadership of Cuba;[75] and indirectly, through influencing the ongoing public debate,[76] the population as a whole.

Over the years, Fidel Castro's speeches have been harshly critical of capitalism. He and the rest of the leadership have been very explicit that they have introduced markets and market-like mechanisms against their will and that they have caused problems for the goal of socialism;[77] yet they believe they can prevent a restoration of capitalism.

> Capitalism and social development always have been, always
> are, and always will be irreconcilable. Capitalism and plunder,
> plunder within and outside the country, are inseparable. Capital-
> ism and unemployment are inseparable.[78] There will be no
> transition towards capitalism.[79] We had to establish joint
> ventures in a relatively short time period ... accept foreign
> investment, we had to do what we did in respect to the decrimi-
> nalization of convertible currency.... We are aware of the
> inequalities that it created, the privileges it created, but we had
> to do it and we did it.[80]

In the main report at the Fifth Congress of the PCC in October 1997, Fidel Castro made clear that, contrary to the hopes of numerous proponents of a restoration of capitalism, he had not abandoned his vision of a more humane world in a conversion to "pragmatism":

> Capitalism as a system belongs to prehistory, even though we
> know that it rules the world ... but it has nothing to offer people,
> a wolf wishing to devour another ... a merciless selfishness that
> has nothing to do with what we wish for human beings.[81]

Near the depths of hardships of the economic downturn, the Cuban government allowed fourteen Gallup pollsters into Cuba to ask a series of questions on attitudes toward the socialist revolution.[82] To the point here, 58 percent of the respondents said they thought the revolution on balance had more achievements than failures, while 31 percent of the respondents thought that the revolution had been more of a failure than a success. In a different question, 69 percent identified themselves as communists, socialists, or revolutionaries.[83] This data suggest that roughly two-thirds of the Cuban population opposes (presumably in differing degrees) a return to capitalism, while perhaps one-fourth of the population presumably could be open to such a transformation.

While space limitations prevent any extensive discussion of the issue of democracy in this chapter, it cannot be left out entirely. One of the strongest arguments that capitalism will not become dominant in Cuba is that the majority of the Cuban population is opposed to it. Opposition, if it continues, will serve to block the reintroduction of capitalism by any political leadership that chooses to reintroduce it.[84] However, the population can do so only if it has the ability to effect its political will. Kotz and Weir (1997) argued that this is critical to what happened in Russia: the population as a whole had been so politically marginalized for sixty years that when the leadership took a sharp turn in a different direction the population did not support the restoration of capitalism. The population was unable to effect its will. It is my view that the Cuban population has had much more influence on its leadership over the whole course of government by the revolutionary state; enough so that the Cuban people could prevent the leadership (or a part of the leadership), if there should be such a development, from conducting a return to capitalism.

Popular opinion seems to be expressing itself in numerous recent documents of the CTC, the Cuban labor union federation, that represents the large majority of the 3.8 million people officially economically active in Cuba. A year-long series of meetings and discussions took place in essentially all workplaces, leading up to the April 1996 quinquennial congress of the CTC. The nature of those discussions, and the content of the 168 theses adopted, reflects the continued commitment by Cuban workers to building socialism. Their statements do not seem "imposed on them by the CTC bureaucracy," but something consistent with the two-thirds national opposition to a return to capitalism as expressed in the Gallop poll.[85] Theses 15 to 37 (section II) of the CTC document was entitled "Our Strategy Does Not Lead to Capitalism." The closing political resolution also contained a clear statement to this effect.

> We will defend at any price our national independence, socialist ideas and political power of the Revolution, which is the power of the workers ... our steadfast national unity has been and continues to be based on three pillars: The predominance of socialist forms of production and distribution,....

5. 3. Steps Taken by the Government to Prevent Growing Market Forces from Leading to a Return to Capitalism

Nowhere has the Cuban government put out a policy statement indicating what it plans to do to maintain socialism, what steps it thinks are key to preventing the introduced markets and market-like-mechanisms from leading to a restoration of capitalism. From what Cuban leaders have done, and from the complaints by the proponents of a full restoration of capitalism, it appears their broad approach is as follows: markets and market-like mechanisms will be introduced, but they will be controlled, to the extent possible, so that the market cannot dominate the entire economy, and so that the most undesirable effects of markets will be mitigated, especially for populations in third world countries.

Above, I mentioned the two major controls that investors are interested in seeing relaxed, but think will not be relaxed in the short run: the control on prices, and the control on the direct hiring of labor. A third, very important control for shaping the economy has been regulating the process of investment. There are two aspects to this. Up until the present, essentially all proposed projects involving foreign capital have had a final review at the highest political level of the state, the Council of Ministers. In addition, even though management autonomy has been greatly expanded in state enterprises, the investment process has not yet been turned over to the enterprises, thus constraining the individual enterprises from a drive to make profits. At this point, the state part of the economy still dominates, and it clearly is not capitalist.

Specific regulatory measures or procedures indicate terms of the "conscious" or "planned" control of markets and the economy; they should not be viewed as a check list. Proponents of a restoration of capitalism feel that state enterprises are in the process of gaining control over investment.[86] The argument cited above that prices would have to be de-controlled as the Cuban economy is increasingly integrated into the world economy, and as enterprises are put on a profit or loss basis, is compelling: if they are not, the profit or loss accounting makes no sense. As the volume of foreign investment increases and investors shift from the earlier large enterprises to small and medium foreign enterprises, the process of project evaluation will have to be, and already is in the process of decentralization. The labor markets are likely to be the last to be de-regulated, and Cubans will probably maintain a degree of protection and social benefits unusual for a third world country trying to attract foreign investments. Nevertheless, it is my view that the work force will be radically transformed eventually to resemble a typical capitalist labor market.

At that point, would capitalism be restored? Capitalism not only has markets, but the markets run the economy. If one could have markets and control them, it would not be capitalism. This is precisely the central question to be addressed: can one have extensive markets and market-like-mechanisms throughout the economy and control them, or do markets have a powerful transformational nature that, once unleashed, will inevitably do what they did in Eastern Europe and the Soviet Union?[87] Since the writings of Oscar Lange in the 1930s, there has been a debate about the possibility of "market socialism." Most modern market socialist models give a very strong role to markets in the name of "efficiency," and then impose a few constraints that are intended to minimize the great inequality that markets tend to generate.[88] But the same arguments for "efficiency" which are utilized loosely to justify the extensive use of markets in the first place, argue against the non-market or regulatory measures that are imposed on the model. If people are brought up to pursue efficiency as defined by markets and maximum profits, they would soon come to see the social add-ons—the minimum wage, and so on—as socially harmful, as they have for state-run enterprises in Western and Eastern Europe. The Cubans are very aware that the central issue is: will the markets be consciously controlled by some criteria other than profit maximization, or will the markets come to dominate the whole economic outlook of the people involved and then lead to a removal of all constraints on unfettered markets? The Cubans have developed a terminology to distinguish the two concepts: they call the latter "market socialism" and reject it, and they call the former "socialism with markets," meaning markets they control; and that is their goal.

The key to their control, even after all the above changes have occurred, will be state property in the "heights of the economy." Osvaldo Martinez, then head of the National Assembly commission on the economy and head of the prestigious think tank CIEM (Center for Study of the World Economy), stated: "We are trying to reform state enterprises on the basis of public property."[89] Concern that a few big enterprises could control the performance of the economy has been a fear in capitalist countries since the late 1800s, when it gave rise in the United States to the first anti-trust legislation. With the state owning dominant enterprises in all the basic branches of the economy, the case that it could control the economy through its control of them seems plausible. It has never been tried, so one should not consider it a "known economic fact," but many economists have considered that it could be so for over one hundred years. The state will have at its disposal the usual state tools in a modern capitalist economy, which would add greatly to the power already available through the ownership of the "economic heights": taxes, tariffs, control of the money supply and other influences on the interest rate, and legislative authority for establishing business law.

6. Conclusions

A collapse in its foreign trade precipitated a sharp decline in Cuba's GDP and its population's standard of living in the early 1990s, when the disappearance or decline of the major economies it had traded with necessitated radical reform of its own economy. Cuba rejected the orthodox neo-liberal reforms that have been adopted by Eastern European countries and Russia, and opted instead for a domestically conceived "unorthodox reform" program, which has been successful in stopping the decline and initiating a partial recovery. There are two schools of thought on the essence of this "unorthodox reform." Proponents of a restoration of capitalism in Cuba see it as a delayed and inefficient way of traveling the same path as Russia and Eastern Europe, a path that leads to a capitalist economy. The Cuban government puts the reforms forward as an attempt to build a new type of socialist economy, dramatically different from both the old Soviet economy and the somewhat different old Cuban economy. Central to their project is the attempt to control the markets and market-like mechanisms that they have introduced in the Cuban economy.

ENDNOTES

1. In the 1980s Cuba published extensive annual statistics in the *Anuario Estadísdico de Cuba*. Publication ceased in 1990 with the 1989 issue (itself abbreviated in size and much reduced in the number printed) as part of the sharp reduction that occurred for all printing in Cuba with the onset of the economic crisis. The given percentages are the author's calculations from p. 249 of the 1989 edition.
2. The GDP for 1989 was $19.585 billion; exports were $5.4 billion, 27.6 percent of GDP; imports were $8.1 billion, 41.3 percent of GDP. Author's calculations. Sources for all three quantities given below.
3. There is an important point about the goals of the Cuban economy, how these goals affected its operation, and how both the goals and the operation differed from third world capitalism. These differences became apparent during the initial response to the developing shortages. When grain shipments from the Soviet Union for November 1990 were delayed, the government spread the shortages by reducing everyone's daily bread ration to 3 ounces -- except in Havana, where the prices of bread and eggs that required grain as an input, were allowed to rise. A central goal of the Cuban economy since 1959 has been to assure everyone enough to live on, even when shortages arise. The main point of the September 1990 decree concerned the same issue. Rationing was re-extended to many goods that had come off rationing over the preceding 20 years. See Deere (1991) for more on rationing at the beginning of the "special period" and a discussion on the meaning of rationing throughout the history of the revolutionary economy. Cuba's commitment to protecting the most economically vulnerable Cubans even in hard times is important to understanding why it is presently carrying out what free market advocates refer to as "unorthodox reform."
4. For the period discussed here, the official exchange rate was one Cuban peso to one US dollar. By the early 1990s, all of Cuba's foreign trade was evaluated in dollars, and then GDP calculations used the 1 to 1 conversion. For that one-third of the Cuban economy the 1 to 1 conversion to consider trade value in dollars is certainly appropriate. For the domestic production of basics such as food or construction, there is no carefully worked out conversion factor. As I explain below, the black market prices often loosely used in the U.S. media are certainly not appropriate: one can buy vastly more rationed goods for 20 pesos in Cuba than one can buy goods in the U.S. for a dollar. In December 1994, Cuba introduced a second currency, the convertible peso. This is used interchangeably in Cuba for dollars. Official calculations of GDP now incorporate the convertible peso more as a measure of value, but the whole process of GDP calculation in Cuba has not yet been made fully transparent. Notwithstanding all the problematic issues involved in simply

using a 1 to 1 ratio, that is as justified a value to use as any other to think about the value of the GDP in dollars. On this issue I will give the figures as they are given in pesos, and not make a conversion. Foreign trade figures do not involve this issue, and for them presentation in dollars or pesos is equivalent.

5. *Bohemia* (Havana, International Edition), May, 1995, gave the figures used for 1989 to 1992 and indicated that these were calculated by INIE (the National Institute for Economic Investigations) and CONAS S.A. (A consulting firm associated with—but not part of—the Ministry of Foreign investment). The *Economic Intelligence Unit* (EIU) 1996 (1), gives 1991 to 1993 figures (matching *Bohemia* for 1991 and 1992).

6. Kotz and Weir, 1997, p. 174. The 1996 figure is from Goskomstat Rossii, *Statisticheskoe obozrenie*, Number 1, 1997, p. 10. A full neo-liberal program was only able to be implemented beginning on the first working day of an independent Russia, January 2, 1992; and that is why 1991 has been chosen as the base for measuring the decline. For an outstanding combination of description and political interpretation of the transformation of the USSR and then Russia, see Kotz and Weir, 1997.

7. Hiram Marquetti Nodarse, *Cuba: el desempeño del sector industrial en el periodo 1990 - 1995*, CEEC (Centro de Estudios de la Economía Cubana, University of Havana), 1996, cited in EIUb, 1997(3), p. 25.

8. Small uncertainties always enter when one uses economic figures from speeches. Carlos Lage actually said Cuba that "consumed" that much. If one adds the more carefully stated data in the *Anuario Estadístico de Cuba*, it appears that 13.32 million tons were imported in 1987 and 13.11 million tons in 1988 (CEE, 1989, p. 281). Domestic extraction of crude in those years was 894,500 and 716,800 tons, respectively (CEE, 1989, p. 156) Accepting the assertion by the Cuban government that imports were not cut until 1990, the 13 million ton figure for 1989 appears to be more consistent with imports. Hence we have assumed here that the data given actually referred to imports.

9. Carlos Lage, cited in *CubaInfo*, December 4, 1992, p. 8.

10. CEE, AEC 1987, p. 176.

11. Reed, 1992.

12. American Association for World Health, 1997, p. 19. The report goes on to make a detailed case that this drop in nutrition was not just a result of the economic disruption following the collapse of trade relations with Russia, but its severity was significantly contributed to by the US embargo which included food, a policy that violated international human rights conventions.

13. Balari, 1990, pp. 157-8.

14. CEE, AEC 1987, p. 176.

15. While the Cuban policy of distributing the shortages throughout the population prevented the outbreak of widespread hunger that such a drop would be expected to cause in a third world country, the effects on the population were significant. By 1993 nutritional deficiencies began to emerge in the general population. The median weight of males and females dropped in 1993, with adolescents registering a weight loss of at least two kilograms compared to 1982 figures; children born in 1990 or after were noticeably smaller than those of the same age in 1982; and men and women of age 20 to 60 registered a marked weight loss. Cuba also began to register deficient nutritional status in women at the beginning of their pregnancies, as well as an increase in the incidence of low-birth weight babies. (AAWH, 1997, p. 19) Further, the neuropathy epidemic of 1992-3 that affected over 50,000 Cuban men and women had food shortages (through certain vitamin deficiencies they caused) as a central cause. It should be noted that despite the country wide shortages of food, the Under Five Mortality stayed low (12/1,000 live births, 1994, compared to 47 for Latin America as a whole) and Infant Mortality actually dropped (from 9.4/1,000 live births, 1994, to 7.9 for 1996, compared to 38 for Latin America) due to the policies of trying to protect the most vulnerable in periods of shortages.

16. One must have some understanding of the Cuban economy to understand what the dollars for peso black market exchange rate means. The U.S. media likes to use it to suggest that the average monthly wage of around 200 pesos means that (at about 20 pesos per dollar in 1997) the average Cuban earns $10 per month. That is totally misleading: one can live (poorly) on 200 pesos per month in Cuba (food, shelter, and clothing), while one could not come close to surviving on $10 per month in the US.

In 1989 one could get at low prices enough food and consumer products for a minimally comfortable existence. One generally had pesos left over after buying the basics. Accumulating pesos in itself does nothing for a person, so Cubans then tried to find a way to buy additional consumer products—more or fancier food, electronic consumer goods, etc. The one source for many of these products was the few dollar stores that were set up for foreigners living in Cuba. While Cubans could not shop in these stores, with dollars (many Cubans had dollars then even though it was illegal to posses them, frequently from relatives who lived outside the country) one could sometimes find a foreigner who would buy the goods for you, or more often, you would buy from a Cuban who did have the connections to have someone buy from him—and so a market developed. The important point here is that the black market exchange rate of 7 to 1 then in no way represented the comparative purchasing power of those currencies. Rather, it represented the balancing of supply and demand for the currencies as used in the purchase of luxuries (or nicer basics, like nicer food).

As the crisis began to unfold, more and more products that had been available on ration (or even not rationed) could no longer be obtained through official channels at official prices. This went well beyond luxury goods and even nice basics: examples of products that could frequently only be obtained with dollars were cooking oil, soap, deodorant, and toothpaste. The quantity of even such basics as rice and beans that one could get through official channels dropped sharply, and eventually dropped below what many people needed to feel adequately fed.

Not only the nature of what people bought, but where it was coming from changed. Dollars were being used to buy more and more domestic products. A growing quantity of goods were finding their way into the black market via theft from state enterprises. One example is rum. In 1993 it was difficult to obtain rum from the ration card, but most of the rums being bought by Cubans on the black market in dollars were stolen from state production facilities. Two other (than theft) major sources of goods in the black market were food that was bought and sold outside the state distribution system, and handmade products (handicrafts do not quite capture the idea, for these were not knickknacks or souvenirs, but shoes, pots and pans, etc., things people used for daily life).

While the black market exchange rate can in no way be used to compare the relative standard of living in the two countries, the rapid devaluation of the peso against the dollar did reflect something important about the Cuban economy at that time. Basic goods were less and less available at the maintained low prices, and hence there was more and more demand for dollars to get what one needed for a minimally acceptable existence. The strengthening of the peso after 1994 reflected above all that the peso could then again buy basic goods, above all food.

17. EIUb, 1997(4), p. 6 for 1994-1996. *Granma* (International Edition) January 20, 1998, for the 1997 growth figure.

18. Op. Cit. in endnote 7.

19. There is a general belief in Cuba that many of the goods (especially machinery) that they received from the Soviet Union, even though they were below world prices, were generally inferior to Western goods, thus the Cubans overpaid for such goods. To the extent that this idea is correct, the recovery in the value of the imports could be significantly above this calculated 43 percent due to the shift to importing a much higher percentage of western machinery, though there is no quantitative estimate of this effect.

20. Data for 1992-1993 were taken from EIU Cuba Country Profile 1998/1999 while the updated numbers for 1994-1998 were taken by the editors from EIU Cuba Country Profile 1999-2000. The 1996 figures are listed as preliminary. Interested readers will also find in these figures a breakdown of the 1995 and 1996 merchandise exports into 9 categories, and in *EIUb* 1997(2), p. 25 a breakdown of exports between sugar and non sugar from 1990 to 1996.

21. Study by Havana's Center for the Study of the Cuban Economy (CEEC), cited in *Cuba Business*, May 1997.

22. EIUb, 1996(1), p. 19. The 1996 figure based on the author's calculations of 1996 data cited by EIUb, 1997(4), p. 6.

23. I strongly suspect that such studies have been conducted in Cuba and the data exists in reports in Cuba, given the high ratio of academic researchers to population that has been developed in Cuba over the course of the revolution. However, most of these studies are identified and used by the international community. The results of studies by a few economic institutions now receive greater attention, but results of studies by other social sciences, such as sociology, still generally receive no notice.

24. From the Cuban trade union newspaper *Trajabadores*, cited in *Cuba Business*, September 1996, p. 5. There are some errors in the data presented there resulting from a problem in the use of commas and decimals points that one often gets in switching from Spanish to English data, but that does not affect the ratios I have calculated.

25. There clearly are other important issues. One is the change in the consciousness of the producers, the change in the way they look at the world, the change in the way they look at their relations with and responsibility for others in society, etc. There is no hard evidence that I know of about the extent to which any such changes have occurred to date. This topic will not be addressed here, although the author thinks it is an important factor in this and any economic restructuring.

26. Profits were one criterion used in enterprise evaluation before, but they were secondary to plan fulfillment.

27. In April 1987 Cubanacán was set up as an independent tourist corporation and charged to find foreign partners for hotel projects. Jenkins and Haines, 1994. p. 19.

28. Two slightly different figures reflect this issue of leakages. Jenkins and Haines (1994, p. 75) estimated that in 1994 it was unlikely that much more than 30 percent of tourism revenues generated remained in Cuba, and this is not subtracting the repatriated profits by joint venture investors. This reflects the lack of linkages so that hotels had to import both food and goods to maintain a quality acceptable for the international tourist market. Since 1994 linkages have been improved significantly, especially in food and furniture. A different measure is the cost of earning a dollar. This fell from $.73 in 1993 to $.68 in 1995. (*Cuba Business*, July-August 1996, p. 5).

29. Many of the hotels that cater predominantly or partially to foreign tourists are Cuban owned, contrary to the image that is often projected. Of these, many have a contract for a foreign directed administration, while many others are Cuban administered.

30. EIUb, 1997(1), p. 18.

31. *Cuba Business*, special edition reprint of Gareth Jenkins presentation to the seminar, "Tightening the US Trade Embargo on Cuba: Implications for Trade and Investment," July 8-10, 1996, page 4. Cuba has been very guarded about publishing figures on direct investment, given that the U.S. uses whatever information it can get to pressure investors to withdraw. A private research group in Washington calculated that from 1990 to January 1997, $707 million was committed or delivered, and an additional $4.6 billion was agreed to. (EIUb, 1997(2), p. 27). In 1997 the National Bank of Cuba did release some figures on the national capital account, but the Central Bank accounts, which so far have been accompanied by little elaboration, do not conform to standard international methodology (EIUb, 1997(4), p. 28). They give the following direct

investment figures (dollars, millions): 1993, 54.0; 1994, 563.4 (mostly from the Domos telecommunications deal); 1995, 4.7; 1996, 8.0 (preliminary).

32. The Vice President in charge of the economy, Carlos Lage, cited in *Cuba Business*, special edition cited in the previous endnote, page 4.

33. A report by the Ministry of Finance, *La reforma económica de Cuba en las cicunstancias actuales, 1995*, cited in *Cuba Business*, special edition cited in endnote 31, page 4.

34. *Cuba Business*, July-August 1996, p. 3.

35. Jenkins and Haines, 1994, p. 19.

36. Copies of this law are readily available in Cuba, as the Cuban government wants to get it into the hands of as many foreign entrepreneurs as possible to promote appropriate foreign investment. The Cuba National office of TIPS has published a copy of the law (in English as well as Spanish) that one can get from the Chamber of Commerce, the TIPS office, or often at the airport. In accordance with article 37 of Law 77, section XI on the labor system was expanded on March 27, 1996 by Resolution No 3/96. Also published by TIPS and distributed in the same locations, the Regulations on the Labor System in Foreign Investment establishes the hiring process and labor rights for labor involved with foreign capital.

37. *Cuba Business*, July-August 1993, p. 1.

38. It is certainly not true that Cubans with strong ties abroad (families or colleagues) are all counter revolutionaries. It is true that considered as a whole this group is less supportive of the socialist goal of the revolution than Cubans as a whole.

39. But not the only one. Probably the most important was that there was a situation where people were being driven to daily break the law to maintain a minimally acceptable standard of living (buying food and goods with dollars), in a way that previously had been done on such a regular basis only by people who opposed or did not care about the revolution. This had the potential of undermining the government's broad support (for itself and for the revolution) over time.

40. Statistics from the Ministry of Labor and Social Security, cited in *Cuba Business*, July-August 1996, p. 3. The Ministry of Economy and Planning gave similar but slightly different figures for the end of 1995, cited in EIUb, 1996(3), p.12. It is important to note that there were already 41,200 registered self-employed in 1989, before the beginning of the recent reforms.

41. EIUb, 1996(3), p. 12 refers to these unnamed Cuban economists, but does not cite a specific written report. They refer to an additional 600,000, which would be three times as many, but says there are four times as many. Given the uncertainty of the estimates, either could as easily be closer to the real number. Gareth Jenkins throws out without any indication of his source a claim that the self-employed perhaps number as many as one quarter of the economically active population (*Cuba Business*, September 1996, p. 1). That would suggest almost a million unreported additional self employed workers (1.2 million self employed out of 4.8 million total), a significantly larger estimate and one that seems quite excessive to this author.

42. Although sometimes referred to as coops or coops of a new kind (to distinguish them from the real coops that have existed since the 1960s and were greatly extended in the early 1980s), the issue under contention is how much decision making power the workers have. The cane UBPCs (about half of them) have no say in crop selection, and most of the others have very little. They cannot set prices for the part of the output they deliver to the state (which for cane is all of it), and they have no control over the price of inputs (or credit), which they buy from the state. Since their inception there have been complaints that the UBPCs have not succeeded in their goal of turning enough power over to the workers to make them feel like decision makers (usually referred to as owners) as opposed to employees, something that was a central goal for raising agricultural productivity.

43. EIUb, 1996(3), p. 12 and p. 17.

44. EIUb, 1997(4), p. 19.

45. Jenkins and Haines, 1994, pp. 22-3.

46. Roman, 1995, p. 43. This article is by far the best presentation in English (that I am aware of) of the very interesting nature of the workers' parliaments. To see the correspondence of what the workers expressed as their concerns and desires and the legislation that followed, compare the workers' positions given on page 53 with the legislation passed as summarized briefly on page 54, and in the source in the last endnote. The one issue in which the government decided to go against the desires of the workers in part was the issue of income taxes on peso salaries - here the legislation enshrines the general principle that all income is taxable. (*Granma Weekly Review*, November 9, 1994, p. 7), though it argued that it hoped it would not have to impose such a tax and has in fact not done so to date. See page 55 in Roman (1995) for a careful discussion of this issue.

47. Roman, 1995, p. 54; Jenkins and Haines, 1994, p. 23.

48. EIUb, 1997(1), p. 14; *Cuba Update*, February 1995, p. 14. This issue of *CUBA Update* gives the 1993 and estimated 1994 (and projected 1995) budgets broken down into 6 income categories and 15 expense categories. The EIU table gives the expense side only, but gives the final figures for 1993-1995.

49. EIUb, 1995(1), p. 9.

50. EIUa, 1996-97, p. 13. The UBPCs are not part of the enterprise total; subsidies for them begin in 1994, but they are relatively small at .1 billion pesos for 1994 and .4 billion pesos for 1995. These subsidies are scheduled to be ended as soon as possible. Note that what the EIU lists as enterprise subsidies is actually the sum of what the Cuban accounts list as subsidies and what they list as price support for enterprises, which could cause some confusion: compare the 1993 EIU data to the CU data cited in endnote 48.

51. *Bohemia*, mayo de 1995, p. 11; EIUb, 1997(4), p. 18. Note that recently the money supply has stopped falling: in 1996 it rose a slight 3.1 percent.

52. *Granma Weekly Review*, October 12, 1994, p. 5; *Cuba Business*, December 1994, p. 6 stated that 160 were opened in the beginning.

53. EIUb, 1997(4), p. 18. For example, it is estimated that prices fell by 30 percent in the first 9 months of 1996.

54. Editors' note: By 1998, state organizations were providing (irregularly, but consistently, as available) food to local neighborhoods at prices significantly lower than the prices in the free markets. Most people in Havana claim that this state intervention makes the difference between malnutrition and getting by since salaries have not risen sufficiently to cover the increase in prices of agricultural produce.

55. *Granma Weekly Review*, November 9. 1994, p. 4.

56. The government gets revenue from this through both sales taxes and rents on the selling sites.

57. *Cuba Business*, October 1994, p. 1; December 1994, p. 1.

58. In June 1997 the newly created Banco Central de Cuba (BCC) took over as Cuba's central bank and the BNC became a commercial bank EIUb, 1997(3), p. 15.

59. It is interesting that even in 1984 Cuba was looking for ways to expand its trade with the West, and the BIF was created as part of those early efforts. The bank is actually a wholly owned subsidiary of the CIMEX Corporation, a Panama registered Cuban group with interests in importing/exporting, merchant shipping, and tourism.

60. The first bank was actually a joint venture between the Dutch bank ING and the Acemex Group from Cuba (main interests in shipping and related activities). Bank legislation was not in place at the time; the Legislative Decree Law 84 from 1984 allowed foreign banks to establish representative offices in Cuba, but did not specifically allow them to perform banking services (not surprisingly, it was not widely used). In issuing the license to operate, the Cuban government interpreted Law 84 loosely, and relied on Law 50 that allows it to approve any foreign investment that is good for the Cuban economy (Jenkins and Haines, 1994,

pp. 76-7). This is an excellent example of how the reforms evolved through time. Since then, ING has opened an office in its own name, as the range of activities foreign banks can be involved in has expanded. *Cuba Business*, October 1996, p. 3, gives 12 foreign banks (they mention a 13th, the Havana International Bank, Ltd, but that is a subsidiary of the BNC despite being registered in London) operating in Cuba, but as in any such new field, there is some turnover: EIUb, 1997(3), p. 21 has moved the HIB to the Grupo Nueva Banca from the foreign classification, dropped two Spanish banks, and added a Mexican bank to list 11 foreign banks.

61. EIUb, 1996(4), p. 12; *Cuba Business*, October 1996, p. 3.

62. EIUa, 1996-97, p. 32; EIUb, 1997(2), p. 21.

63. Like the two laws referred to in endnote 36, this law is readily available in Cuba as a TIPS publication.

64. As usual, the free trade zones were the result of a process. The Berroa site had been a bonded warehouse area since 1991, described as the nearest to a free trade zone operating in Cuba up until the new free zone legislation. See Jenkins and Haines (1994. p. 68) for a description of this predecessor structure. Note that the operation of the zones is done by Cuban companies such as CIMEX which operates Berroa, and Almacenes Universales that operates Wajay. (EIUb, 1997(3), p. 26).

65. For more on the goals and nature (customs, taxation, finance, labor, etc.) of these free trade zones, see *Cuba Business*, summer 1997, p. 3.

66. Mesa-Lago, 1994, p. 68.

67. EIUb, 1997(3), p. 8. In line with the point I will make below that they feel that a restoration of capitalism is inevitable, they go on to argue that this limitation will subside and why. This limitation is likely to subside, however, as the need to integrate the domestic economy with the external sector increases the use of international pricing.

68. EIUb, 1996(4), p. 3.

69. Cited in Jenkins and Haines, 1994, p. 15.

70. From an article in *Actualidad Económica*, cited in *Cuba Business*, June 1995, p. 5.

71. EIUb, 1997(3), p. 7.

72. EIUb. 1997(3), p. 12. A listing of the specifics that underlie this position that Cuba is in is a process of introducing capitalism while at the same time denying it:

The restoration of capitalism is roundly rejected, but the progressive introduction of market mechanisms into the economic system is not defined as capitalism. Important barriers have been crossed, with the acceptance of foreign investment and opening of free agricultural markets. The capitalist reforms which are rejected are becoming more flexibly defined. Wholesale privatization is rejected, although partial privatization has been conceded (for example, in telecommunications); a free property market is ruled out, although foreign investors have obtained leasehold arrangements which can become tradeable assets; private ownership of productive capital is rejected, but the self-employed and foreign investors blur the lines of distinction; the surrender of state control of economic development is denied, but foreign investment and the reorganized financial system allocate investment spending by market criteria; and excessive disparities income and wealth will not be tolerated, even though increased inequality has been accepted as a cost of adjustment. The PCC congress has the task of forging unity and ideological consensus amid such uncertainties in a period of profound change (EIUb, 1997(3), p. 15).

73. EIUb, 1997(4), p. 8.

74. *The Economist*, January 17- 23, 1998, p. 3.

75. As was just discussed above, groups like the Economist Intelligence Unit hold that the pronouncements by the political leaders of the need to maintain socialism are cynical covers for the transition to capitalism. If one agrees with that position, of course the quotes I include to establish the stated commitment of the

Cuban leadership to socialism do not mean that group is in fact a factor that will impede a return to capitalism. I do not, however, accept that position.

76. It is hard to seriously study contemporary Cuba without admitting there is a far reaching public debate going on there about what sort of future Cuba should aspire to, despite the false image of the lack of debate commonly served up by the U.S. government and media. The Economist Intelligence Unit, a staunch opponent of both the present economic structure and political order in Cuba, acknowledges that this public debate is going on, while seeing it as at least partially if not largely controlled. They are thus allowing a public debate to reassess the meaning of socialism while reaffirming its validity (EIUb, 1997(3), p. 7).

77. While the position stated in the text is the general Cuban position on markets, occasionally the very different position is put forward that markets and joint ventures (and management practices, labor practices, accounting, etc. learned from joint ventures and then spread to the rest of the economy) can be incorporated into socialism and can help increase efficiency. "Ultimately we will not just save socialism. Ultimately, our socialism will be truly improved. .... Much of the experience that we are acquiring now will serve us in good stead to have a more efficient, perfect and more rational socialism, better adapted to human reality. That is my hope." (Castro, *CubaInfo*, September 14, 1995, p. 5) This latter current of thought could suggest shifting the ever changing strategies for developing socialism in Cuba in the direction of market socialism. Numerous foreign economists friendly to Cuba have advised Cuba to do this for years. It was never popular in Cuba before the special period, and it represents the antithesis of Cuba's last experiment before the special period, the 1996-1990 rectification process.

78. Castro, *Granma Weekly Review*, August 23, 1995, p. 6.

79. Ibid., p. 11.

80. Ibid., p. 9.

81. *Granma Weekly Review*, November 23, 1997, p. 10. His speeches over the years appear in many collections. Two recent works reflect his continued commitment to the same ideas he has espoused over the years: Castro 1994 and Castro 1996.

82. The Costa Rican firm associated with Gallop, CID-Gallop, conducted a scientific random (except that, due to bureaucratic problems, they were blocked from interviews in the eastern third of the island, where people have traditionally been more pro- revolutionary on average than in Havana) survey of 1,002 adults. For a brief review of some of the results, see *Cuba Update*, February 1995, p. 9.

83. Twenty-four percent considered themselves not integrated into the revolution. My concern here is what percent of the Cuban population oppose capitalism. Considering oneself revolutionary in Cuba certainly falls in that category - above all it means one identifies with the Cuban revolution, and that has been anti-capitalist. The break down of this 69 percent into its three component parts reflects a lot about Cuban attitudes toward the system in the Soviet Union (the term "communism" certainly referred to that, though the term "socialism" sometimes referred to that and sometimes referred to European Social Democracy) as of 1993, and their tremendous national pride, which is an important factor in any considerations on the future of Cuba: 10 percent identified themselves as Socialists, 11 percent identified themselves as Communists, and 48 percent identified themselves as Revolutionary.

84. Which I do not think at present it is trying to do, but as I have argued above, other observers of Cuba such as the Economist Intelligence Unit do think it is.

85. Approximately 70,000 proposals were made in the meetings, and many changes in the final form of the theses followed from these proposals.

86. EIUb, 1997(3), p. 7.

87. Recall there were always some markets and market-like-mechanisms in the Soviet Union, and few would call that a capitalist economy where markets ruled. The question is if when one has as many markets and market-like mechanisms as the Soviet Union had following the reforms of the 1980s, a critical mass of

markets exist and they will inevitably transform the economy into capitalism, or if instead the restoration of capitalism in the Soviet Union was caused by other factors so that one could have extensive markets and still not return to capitalism.
88. For a well known modern example of this type, see John Roemer, 1994.
89. Cited in Jenkins and Haines, 1994, p. 16.

REFERENCES

American Association for World Health (1997) *The Impact of the U.S. Embargo on Health & Nutrition in Cuba*, Executive Summary. Self Published. Copies can be obtained from the AAWH.

Balari, Eugenio (1990) "Agricultural Policy with Social Justice," in Sandor Halebsky and John Kirk (editors) *Cuba in Transition* (New York: Praeger Press).

Castro, Fidel (1996) *Cuba at the Crossroads* (Melbourne: Ocean Press).

Castro, Fidel (1994) *Che: A Memoir by Fidel Casto* (Melbourne: Ocean Press).

Comité Estatal de Estadísticas (CEE) *Anuario Estadístico de Cuba* (AEC) Yearly, suspended after 1989.

Cuba Business, Newsletter, almost monthly.

CubaInfo (CI), Newsletter published by the Cuba Policy Project at John Hopkins University, School of Advanced International Studies.

Cuba Update (CU) Publication of the Center for Cuban Studies, New York.

Deere, Carmen Diana (1991) "Cuba's Struggle for Self-Sufficiency," *Monthly Review* (July-August), pp. 55-73.

Economist Intelligence Unit (EIUa) Country Profile Cuba. Various years since 1986-87.

Economist Intelligence Unit (EIUb) Cuba, Dominican Republic, Haiti, Puerto Rico Country Report. Published quarterly.

Granma Weekly Review (GWR) A Cuban government newspaper, Havana, Cuba.

Edelstein, Joel (1995) "The Future of Democracy in Cuba," *Latin American Perspectives*, Volume 22, Number 4, pp. 7-26.

Fitzgerald, Frank (1994) *The Cuban Revolution in Crisis* (New York: Monthly Review Press).

Fuller, Linda (1992) *Work and Democracy in Socialist Cuba* (Philadelphia: Temple University Press).

Halebsky, Sandor and John Kirk (editors) (1992) *Cuba in Transition* (New York: Praeger Press).

_____ (editors) (1990) *Transformation and Struggle: Cuba Faces the 1990s* (New York: Praeger Press).

Harris, Richard (1992) "Bureaucracy vs Democracy in Contemporary Cuba: An Assessment of 30 Years Organizational Development," in Halebsky and Kirk (1992), op. cit.

Jenkins, Gareth and Lila Haines (1994) *Cuba: Prospects for Reform, Trade, and Investment* (New York: The Economist Intelligence Unit).

Kotz, David with Fred Weir (1997) *Revolution from Above* (London: Routledge).

Lutjens, Sheryl (1992) "Democracy in Cuba," in Halebsky and Kirk (1992), op. cit.

Mesa-Lago, Carmelo (1994) *Are Economic Reforms Propelling Cuba to the Market?* (Miami: University of Miami).

Reed, Gail (1991) "Making Due in the Special Period," *Cuba Update* (September), pp. 17-19.

Roemer, John (1994) *A Future for Socialism* (Cambridge: Harvard University Press).

Roman, Peter (1993) "Representative Government in Cuba," *Latin American Perspectives*, Volume 20, Number 1, pp. 7-27.

Roman, Peter (1995) "Workers' Parliaments," *Latin American Perspectives*, Volume 22, Number 4, pp. 43-58.

World Bank (1992) *World Development Report*.

14

Caribbean Convergence:
Cuba-CARICOM RelationsThrough 1995

John Walton Cotman

Cuba and the nations of the Caribbean Community and Common Market (CARICOM) have improved remarkably their diplomatic and economic relations. After the United States' invasion of Grenada in 1983, Havana's ties with the anglophone Caribbean deteriorated dramatically. Since the collapse of the Soviet bloc this trend has been reversed. Policymakers in Cuba and the CARICOM states fear that the realities of the post-Cold War global market will overwhelm Caribbean economies. They have been actively promoting regional economic integration in order to optimize their chances for economic survival in the twenty-first century. Despite significant impediments, including efforts by U.S. officials to prevent and reverse Cuba-CARICOM diplomatic and economic cooperation, it has expanded and institutionalized.

1. Introduction

In 1983 Cuba's relations with the anglophone Caribbean deteriorated precipitously following the United States' invasion of Grenada. That action reversed a trend of expanding ties set in motion when Jamaica, Trinidad-Tobago, Guyana, and Barbados—the "Big Four" of the Caribbean Community and Common Market (CARICOM)[1]—had jointly established diplomatic relations with Havana in late 1972. By the time of the dissolution of the Soviet Union in December 1991, the deterioration of Cuba's relations with CARICOM had been reversed dramatically. It appears that the survival of Cuban socialism in the post-Cold War era could rest, in part, on Havana's heightened cooperation with the former British West Indies. This chapter examines Cuba's expanding political and economic ties with the English-speaking

Caribbean through 1995. The chapter will address the following issues: (1) Cuban and CARICOM views on the contemporary global political economy, regional integration and economic development; (2) Cuba's relations with CARICOM nations in the 1990s; and (3) a review of actual and potential collaboration in tourism, trade, multilateral economic negotiations, and investments.

2. The Communist Party of Cuba (PCC) Views on the Global Political Economy, Integration and Development

Havana's support of regional integration has a long history.[2] For Cuban policy makers the harsh realities of the post-Cold War global political economy pushed the integration option to the forefront. This was evident in the proceedings of the Communist Party of Cuba (PCC) Fourth Congress at the close of 1991:

> The world economy is also showing the tendency to consolidate into large economic blocs. [...] The existence of these blocs [...] increasingly marginalizes the developing nations. It creates the urgent need for the unity and economic integration of these nations.[3]
>
> We have to begin [...] by regional and intra-regional agreements that can become broader channels for Latin America's economic integration. [...] The Fourth Congress reaffirms our country's interest in integration and cooperation with the rest of Latin America, and reiterates the position expressed by President Fidel Castro [...] to the effect that we could offer preferential terms to Latin American investors to encourage this process.[4]

Having lost 85 percent of its foreign trade with the collapse of the Soviet bloc, reeling from an estimated 51 percent decline in foreign exchange earnings from 1989 through 1992, and facing the U.S. economic embargo, Cuba's economy contracted considerably. Economists estimated that for 1991 there was a 20 percent decline in the global social product (GSP)—the sum of the gross values of agriculture, fishing, industry, construction, transport, communication and trade.[5]

With the socialist model—indeed, basic human survival—in jeopardy, the PCC outlined an economic strategy in late 1991. It emphasized the following: (1) achieving national food self-sufficiency as soon as possible; (2) increased hard currency earnings via a rapid expansion in tourism, traditional exports, and exports of biotechnology products, medicines, and sugar derivatives; and (3) securing a sufficient and reliable energy supply while reducing the consumption of imported oil.[6]

On July 15, 1992, the Cuban National Assembly voted to revise the republic's Constitution to entice foreign investment into the beleaguered economy.[7] By mid-1993 the economic signs were not encouraging. A tightened U.S. embargo drained Cuba's meager resources. Domestic agriculture could not meet Cuba's food requirements, and a dismal sugar harvest and unresolved energy crisis further strained the foreign exchange reserves and hampered domestic production. The impact of these setbacks led to a "re-definition of Cuba's economic model and its system of economic management."[8] Cuban policymakers are now attempting to manage "the uneasy relationship between socialist aims and market mechanisms."[9]

In April 1994 Cuba abandoned the economic administrative structures designed for its former ties with the USSR and Eastern Europe. Cuban public companies—especially in tourism—have been given greater autonomy to purchase, market, and negotiate directly with foreign investors. To attract regional investors and facilitate economic integration, 100 percent stock ownership options are available for Caribbean and Latin American firms. The tourism sector is the leader in the drive to attract foreign capital and generate foreign exchange. Speaking in New York City in June 1995, a Cuban official announced pending changes in the laws on foreign investment. Cuba would permit: (1) up to 100 percent ownership of Cuban firms by all foreign investors; (2) Cuba would establish "very strong guarantees protecting foreign investors against nationalization and expropriation of property"; and (3) direct employment of Cubans by foreign firms.[10]

Given the gravity of the economic crisis, despite the end of the economic free-fall in 1994, the Castro government has accelerated the late 1989 policy of "actively restoring" links with CARICOM states and entrepreneurs.[11]

3. CARICOM's Views on the Global Political Economy, Integration and Development

Meeting in Grenada in July 1989, the 10th Meeting of the Conference of Heads of Government of the Caribbean Community established the Independent West Indian Commission to create, via CARICOM wide consultations, a strategic plan to prepare "the peoples of the West Indies for the twenty-first century."[12] The central challenge facing the anglophone Caribbean was expressed by then President of Guyana, Desmond Hoyte:

Huge economic groupings are going to dominate the world
economy and there will be no place for countries that try to go it
alone. Certainly the member states of CARICOM cannot face the
powerful groupings individually. We have to combine our forces
to obtain maximum leverage in any negotiations with them.[13]

The West Indian Commission leaders met with President Fidel Castro in
March 1992.[14] In their view:

Cuba, its economic life dislocated and threatened by the breakdown in its links with Eastern Europe and the former Soviet Union,
but with its ten million well-educated people, advanced technology
in many areas, and unlimited tourist potential, offers a huge
challenge to enlightened statesmanship and entrepreneurial skills
in the Community.[15]

In July 1992 the West Indian Commission presented its findings and
recommendations. They provided the foundation of current CARICOM policy.[16]
Formal recommendations concerning regional strategy included:

1. That CARICOM bridge the divide between its Member States
and other states and territories of the Caribbean and Latin America,
recognizing the advent of an increasingly "Caribbean Basin"
approach to international negotiations and development issues, as
well as the changes within and among Latin American countries;
8. That CARICOM initiate proposals for the establishment of an
Association of Caribbean States [ACS] directed to both economic
integration and functional cooperation with the other Caribbean
Basin countries;
9. That the ACS be open to all CARICOM Member States, the
other island states of the Caribbean and the Latin American
countries of the Caribbean littoral; the ACS should allow for a
variety of arrangements appropriate to its membership.[17]

The Commission also proposed that member states wholeheartedly adopt "an
export propelled strategy" to succeed in the global economy.[18] Given Havana's
emphasis on expanding its Caribbean relations, the Commission recommended that

CARICOM: (1) "play a distinct role in assisting the process of normalizing Cuba's relations in the Hemisphere"; and (2) oppose Washington's embargo of the island.[19]

4. Washington Steps In

On October 23, 1992, President George Bush signed the Cuban Democracy Act, thereby tightening Washington's embargo of Cuba. Democratic presidential hopeful Bill Clinton's position on the legislation was unequivocal: "I believe in it, and I will enforce it."[20] The extraterritorial provisions of the act had inauspicious implications for the budding CARICOM-Cuba alliance. The United States legislation threatened and "prohibited" other countries and non-U.S. firms from exporting goods to Cuba that contain in excess of 20 percent U.S. inputs, and prohibited other economic activities such as trading with, shipping to, or traveling to Cuba.[21]   The Caribbean Community Heads of Government met in Dominica in late March 1993. They addressed increased "cooperation" with Cuba via the proposed CARICOM-Cuba Joint Commission.[22] Despite the rift caused by the invasion of Grenada a decade earlier, Prime Minister Eugenia Charles—an outspoken backer of the intervention—vowed in March 1993 that "we in Dominica are already trading with Cuba and we are going to continue doing so as long as it can pay."[23]

The Office of Foreign Assets Control of the U.S. Treasury Department chose June 29, 1993 to publish new regulations strengthening the embargo of Cuba in line with the Cuban Democracy Act of October 1992. During the CARICOM summit, President Clinton—on July 6, 1993—issued an executive order calling for its implementation.[24]

The 14th CARICOM Summit Conference of Heads of State was held in Nassau, the Bahamas, between July 5-8, 1993. The Conference marked a watershed in Caribbean Community ties with the largest isle of the Greater Antilles. The summit resolved to create the CARICOM-Cuba Joint Commission to aid economic, scientific-technical, and cultural exchange.[25] Much to the chagrin of policymakers in the Clinton Administration and the U.S. Congress, the accord respected Havana's request to omit language regarding human rights and democracy in Cuba found in earlier drafts. United States officials at the summit argued that CARICOM was remiss for "rewarding" Havana with improved ties without obtaining any commitment from Cuba to revise its political system.[26]

Opposition to the joint body from Washington continued after the Nassau summit.[27] However, elected leaders from Kingston to St. George's let it be known that support of the accord was unshakable. St. Lucia's Prime Minister, John Compton, reasoned that CARICOM's position was consistent, as similar joint commissions had been set up with Venezuela and Mexico. He added, "I do not think the U.S. will be happy at what CARICOM has done, but the Cold War is over and should not be fought in the Caribbean."[28]   One of Washington's strongest Caribbean allies, Grenada's Prime Minister Nicholas Brathwaite, defended the CARICOM-Cuba Joint Commission: "Mexico and Canada never broke ties with Cuba, yet the U.S. is joining with these two to create the North American free-trade agreement."[29]

Pressure from the U.S. capital against advances being made in CARICOM-Cuba collaboration escalated with the delivery of a letter dated July 26, 1993 from Robert G. Torricelli and three other members of the United States Congress to CARICOM leaders:

> We are writing to express our shock and dismay over press reports that CARICOM has agreed to establish a joint commission to explore technical cooperation with Cuba.
>
> We are particularly outraged that, according to the reports, language that would have linked technical cooperation with Cuba to improvements in human rights and movement toward democracy in that country was deleted from the document. Your countries, which represent the best in human rights in our hemisphere, should be in the forefront of those critical of dictatorship and repression in Cuba.
>
> We had hoped that it would be possible to construct a free trade area in this hemisphere based upon our countries' shared commitment to democratic values. Regrettably, those of us who have promoted this concept in the Congress must now reconsider our support for it. It is simply not possible for us to support the extension of trade benefits to the Caribbean region if we believe that the ultimate beneficiary will be the Cuban dictatorship.
>
> We strongly urge you to reconsider and rescind this unfortunate action.[30]

United States' pressures, however, have had the opposite effect, not only on CARICOM but also on the global community. Each year since 1992 the countries of the United Nations General Assembly have voted consistently and increasingly against the U.S. embargo of Cuba.[31] CARICOM Prime Ministers Hubert Ingraham of the Bahamas, Erskine Sandiford of Barbados, P. J. Patterson of Jamaica, Patrick

Manning of Trinidad and Tobago, and the late President Cheddi Jagan of Guyana attended an August 30, 1993 luncheon meeting at the White House hosted by President Clinton. The Caribbean leaders and the U.S. president differed in their assessments of the CARICOM-Cuba Joint Commission.[32] At a press conference in Washington on August 31, 1993, Prime Minister Patterson stated that, if Presidents Clinton and Castro requested an outside mediator to settle their disputes, CARICOM would be willing to act in that capacity.[33]

In late summer 1993, CARICOM Secretary-General Carrington made public an ambitious plan to integrate the Caribbean Community into the regional economy. CARICOM's market of almost six million, with US$11 billion in world trade—vulnerable to the vicissitudes of the post-Cold War global economy—would seek its salvation in the proposed Association of Caribbean States (ACS).[34] As envisaged by CARICOM leaders, the Association of Caribbean States would be an intergovernmental institution concerned with economic and social development. Its mandate would exclude political and security matters. Members would be free to participate at whatever level desired. Although designed to promote economic cooperation among member states, the ACS would also seek to facilitate regional cooperation among non-governmental entities.[35]

Improved relations between the Caribbean Community and Common Market and socialist Cuba were reaffirmed and institutionalized in Georgetown, Guyana on December 13, 1993. In the presence of representatives from the Organization of Eastern Caribbean States, Cuba, and other anglophone Caribbean countries, CARICOM's Secretary-General Edwin Carrington and Havana's Minister of Foreign Trade Ricardo Cabrisas Ruíz signed documents establishing the CARICOM-Cuba Joint Commission. Cuban policy-makers saw this setback for the Clinton Administration's foreign policy as a significant boost to their strategy for overcoming economic collapse. The accord codified areas of cooperation including: biotechnology, pharmacology, medical equipment, transportation, trade, pooling of data on commerce, investment, human resources development, and tourism.[36]

Details of the expanded ties would be set, implemented, and supervised in the various "working groups" of the joint body. During a press conference announcing the accord, CARICOM's Secretary-General urged private capital in the anglophone Caribbean to take advantage of the opportunities in Cuba. Cuban Minister Cabrisas said that in spite of its profound crisis, Cuba's new economic policies should find a favorable response within the Caribbean private sector. Havana's trade minister noted that in less than three years, trade between Cuba and the regional states had increased by 400 percent. In addition, Cuba's internal hard currency market was expected to generate $500 million in 1994 alone. Cabrisas emphasized the importance of "becoming partners and encouraging common interests in the [region], in such a manner that the progress of some is not made at the expense of the others, but rather that progress be shared by all." He pointed to the profit potential in Cuba's expanding tourism industry and predicted that imports of consumer goods for that sector would reach $400 million by 1995. [37]

The formal launching date of the ACS, July 24, 1994, was made public on April 4, 1994 at a CARICOM meeting in Kingston. Those in attendance indicated that U.S. officials pressured CARICOM to exclude Cuba from the proposed body.[38] Table 1 shows the ACS membership.

5. Cuba-CARICOM Economic Cooperation

5. 1. Tourism

Tourism in Cuba has grown steadily in the 1990s, with 398,400 visitors in 1991 and 620,000 in 1994. Cuba's 1992 figure totaled only 6 percent of CARICOM's 8-million-plus visitors. Although Cuba surpassed the hotel capacities of the Bahamas, Jamaica, and Barbados (the leaders in CARICOM tourism) in 1992, the largest Caribbean island could not match the number of visitors, tourism revenue, or hotel occupancy rate of the three.[39]

Tourism is seen as Cuba's future main source of hard currency.[40] The island's top hard-currency-generating exports sugar, nickel, and petroleum fell by 68 percent, 48.5 percent and 100 percent, respectively, between 1989 and 1992. Gross revenues from tourism increased from 4.8 percent to 23.3 percent of total export earnings, and from 4.5 percent to 17.7 percent of total foreign exchange earnings during the same period. In 1992 gross tourism revenues of $500 million were second only to sugar exports, $1,250 million, in foreign exchange earnings. In the years since, gross income from tourism has surpassed that of sugar exports, although the ratio of net profits is still behind that of the sugar industry.[41]

The centrality of tourism to Havana's economic policy was evident in a reshuffling of Cuba's state bureaucracy. In April 1994 the National Tourism Institute (INTUR) was upgraded to the Ministry of Tourism, and the PCC Political Bureau member Osmany Cienfuegos was selected to head it. In mid-1994 Abraham Maciques, a leading tourism official, said , "We are prioritizing the sector. Without a doubt, it's an important source of immediate hard currency for the country."[42]

Table 1: Members of the Association of Caribbean States (ACS) (Founded July 24, 1994 in Cartagena, Colombia)

Region/Regional Group	Members	Associate Members (nonvoting observers)
Caribbean Community and Common Market (CARICOM)	Antigua-Barbuda, Bahamas, Barbados, Belize, Dominica Grenada, Guyana, Jamaica, St. Kitts-Nevis, St. Lucia, St. Vincent & the Grenadines, Trinidad and Tobago.	Montserrat
Caribbean Basin	Cuba, Domincan Republic, Haiti, and Suriname.	
Central America	Costa Rica, El Salvador+ Guatemala, Honduras, Nicaragua, and Panama.	
Group of Three (G3)	Colombia, Mexico, Venezuela.	
British Dependencies		Anguilla, Bermuda, British Virgin Islands, Cayman Islands, Montserrat, Turks and Caicos Islands.
French Departments		Guyane, Guadaloupe, Martinique, St. Barthélémy, and St. Martin.
Netherlands Antilles		Aruba, Bonaire, Curacao, St. Maarten, St. Eustatius, Saba.
U.S. Dependencies		Puerto Rico+, U.S. Virgin Islands+.
Total Membership	25	10#

Source: "The Association of Caribbean States," *CC Press Release*, #65 (July 28, 1994), CARICOM Secretariat, Georgetown, Guyana; *CubaINFO*, Volume 6, Number 10 (August 5, 1994), p. 4; Phil Gunson, Greg Chamberlain, and Andrew Thompson, (editors) *The Dictionary of Contemporary Politics of Central America* (New York: Simon & Schuster, 1991), pp. 20-326; *Gramma International* (GI), March 30, 1994, p. 14; GI, July 20, 1994, pp. 1, 7; *CubaINFO*, Volume 6, Number 5 (April 8, 1994), pp. 7-28; *Caribbean Update*, Volume 10, Number 4, (May 1994), p. 1; *Caribbean Update*, Volume 10, Number 5 (June 1994), p. 1; GI, August 17, 1994, p. 10; Cuba Foreign Trade, July-December 1994, pp. 62-63.
+ Did not send delegates to founding conference of ACS. They are considered potential members.
# French colonies counted as one; the Netherlands colonies counted as one.

Participating in a June 1994 joint meeting of the Caribbean Tourism Organization (CTO) and Caribbean Hotel Association (CHA) with Cuban tourism officials in Havana, CTO General-Secretary Jean Holder rejected the idea that Cuba was an unwelcome competitor in the Caribbean market. In his view the competition threatening Caribbean-based tourism emanated from North American, European, and Asian tourism interests. Havana's tourism minister Osmany Cienfuegos and Cuban Foreign Minister Roberto Robaina embraced the CTO and CARICOM policy of cooperative regional tourism development. With its June 1992 admission to the CTO and January 1994 induction into the Caribbean Hotel Association, Havana joined the key institutions promoting regional tourism. In late January 1995 Cuba hosted the 20th Conference of the Caribbean Tourism Organization Board of Directors and the 9th Meeting of Tourism Ministers in Havana.[43]

Given the impressive recent growth of Cuban tourism, the potential size of its market undoubtedly has attracted the attention and interest of the anglophone Caribbean tourist sector. The CARICOM entrepreneurs can consider Cuban requests to supply consumer goods to its tourism facilities. The CARICOM capital has the opportunity to share—on more favorable terms—in the 19 to 22 percent profits realized by foreign joint investors in Cuban tourism. But perhaps the greatest inducement for CARICOM companies to participate is the opportunity to establish a presence in the market before Washington lifts its embargo. Caribbean investors could reap substantial earnings in the expected boom associated with the arrival of U.S. visitors. The CARICOM firms face the risk of waiting too long and losing out to U.S. financial capital once it is allowed to invest in the Cuban economy.[44]

Two major impediments to anglophone Caribbean cooperation with Cuban tourism are U.S policy and the possible failure of the Castro regime economic strategy and the consequent societal collapse. The trend in CARICOM capitals is to challenge the embargo, so that this constraint should carry less weight as time passes. However, if the Cuban strategy is successful two other factors act to limit CARICOM participation in Cuban tourism. First, Cuba is seeking large scale investment.[45] Does CARICOM have the large investors to provide the sizeable capital outlays required? Second, tourism minister Cienfuegos has made it clear that "national crafts and other Cuban products will replace imported goods in our stores." It appears that the medium-to-long-term prospects are that demand for foreign commodities in the tourism sector will decline.[46]

From the perspective of Havana officials, cooperation with CARICOM in tourism via the CTO, CHA and Cuba-CARICOM Joint Commission will prove to be beneficial in the areas of marketing, training of personnel, and air transportation. Membership in CTO and CHA allows Cuba to share in marketing efforts aimed at South America and the Caribbean. Joint marketing reduces promotional expenses. The CTO and Cuban experts agree that the isle "could benefit greatly from the marketing agreements the CTO has in Europe, even though Cuba does not belong to the Lomé Convention that provides its signatories with preferential treatment."[47]

Jamaica is Cuba's closest CARICOM neighbor. The second leading tourist destination in the anglo-Caribbean hosted 299,835 non-U.S. stayover visitors in 1991.[48] Jamaica leads CARICOM in cooperation with Cuban tourism. Former Cuban Foreign Minister Ricardo Alarcón and Jamaican Foreign Trade Minister David H. Coore signed three accords in Havana in early February 1993. One of these accords dealt with joint ventures in tourism. In fall 1993 officials from Kingston and Havana firmed up plans to add the larger isle as a second destination for vacationers in Jamaica from Europe and Canada. New sea routes opened between the islands in late 1993. The Cuban airline Cubana commenced direct, weekly flights to Jamaica in mid-1993.[49]

Another joint project is the four-star "ClubVaradero" at Cuba's premier resort involving the Jamaican company SuperClubs. Since 1991 SuperClubs has operated the 270-room complex owned by Cubanacán S.A. The Jamaican group has a management contract that taps its expertise in all-inclusive tourism and efficient service. ClubVaradero's director of operations noted with pride that "our revenue per tourist is the highest in Cuba." SuperClubs head John Issa, the "Caribbean Hotelier of the Year" in 1994, hopes to soon manage a second, new Cubanacán facility nearby. Hugh Maitland-Walker operates Tourwise Limited. It runs weekly charter flights from Montego Bay to Havana and Varadero. Jamaica's participation in the Cuban tourism market pales in comparison with Spain, the leader in Cuba's holiday industry. In July 1994 Spanish financial capital was represented by 32 companies.[50]

By 1995 tourism links with other CARICOM nations were few, but expanding. Documenting this trend has become more difficult since the mid-1990s as Havana further restricted information on its foreign partners in tourism due to heightened pressure from Washington. During a November 1993 visit to Trinidad, Cuban Foreign Minister Robaina discussed multidestination tourism with Prime Minister Manning. A Cuban official mentioned "business associations in tourism with the Bahamas," but no details were given. Cooperation with the Bahamas—the second closest CARICOM nation—would be advantageous to Cuba. With 3.7 million foreign guests in 1992, it led CARICOM in tourism. The 758,000 non-U.S. visitors in 1992 provided the largest pool for potential CARICOM-Cuba collaboration in the foreign travel industry.[51]

5. 2. Trade and Investment

Despite increased Cuban efforts to expand trade in the English-speaking Caribbean, there are formidable obstacles including the following: (1) the global economic recession; (2) impediments from Washington; (3) noncomplementary trade profiles; (4) indebtedness and lack of credit; (5) inadequate intra-regional transport infrastructure; (6) increasing dominance of Latin American economies in Cuban trade; (7) smallness of most CARICOM national markets; (8) Cuba's goal of food self-sufficiency; and (9) the competitiveness of Cuban and CARICOM non-traditional exports.

The U.S. embargo should have the greatest influence in those nations where the U.S. is a major economic player. The CARICOM's top four economies (in GDP) for 1991 were Trinidad, Jamaica, the Bahamas, and Barbados.[52] Using U.S. investment as percentage of GDP as an index of U.S. influence, the embargo should be most effective as an impediment to trade with Cuba in the Bahamas (125 percent). It should have appreciably less impact in Jamaica (22.2 percent), Barbados (22.1 percent) and Trinidad-Tobago (9.4 percent). [53]

In general, the CARICOM and Cuba do not possess complementary trade profiles for major imports and exports.[54] Priority imports for Cuba during the "Special Period in Peacetime" are crude oil, food (wheat, beans, animal feed and rice), plus various capital goods and industrial raw materials. Trinidad is a potential source of oil, and perhaps capital goods and raw materials. Guyana imports a principal Cuban export, tobacco. St. Vincent could also turn to Havana as a supplier of tobacco.55

The important point for Havana is to continue the tendency of increasing Caribbean commerce evident through the mid-1990s. Cuba-CARICOM trade was valued at 6.73 million pesos (.052 percent Cuban foreign trade) in 1987, and US $17.5 million (.51 percent Cuban foreign trade) in 1993. Between 1993 and 1994 Cuba-CARICOM trade doubled in value to US $35 million, but the 1994 amount was skewed by Cuba's fuel and lubricant imports via brokers in CARICOM countries. Data on trade with Barbados and Trinidad illustrate the negligible role of Cuban exports in their foreign trade, as well.[56]

For the most part, expanded trade will be in non-traditional and minor exports. For Cuba these goods and services include: pharmaceuticals, salt, cement and other building materials and services; steel products, agricultural equipment and spare parts; plus sugar cane based by-products, technology and consulting services. Published reports indicate that Cuba has exported medical equipment and salt to Guyana since 1990. Guyana is interested in furniture and wood product exports to Cuba. Trade ties are advancing with Jamaica. Cuba has opened an office for its iron and steel company ACINOX S.A. in Jamaica. Exports to Jamaica include an asphalt paving plant, plus bathroom tiles and fixtures. Jamaica exports fruit juices and water conditioner parts, and a firm from Dominica sells toiletries to Cuba. [57]

Debt and Cuba's bad credit rating are trade impediments to be overcome. The CARICOM's four major importers in 1992 were straddled with significant debt loads. On a per capita basis for 1992 indebtedness was as follows in millions of U.S. dollars: Jamaica, $1,495; the Bahamas, $1,972; Trinidad, $1,763; Barbados, $2,721. For Havana, the per capita figures in 1992 were $2,950 for its total debt—including outstanding debt in rubles to the former USSR—and $572 for its hard-currency debt.[58]

Cuba is expanding and improving its warehouse and customs facilities. To augment its limited shipping ties with CARICOM, Havana inaugurated new sea transport routes in mid-1993, initially with Jamaica. Unfortunately for current and prospective CARICOM exporters, they face serious competition from Latin American exporters in the Cuban market. In 1994 Latin America became the socialist isle's main trading partner, responsible for 40 percent of its foreign trade. The size of CARICOM markets, with the exceptions of Jamaica and Trinidad-Tobago, will be a brake on Cuba's exports as well. Cuban policymakers hope to reduce dependence on foreign food and animal feed, thereby eliminating a market for CARICOM goods. An essential issue to be addressed concerning increased commerce is whether CARICOM and Cuban commodities are competitive in terms of price and quality. If not, expanding trade in nontraditional goods would not fare well.[59]

Given the limited—but real—prospects for increased trade, what forces are favoring this trend? For CARICOM nations a decisive factor is the pernicious impact of the North American Free Trade Agreement (NAFTA). A 1994 World Bank study concluded that the Caribbean Basin would lose substantial export markets in the wake of NAFTA. Jamaica was expected to lose 45 to 60 percent of its exports. Dominica, St. Lucia, and St. Vincent also face sizeable export losses. If stable, the Cuban market is large enough to absorb significant quantities of the CARICOM's minor and non-traditional exports. Cuba has shown a willingness to engage in barter and other forms of non-currency commerce in the region. Additionally, in its drive to diversify and expand trade the Castro government has prioritized Latin America and the Caribbean.[60] A potential—and potent—rationale for Havana's interest in solidifying trade relations with CARICOM concerns the enhancement of Cuba's position in international trade talks:

> Since the CARICOM countries have long played a highly influen-
> tial role in ACP/Lomé affairs and since Cuba would as a former
> colony of one of the EC countries (i.e., Spain) appear to have the
> basic credentials to join ACP and become a party to the Lomé
> accords, significantly improved Cuban/CARICOM ties could
> markedly enhance Havana's membership prospects. Such a move
> could contribute greatly to Havana's efforts not only to stabilize,
> but hopefully also to expand its trade/aid links with Western
> Europe.[61]

For the anglophone Caribbean policymakers, "The importance of deeper CARICOM integration allied to closer Caribbean cooperation arises also from the need to strengthen our negotiating hand." During an April 1995 interview in Havana, Ministry of Foreign Trade, and Latin America and Caribbean regional integration expert Fernando Suárez-Murias Pella was asked if Cuba collaborated with CARICOM in trade negotiations on primary commodity exports. He replied, "It's not our purpose, but it could be useful." He said Cuba-CARICOM relations are still in their infancy, but noted that joint negotiations could be placed on the agenda in the future.[62]

The opportunities for joint bargaining are real given the configurations of Cuban and the CARICOM's exports. Cuba, Barbados, Belize, Guyana, Jamaica and St. Kitts-Nevis all depend to a significant degree on sugar exports; the Bahamas, Belize, Jamaica and Cuba on citrus exports; Cuba, the Bahamas, Belize, Guyana and St. Kitts-Nevis on seafood exports; and Cuba and Jamaica on coffee. It should be cautioned, however, that exporting similar commodities can generate competitive friction. For example, " Jamaican representatives [...] have accused Cuba of dumping cheap citrus products into CARICOM because of its ability to produce using cheap labor."[63] Cuba is finding interest in its direct investment and joint venture offers, outside tourism, among anglo-Caribbean entrepreneurs. It is soliciting financial capital, technical and management expertise, and raw materials in petroleum refining, the chemical, machine, and nickel industries; construction equipment manufacture, materials and technology; citrus production, financial services, and its textile industry. As of July 1994 Cuban sources reported 146 joint ventures with foreign capital, with 130 more under negotiation. A dozen of those in operation involved financial capital of Caribbean (including non-CARICOM) origin. One U.S. analyst noted the Jamaican private sector's upbeat assessment on investing in the socialist economy. Business deals are being discussed with the Bahamas, Trinidad and Tobago, and Guyana. Barbados and Cuba signed a bilateral investment accord—a first between Havana and a Caribbean nation—in February 1996. Policymakers in Havana are also proposing Cuban investments in CARICOM businesses, for example, Guyana's bauxite industry. While on the increase, CARICOM's investments are and will continue to be—at best—of secondary importance to Cuba's economy. Cuban direct financial investment in CARICOM nations will be of no appreciable importance given current economic realities. However, Cuba could make investments in the form of materials, skilled labor and technology in lieu of hard currency.[64]

6. Conclusion

The configurations of economic power in the highly competitive post-Cold War global system have energized the convergence of foreign economic policy and diplomatic relations between the Caribbean Community and Common Market, CARICOM member states and business interests, and the Republic of Cuba. Policymakers in Caribbean capitals recognize that they face growing economic marginalization, and see regional integration as a risky but necessary strategy to maximize chances for national economic well-being in the coming millennium. Despite efforts by President Clinton and leaders of the United States Congress to prevent and reverse Cuba-CARICOM cooperation, it has increased and become institutionalized. The view from the Caribbean is that cooperation brings measurable immediate benefits that could expand considerably in the next decade and beyond. For Cuba an alliance with CARICOM provides: (1) a key partner in tourism promotion; (2) a secondary source of management expertise in tourism; (3) a minor source of capital investment; (4) new, small markets for non-traditional exports; and (5) an important ally to aid regional integration and oppose the U.S. embargo. Benefits accruing to the CARICOM nations are: (1) an essential ally in regional integration efforts; (2) a partner in the top priority tourism industry; (3) profitable investment openings; (4) a market for minor and non-traditional exports; and (5) preferred access to a sizeable regional market without competition from U.S. firms. Given these benefits, plus future prospects for advantageous economic ties, cooperation between the anglophone Caribbean and socialist Cuba should expand.

ENDNOTES

1. The full members of CARICOM (founded in July 1973) are: Antigua-Barbuda, the Bahamas (not member of Common Market), Barbados, Belize, Dominica, Grenada, Guyana, Jamaica, Montserrat, St. Kitts-Nevis, St. Lucia, St. Vincent and the Grenadines, Suriname and Trinidad-Tobago. The British Virgin Islands, and Turks and Caicos islands are "observers" at CARICOM heads of government conferences and full members of all CARICOM bodies, except that related to foreign affairs. Other nations that have requested and received observer status in CARICOM are: Anguilla, Bermuda, the Cayman Islands, Colom bia, Cuba, the Dominican Republic, Haiti, Mexico, the Netherlands Antilles, Puerto Rico, and Venezuela. Source: Phil Gunson, Greg Chamberlain and Andrew Thompson, eds., *The Dictionary of Contemporary Politics of Central America and the Caribbean*, (New York: Simon & Schuster, 1991), pp. 62-63; *Granma International (GI)* August 16, 1992, p. 13; "Suriname Signs Instruments of Accession To CARICOM," *CARICOM Press Release* No. 41 (June 27, 1995), CARICOM Secretariat, Georgetown, Guyana; *Granma International*, October 12, 1994, p. 15. For a penetrating study of CARICOM's history and contemporary politics see H. Michael Erisman, *Pursuing Postdependency Politics: South-South Relations in the Caribbean* (Boulder: Lynne Rienner Publishers, Inc., 1992).

2. Communist Party of Cuba, *Programmatic Platform of the Communist Party of Cuba* (Havana, 1976), p. 125; "3rd Congress of the Communist Party of Cuba. Resolution on International Policy," *Granma Weekly Review*, February 23, 1986, p. 2; "Resolution on Foreign Policy," in *Island in the Storm: The Cuban Communist Party's Fourth Congress*, Gail Reed, ed. (Melbourne: Ocean Press, 1992), p. 148; Juan Valdés Paz, "Cuba's Foreign Policy Toward Latin America and the Caribbean in the 1980s," in Jorge I Dominguez and Rafael Hernandez *(editors) (1989) U.S.-Cuban Relations in the 1990s* (Boulder: Westview Press), pp. 185-186.

3. "Resolution on Foreign Policy", p. 146.

4. Ibid., p. 148; See also Gail Reed, "Ten Years After Grenada: Cuba and the Caribbean" [with interview of Cuban Vice-minister of Foreign Relations Ramón Sánchez Parodi], *Cuba Update*, Volume 14, Number 6 (1993), p. 20.

5. *Granma International*, May 4, 1994, p. 16; see Table 2 in Claes Brundenius, *Revolutionary Cuba: The Challenge of Economic Growth with Equity* (Boulder: Westview Press, 1984), p. 31.

6. "Resolution on the Country's Economic Development", pp. 133-136; Susan Kaufman Purcell, "Collapsing Cuba," *Foreign Affairs* Volume 71, Number 1 (1992), pp. 135-136.

7. *CubaINFO*, Volume 4, Number 8 (1992), p. 5.

8. Gail Reed, "Reshaping the Cuban Strategy: Thoughts from Cuban Economists," *Cuba Update*, Volume 14, Number 6 (1993), p. 11.

9. Gail Reed, "Tourism: The Front Runner," *Cuba Update*, Volume 15, Number 3 (1994), p. 13.

10. "Reshaping the Cuban Strategy," pp. 11 - 12; "Cuba Shuffles Economic Bureaucracy," *Washington Post*, April 23, 1994, p. A26; "Tourism: The Front Runner," p. 13; *Granma International*, February 16, 1994, p. 7; "The Cuban Economy in the 1990s," p. 122; *CubaINFO*, Volume 7, Number. 9 (June 29, 1995), p. 8.

11. *Granma Weekly Review*, December 10, 1989, p. 11; *Granma International*, May 4, 1994, p. 16; "Ten Years After Grenada," p. 19; Gail Reed and Jorge Miyares, "Cuba and the Caribbean - Once More with Feeling," *Cuba Update*, Volume 15, Number 1 (1994), p. 15; *Granma International*, July 27, 1994, p. 15; *Granma International*, July 13, 1994, p. 6. Note: Cuba's economy reportedly grew by 0.7% in 1994. Source: Deputy Minister Raul Taladrid and Director of Developed Countries Rafael Roqueta, Ministry of Foreign Investment and Economic Cooperation, interview by author, 25 April 1995, Havana; Fernando Suárez-

Murias Pella, Ministry of Foreign Trade specialist on Latin America and Caribbean economic integration, interview by author, 19 April 1995, Havana.

12. *Time for Action: The Report of the West Indian Commission* (Black Rock, Barbados: The West Indian Commission, 1992), pp. 527-528.

13. Desmond Hoyte, "Making the Quantum Leap: Imperatives, Opportunities, and Challenges for CARICOM," *Caribbean Affairs*, Volume 2, Number 2 (1989), pp. 55-56.

14. *Time for Action*, p. 11.

15. Ibid., p. 22.

16. Ibid., pp. 408-409, 444-447.

17. Ibid., p. 457.

18. Ibid., p. 96.

19. Ibid., pp. 457, 429.

20. *CubaINFO*, Volume 4, Number 12 (1992), p. 1.

21. Andrew Zimbalist, "Dateline Cuba: Hanging on in Havana," *Foreign Policy*, Number 92 (1993), pp. 158-160; *Granma International*, October 6, 1993, pp. 7-9.

22. *Caribbean UPDATE*, Volume 9, Number 4 (1993), p. 1.

23 *Caribbean UPDATE*, Volume 9, Number 4 (1993), p. 5.

24. *CubaINFO*, Volume 5, Number 9 (1993), p. 3.

25. "CARICOM-Cuba Commission Get Approval," *Barbados Advocate*, 8 July 1993; Alisa Valdés, "International Support for Cuba Continues. The Caribbean Community," *Cuba UPDATE*, Volume 14, Number 5 (1993), p. 15; *Caribbean UPDATE*, Volume 9, Number 4 (1993), p. 1; *CubaINFO*, Volume 5, Number 9 (1993), p. 7; *Granma International*, July 21, 1993, p. 3.

26. Ibid.; *Caribbean UPDATE*, Volume 9, Number 8 (1993), p. 2.

27. *CubaINFO*, Volume 5, Number 11 (1993), p. 1

28. *Caribbean UPDATE*, Volume 9, Number 8 (1993), p. 2.

29. Ibid.

30. 103rd Congress, House of Representatives. Committee on Foreign Affairs. Letter from Robert G. Torricelli, Chairman, Subcommittee on Western Hemisphere Affairs; Ileana Ros-Lehtinen, Subcommittee on Western Hemisphere Affairs; Robert Menendez, Subcommittee on Western Hemisphere Affairs; Lincoln Díaz-Balart, Dated July 26, 1993. Received by Caribbean Community and Common Market Secretariat, Georgetown, Guyana. Photocopy.

31. *Granma International*, December 6, 1992, p. 5; *Granma International*, November 10, 1993, p. 1; *Granma International*, November 17, 1993, p. 7; *CubaUPDATE*, Volume 4, Number 14 (December 4, 1992), pp. 1-3; CI Volume 5, Number 14 (November 5, 1993), p. 1; Julia Preston, "U.N. Urges United States To End Cuban Embargo," *The Washington Post*, October 27, 1994, p. A18; *Granma International*, November 9, 1994, p. 13; *Granma International*, November 15, 1995, p. 2.

32. *CubaINFO*, Volume 5, Number 11 (1993), p. 1.

33. Ibid.

34. *Caribbean UPDATE*, Volume 9, Number 8 (1993), p. 1.

35. *Granma International*, November 3, 1993, p. 14.

36. Bert Wilkinson, "Cuba, English-Speaking Caribbean Sign Agreement to Set Up Regional Group," Associated Press wire report "34133 AM-FL-Cuba-Caribbean AP-RG LOCAL NEWS RUSH 431 12/13 6:55 PM"; *CubaINFO*, Volume 5, Number 16 (1993), p. 5; *Granma International*, December 29, 1993, p. 16.

Note: The Second CARICOM-Cuba Joint Commission met in Havana on 17-18 January 1995. It assessed current collaboration programs and extended the areas of cooperation. For details see: "CARICOM-Cuba

Joint Commission Meets," *Caricom View*, Volume 2 (February 1995), p. 6. At this meeting Cuba's foreign trade minister announced Cuba's National Assembly would soon ratify the ACS Treaty. Source: "Statement Made by Cuban Foreign Trade Minister Ricardo Cabrisas at the Second Meeting of the Cuba-CARICOM Joint Commission," [17 January 1995, Havana], photocopy, 4.

37. Ibid.; On Cuba's July 1993 legalization of hard currency holdings by all citizens see *CubaINFO*, Volume 5, Number 10 (1993), pp. 7-8; *CubaINFO*, Volume 5, Number 11 (1993), pp. 7-8.

38. *Granma International*, March 30, 1994, p. 15; *CubaINFO*, Volume 6, Number 5 (1994), pp. 7-8.

39. Susan Kohler-Reed, ed., *Caribbean Basin Commercial Profile 1994* (Miami: Caribbean Publishing Company, Ltd., 1994); *CubaINFO*, Volume 6, Number 3 (February 18, 1994), pp. 10-11; María Dolores Espino, "Tourism in Cuba: A Development Strategy for the 1990s?" *Cuban Studies*, Volume 23 (1993), pp. 58-59; "Tourism: The Front Runner," p. 13; Susan Kohler-Reed, ed., *1995 Caribbean Basin Commercial Profile* (Miami: Caribbean Publishing Company Ltd., 1994), pp. 118, 121, 193, 200; Gerardo Gonzalez Nuñez, *Centro de Estudios sobre América*, April 10, 1995, Havana; *CubaINFO*, Volume 7, Number 7 (May 18, 1995), p. 11; *Granma International*, April 27, 1994, p. 8; *Granma International*, June 1, 1994, p. 7; H. M. Erisman, "Cuba's Macrostrategy in Latin America: A Feasibility Analysis," Paper presented at 18th LASA Congress, Atlanta, March 1994, p. 7; *CubaINFO*, Volume 6, Number 3 (February 18, 1994), pp. 10-11; *CubaINFO*, Volume 6, Number 5 (April 8, 1994), p. 11; José Luis Rodríguez, "The Cuban Economy in a Changing International Environment," *Cuban Studies*, Volume 23 (1993), pp. 40-41; L. Willmore, draft paper from Internet "Recent Economic Reforms in Cuba," November 14, 1994, p. 7; *Cuba Trade Directory* (Havana: Chamber of Commerce of the Republic of Cuba, 1993), p. xvi; Director of Operations Abe Moore, SuperClubs ClubVaradero, interview by author, 17 April 1995, Cuba.

40. "Cuba Shuffles Economic Bureaucracy," *Granma International*, April 20, 1994, p. 13; "Tourism: The Front Runner," p. 16, *Granma International*, March 2, 1994, p. 7.

41. Ernest H. Preeg, *Cuba and the New Caribbean Economic Order* (Washington: Center for Strategic and International Studies, 1993), p. 16; "Tourism in Cuba," p. 58; "Cuba's Macrostrategy," p. 7.

42. "Cuba Shuffles Economic Bureaucracy," *Granma International*, April 20, 1994, p. 13; "Tourism: The Front Runner," p. 16, *Granma International*, March 2, 1994, p. 7.

43. *Granma International*, July 13, 1994, p. 8; *Granma International*, June 1, 1994, p. 9; "Cuba Joins Tourism Group," *The New York Times*, June 23, 1992, p. D7; *Granma International*, June 29, 1994, p. 8; *CubaINFO*, Volume 6, Number 3 (1994), p. 10; *Granma International*, July 27, 1994, p. 9; *Granma International*, February, 1 1995, p. 3.

44. *Granma International*, December 29, 1993, p. 16.; "Reshaping the Cuban Strategy," p. 11; "Tourism: The Front Runner," p. 16; *CubaUPDATE* Volume 15, Number 1 (1994), p. 20.

45. *Granma International*, June 1, 1994, p. 7.

46. *Granma International*, June 1, 1994, p. 9.

47. "Cuba Joins Tourism Group," *Granma International* July 13, 1994, p. 19, and "Ten Years After Grenada," *Granma International*, July 27, 1994, pp 8- 9.

48. The distance from Kingston to Santiago de Cuba is 150 miles; from Kingston to Havana is just under 500 miles. Source: *The New Rand McNally College World Atlas* (Chicago: Rand McNally & Company, 1983), p. 133; *Caribbean Exporters 1993/94: A Directory of Exporters and Producers in the Thirteen Member States of the Caribbean Community (CARICOM)* (Georgetown, Guyana: CARICOM, 1993), p. 95.

49. *Granma International*, February 14, 1993, p. 6; *Granma International*, February 21, 1993, p. 11; *CubaINFO*, Volume 5, Number 2. (1993), p. 4; *CubaINFO*, Vol. 5, No. 13 (1993), p. 10; *Granma International*, June 1, 1994, p. 9; *CubaINFO*, Volume 5, Number 12 (1993), p. 8; *Granma International*, October 13, 1993, p. 11; *Granma International*, December 22, 1993, p. 9; *Granma International*, June 16,

1993, p. 7; *Granma International*, September 22, 1993, p. 5; *Granma International*, January 5, 1994, p. 7; *Granma International*, May 31, 1995, 9; *Granma International*, April 26, 1995, p. 8.

50. Abe Moore, Director of Operations-Cuba, SuperClubs ClubVaradero, interview by author, 17 April 1995, Varadero Beach, Matanzas; Eduardo Fagundo, Marketing and Sales Manager, SuperClubs ClubVaradero, conversation with author, 7 April 1995, Matanzas; Vice President Carlos Garcia Hernández Cubanacán, S.A. [Corporacion de Turismo y Comercio Internacional, S.A.] interview by author, 21 April 1995, Havana, Cuba; *CubaINFO*, Volume 4, Number 1 (1992), p. 6; *Caribbean UPDATE*, Volume 9, Number 4 (1993), pp. 5-6; *Granma International*, October 20, 1993, p. 9; *Granma International*, July 7, 1993, p. 3; "Tourism: The Front Runner," p. 16; *CubaINFO*, Volume 6, Number 9. (1994), p. 10; *Caribbean UPDATE*, Volume 10, Number 8 (1994), p. 2.

51. Carlos Garcia Hernández interview; Alberto Velázquez Sánchez, Commercial Vice President AeroCaribbean Air Company, S.A., interview by author, 19 April 1995, Havana; *Granma International*, June 7, 1995, p. 9; "Ten Years After Grenada," p. 19; *World Atlas*, p. 133; also see note 39.

52. See Table 2; The Bahamas is a member of the Caribbean Community, but not its Common Market.

53. Caribbean Basin Commercial Profile 1994, pp. 14, 30 ff.; Jan Svejnar and Jorge Pérez-López, "A Strategy for the Economic Transformation of Cuba Based on the East European Experience," in Carmelo Mesa-Lago, ed., *Cuba After the Cold War* (Pittsburgh: University of Pittsburgh Press, 1993), p. 342; *CIA World Fact Book 1994*; *Caribbean UPDATE*, Volume 9, Number 1 (February 1993), p. 5; *Cuba & New Caribbean Economic Order*, pp. 16, 18; *Caribbean UPDATE*, Volume 11, Number 1 (February 1995), p. 6; Alfonso Casanova Montero, "La economia de Cuba en 1993 y perspectivas para 1994," *Economia Cubana*, Number 16 (July 1994), pp. 3-14.

54. Caribbean Basin Commercial Profile 1994, pp. 38 ff; *Cuba & New Caribbean Economic Order*, p. 16; *CIA World Fact Book 1994*.

55. Carmen Diana Deere, "Cuba's Struggle for Self-Sufficiency," *Monthly Review*, Volume 43, Number 3 (1991), pp. 62-63; footnotes 6-8; James Brooke, "Latin America's Oil Rush: Tapping Into Foreign Investors," *New York Times*, July 11, 1993, p. F5; *Time For Action*, p. 187; *Granma Weekly Review* (GWR), May 13, 1990, p. 5; see also note 56.

56. *Granma Weekly Review*, May 13, 1990, p. 5; Luis Suárez Salazar, "Cuba's International Relations with Latin America and the Caribbean: Towards a New Stage?" in H. Michael Erisman and John M. Kirk, (editors)*Cuban Foreign Policy Confronts a New International Order* (Boulder: Lynne Rienner Publishers, Inc., 1991), p. 112; H. M. Erisman, "Cuba's Macrostrategy," op. cit., (endnote #39), pp. 7- 8; *Caribbean UPDATE*, Volume 9, Number 5 (1993), p. 7; Fernando Suárez-Murias Pella interview, op.cit (endnote #11); *Cuba & New Caribbean Economic Order*, p. 16; *Caribbean Basin Commercial Profile 1994*, pp. 59, 232; *Economic Survey of Latin America and the Caribbean 1991, Volume 1* (Santiago: Economic Commission for Latin America and the Caribbean, 1993), p. 182. Note: the calculation of percentage Cuban foreign trade assumes 1 Cuban peso = US $1.

57. "Ten Years After Grenada," p. 20; Julie M. Feinsilver, *Healing the Masses: Cuban Health Politics at Home and Abroad* (Berkeley: University of California Press, 1993), pp. 126-127, 143, 147, 195; *Granma Weekly Review*, May 13, 1990, p. 5; *Granma International*, June 22, 1994, p. 7; *CubaINFO*, Volume 6, Number 8. (1994), pp. 6-7; *Granma International*, June 15, 1994, p. 6; *Granma International*, April 20, 1994, p. 6; *Caribbean UPDATE*, Volume 9, Number 4 (1993), p. 5; "Cuba and Caribbean-Once More," p. 15; "Cuba, English-Speaking Caribbean Sign Agreement."

58. Carmelo Mesa-Lago, "Cuba's Economic Policies and Strategies for Confronting the Crisis," in *Cuba After the Cold War*, Carmelo Mesa-Lago, ed. (Pittsburgh: University of Pittsburgh Press, 1993), p. 201.

59. Deputy Minister Raul Taladrid and Director of Developed Countries Rafael Roqueta, Ministry of Foreign Investment and Economic Cooperation, interview by author, 25 April 1995, Havana; Fernando Suárez-Murias Pella interview; Minister of Construction Homero Crabb Valdes and Edilberto Martínez Noa of Quality Couriers International, S.E.A., interview by author, 18 April 1995, Havana; Joaquin Oramas, *Granma International*, March 1, 1995, p. 11; *Granma International*, October 19, 1994, p. 7; *Granma International*, July 27, 1994, p. 7; *Granma International*, June 16, 1993, p. 7; "Cuba and the Caribbean-Once More," p. 15; *Granma International*, July 6, 1994, p. 5; "Cuba's Macrostrategy," p. 18; "Cuba's Economic Policies and Strategies," p. 229; *Healing the Masses*, pp. 126-127, 135-136, 143.

60. *Caribbean UPDATE*, Volume 10, Number 7 (1994), pp. 1-2; "Cuba's Economic Policies and Strategies", pp. 208-209; *Granma International*, October 20, 1991, p. 8; *Granma International*, May 4, 1994, p. 16.

61. "Cuba's Macrostrategy," p. 12; *Granma International*, June 8, 1994, p. 12; ACP refers to African-Caribbean-Pacific group of former European colonies.
Note: A leading Cuban scholar of Havana's Caribbean policy agrees with Erisman that the potential joint negotiating power of Cuba and CARICOM is key to understanding the convergence of interests between Cuba and the anglophone isles. Gerardo González Núñez, Centro de Estudios sobre América, conversation with author, 10 April 1995.

62. *Time for Action*, pp. 66-67; Fernando Suárez-Murias Pella interview, op.cit.

63. On collaboration in regional economic bodies see John Walton Cotman, "Cuba and the CARICOM States: The Last Decade," in *Cuba's Ties to a Changing World*, Donna Rich Kaplowitz, ed. (Boulder: Lynne Rienner Publishers, Inc., 1993), pp. 149-150; *Caribbean UPDATE*, Volume 8, Number 12. (1993), p. 2; see also note 54.

64. *Granma International*, June 22, 1994, p. 7; *CubaINFO*, Volume 6, Number 8 (1994), pp. 6-7; "Cuba and the Caribbean-Once More," p. 15; *Caribbean UPDATE*, Volume 10, Number 7 (1994), p. 7; *Cuba & the New Caribbean Economic Order*, p. 67; Carlos A. Batista Odio, "La Integración Latinoamericana y Cuba: Los Desafios de la Política de Estados Unidos," Paper presented at 18th International Congress of the Latin American Studies Association, Atlanta, 10-12 March 1994, p. 10; *Granma International*, July 27, 1994, p. 7; *CubaINFO*, Volume 6, Number 9 (1994)), p. 10; *Granma International*, April 20, 1994, p. 6; "Cuba, English-Speaking Caribbean Sign"; for summary of joint venture terms offered by Cuba see "Tourism: The Front Runner," p. 16; *CubaINFO*, Volume 8, Number 3 (1996), p. 7.

15

Health Tourism: A Niching Strategy for Marketplace Survival in Cuba

Sharon L. Oswald and Tony L. Henthorne

The Cuban health care system has long enjoyed a worldwide reputation for superiority in medicine. However, with the dismantling of the Soviet Union, this reputation was not providing the hard currency necessary for the country's economic survival. Health tourism, a specialized, under-served niche in the hotly competitive realm of Caribbean tourism, became the shining star of the Cuban government's hope for resurgence into the global marketplace. With the exploitation of health tourism through a for-profit entity, Cuba appears to be heading down a path untraveled for nearly four decades.

1. Introduction

With the continued rapid growth in global competition, more and more countries are under increasing pressure to find a distinctive competitive competency—an industry, service, or resource that will set that country apart from the pack. For countries with the natural resources conducive to "curative health," health tourism may be just such a competency.

Goodrich and Goodrich (1987, p. 217) define health tourism as "the attempt on the part of a tourist facility (e.g., hotel) or destination (e.g., Baden, Switzerland) to attract tourists by deliberately promoting its health-care services and facilities, in addition to its regular tourist amenities." Countries claiming a niche in health tourism generally possess good natural resources, including mineral waters, a stable comfortable year-round climate, and active, calming scenery. Israel, Hungary, Austria, Switzerland, the Bahamas and even the United Kingdom have all been quick to jump on the health tourism bandwagon in recent years. Many of the world's best-known resorts literally sprang up around thermal springs and concomitant curative facilities, such as Baden-Baden in Germany and Hot Springs, Arkansas in the United States (Niv, 1989; Goodrich & Goodrich, 1987).

One country possessing all the right qualities for a thriving health tourism industry is Cuba. Once considered a paradise destination for American tourists, Cuba is rich in all the natural amenities to support a thriving spa and hot springs industry. However, the competitive playing field is a worldwide hotbed of continuous activities. Additionally, the Cuban facilities are in serious need of upgrading and refurbishment, translating into an extraordinary investment for a country still on the brink of bankruptcy and still trying to recover from the devastating blow to its economy caused by the fall of the Soviet empire. The reality of Cuba thriving as a Caribbean spa destination becomes even more complex when you consider that a customer orientation is not a strong point for this island nation. The preclusion of U.S. tourists (Goodrich, 1994; Harrison, Hall, & Harrison, 1992) only adds to the dismal prospects of Cuba as a spa destination.

An examination of what truly was Cuba's distinctive competency—a renown health care system—resulted in the Cuban government embarking upon a unique twist to health tourism. By applying Michael Porter's (1980) niche strategy concept, Cuba has become a "tourist" destination for affordable, highly technical medical treatment. This chapter will look at health tourism, "Cuban style," first by discussing separately the Cuban medical system and then showing how the intertwining of medical expertise and niche tourism is Cuba's strategy for marketplace survival. Finally, we will provide a case study of one of Cuba's premiere tourist hospitals.

2. The Cuban Health Care System

The Cuban health system guarantees free medical accessibility to the entire population, covering the spectrum from vaccinations to sophisticated interventions. Prior to the 1959 revolution and not unlike other developing countries, Cuba lacked comprehensive primary health care. However, following the Revolution, when approximately 50 percent of the country's nurses and physicians fled, a redistribution of income occurred among those who remained. New priorities were set for the country with health care at the top. The government committed itself to substantial changes in the delivery and availability of health care. In the ensuing years, emphasis was placed on health promotion and primary medical care, health maintenance and family planning, medical education and high technology medical treatment (Tancer, 1995). Between 1965 and 1985, Cuba greatly expanded its medical corps and populated the rural areas with sufficient physicians to fully support the population (*Economists*, 1996; Swanson, 1987).

Much of the achievement in medical care is due to the unprecedented commitment of the government to medical education. Serving the 11 million Cuban citizenry are approximately 60,000 medical doctors, 50,000 dentists, 75,000 nurses, and 125,000 technicians or paramedics. Likewise, the number of free health facilities owned and operated by the Ministry of Health is astonishing for a population of this size. In 1996 there were 284 hospitals, 440 polyclinics, 268 dental clinics, 208 homes for pregnant women, 182 homes for the elderly, 26 homes for the disabled, 11 research institutions, 25 blood centers, and a number of AIDS sanitariums. Some 5,000 students enter medical schools annually (Cardenas, 1997). This concentrated focus on health care by the Castro regime has led to some astonishing outcomes for the small island nation. Today, health statistics (e.g., mortality and morbidity rates) and facilities are comparable to most developed countries. For example, in 1993, infant mortality in Cuba was 9.4 per 1000 live births. This compares favorably to 8.3 per 1000 live births for the same time period in the United States. In fact, Cuba is so far advanced that when the World Health Organization recently established its goal of Health for all by the year 2000, Cuba was viewed as the model country. Cuba's primary health model of free, quality care for all had already met and exceeded the World Health Organization's standards some ten years earlier (APHA, 1985; Swanson, 1987; Officials of Hermanes Ameijenes Hospital, 1997).

The previously close relationship between Cuba and the former Soviet Union helped to support and bring further recognition to Cuba's health system. Following the disaster at Chernobyl, Cuban hospitals cared for more than 6,000 children. Nonetheless, Cuba's achievements in health are not just recognized in Eastern Europe. During better times, prior to the fall of the Soviet Union, Cuba established a strong reputation among Third World countries as a leader in the health care field. This reputation was further bolstered by the large investments made by the government in the biotechnology industry. Biotechnology efforts were focused on vaccinations and anticholesterol drugs (Miller & Henthorne, 1997).

Technology alone did not gain Cuba its worldwide reputation of superiority in medicine. Cuban physicians are renown for their achievements in transplants—kidney, heart/lung, bone marrow, and scalp—as well as their advances in new medical treatments. Work is presently underway at one of the eleven research centers throughout the island on a mechanical heart. Additionally, Cuban hospitals have also been recognized for their treatment of diving injuries throughout the Caribbean.

For decades, the Cuban people enjoyed comfortable—though by no means extravagant—livelihoods based in large part upon economic subsidies received in exchange for at least nominal allegiance to the Soviet Union. With the dismantling of the Soviet Union came a re-examination and reorientation of priorities. Further problems erupted for Cuba as a result of U.S. policy. The trade embargo by the U.S. was tightened with the 1992 Torricelli Bill, which barred U.S. subsidiaries in other countries from doing business with Cuba. As a result of this and other bans imposed by the U.S. government, foreign aid to Cuba virtually disappeared (Cardenas, 1997; Kuntz, 1994). Despite the commitment to health, Cuban medicine and health care today suffer the same shortages as the rest of the country. As noted by Cardenas (1997), "Getting an aspirin in Cuba is next to impossible; however, if you need heart surgery or a liver transplant your medical care will be excellent." Medicine, medical equipment, and other health-related materials required hard currency. Unfortunately, expenditure of hard currency in the health care sector plummeted from $227 million (US$) in 1989 to $74 million in 1994 (Miller & Henthorne, 1997).

New methods for the generation of hard foreign exchange became a mantra of the Cuban government. Tourism, viewed by many Caribbean countries as the "last resort" (Pattullo 1996) and long shunned by Castro as imperialistic, elitist, and exploitive of the population, became the shining star upon which the country would peg its greatest hopes for not only economic survival, but for its resurgence in the global marketplace. Possibly unable to effectively compete "head to head" with the established tourism destinations of the Caribbean (e.g., Jamaica and the Dominican Republic), Cuba sought out a specialized, under-served, "niche" in the hotly competitive realm of Caribbean tourism—health tourism. The strategy was a very conscious decision—people value their health. "If people are nervous about keeping their jobs or having enough to pay the rent, they postpone vacations and big-ticket items" (Dickinson & Vladimir, 1997, p. 210). However, if they can find quality health care and, at the same time, enjoy the Caribbean experience, the journey becomes "more affordable."

3. Niche Tourism

A niche marketing strategy, like that implemented by Cuba, means finding an identifiable market segment—distinguishable by size, need, and/or objective—and attempting to dominate it (Cohen, 1998). The foundation for a successful niche strategy is that one entity can serve a specific segment of the market more effectively or efficiently than the competition.

While the competition is searching for the high-profile, high growth markets, the niche players are searching for the out-of-the way markets and specialty segments where the competition is less intense. Although the breadth of the target niche is clearly a matter of sufficient customer base, the essence of the niche strategy is "the exploitation of a narrow target's differences from the rest of the industry" (Porter, 1985, p. 15). This strategy can and does work because the niche may not be large enough to be worthwhile to larger competitors. Dominating in such a niche strategy involves the bundling of unique provider attributes which appeal to a substantially large sub-group within the larger market segment (Kotler, Bowen, and Makens, 1996). This is a real advantage because the entity that practices a niching strategy may be smaller, yet be the superior provider in the niche. This method of competition has been aptly labeled "guerrilla against gorilla" (Dalgic and Leeuw, 1994).

One niching strategy, identified by Drucker (1985), is particularly applicable to the present case: the specialty skill niching strategy. The specialty skill strategy can be used when the competing entity has a particular skill or set of skills that are visibly lacking in their competitors. In other words, they do something better than any of their competition; it is their distinctive competency (Porter, 1985). Cuba does this in health care. Cuba has long been recognized as a superior provider of affordable, yet technically advanced, health care services in the Caribbean and beyond. No other Caribbean country has the reputation or could conceivably rapidly develop the reputation currently enjoyed by Cuba. Nor does any other Caribbean country have such an highly educated population with which to exploit its reputation. It is estimated that 95 percent of the adult Cuban population can read and write (Kuntz, 1994; APHA, 1985). Thus, a niche in highly technical health services directed at the tourist market seemed a natural avenue for Cuba to pursue. Combining this recognized superiority with Cuba's ideal location and marketable attributes make it a natural tourist attraction of, in many eyes, unparalleled opportunity. Promoting and exploiting this distinctive advantage appeared to the Cuban government to be one method of capitalizing on this "unparalleled opportunity;" a relatively easy and low cost method of entering into the hotly competitive world tourism field. With the competition tight for tourist dollars throughout the Caribbean and with Cuba's inability, at present, to draw from the large and lucrative U.S. tourist market, Cuba was at a distinct competitive disadvantage for the mainstream Caribbean traveler. However, with its surplus of highly trained and skilled medical personnel, its reputation for specialized medical care, and the lack of large well established competitors, Cuba had all the accouterments for the development of specialized tourism devoted solely to health.

While many of the South American neighbors were previously bypassing Cuba for more costly medical care in the U.S., the government chose to strengthen its position in the health care arena by touting comparable care at considerably lower prices. By continuing to pay low wages, Cuban officials were looking at profit maximization while undercutting its competitors' pricing strategies.

The early successes experienced by Cuba in the burgeoning health tourism industry became instrumental in Cuba's very conscious decision to focus additional attention and resources, albeit limited, to this niche. Health tourism quickly came to be viewed as a means to help bolster or even ensure the country's economic survival. Additionally, tourism geared towards "curative health" appealed more to the Castro government as being "non-exploitive" of the population, yet allowing Cuba to become known world-wide as a desirable tourist destination. With the ratios of physicians to population far exceeding most developed nations, it would allow for more full utilization of talents while, at the same time, bringing hard currency to the government.

In carrying out a strategy of such magnitude, Cuba has been forced to flirt with and even embrace some market-oriented principles. The basic demographics and psychographics of this targeted health tourism market are very different from that of other visitors. Generally, this market is more upscale and demanding of quality service and care. While the highly competent health care component was undoubtedly present, Cuba was sorely lacking in the areas of efficiency, customer service, and promotion— all key components to making such a niche strategy work. In fact, survival using a niching strategy is largely dependent on the ability to be efficient and focused, coupled with an offer of exceptional customer service (Porter, 1985). Employee job proficiency is particularly important in the medical tourism industry due to the large number of "customer contact" employees needed. Bitner (1990) describes the delivery of a service as a "performance," featuring the employees who provide the service and the customer. It is during this performance that the actions and behaviors of service employees become the "crucial determinants of service quality as perceived by the customers" (Hartline & Ferrell, 1993, p. 1). Therefore, adequate employee training and job proficiency is critical to marketplace success. This is especially true when the niche market is medical care. In a country where medical personnel are paid barely livable wages, efficiency and quality customer service have not been high on the list of individual priorities. No incentives existed. Consequently, and interestingly, the strategy for marketplace survival in Cuba was to engage in the tactics of a market economy. Research suggests that the provision of quality care for travelers can often result in the most rapid return on monies invested

(Plock, 1996). This was obviously something of paramount importance to Cuba. Therefore, to compete effectively in health tourism, Cuba had to develop a for-profit entity, complete with built-in (albeit modest) employee incentives and an emphasis on highly skilled, proficient, customer-oriented, service providers.

4. Health Tourism Niche via Cubanacán

Health tourism in Cuba falls under the jurisdiction of Servimed which, in turn, falls under the auspices of Cubanacan, the government's for-profit umbrella agency for tourism. The placement of Servimed under Cubanacan was a deliberate business decision. In following the niche strategy concept, Servimed operates its facilities more as customer-oriented tourist destinations than traditional health care facilities, and it is strictly a commercial enterprise. Working closely with the Ministry of Health, Servimed owns and operates hospitals and polyclinics throughout the island dedicated strictly to the health care needs of tourists. Servimed is a for-profit venture separate from the Cuban health system; consequently, services are not free. Payment in a Servimed facility may be made in US dollars, or through insurance provided by one of the 86 worldwide insurance companies that have elected to do business with the Cuban government. Another marketing advantage—the cost of a visit to a Servimed facility is considerably less than one might find in other developed countries: $20 for an office visit and $25 for x-rays.

Servimed polyclinics are located throughout Cuba, with particular emphasis on the tourist areas. The polyclinic at Varadero Beach resembles an emergency care clinic in the U.S. The waiting room is pleasant and clean and there is an unmistakably sterile odor in the air. Examining rooms are modern and well-equipped. Interestingly, Cuba's full employment was evident at the Varadero Clinic where staffing levels are constant year round. The clinic employs five physicians, eight licensed nurses (one of whom serves as nursing director), one laboratory technician, one x-ray technician, one dentist, two pharmacists, and five other management and business office personnel. However, Servimed employees are all handpicked and focused on customer service. Some research suggests that this knowledge of being "singled out" is an intrinsic reward in itself, which, in turn, plays an important role in customer-oriented behavior (Hoffman & Ingram, 1992).

Clinic officials indicated that patient loads during the high tourist season averaged from eight patients per day to a maximum of 22 patients. Similar to most resort areas, typical ailments include over-eating, skin damage due to overexposure to the sun, and motorcycle accidents (Clift & Page, 1996).

While Servimed operates specialty hospitals throughout Cuba, non-specialty "tourist ailments" are handled at one of several full-service, top national hospitals. Because the method of payment and the level of service differ for tourists, as compared to the general population, specific hospital floors are designated in these facilities for health tourism. For example, Hermanos Ameijeiras Hospital, a 1400 bed tertiary care, multi-specialty facility located in the heart of Havana, has 112 beds designated solely for health tourism. However, it should be noted that the hospitals housing tourism floors are truly the finest hospitals in the country. Hermanos Ameijeiras is noted for achievements in bone marrow, kidney, heart, lung, and scalp transplants.

Servimed teamed up with Italian-owned Finmed in 1996 to announce a health tourism joint venture—Mediclub. The 200-room facility was slated to open in 1998 in Santa Lucia, on the north coast of Camaguey Province. This facility would provide clinical and stomatological treatment, as well as specialized therapy using medicinal mud (*Business TIPS* [on-line], 1996).

Despite the recent joint venture, Cuban-owned Servimed specialty facilities are the cog in the health tourism wheel. Hundreds of individuals are treated annually in the Underwater Medicine Center in Cardenas, Matanzas (near Varadero) because of its hyperbolic chamber and success rate in treating diving accidents. Anti-stress centers are located throughout the mountains of Holguin and Santiago de Cuba Provinces, serving the Caribbean as mental health get-aways for rest and medical care. Weight loss and other medically oriented spas are gaining recognition, such as Santa Maria del Rosario Spa in San Diego de los Banos, Pinar del Rio Province (Miller & Henthorne, 1997). However, one of the most talked about Servimed facilities in Cuba is Havana's world renowned Ophthalmology Surgery Center.

5. Case Example: Camilo Cienfuegos International Ophthalmology Center

Located in the center of Havana, Camilo Cienfuegos is an internationally acclaimed Servimed hospital dedicated to degenerative diseases of the retina. Its medical director, Dr. Orfilio Pelaez, has gained worldwide recognition for his treatment of retinitis pigmentosa. The hospital also provides a comprehensive medical care plan for its patients, including the specialties of internal medicine, pediatrics, odontology, anesthesiology, and gynecology.

The treatment of retinitis pigmentosa is what brings patients to Camilo Cienfuegos. Retinitis pigmentosa, also known as night blindness, is a degenerative hereditary disease of the eye that may lead to total blindness. Pelaez and his team of Cuban physicians and scientists have spent some 40 years devoted to studying potential therapies to stop the progress of this disease. Pelaez's treatment consists of a surgical technique associated with ozonotherapy, electrostimulation and vitamin therapy. Surgical indications and outcomes following Pelaez's treatment depend on the stage and manner of progressions of the disease. Better responses are likely obtained among patients in the earlier stages of the disease. While a cure for retinitis pigmentosa is yet to be discovered anywhere in the world, Pelaez has had a noted success rate. Statistics gathered at Camilo Cienfuegos indicate that visual sharpness improvement is evident in 70 percent of the patients. As a result of his noted success, physicians around the world travel to Cuba annually to train with Pelaez and his staff at Camilo Cienfuegos (Pelaez & Staff, 1997; Patient Information Brochure, 1997).

Upon entering the ninety-room, seven-floor facility, Camilo Cienfuegos appears every bit as comfortable and modern as any of the finest U.S. private and specialty hospitals. Patient rooms are comparable to private and semi-private rooms in top of the line U.S. facilities, both in décor and amenities. Private suites, available for the more affluent, are donned with leather furniture, color television, and a vase of flowers on the coffee table in the "living area." The bedrooms in the private suites look much like home: wooden dresser and headboard, a leather chair, and matching curtains and bedspread. Patient dining areas are located on each floor for those patients who prefer to socialize during their stay. At the end of one hallway stands a beautiful Steinway piano—a gift from three former patients: Canadian, German, and American.

Accommodations are not the only impressive aspects of Camilo Cienfuegos. Computerized diagnostic and treatment technologies are among the finest in the world. Clearly, the computer capabilities at Camilo Cienfuegos surpass anything found in any Cuban university.

The staff of Camilo Cienfuegos consists of only the top graduates and/or experienced nurses. A staff specialist heads each floor. The sixty-plus registered nurses assigned to the seven floors receive continuous training in both nursing and computer skills. While the nursing staff is paid equal to those in non-Servimed hospitals, a wage much too low on which to comfortably live, these nurses are often rewarded with bonuses once or twice a year. The nursing staff implied that it was considered an honor to be selected for a Servimed facility. However, the requirements are much more stringent. For example, at Camilo Cienfuegos nursing personnel are required to speak a second language — preferably English, although Portuguese and Italian may be acceptable. But the staff does not seem to mind the more stringent requirements; instead, they are focused on providing good customer service (Pelaez & Staff, 1997; Patient Information Brochure, 1997). Research suggests this satisfaction with work—being singled out as the "cream of the crop"—is the primary determinant of good customer service and, ultimately, customer satisfaction (Hartline & Ferrell, 1993). This might explain why, despite little more than word-of-mouth advertising, 1000 to 1500 patients visit this facility annually from some 65 countries, keeping the hospital at a steady 90 percent occupancy rate. While Brazilians and fellow South Americans rank highest among the tourists who frequent this facility, patients from Canada, Spain, Korea and the Arabian countries can likely be found at Camilo Cienfuegos. The U.S. government's preclusion of its citizens to travel to Cuba has not stopped the many individuals who find their way to Camilo Cienfuegos by way of Canada or Mexico (Pelaez & Staff, 1997; Patient Information Brochure, 1997).

6. Conclusions

Strategies for managing tourism growth in micro-destinations, like the Caribbean, must be based on "securing tourism markets that match their resources and use their competitive and comparative advantages" (Reid & Reid, 1994). Hard-pressed to compete for the broad-based Caribbean tourism dollar, Cuba has discovered what may be a profitable niche. Cuba has dedicated itself to international prominence in health tourism. Additionally, in an effort to bolster its position, Cuba has appropriated substantial resources to developing a marketing-oriented approach.

Despite the hardships placed on Cuba by the Torricelli Bill and subsequent bans imposed on Cuba by the U.S. government, Cuba has vowed to become a player in the global marketplace. In its dedication to health tourism, the Cuban government is achieving this goal. By exploiting health tourism through a for-profit entity, Cuba is treading waters nonexistent in forty-odd years. Through the institution of pricing policies that undercut the U.S. and other first world markets, Cuba is adapting to the laws of competition and profit maximization. By introducing a customer orientation into its product delivery, Cuba is carving out its own niche in the tourism market. Interestingly, for a country still under the auspices of a planned economy, Cuba's distinctive competency has all the trappings of a market economy.

REFERENCES

American Public Health Association (1985) "Government Responsibility and the People's Health," in *Program and Abstracts of the 113th Annual Meeting of the*

American Public Health Association (Washington D.C.: American Public Health Association).

Bahamas Tourism Statistics (1987) (Nassau, Bahamas: Ministry of Tourism).

Bitner, M.J. (1990) "Evaluating Service Encounters: The Effects of Physical Surrounding and Employee Responses," *Journal of Marketing*, Volume 54 (April), pp. 69-82.

Business TIPS (Technical Information Promotion System) on Cuba. August, 1996. http://www. cubaweb.cu/tips/index.html.

Cardenas, A.D. (1997) Dean, College of Economics, University of Havana, Personal Interview.

Clift, S. and S.J. Page (1996) *Health and the International Tourist* (London: Routledge Press).

Cohen, W. A. (1998) *The Marketing Plan* (2nd edition) (New York: John Wiley & Sons, Inc.).

Dalgic, T. and M. Leeuw (1994) "Niche Marketing Revisited: Concept, Applications, and Some European Cases," *European Journal of Marketing* Volume 28, Number (4), pp. 39-55.

Dickinson, B. and A. Vladimir (1997) *Selling the Sea: An Inside Look at the Cruise Industry* (New York: John Wiley & Sons, Inc.).

Drucker, P. F. (1985) *Innovation and Entrepreneurship* (New York: Harper & Row).

Economist (1996) "Heroic illusions: A Survey of Cuba," April 6.

Goodrich, J. N. (1993) "Socialist Cuba: A Study of Health Tourism," *Journal of Travel Research* (Summer), pp. 36-41.

Goodrich, J. N. (1994) "Health Tourism: A New Positioning Strategy for Tourism Destinations," *Global Tourist Behavior*, pp. 227-238.

Goodrich, J. N. and G. E. Goodrich (1987) "Health-Care Tourism: An Exploratory Study," *Tourism Management* (September) pp. 217-222.

Harrison, D., D. R. Hall, and D. Harrison (1992) *Tourism Development in Cuba* (London: Belhaven Press).

Hartline, M. D. and O. C. Ferrell (1993) *Service Quality Implementation: The Effects of Organizational Socialization and Managerial Actions on Customer-Contact Employee Behaviors.* Technical Working Paper for the Marketing Science Institute, Report No. 93-122, Cambridge, Massachusetts.

Hoffman, K. D. and T. N. Ingram (1992) "Service Provider Job Satisfaction and Customer-Oriented Performance," *Journal of Service Marketing*, Volume 6, Number 2 (Spring), pp. 68-78.

Kotler, P. (1997) *Marketing Management: Analysis, Planning, Implementation, and Control* (7th edition) (Upper Saddle River, New Jersey: Prentice-Hall).

Kotler, P., J. Bowen, and J. Makens (1996) *Marketing for Hospitality and Tourism* (Upper Saddle River, New Jersey: Prentice-Hall).

Kuntz, D. (1994) "The Politics of Suffering: The Impact of the US Embargo on the Health of the Cuban People," *International Journal of Health Services*, Volume 24, pp. 161-179.

Miller, M. and T. Henthorne (1997) *Investment in the New Cuban Tourist Industry: A Guide to Entrepreneurial Opportunities* (Westport, Connecticut: Quorum Books).

Moraguez, M. M. (1997) Specialist in Ecotourism and Marketing, College of Economics, University of Havana, Personal Interview.

Nayeri, K. (1995) "The Cuban Health Care System and the Factors Currently Undermining It," *Journal of Community Health*, Volume 20, Number 4, pp. 321-334.

Niv, A. (1989) "Health Tourism in Israel: A Developing Industry," *Economic and Tourism Consultancy*, Volume 44, Number 4, pp. 30-32.

Officials of Hermanes Ameijenes Hospital, Personal Interview, 1997.

Patient Information Brochure, Camilo Cienfuegos International Ophthalmology Center, 1997.

Pattullo, P. (1996) *Last Resorts: The Cost of Tourism in the Caribbean* (London: Cassell Press).

Pelaez, O. and Staff (1997) Medical Director Camilo Cienfuegos, Personal Interview.

Plock, Ernest (1996) "The Global Healthcare Services Market is Growing Fast as Foreign Consumers Look for Better Medical Care," *Business America*, Volume 117, Number 7 (July), pp. 18-20.

Porter, M.E. (1985) *Competitive Advantage* (New York: Free Press).

_____(1980) *Competitive Strategy* (New York: Free Press).

Reid, S. D. and L. J. Reid (1994) "Tourism Marketing Management in Small Island Nations: A Tale of Micro-Destinations," *Journal of International Consumer Marketing*, Volume 6, Numbers 3-4, pp. 39-60.

Swanson, J. M. (1987) "Nursing in Cuba: Population-focused Practice," *Public Health Nursing*, Volume 4, Number 3, pp. 183-191.

Tancer, R. S. (1995) "The Pharmaceutical Industry in Cuba," *Clinical Therapeutics*, Volume 17, Number 4, pp. 791-798.

16

External Finances and the Limits of Economic Growth in Cuba: 1996-1997

Julio Carranza

This chapter provides information about developments in the Cuban economy between 1996-1997 and the degree to which external financing has been at the heart of Cuban economic recovery. The Cuban government is advised to continue making internal adjustments that would enable the country to maintain its heralded social gains while at the same time increasing internal economic efficiency.

External finances constitute a point of contention in the contemporary Cuban economy. The economic revitalization that has been achieved since 1994 has not allowed Cuba to free itself from the burden of external debt, the inequalities of the balance of payments, and the lack of stable sources of financing. The fundamental issue is to acknowledge the duration of these inequalities and identify alternative strategies for overcoming these problems.

The tension from external finances goes back to the early 1980s when global economic tendencies and pressures from the United States embargo caused a drastic reduction of credits in U.S. dollars. During the 1970s, Cuba had succeeded in obtaining important sources of financing from several capitalist countries. However, since 1979 the situation changed, the price of sugar dropped, interest rates increased, and inflationary pressures increased in the industrialized economies. These developments were all exacerbated by the economic pressures from the United States.

By the middle of 1982, the Cuban government asked its creditors to re-negotiate its debt—which at that time amounted to 2.914 billion dollars. As a result of this request, Cuba obtained a reasonable agreement that did not, however, free the country from its economic problems. On the contrary, the problems were worsened due to the constant, negative developments in the sugar markets. In 1984 and 1985 a new debt repayment schedule agreement was reached.

In 1986 additional factors aggravated the economic problems in Cuba, and, thus, the possibilities to fulfill the demands of the debt repayment program, even under the more favorable conditions negotiated in the previous two years. The availability of currency was affected by the fall of oil prices, because through the agreements with the Soviet Union, Cuba was able to export Soviet oil that was saved as a result of Cuban national austerity. In addition, the American dollar, which Cuba used for international exchange, was devalued in 1986. Furthermore, unfavorable weather conditions affected Cuban exports. This situation compelled the government of Cuba to request new renegotiations of its debt. Although Cuba succeeded in having the governments of the creditor countries sign an agreement, the banks declined the new credits which were derived from such agreements. Given these conditions, it became impossible for the Cuban government to continue making the corresponding payments that had been suspended since the second half of 1986. Since that date, the Cuban economy practically lost access to both medium and long-term international credits in dollars.

During the years 1982-1988, the socialist countries maintained relations with Cuba on much more favorable terms within the context of an economic integration with those countries. In reaction to the closing of credits from the West, the Cuban government increased aggressively its commercial and financial relations with the socialist countries. By 1989, more than 86 percent of Cuba's external trade was with the socialist countries. With the dissolution of the Soviet Union and therefore the elimination of the Council of Mutual Economic Assistance (CMEA), this compensation was lost. The Cuban economy was suddenly and totally exposed to the global market where it had lost all its credits. Furthermore, the North American market, the closest and most important for Cuba, remained closed because of an embargo policy that was further reinforced by the Torricelli (1992) and Helms Burton (1996) laws.

The Cuban economy entered a new phase in 1990. Characterized by a double process of profound economic crisis and major changes in the organization of the internal economy, the country began a process of insertion into the international circles of capitalist commerce, finance, and investment.

Between 1989 and 1993 the GNP decreased by 37.8 percent; from 1994 to 1996 an increase of 10.4 percent was achieved (7.8 percent during 1996). However, in both periods there was an increase in the country's external debt in dollars. The increased debt was not due to increments of long and medium-term credits—which remained virtually closed—but because of other factors over which Cuba had no control. The accumulation of unpaid interest and the need for short-term credit with very harsh conditions escalated after 1994 when the recovery of the economy demanded increased imports.[1] By 1996, the short-term credits were approximately $2.4 billion dollars.[2]

Variations of the dollar's exchange rate in international markets have also influenced the level of Cuba's debt. After 1994, there has been a tendency for the value of the dollar to appreciate, and this resulted in the re-valuation of the Cuban currency. In 1996 this factor caused a slight (39.5 million dollars) reduction in Cuba's debt. In 1994 the debt in dollars was 9.08 billion dollars, it rose to 10.5 billion in 1995, and in 1996 it fell slightly to 10.466 billion dollars.[3]

Energy deficiency has fiercely affected the economy, especially the national industry. The growth in productivity has brought an increase in the consumption of energy and fuel, which must be imported; and every rise in the cost of fuel in the international market meant an increase in Cuba's foreign debt.[4]

As we can see in the following table, the relation of debt to GNP (market prices) has not facilitated an economic recovery.

Table 1: Relation of Debt as percentage of GNP (market prices)

1990	1991	1992	1993	1994	1995	1996
34.0	NA	52.1	58.2	47.3	48.5	46.4

Source: Author's calculations

If the GNP were measured with an economically grounded exchange rate,[5] and not with the official rate (1 peso = 1 U.S. dollar, an artificial overvaluation of the Cuban currency), this relation would have been much higher. Between 1993 and 1994, the deterioration of the debt to GNP ratio was noticeably reduced (market prices) due to two fundamental reasons. First, Cuba was able to reduce its debt with Mexico through an exchange transaction of debt versus investments (swaps) in the areas of construction materials and telecommunications. Second, in that year Cuba experienced a remarkable price increase as part of the crisis alleviation policy of internal finances, which had a great impact in the growth of the GNP, as measured in market prices.

The relation between debt and exports of goods and services also shows tensions, while the relation of debt repayment service versus exports cannot be measured, although this is the most appropriate indicator to assess the impact of Cuba's debt upon the country's resources. The amount of the annual payments has not been officially reported, but it is known that the debt ratio has been reduced.

Table 2: Relation of Debt as a Percentage of Goods and Services

1993	1994	1995	1996
446	357.3	357.8	273

Source: Author's calculations

The reduction in this relation between 1993 and 1994 is mainly due to the reasons previously mentioned with regards to the swaps with Mexico. The best result (corresponding to the year 1996) is due to the growth in exports that year—as well as to the slight reduction of the debt—thanks to the revaluation of the dollar. It is important to point out two evident facts in this chart. First, the increase in the exports of goods and services corresponding to the growth period 1994-1996 has allowed a favorable reduction of the debt. Second, however, the relation continues to be tense, and the debt reduction is still insufficient.

As shown in Tables 1 and 2, the recovery of the GNP that has been achieved since 1994 has not been able to free Cuba from the burdens of external debt. It is necessary to keep in mind that these calculations do not include Cuba's debt with the former socialist European countries (of which the Soviet Union is the most important). The Soviet debt has taken a complicated negotiating course, in the sense that there are no longer the participants, the institutions, the currencies, and most importantly, the countries to which the debt was contracted. Instead, there has been a radical change in the conditions of the economic agreements under which they were created. This takes us to an unconcluded discussion regarding the amount, payment conditions, etc. Both sides are willing to find a reasonable and progressive solution. At this moment, however, that debt does not pose a strong enough pressure on the Cuban economy. Yet it is a problem that can neither be forgotten nor neglected.

2. Debt Structure

The major burden of external debt can be summarized as 80.9 percent corresponding to principal, and 19.1 percent to the overdue interest payments. Sixty percent of the total debt is concentrated in five creditor countries: Japan, Argentina, Spain, France, and the United Kingdom. Two Latin American countries appear as creditors, Argentina with 12.8 percent, and Mexico with 4.4 percent.

Table 3: Structure of the Debt by Countries (1996, in percentages)

Japan	15.7	Mexico	4.4
Argentina	12.8	Switzerland	2.6
Spain	12.1	Germany	2.2
France	10.2	Austria	2.1
United Kingdom	9.8	Other Countries	23.2
Italy	4.9		

Source: *Economic Report 1996 BNC* (Cuban National Bank).

Table 4: Structure of the Debt by Currency (in percentages)

Mark	26.4	Canadian Dollar	5.4
Yen	19.1	French Franc	4.4
USD	22.0	Sterling Pound	3.0
Swiss Franc	7.6	Other Currencies	6.8
Peseta	5.3		

Source: *Economic Report 1996, BNC* (Cuban National Bank).

3. Balance of Payments

Table 5 presents the changes in the balance of payments, in order to consider the implications in the national economy and its alternatives. To better understand the balance of payments, it is necessary to explain some of its elements. The account of the long-term capital flows in 1994 includes not only what corresponds to that year, but also the accumulation up to that date. The reason is that the statistical records of the previous years were not officially presented, so they were added onto the other

Table 5: Balance of Payments (Cuba) in millions of dollars.

	1994	1995	1996	1997
Balance of the Current Account	-260.2	-517.7	-137.2	-515.1
Balance of Trade	-971.4	-1484.3	-1760.7	-2468.1
Exports of Goods and Services	2552.8	2935.6	3834.4	4132.7
Goods	1381.4	1507.3	1849.6	1860.7
Services	1160.4	1418.9	1841.3	2072.0
Income	11.0	9.4	143.5	200.0
Imports of Goods and Services	3283.2	4099.5	4715.3	5548.8
Goods	2352.8	2991.6	3610.3	4328.8
Services	496.6	573.7	468.9	520.0
Revenue	-433.8	-534.2	-636.1	-700.0
Ordinary Transfer (net)	470.2	646.2	743.7	900.0
Long-term Capital	817.4	24.2	233.8	
Direct Investment	563.4	4.7	8.0	
Other	254.0	19.5	225.8	
Other Capital (net)	-555.0	572.0	-89.0	
Reserve Variance	-2.2	-78.5	7.6	
Memo Accounts Reappraisals of Assets and Liabilities	-617.0	-533.7	-847.5	

Source: Economic Report of the Cuban National Bank of the corresponding years. Figures for 1997 are the author's estimations.

year so that the information would not be lost. This explains the remarkable difference between 1994 and 1995-1996 in the entry of "Direct Investment."

The division of the relations between the different accounts reveals the persistent deficits of the balance of payments, even in those years during which the recovery process of the GNP began. The commercial deficit was increased by 52.8 percent in 1995, 18.65 percent in 1996, and 28.7 percent in 1997. In addition to the increase in imports, the result has heavily affected the deterioration in terms of exchange trade, which in 1996 was 21.3 percent and 1.5 percent in 1997.

The deficit in the balance of goods and services grew by 59.3 percent in 1995; and it only dropped to 24.3 percent in 1996, and grew again by 37.8 percent in 1997 despite the growth in export of services such as tourism, air transportation and international communications during that year. These have been three of the most dynamic sectors of the Cuban economy in the last few years.

The deficit in the current account grew by 98.9 percent in 1995, it then dropped by 73.5 percent in 1996, and then increased again by 73.5 percent in 1997. The item that somewhat compensated for this deficit has been money transfers which have grown from 470.2 million dollars in 1994, to 646.2 million dollars in 1995, and an estimated 743.7 million for 1996 and 900 million for 1997. These figures include remittances and donations, the biggest part of which comes from remittances by Cubans living overseas to their relatives on the island. Of this, the largest portion arrives to the island through informal channels, because the restrictions imposed by the embargo have prevented direct transactions from the U.S. At the beginning of 1998, the United States government allowed the Cuban communities to send directly up to $300 every three months. This is part of a set of measures that includes, as well, the reestablishment of direct flights between Miami and Havana, which were suspended in 1996 as a consequence of the incident involving the airplanes. These new measures may help the inflow of capital from the U.S.

However, hoping that this factor alone would allow a major expansion and impact on the Cuban economy necessitates the need for deep reflection upon this issue. In order to overcome the current figures with money transfers, there would have to be a profound change in the economic policies that would allow this capital to be used for small and medium size family investment, as well as seeking new channels to increase domestic savings. However, a decision of this nature cannot be taken for the exclusive purpose of stimulating these net transfers because such a decision would touch upon a very sensitive area of the economic model which is being built. A decision—positive or negative—about this issue, has to be part of a global analysis regarding the economic changes and the quality of the reconfiguration that has to take place.

The registered introduction of "Direct Investments" is still very low, despite the expectations and the importance that has been attached to this factor in the national financial recovery strategy. It is necessary to distinguish between the figures, much higher, of the capital involved in the different negotiations taking place, and that of the capital already invested in the country, which is what is reflected in the balance of payments.[6]

The account "Other Capital," which includes short-term assets and debits (in addition to errors and omissions) was a negative figure of 555 million pesos in 1994; it became a positive figure of 572.5 million dollars in 1995, and a negative of 89 million in 1996. These movements are due to various reasons: first, the fact is that errors and omissions are included, which works as an adjustment account; and second, the diverse impact that the short-term credits have had, depending on its amount and payment moment, that have been derived from the GNP recovery. For the year 1996 the result of this account reflected a net increase in the net short-term assets.

4. Final Considerations

Analysis of external finances allows us to establish the differences between the resources generated and the resources which are actually available. In this sense, it becomes important to keep in mind the different proportions. The Cuban economy has managed to reverse the strong setback relative to economic growth between 1990 and 1993. Although the growth rate is still very far from the levels reached in the 1980s, it has nevertheless relatively improved the situation. Cuba is now in a more favorable position to allow the country to definitely and strategically overcome the economic crisis.

However, as we have seen, the growth of the economy has not overcome, and in many cases has caused, the balance of payments disequilibrium. By the end of 1997, it was evident that the situation was tense when compared to the end of 1996. A key issue within the current context is to determine the duration of these imbalances.

The deficits are out of proportion, and they constitute an obstacle to open international credits and to the support of international financial institutions. This last problem is further aggravated by the hostile policies (pressures) of the United States' embargo.

Two fundamental questions are necessary to put the imbalances in perspective: what is the level of manageable imbalance, and for how long? How should the available resources be utilized? This last question refers to the determination of the appropriate proportion between investment and consumption, and more specifically between investment in those sectors that produce exportable goods and investment in those sectors that produce goods for the internal market, as well as between the personal consumption and social consumption.

The answers to these questions become more complex if one keeps in mind that the crisis has driven investments as much as consumption to dramatically low levels, and economic recovery in the last few years has been minimal. In this context the need to continue generating external resources is quite evident. There is also the need to encourage internal savings on the basis of greater efficiency. To conclude this chapter, an attempt is made to analyze thoroughly the alternatives relative to any successful attempt to manage the economic crisis.

The current model of accumulation, with high external dependency, does not allow Cuba to sustain a high rate of growth. It is necessary to determine and maintain the growth rate of the GNP at a level that would not aggravate the external imbalances. Furthermore, it is necessary to prioritize the growth of the sectors that generate income in foreign currency based on a dynamic policy that would have greater productive repercussions and also integrate the internal economic sectors. Strategically decisive should be the systematic restructuring of industrial policies of the country (its model of accumulation) in order to lower the degree of external dependency and to enable Cuban industries to be competitive in the global economy.

The aforesaid demands a complex and precise design of an accumulation policy. With this, Cuba would bring into play variables that are important for the future of the country not only on the economic terrain, but also in the political and social areas. In fact, the search for a quick structural change in terms of the growth of competitive exports has been the recent experience of many Latin American countries, and they have resulted in high social costs and political crises. The Latin America method, under pressures from international financial organizations, has been to devalue currencies and liberalize their economies by deregulating and privatizing the nation's assets without limitations.

In Cuba, we have to confront this process by using a different model. We have the possibility of measuring and planning the most adequate proportions, both economically and politically. The combined utilization of market mechanisms is necessary and includes the opening of new areas and the establishment of an exchange rate economically grounded in terms of these objectives and with directive mechanisms and strategic planning. It is necessary to keep in mind, for example, that an excessive reduction in imports and products for the internal market could reduce consumption beyond the politically advisable levels.

The issue of interest rates deserves an in-depth analysis because the expression "economically grounded exchange rate" is inaccurate and insufficient to explain what we really mean when we refer to it. The exchange rate acquires major importance as an instrument of economic policy only when the internal markets reach a greater structure and development within a decentralized economy including the existence of currency markets regulated by the state. This, in turn, gives way to an internal convertibility of the national currency. Within this context the exchange rate works as a valuable instrument to achieve the objectives established by the development strategy. In the current conditions its role is passive.

Foreign investment constitutes a fundamental and essential point in this strategy. In it, there is an irreplaceable source of capital, markets, and cutting edge technology. However, it is also a vehicle of severe risk potentials. It is very important that foreign investment policy continues to use the adequate safeguards that do not compromise the economic sovereignty of Cuba. We should prevent the inflow of foreign investment from becoming so basically structured by incentives that it gains access to a qualified labor force at relatively—perhaps ridiculously—inexpensive rates of pay. This would establish an excessive transfer of funds from the country, and, in the medium-term, would affect the expectations and interests of the workers.

Cuba should accomplish a greater orientation of foreign investment toward the competitive products that generate a greater inflow of foreign currency. We have noticed lately that there is an excessive tendency to dispute areas in the captive internal market that have been structured since the remissions from Cubans overseas, tourism, and the needs of factors of production within the national economy.

There are two fundamental and sensitive problems that affect the development of the country and its re-insertion in the global economy, issues of strategic importance that require further debate: (1) To increase the efficiency of the internal economy, an area where Cuba has been making progress in the last few years through the economic changes that the government has implemented. However, this process has to be analyzed with more coherence, depth and detail; (2) Re-negotiation of the debt. Here is another occasion to remedy the inequalities of the external finances. The Cuban National Bank has held informal meetings with the Secretary of the Club of Paris, with the purpose of establishing a continuous dialogue that allows us to re-initiate analysis of the Cuban external debt. This issue requires taking into account the pressures imposed by the United States government as part of its aggressive policy towards Cuba.

The options may create the conditions to increase the payments, analyze and alter the transactions of debt-investment and debt-exports, transactions that allow us to convert short-term credits into long-term credits. We might consider purchase of the Cuban debt in secondary markets (this transaction is limited because when it begins, the exchange rate immediately increases). There might be greater utilization of the different techniques of financial engineering such as Commodities Linked Transactions (CLT), or others that might help improve the quality of the external financing.

As we have seen, the study of external finances constitutes a fundamental issue in the analysis of the current Cuban economy and its panorama. Its revision brings about more global considerations that results in other ideas of economic changes and the resistance against international pressures. While the Cuban government and the Cuban people have advanced a great deal, it is necessary to continue analyzing and improving our position in the new global context.

ENDNOTES

1. In the work by Hiram Marquetti Nodarse, *La deuda externa de Cuba en monedas convertibles: evolución y perspectivas de solución* CEEC, 1996, we can find an interesting presentation of all this process.
2. Interview with the Secretary of Planing and Finance, José Luis Rodriguez, by the Spanish newspaper *El País*, in January 1997.
3. Annual reports from the Cuban National Bank (BNC).
4. See Hiram Marquetti, *Evolución del sector industrial en 1996*, and the "Informe sobre los resultados económicos de 1996 y el plan económico y social para 1997," in *Granma*, December 27, 1996, where it is stated: "the physical consumption of fuel and lubricants, excluding the population, grew eight percent, which is a higher figure than the 7.8 percent growth in GNP. In terms of value, energy consumption grew by 24 percent."
5. On the meaning of the expression "economically grounded exchange rate" we will expound later.
6. The "*Informe sobre el Plan Económico y Social para 1996*" presented by the Secretary of Planing and Finance explains that the commitment of the foreign investment until that date was 2.1 billion dollars. See *Granma*, December 27, 1995.

17

The Urban Challenge in Cuba: Socially and Environmentally Sound Research in "Tropical Suburbia[1]

Julia R. Nevárez

This chapter reflects upon the experience of the author who conducted research in Cuba in 1993 and 1994, during the "Special Period." The joint research project involved community organizations from Pogolotti District, a suburb in the City of Havana, professors and students from the Center for the Study of Tropical Architecture, and the Environmental Psychology Ph.D. Program of the City University of New York (CUNY).

1. Introduction

To identify urban problems and offer solutions were the main goals of the research agenda for the professors and students from the City University of New York (CUNY) and the Center for Tropical Architecture,[2] as they identified and evaluated the conditions for open space in Pogolotti (Boveland and Berg, 1993). The research methods included interviews with residents of the neighborhoods in the Pogolotti District and walks through the neighborhoods to identify the conditions of open space in the district. Based on interview research results, the community representatives, professors, and students conceived a plan for the construction of a children's playground and vegetable garden (Nevárez, 1993). Another research component involved the on-going evaluation of the development of the children's community garden (Low, Oliver, Nevárez and Tillet, 1994).

The purpose of the garden space was twofold: (1) to provide a public open space for community residents; and (2) to develop sustainable development techniques. The objective of creating a public open space was to improve and sustain social relations among the different groups in the community. With the exception of the streets, there was a lack of formal public spaces for communal recreational activities. Additionally, limited means of transportation restricted Pogolotti residents' access to leisure activities in Havana's downtown (movie theaters, the Malecon, or Old Havana).

The sustainable development component was suggested by way of introducing the technique of composting, whereby members of the community would collect organic residue to be used in the children's vegetable garden. The technique of composting was viewed as a long-term opportunity to promote sustainable development strategies to increase food availability. This experience took place during the "Special Period" when the collapse of the Eastern bloc and its subsequent impact on the Cuban economy forced the population into a situation of serious economic hardship with food shortage.

Some background information regarding urbanism in Cuba, the "Special Period," the Pogolotti District, and early initiatives by the Cuban revolutionary government to bridge the gap between rural and urban areas, particularly the *Cordón Urbana de La Habana*, (Havana's Urban Greenbelt) is necessary to understand the positive and negative features of our research project. The community garden is discussed as a vehicle to promote social and environmentally sound initiatives in the context of broader urban issues. Yet the specifics of the location under study are always moderated by the effects of Cuba's "Special Period." Finally, I will discuss some of my own reflections about the research project and the limitations for outside researchers and for local residents.

2. Background Notes: Urbanism, the "Special Period," and Pogolotti

Since the Spanish colonial period, cities in Cuba developed near the ports. The distribution of urban agglomeration was determined by a transportation network system based on an export economy. The insertion of land transportation, such as railroads and highways, connected the ports to new developing centers. During the early part of the twentieth century, new forms of transportation were mainly determined by the requirements of the sugar industry.

The latifundio economy of the nineteenth century in Cuba resulted in the formation of a large rural wage workers sector, which strongly influenced the urbanization process. Due to the seasonal character of the sugar economy, this population of workers moved back and forth between the rural areas and the city, creating distinct patterns of development between the city and rural areas in Cuba

(Pérez-Stable, 1993). The advantages of the urban areas over the rural areas were mainly reflected in housing, household goods and wages. The rural areas had a housing shortage in addition to a dispersed population.

After the revolution of 1959, the state accomplished relative success with policies aimed at promoting national development of the island. Some of these policies were designed to help diminish the gap between urban and rural areas. Three laws were implemented to improve the rural and urban conditions in Cuba: the First Agrarian Reform Law; the Second Agrarian Reform Law; and the Urban Reform Law (Acosta & Hardoy, 1971). The main objective of the First and Second Agrarian Reform Laws was to gradually redistribute rural land. The redistribution consisted of transforming the ownership of lands to peasant proprietors and to the state.

The Urban Reform Law, in a different setting, gradually transformed the ownership of properties to urban dwellers, and made other changes.[3] Under the Urban Reform Law, the function of land bordering Havana was also re-defined. According to Acosta and Hardoy (1971), the Havana Urban Greenbelt (*El Cordón urbano de La Habana*) was developed under the Urban Reform Law to promote self-sufficiency rather than dependency on more distant rural products.

Residents of the Province of Havana began to implement a special regional program in 1967. The Havana Urban Greenbelt, which included twelve to fifteen kilometers of land moving outward from the city limits and encircling the city, was to be allocated for agriculture and landscaping. This initiative incorporated small farmers into the economic programs of the Revolution, created water reservoir ponds and new towns, promoted urban folks' participation in agricultural tasks, and created urban parks such as the Zoological Garden, Botanical Garden, Lenin Park, and Metropolitan Park that was contiguous to the Pogolotti Community. The Urban Greenbelt initiative helped supply much needed water in the city as well as recreational public spaces. However, one of the main social changes that this program brought to the city was the conversion of agriculture into an urban civilian activity.

Pogolotti District was exposed to self-sufficiency practices similar to what has been recently called "sustainable development." Although different in its origins, the objective of implementing agricultural production in the urban context is a mode for developing self-sufficiency in the production of basic resources, such as food. The origins of sustainable development sprout from environmental movements and an awareness of global environmental issues. However, it is at the local level that remedies and alternatives are concretized (Adams, 1990).

This urban agricultural effort was not something new to the Cuban society in the 1990s. By being subjected to the U.S. embargo, even before the Soviets stepped in to do business with Cuba, the revolutionary leaders were trying to develop new options for the development of an independent and diversified economy. Throughout the twentieth century, in fact, the goal of self sufficiency was always part of the Cuban agenda. However, this chapter cannot discuss the success or failure of a diversified Cuban economy, neither earlier in the century nor under the revolutionary government. Suffice it to say that with the collapse of the Eastern European Bloc and the disintegration of the Soviet Union, Cuba's capacity to survive against the U.S. embargo was threatened. With the collapse of the Eastern Bloc and the end of trade agreements, the government in Cuba could no longer provide all the services and resources it had made available to the Cuban population.

The effort to create the children's community garden in Pogolotti is one instance of the insertion of agricultural practices into an urban context for sustainable development. These efforts were prompted by the critical situation of the "Special Period". The project was then supported by a pre-existing culture of urban agriculture already in place due to previous efforts such as those promoted by the Havana Cordón initiative. Pogolotti's location made it especially attractive.

3. Pogolotti: "Tropical Suburbia" at the Edge of the City

Pogolotti is a suburb in Marianao, located at the southwest edge of Havana City. Built in 1911, Pogolotti was the first urban enclave for working class residents. Approximately 2,590 residents, most of them between the ages of twenty-six and fifty years, live in Pogolotti and are linked to downtown Havana by paved roads. The population essentially moves in public buses and on bicycles. The majority of buses are old models, and the number is insufficient. All the vehicles are very crowded at all hours. Urban transport is one of the most burdensome problems that city dwellers face on a regular basis.

The District of Pogolotti includes three distinct neighborhoods—Finlay, Pogolotti, and the Isle of Dust.[4] The size of the houses, the open spaces for community use, and the width of the streets gradually diminish throughout the three neighborhoods from Finlay to the Island of Dust. Finlay has the largest residences with front and back yards alongside wide paved streets. The spatial organization in this neighborhood suggests affluence when compared with the two other neighborhoods. People use their backyards or any other available land in their property to grow vegetables, keep chickens and/or pigs. The houses in Finlay, by having more spacious backyards, enjoy the use of more land for gardening. Residences in Pogolotti are aligned in rows that are narrower compared to Finlay, with small front yards and back yards. Residents have altered the shape of their houses to replace the original peaked roofs by cement roofs that support additional levels of rooms and residential space. The streets of Pogolotti are narrow and some of them are unpaved. Both Finlay and Pogolotti have fewer trees than the Isle of Dust, which is contiguous to the Metropolitan Park, an area with more lush green bushes and trees.

The Isle of Dust houses are shacks made of wood and sheet metal, built firmly along narrow alleys. The surrounding front and back yards in the Isle of Dust are sparkling clean in appearance. Another distinctive demographic characteristic of the Isle of Dust is that most residents belong to the African religion of Abacuá in which the "Ceiba" tree is a sacred icon. The predominant religious belief of Finlay and Pogolotti residents is Catholicism.

Pogolotti was selected as the locale for the community project because it had already in place a community organization to deal with urban issues from the local initiative perspective. Even though there were no visible social tensions in the community, the idea of developing the children's community garden was also conceived to provide a space for recreational activities where members of different age groups and different social groups (i.e., members of the three neighborhoods and religious backgrounds) could enjoy an open space for communal activities.

4. Alternatives, Possibilities and the Pitfalls
of Collaborative Efforts for Social and Environmentally
Sound Community Projects

Local communities are the most basic units to promote sound social and environmental projects that may also be able to advance economic initiatives. The scale in which this attempt was proposed in the Pogolotti community was the most basic one. By promoting community involvement and the introduction of new technologies such as composting in this neighborhood, it was possible to plan the development of a children's community garden as a space for social interaction, environmental awareness, and sustainable food production.

The "Special Period" has offered the opportunity to accept the challenges raised when traditional ways are no longer effective means of producing goods. There is a sense of empowerment for people participating in the transformation of their environments.[5] For the Cuban people the "Special Period" is still a challenge for the transition between a highly centralized government and the development of local initiatives. In dealing with alternatives for the production of food the technique of local organic composting was essential, given the lack of other fertilizers. The transitional character of the "Special Period" suggests that many new adaptations for survival may become more long-term conditions for domestic food production. This process helps illustrate the connections between broader historical trends and the specifics of local applications. These connections are not always smooth.

A community organization network, the Integrated Development Workshops, worked with the development of grassroots solutions to urban problems. The main principles that guided the community workshops were to develop local initiatives utilizing local knowledge and resources, and to diminish the dependency on the centralized Cuban government. The trajectory of this process, however, seemed to lead to conflict between former and new modes of community organizing, principles, and initiatives. In terms of leadership, this was shown in the change of workshop leaders twice during the time of our research project. These changes affected the process of building contacts and developing working relations for research purposes. The process of continuity was challenged each time different and new persons were introduced, and this involved also getting re-acquainted with different leadership styles. This was as true for local residents as it was for the students and professors who came from New York City to participate in the project.

The clash between new ways of developing local initiatives and former centralized government practices was also visible in the attempts to determine where the community children's garden was to be built. There were open spaces available in the community for the children's garden; they included publicly and privately owned, neglected or abandoned spaces, under-used lots and garbage dumps. However, the process to obtain government approval for the construction of the children's garden at any of the specific sites considered was lengthy and the site was changed a couple of times because of conflicts of usage with community members who already utilized those spaces. At that time, 1993-1994, later assessed as the two worst years for living conditions by the Cuban population, the potential value of animal grazing for production of milk—and possibly for some very rare meat—may have been a highly significant psychological factor.

A plan for the use of land and the vegetable garden was proposed, based on the research results. However, during the time in which I participated in the research, the community children's garden could not be constructed. In another research context like New York City, some conditions such as availability of tools, other materials, and the means to transport them are usually taken for granted. A researcher who comes from abroad may take a great deal for granted. A researcher working on the island of Cuba requires a time-consuming process of familiarizing herself or himself with the local Cuban political system and society.

Another unanticipated hindrance was the overwhelming number of simultaneous projects and initiatives in which the Workshop for Integrated Development was involved. The community-based organization was itself over-worked due to the critical situation of the "Special Period" and the precarious sources to satisfy the most basic needs. For instance, the workshop was also involved in the construction of housing units by community members who were using new technologies and materials locally produced. Because of the local character of these initiatives, the capacities and abilities of the community members were stretched to the limit.

Finally, the research component for the community children's garden was planned to include the documentation of the process with two components: the first included documentation by the CUNY team while visiting; and the second documentation on a daily basis done by community residents. It was unrealistic to place this emphasis as a priority, when the entire population of the community had to deal with more pressing daily issues such acquiring food the moment it became available, building a much needed housing unit, or commuting long distances by bicycle to and from work. Among the increasingly burdensome routines of everyday life, especially the worsening means of transportation and communication, community people faced too many time-consuming tasks to follow a garden project that would have no redeeming value until sometime in the future.

5. The Identities of "in-between"

The research process raised issues that I would like to call "identities of in-between." I refer to the gray areas where different aspects of our identities intersect, according to the different contexts in which we perform. More specifically, "in-betweenness" includes, for me at least, to be a Puerto Rican graduate student in a New York City University working as a researcher in Cuba. Other aspects of these "in-between" identities include gender, age, and previous experiences that shape a person. These personal conditions are unavoidably exposed and negotiated through the politics of personal interaction, which involves the act of balancing the different components of identity.

This is particularly true when these identities have been affected by controversial historical trajectories such as those between the United States, Cuba, and Puerto Rico. These trajectories have affected and are elements of identities of "in-between" for all the participants involved simultaneously in the research, in the development of the community children's garden, and the social relations among all of us. The negotiation of these identities produced lasting memories, experiences in working in different contexts and adapting strategies of flexibility and tolerance. But the different ways in which we all understand reality also exacerbated the tensions of the research project.

Especially relevant for me as a researcher coming from North America was the challenge to understand the notion of private property in Cuba. This was particularly important when deciding a recommendation for the site of the community garden. It was hard to grasp an understanding of the formal ways to re-define the use of a public space in a context in which almost everything is state-owned. In this situation there surfaced conflicts of territoriality and control relative to the local level and the researchers' various anticipated roles and agendas that made the decision of site selection even more complex and far more time-consuming than originally anticipated. Many of these issues also raised critical questions about the relevance of conducting academic research versus the need to create satisfactory daily life conditions where basic needs are met. These, of course, are not particular to this one research experience in Cuba, but this experience did expose many of these contradictions.

6. Conclusion

According to recent information made accessible by informal sources, the development of urban vegetable gardens has spread over the past five years since our research, and they are now flourishing in the City of Havana. It seems that the challenge of developing sound environmental strategies is well underway in the urban context of Havana. At least a major reason is because the "Special Period" brought hardships so severe that change was not only possible but also critical for survival. Other changes that point to structural reform of the economy are also being implemented —tourism, self-employment, and legalization of the U.S. dollar, which have been analyzed elsewhere. By concentrating on situations which facilitated and hindered the creation of the community children's garden in Pogolotti, and by explaining aspects of the historical and global economic context, the chapter has, presumably, helped to show links between larger urban issues and local concrete practices.

My retrospective view of conducting research under conditions of economic hardship of everyday life in Cuba shows that the problems of the "Special Period" necessitated some adjustment, patience, and a great deal of time unanticipated by researchers from abroad. The changing articulation between local leaders and the central government regarding local initiatives seem to be responsible for at least some of the delays in the implementation of the construction of the children's garden during the two years we were working on the research project. Among the factors that facilitated the community children's garden initiative was the eagerness of community members to be involved in the research and decision-making process. That factor, more than anything else, probably helps to explain the good news arriving in recent years about food availability in Cuba.

ENDNOTES

1. "Tropical Suburbia" is used here to describe the location where the research was conducted, along the periphery of the City of Havana. Special thanks to Jill Hamburg and Carlota Pasquali who provided helpful comments on this chapter.
2. The research project was funded by the CUNY-Caribbean Exchange Program at Hunter College. The institutions participating in this collaboration included the Environmental Psychology Ph. D. Program, Graduate School and University Center, CUNY, and the Center for the Study of Construction and Tropical Architecture, Instituto Superior Politécnico Jose Antonio Echevarria, Havana City, Cuba. Professors and students from both institutions participated in the research project.
3. The Urban Reform Law transformed privately owned properties to state-owned, after which families already living in urban dwellings could become owners. Thus, the properties of those who left Cuba after the revolution became state property and were redistributed to the urban population.
4. The Island of Dust is located on a hillside and is so named due to the limestone that was emitted by a nearby factory. At the time of our visit the factory was not polluting the air.
5. Here, I do not mean to romanticize the "Special Period" or simplify the dramatic impact and hardships it has caused. I am drawing from the attitudes of community residents in Pogolotti who have seen it as a challenge.

REFERENCES

Acosta, M. and J. E. Hardoy (1971) "Urban Reform in Revolutionary Cuba," *Antilles Research Program* (translator Mal Bochner), Connecticut: Yale University.
Adams, W. (1990) *Green Development: Environment and Sustainability in the Third World* (New York: Routledge).
Boveland, B. and B. Berg (1993) *Report on Open Space in Pogolotti*. Report submitted to the CUNY-Caribbean Exchange Program, Hunter College, New York.
Low, S., J. Nevárez, C. Oliver, and L. Tillett (1994) *Report on the Children's Community Garden, Pogolotti District, City of Havana, Cuba*. Report submitted to the CUNY-Caribbean Exchange Program, Hunter College, New York.

Nevárez, J. (1993) *Report on the Development of an Environmental Educational Program: Experimental Children's Garden, Pogolotti District, City of Havana, Cuba.* Report submitted to the CUNY-Caribbean Exchange Program, Hunter College, New York.

Pérez-Stable, Marifeli (1993) *The Cuban Revolution: Origins, Course, and Legacy* (New York: Oxford University Press).

18

Biodiversity in Cuba

Jorge Ramon Cuevas

Cuba's diversity of flora and fauna is sketched, showing that its large quantity of species is matched in impressiveness by the percentage of species native to only Cuba and/or the archipelago of Cuban islands. The author makes the point that all global structures and productive processes are relevant to one another and to various ecosystems of land and sea. It also calls for greater sharing of the responsibilities for preservation of biodiversity, endangered species, and the lands important for future survival of the earth and its peoples.

Biodiversity is basically an ecological issue, but the current problems the planet is experiencing are related to all the structures of our global society. Biodiversity encompasses all the species of plants, animals and other forms of life, their genetic material and the ecosystems to which they belong. However, not all countries are equally endowed or diverse. Tropical forests, for example, comprise only 7 percent of the earth's surface, but they contain at least 50 percent of all species.

The fact that the richest countries display the least biological diversity and that the poorest countries are the owners of the greatest reserves of these resources underscores the interdependency of all nations. It is urgent that we mediate common strategies for sustaining biodiversity, for sharing responsibility for its preservation as well as its benefits.

This chapter is a revised version of an article entitled "An Assessment of Biodiversity in Cuba," which was originally published in the 1995 Inter-American Dialogue Report, *The Environment in the U.S.-Cuban Relations: Opportunities and Challenges*. The publisher acknowledges the permission of the Inter-American Dialogue to publish this chapter.

Biological resources are renewable, but they are being exploited globally at a rate exceeding a sustainable yield of renewal. The excessive and unsustainable consumption of resources by a small but rich minority of the world's population, together with the destructive effects of the poor and starving of the world in their desperate attempts to survive, have destroyed or excessively exploited habitats throughout the entire world.

The underlying causes are fundamentally social, economic and political. Historically, the industrialized countries have obtained the greatest benefits from the exploitation of biological resources of the planet. But, given the economic and social disparity of the genetically rich and the technologically rich, there is an increasing pressure to ensure that those who benefit the most from living resources contribute more to the cost of guaranteeing that these resources are properly described, satisfactorily preserved, sustainably employed, and accessible to everyone.

It is gradually being recognized that biological diversity must be protected and simultaneously utilized. Using biodiversity in a sustainable and equitable fashion means prudently managing biological resources so that they might last to better the human condition.

From a geographic point of view, Latin America and the Caribbean possess a wide variety of unique species and ecosystems in the world, but like other regions of the planet, these treasures are highly threatened for a variety of reasons. Among these reasons, the following stand out: the deterioration and fragmentation of their habitats, the introduction of foreign species, agriculture, agroforestry practices, and climate changes.

Within this region, some islands are very rich in biodiversity, particularly in their marine ecosystems. It is well known that coral reefs exhibit as much diversity of species as do tropical forests. In addition, this high level of biodiversity is complemented by a high endemism, which has its fundamental origin in the natural isolation of the islands. Generally, the majority of island states are small, isolated islands that have very fragile ecosystems, and this results in a very interdependent relationship between the environment and human activities.

1. Cuban Location and its Riches

Because of Cuba's position between North and South America, it has been rightly said that it looks out onto all the roads of the world. Its privileged geographic position confers ecological characteristics on its territory that seem unequaled on the rest of the planet. This, coupled with the complexity and diversity of rocks and types of soil present in the archipelago, have given rise to a high level of biological diversity—probably the highest in the Caribbean islands.

Cuba, as a geomorphological phenomenon, is of Middle Eocene age; that is, the stability of the biotopes or surrounding land and marine ecosystems were achieved beginning with this period. Many large areas, such as the Sierra de los Organos, Sierra del Rosario, Sierra del Escambray, Sierra Maestra and northern parts of the eastern provinces (Moa and Baracoa) probably have remained above the surface since that period. The biological diversity of the Cuban archipelago is characterized by remarkable treasures in the natural environment as well as by the high level of endemism of its biotic resources.

The Cuban archipelago has an area of 110,922 kilometers and comprises two principal islands, Cuba and the island of Youth (*Isla de la Juventud*, formerly called the Isle of Pines), and 4,195 smaller islands and keys. Seventy-five percent of the territory is made up of plains, 18 percent mountains, and the remaining 4 percent moist soil areas. The high level of biodiversity can also be appreciated in the various ecosystems and landscapes, which range from semideserts and arid mountains to tropical rain forests. The island shelf displays the relief of a very shallow, submerged platform with a total area of 67,831 kilometers.

The mosaic of lithologies and soils has given rise to greater variations in substrate, unequaled in the Caribbean islands, which are predominantly of karstic origin. The soils have been produced mainly from sedimentary limestone rocks, which alternate with other derivatives from different substrata.

The differences of soils, lithologies, and climate are responsible for the wide variability and endemism (native only to Cuba) of the types of vegetation and ecosystems in Cuba. The endemism in the Cuban archipelago is ten times and sometimes one hundred times greater than in the majority of European countries, and other new endemic species in Cuba are continually being discovered. There are more endemic species in Cuba than in the unlimited Siberian expanses of the former Soviet Union and probably more than in the entire Amazon region of Brazil.

The density of species, that is, the number of species per square kilometer in Cuba is six times greater than in Texas, seven times greater than Spain's, nine times greater than Chile's, twenty-two times greater than Nigeria's, thirty-six times greater than in India and China, and forty-two times greater than Australia's.

2. Cuban Flora

In Cuba, the flora of vascular plants consists of 6,700 species, with an endemism of 51.4 percent. This represents the greatest diversity of flora within the Antilles, which has seventy genera and more than 3000 endemic lower taxa.

Of our flora, one in seven plants offers economic value as a plant used in medicine, food, textiles, etc. A quick calculation reveals that in Cuba there are no less than five hundred species that could contribute to the well-being of humanity.

The Cuban flora has one of the highest levels of endemism in the world, surpassed only by the Cape region in South Africa, Hawaii, and some parts of Australia. The families of plants with the most species are Poaceae and Astaraceae with four hundred species each. They are followed by Rubiaceae, Euphoribiacaeae and Leguminoceae, each having approximately three hundred species (COMARNA, 1993). If we analyze the distribution of the endemic species into genera, we find that some of these exist almost exclusively in Cuba where they are 100 percent endemic.

Among the various factors that have assisted the speciation process, we can point to the geological isolation that the Cuban territory has experienced since early times: insularity, the wide range of soils and geology, the different altitudes and the changes in climate, among others.

The study of Cuban vegetation shows that at the time of the conquest (1492), approximately 95 percent of Cuba was covered with forests. "The island is three hundred leagues long and one can walk it completely under trees," wrote Padre Bartolome de las Casas shortly after its discovery. Notwithstanding this assertion by the illustrious priest of Spain, some authors suggest that during the period of the discovery, between 70 to 80 percent of Cuba's surface was covered by forests.

Since then, the policy of plundering directed at Cuba's natural resources has grown; by 1900, the presence of forests already had declined to 54 percent. By 1959, this destruction had reduced the forested area to the alarming figure of 13 percent. The policy of reforestation today in Cuba has led to an increase in wooded surface areas, up to 18. 7 percent in 1990 (ICGC, 1978) and presumably will continue to produce more trees and forest areas.

As the forests were being cut down to make way for agriculture, one light-loving plant gradually became master of the landscape: the Royal Palm, which is our national tree. No one can imagine the Cuban landscape without its palms; there are more than one hundred species with 90 percent endemism. The destruction of Cuban forests is responsible for the fact that 16 percent of Cuban plants are threatened with extinction; approximately 2 percent are already extinct.

3. Cuban Fauna

Around 50 percent of Cuban fauna is understood in a general way, but is far from being well understood. At this time it numbers around 14, 000 described species, of which it is estimated that 10 percent are already extinct. Cuba also exhibits a large number of micro-organisms about which information is very deficient; it requires a very serious investigative effort. Column 3 of Table 1 reveals how little we know at this point about how many various species we have discovered and classified.

Almost 40 percent of the species reported in the last twenty years are new scientific contributions. For example, until 1970, only four species of living hutias (a group of Cuban mammals) and seventeen species of gadflies were known. Recently, the number has climbed to nine species of hutias and thirty of gadflies. in 1965 twelve species of ticks had been reported, and this number has increased, thus far, to thirty. Regarding terrestrial fauna, the rate of endemism in some groups can reach figures above 90 percent, as in terrestrial mollusks and amphibia.

For centuries, the indiscriminate exploitation of the forests and uncontrolled removal of specimens of fauna caused the fauna to decline noticeably until recent years. Numerous species have become extinct, as is the case with the Cuban Macaw (Ara cubensis). Yet other populations, for example, the ivory-billed woodpecker (Campephillus principalis), the almique (Soledonon cubanus) and the St. Thomas gallinule (Cyanolinas cerverai), were reduced at an alarming rate, and are at present in serious danger of extinction.

Table 1: Current Knowledge of Cuban Fauna

Kingdom and Subdivisions (estimates)	Number of Known Species	% known
INSECTA	**6238**	**60**
Orthptera	250	40-70
Dermoptera	19	40-70
Isoptera	22	90
Odonata	85	80
Hemipera	549	40-70
Homoptera	650	40-70
Lepidoptera	800	40-70
Diptera	929	40-70
Coleoptera	2170	40-70
Hymenoptera	910	40-70
ARACHINIDA	**1324**	**40-70**
Araneae	718	40-70
Acarina	606	40-70
MOLLUSCA (Terrestrial)	1700	70
CRUSTACEA (Terrestrial & fresh water)	60	40-70
NEMATODA TREMATODA, & CESTODA (Zooparasites)	600	90 (vertebrate) 15 (invertebrate)
REPTILIA	105	60-80
AMPHIBIA	42	40-70
PISCES (Fresh water)	58	40-70
AVES	330	100
MAMMALIA	88	100

4. Migratory Birds

Thus far, 350 species of birds have been reported in Cuba, of which 116 are terrestrial and 92 are aquatic birds found in different categories that breed in North America and utilize the Cuban archipelago in the course of their migration.

Various factors affect the state of the migratory bird populations in their change of residence and stay in the Caribbean: the climate, the distance from North America, the size of the areas of hibernation, indiscriminate hunting, the capture of birds for ornamental use and the conditions of preservation of the habitats. In Cuba, investigations are being carried out on the density, diversity, and activity of terrestrial bird communities in different ecosystems and locations, some of which are within protected areas and natural reserves of the biosphere.

Among the regions where the greatest number of coastal migratory birds have been detected are: the Sabana-Camaguey Archipelago, the Canarreos Archipelago, the Colorados Archipelago, the Zapata Peninsula, and the delta of the Cauto River (Torres et al., 1989). In the Zapata swamp, eight types of habitat have been evaluated thus far during the period of winter residency from 1988 to 1992. Of approximately 40 species, 648 permanent resident birds and 490 migratory birds were captured and banded.

The Cuban archipelago features the largest submerged island area in the Caribbean, in which there is a great heterogeneity of environmental conditions, that is, a high level of diversity of ecosystems, which also accounts for the great diversity of organisms that live in them.

Among the marine ecosystems, the coral reefs require special attention because of their size, extraordinary beauty, state of preservation and their role in the protection of the coasts, especially the beaches, which occupy more than 1,000 kilometers along the coast and sustain extensive tourist and recreational facilities.

Due to the continuity of its ecosystems, marine endemism is less common than in the terrestrial ecosystems. On the other hand, the lack of systematic studies in the majority of Caribbean islands and the Gulf of Mexico makes it difficult to determine the existence of endemic or endangered species, except in the cases of very charismatic species, such as cetacea, turtles, large-sized fish, etc. Table 2 lists the number of endangered species that we have been able to determine in the four groups of vertebrates as of 1988.

In spite of the fact that our knowledge of Cuban diversity is still incomplete. it is clear that there exists a great richness in biological resources. Nonetheless, we should take into account that Cuba ranks fourth in the New World in the destruction of its ecosystems, preceded only by Haiti, Puerto Rico, and Barbados. Therefore, it is obvious that there is a need to pay special attention to the preservation of its ecosystems and the establishment of strategies of rational, sustained use and management

Table 2: Endangered Species of Vertebrates (Perea et al., 1993)

Group	Number of Endangered Species
Birds	46
Reptiles	51
Amphibians	20
Mammals	12

The principal criteria currently employed to establish Units of Preservation *in situ* are: the presence of biological richness, the existence of preservation sites for fauna, the protection of watersheds, the existence of unique or representative vegetational formations and associations, or the presence of endemic species and genetic resources and geomorphological or landscape value.

In Cuba, there is a National System of Protected Areas, the result of coordinated efforts of several scientific institutions and the Ministry of Agriculture. There are currently 65 protected areas with different categories of management that occupy 1,370, 246 hectares, a significant 13.6 percent of Cuban national territory.

The tendency to create protected areas at the global level in the regions of Latin America and the Caribbean demonstrates the concern for the preservation of biodiversity. In this greater region, 2,000 protected areas have been established, which cover a surface area greater than 200 million hectares. In spite of this, the existing protected areas are not sufficient to guarantee the region's preservation of biodiversity. Governmental organizations, under whose responsibilities these areas fall, lack policies, strategies and adequate legislation. Furthermore, the protected areas are vulnerable to ongoing conflicts with the productive sectors and the agricultural areas that surround them, and end up as isolated or fragmented areas of extensive lands that were previously habitats for many species of animals and plants (FAO, 1994).

5. Cuban Scientific Institutions in the Study of Biodiversity

Sixty scientific institutions in Cuba collaborate with the inventory of biodiversity. Twenty-five percent of the 500,000 university graduates in the country work in these institutes. In the last five years alone, 42,361 professionals have graduated in the field of biology.

Cuba also has a tradition in the development of naturalists and scientists. Since the 19th century, Cuban scientists have distinguished themselves with their investigations in this field. We can mention, among others, Felipe Poey, Carlos de la Torre and Carlos J. Finlay, who, in addition, contributed to the creation of databases and collections that today are still fundamental in the study of biodiversity in the Americas.

The Ministry of Science, Technology and Environment was responsible for the creation of a National Center for Biodiversity, assigned to the Institute of Ecology and Systematics (IES). This center will be capable of carrying out quick ecological evaluations of different areas of the Cuban archipelago, including critical areas, endemism, and fragmented areas. An attempt is being made to create a central data bank on Cuban biodiversity with information compiled by the EIS and all of the Cuban scientific institutions related to biology. This will permit the development of a national, regional, and global strategy for the use and preservation of these areas.

There are also a large number of non-governmental scientific associations, created under the protection of the Law of Associations (1985). The leading association, Pro Nature, brings together more than 5,000 members, and counts among them laborers, housewives, and nature-loving professionals.

6. An Appeal for Common Action to Preserve Biodiversity

We need an important international instruments for promoting changes in the way that societies interact with their natural environment, and with one another. The developed countries from the North have seen their biodiversity drastically reduced in the last few years due to excessive exploitation, and the use and abuse of natural habitats. Furthermore, they desire to have access to the rich, biological resources of the countries from the South. On the other hand, the South wants technical and financial assistance for better use of its resources so that the resources as well as the benefits will be sustainable.

The preservation of biodiversity is an issue for everyone. It is incumbent on all of us, in the same way for governments as it is for scientists, non governmental organizations, industrial sectors and individuals. Collaboration among these sectors must be strengthened in order to ensure a more active and the broadest possible participation in complementary preservation activities. The global society must recognize that biological diversity must be protected and simultaneously utilized. Conserving biodiversity means taking productive measures for genes, species, habitats and ecosystems. In the words of Mr. Edouard Saouma, "Getting the formula right for calculating the cost of preservation into the cost of production, is a challenge that we must face in order to fulfill our responsibility to future generations and to stop the constant abuse of biodiversity" (Shand, 1993).

The cost of preserving biodiversity is much less than the punishment for permitting its degradation; we will not be able to recover the losses. Therein lies the challenge for each and every one of us.

REFERENCES

Borhidi, A. and O. Muniz (1981) *Catalogo de plantas amenzadas o extinguidas* (Havana: Editorial Academia).

COMARNA (National Commission for the Protection of the Environment and the Rational Use of Natural Resources) (1993) *Programa nacional sobre medio ambiante y desarrollo. Adessuasion cubana al documento "Agenda 21,"* agreed to in the UNCED, 1993 (Havana: COMARNA).

Godinez, E. and R. Martinez (1991) *Aves migratorias en vuelo detectadas por radar sobre La Habana* (En II Simposio de Zoologia, Cuba).

ICGC (Cuban Institute of Geodesy and Cartography) (1978) *Atlas de Cuba XX Aniversario del Triunfor de la Revolucion* (Havana: ICGC).

FAO Regional Office in Latin America and the Caribbean (1993) *Informe del taller internacional sobre politicas de los sistemas de areas protegidas en la conservación y uso de la biodiversidad en America Latina.* Iguazú National Park, Argentina, September 27 to October 1, 1993.

Perea, A., O. Garrido, J. Estrada and H. Gonzalez (unpublished, 1993) *Especies de vertebrados amenzadas,* Havana, Cuba.

Shand, Hope (1993) *La diversidad de la naturaleza, un patrimonio valioso.* Dirección de Información (Rome: Food and Agricultural Organization).

PART 3

THEORIZING
POLITICS

19

The Stability of Cuba's Political System

Benigno E. Aguirre

This chapter questions the capacity of competing theories to explain the long-term stability of the Cuban regime that grew out of the revolution of 1959. Peter Berger's theory of legitimacy is shown as a relevant guide to understand the durability of the revolutionary state, Castro's style of governance, the institutional arrangements, and the popular internalization that still embraces the values of the revolution. Because elite viability rests on social or cultural values that have been weakening since the 1970s, those who want to see peaceful change in Cuba should challenge the system by supporting other cultural values and the cultural opposition that exists on the island.

1. Introduction

It is the thesis of this essay that the political stability of Fidel Castro's government during the post-1989 period in the face of seemingly insurmountable national problems must be understood as a function of both the continued legacy of the legitimacy of revolutionary institutions and practices created by Castro's government during the 1959-1989 period and the presence of a determined leadership and elite in power. Alternative explanations of Castro's political resiliency do not take us very far.

2. The Anomaly

In the aftermath of the disintegration of the Soviet Union and the emergence of democracy in the countries of Eastern Europe and Russia, most informed commentators anticipated the occurrence of very significant political changes in Cuba. It was recognized that the Castro government's almost total economic dependence on the Soviet bloc of nations made his continuation in power untenable.

Moreover, it was believed that the collapse of the socialist camp would deprive the government of support for its socialist ideology, fatally discrediting the regime of any claims on its citizens.   Yet the seemingly unthinkable occurred, and Castro's government is still in power more than a decade after the miraculous year of 1989. The prognosis is of continued control by the Castro brothers of the reigns of political power in Cuba. How can we explain it?

3. The Usual Suspects

Montaner (1995), representing a well established explanation of the resiliency of the Castro regime, argues that Castro is a typical Latin American *caudillo* who is able to hold on to power because he does not share it with anyone else. From this perspective, other high officials of the revolutionary government are useful marionettes, doing Castro's will out of personal convenience and fear. The majority of the Cuban people also do not rebel because of fear of the secret police and other organs of repression. In a theme which I wish to revisit later because it is close to my own view, Montaner mentions that Castro stays in power because there are no alternatives in the island, *no tiene hacia donde caer*.

The problem with this and other similar explanations is the absence of a recognition of the political legitimacy of Castro's government. I would argue that it is much more plausible to assume its legitimacy, understood not as the relative approval of the government by the public but as the ability of the government to provide explanations to the public to any "questions about the why of institutional arrangements" (Berger, 1990, p. 29). The government has been in near absolute power for forty-one years during which it has aggressively carried out a more or less cogent national cultural policy. Importantly, Montaner acknowledges the presence of a "revolutionary clan" of a million people who are supporters of the government, but their existence does not form part of his explanations of the political stability of the regime. Yet they need to be made part of it.

4. Peter Berger's Theory and Political Legitimacy

Berger's (1990) celebrated opus on the sociology of social organization provides us with clear directives to clarify the origins and mechanisms of the legitimacy of Castro's government. Berger begins with the person and his or her involvement in three dynamically interrelated "moments" in the process of society: externalization, objectivation, internalization. It is worthwhile to remind ourselves that Cubans are human beings who fulfill their lives through their involvement with physical and social worlds external to themselves and who socially construct and reconstruct their locations in society in the presence and with the assistance of others. Berger reminds us that society is "human meaning externalized in human activity." The institutions of a society, its myths and rituals, are dependent on the externalization which is an intrinsic part of being human.

Institutions also take on lives of their own, become objects, controlling and channeling the actions of human beings. Berger thus explains social control and societal coercion as derived from the process of objectivation, as the society that is created by human interaction becomes relatively independent of it. This society, or social world in Berger's terminology, not only places restrictions but also becomes a guide to the anomie which in its absence would otherwise ensue; it is what allows its members to understand and make sense of their lives. Finally, Berger's concept of internalization completes the logical circle of his argument. It is the "reabsorption into consciousness of the objectivated world in such a way that the structures of this world come to determine the subjective structures of consciousness itself" (Berger, 1990, p. 15). Ideally, through socialization human beings incorporate in their consciousness the objective features of their societies even as they recognize the external, object-like quality of these features. They learn to represent and express these objective features as part of themselves:

> ...the objective facticity of the social world becomes a subjective facticity as well. The individual encounters the institutions as data of the objective world outside himself, but they are now data of his own consciousness as well. The institutional programs set up by society are subjectively real as attitudes, motives and life projects (Berger, 1990, p. 17).

After four decades in power, Castro's government has been able to direct, shape, and order the socially constructed world of Cubans on the island. This is not merely the result of the government's organized efforts at social control and the use of force, however effective and oftentimes brutal they may be. It also results from its ability and willingness to shape the institutions and practices of the society, the "object like" features which confront individual Cubans from the moment of their births. It is a totalitarian government in control of a social and political system that does not permit the free expression of dissenting viewpoints and opinions. Importantly, however, this totalitarianism also serves to create legitimacy for the government. Berger (1990, p. 29) defines legitimacy as objectivated factual knowledge "that serves to explain and justify the social order". Legitimization is what passes for knowledge in a given society at a given time, not only the ideas of intellectuals but also the ethno knowledge of the folk. Berger differentiates between self legitimating facticities and secondary legitimations, which occur as people react to challenges to the established explanations. They range from statements of facts, "this is the way it is," to myths, legends and folk tales, to abstract all encompassing conceptual systems legitimating the organization of the society and its political system.

The Cuban government's monopoly of information and interpretations, its total command of formal education and its assiduous attention to it, its ability to create facts, has rendered its favored explanations formidable channels used by Cubans to make sense of their world. In turn, this usage provides legitimacy to the government. There is nothing unique about this, for as Berger points out for the general case, the very existence of language and a set of institutional arrangements generate legitimacy for the established organization of the society. Thus an important although usually unrecognized reason Castro's government remains in power despite the enormous contemporary crisis, and however inefficient its control, is that most people in Cuba construct their lives in ways that affirm and make possible the present government's control of the state. The effects are circular, of course, and the "proper" construction of lives is made more probable by the government's near hegemony over the interpretations available in the island and its careful attention to the timely provision to the public of such interpretations.

While it is not possible in this short chapter to prove the existence of this official, privileged effort at ideological construction, examples abound. In programmatic fashion, three days prior to the arrival of the Pope John Paul II to Cuba in January 1998, Fidel Castro, in a lengthy six hour televised interview, portrayed the distinguished visitor as the foremost anti-imperialist leader of our time. Or, in another context, a visiting Cuban citizen spoke to me matter-of-factly about the "auto golpe" (self inflicted coup) of Mikhail Gorbachev during a perilous period of political instability in Moscow. In this and other cases it is possible to observe the operation and effects of this hegemonic control by the Cuban government of the "explanations" available to Cubans about significant events affecting their lives.

In sum, then, a fuller understanding of the remarkable political stability of the Cuban government would require attention not only to the repressive apparatus of the state, but also to the probably much more important processes of externaliza-tion, objectivation, and internalization taking place in Cuba. In such explanation it would also be necessary to consider the government policies and programs designed to reshape the political culture of the Cuban nation during 40-odd years of uninterrupted governance.

5. The Continued Viability of Elites

Another key reason for the continuation of Castro's government is the continued viability of the Cuban Communist Party (PCC) and the political elites of the government. Montaner assumes that such structures are moribund and thus fails to recognize their continued importance despite important contemporary transformations in their forms and functions. Yet some facts would argue against his interpretation.

For one, the PCC continues to have congresses and its members continue to act decisively in defense of the government, as shown, for example, in their importance in leading and organizing the rapid action brigades that were mobilized between 1992 and 1996 to terrorize people perceived as oppositionists or threats to the regime. Second, the top officer corps of the armed forces continues to act in accord with the political leadership. There has not been serious schisms or open clashes, and in fact, the execution of General Ochoa cemented even more firmly Castro's control over all security systems and compromised many of the top military leaders in the execution of their comrade and national hero. The national police, the courts, and all other institutions of the society continue to operate, albeit with difficulties, but showing the continued willingness of leading cadres to make them work.

The same can be said of new programs to adjust to the crisis, such as tourism and foreign investment. The facilitation of the emigration of many professional and artistic members of the Cuban elite to Spain and other countries in Europe, and to the United States, also shows the government's concern for their welfare. The widespread notion that Castro governs without the active support of these elite elements is in my view a mistake. It does not help us understand the present and future prospects of Cuban society. Rather than assuming the widely held view that once Fidel Castro ceases to exercise power Cuba will experience political chaos and civil war, the view of elite viability advanced here suggests a different outcome. It is much more likely to expect the continuation of the present system of elite governance, the gradual transformation of the political system, and a limited opening to US investment and influence. The decentering of Castro is an important first step to gain this alternative view of the future.

6. What is to be done?

A cultural point of view is indispensable to structure effective efforts to bring about political change in Cuba. Since the late 1980s, the cultural hegemony of the Cuban government has weakened rapidly. The symptoms are well-known, as shown by the virulence of the shadow institutions that exist in the society, shadow arrangements that are not supposed to exist even as they facilitate the operation of the legal institutions. Great discontent generated by the dollarization of the economy, the new lyrics in Cuban salsa, the growth of the Catholic Church, and the increased activities of a small dissident movement with transnational organizational ties are the symptoms of weakening hegemony.

I would venture to guess that the potential threat this emerging pluralism poses to the legitimacy of the government is one of its important concerns today. Interestingly, however, most observers of the Cuban scene do not recognize the importance of this emerging culture of opposition as a mechanism of political change. Rather, they continue to emphasize Castro's charisma, his alleged *caudillismo*, and state repression as the reasons for his continued hold of the state and the absence of change. Berger's work helps us to see the problem from a different angle. Those who would like to see peaceful change in the political system of Cuba and the amelioration of the present economic and cultural crisis of the nation must recognize the need for persistent, effective efforts to strengthen its culture of opposition, the need to facilitate cultural emergence in the island outside the control of the government. The work of artists and intellectuals, eternal creators of alternative futures and critics of the present, is central to this project of cultural reconstruction that would express and make available to Cubans alternative explanations. Once oppositional culture gains sufficient ground, Castro will have lost much legitimacy within the population and political change would become much more likely than it is today.

REFERENCES

Berger, Peter (1990) *The Sacred Canopy* (New York: Doubleday).
Montaner, Carlos Alberto (1995) *Cuba Hoy. La Lenta Muerte del Castrismo* (Miami, Florida: Ediciones Universal).

20

Competing Perspectives on Democracy in Cuba

Edward J. McCaughan

What does democracy mean for Cuba and to Cubans at the onset of the twentieth century? On the basis of forty-three interviews conducted with a range of intellectuals in Cuba, this chapter summarizes key elements of the ongoing debates about democracy in Cuba. Three major conceptions of democracy might be labeled as currents representing liberalism, state socialism, and a new and renovative trend that reflects the other two conceptions as historically failed systems without creative democratic norms.

1. Introduction

The rapid disintegration of the Soviet bloc and the supposed end of the Cold War created a moment filled with great danger as well as great potential for Cuba. On the one hand, the frayed legitimacy of Cuba's authoritarian socialist regime is completely intertwined with its ability to defend Cuban sovereignty, maintain the social accomplishments of the revolution, and democratize its political system. These are no small tasks given the nation's deep economic crisis and unrelenting hostility from the United States government and the right-wing exile community. On the other hand, the very severity of the crisis has shattered many old dogmas and opened an intellectual space within Cuba for rethinking the question of democracy and its relationship to socialist alternatives in a post-Cold War world of globalized capitalism.

As part of a larger comparative study of how left intellectuals in Cuba and Mexico were rethinking important questions of democracy, socialism and national sovereignty in the 1990s, I interviewed 43 Cuban intellectuals in the winter of 1993.[1] Based on those interviews and on recent writings from Cuba, this chapter will summarize key elements of the current debate about democracy in post-Soviet Cuba.

Three principal currents of thought are identified. The first two advocate conceptions of democracy that still adhere closely to the historical ideologies of state socialism and liberalism. A third, renovative current seeks to transcend the orthodoxy of these old ideologies. The three tendencies—liberal, state socialist, and renovative—do not correspond precisely with past political or ideological affiliations, or with generations, but rather reflect the paradigm crisis, shake-up, and realignment taking place in response to recent changes inside Cuba and world-wide. Following a brief summary of the state socialist and liberal tendencies, the ideas of the renovative current will be explored in more detail.

2. State Socialist and Liberal Perspectives on Democracy

State socialist perspectives tend to define democracy in the broadest of terms, extending beyond the formal political arena to include the substantive goals of economic equality and social justice—not as prerequisites for democracy but as part of its very definition.[2] For the orthodox socialist current in Cuba, democratization is understood primarily in terms of greater social equality and the state's defense or advocacy of working class interests—a view which tends to conceal the party's domination and its privileges in acting as the class' fiduciary. The participatory aspect of democracy is frequently emphasized by this current, but without reference to the need for civil society's autonomy from state and ruling party.

State socialist views on democracy remain very influential but no longer hegemonic among the revolution's intellectuals. In essence, this perspective says the Cuban political system is the most democratic, most participatory in the world, requiring only some fine-tuning. For example, a Communist Youth Leader expressed the opinion that, "The Eastern European regimes were perfectly democratic and it would be difficult to come up with a more participatory system than Cuba's Poder Popular."[3] Another young Communist militant said: "I don't know of a better system. Besides, the youth are not concerned with democracy, which is a foreign discourse used against Cuba."[4] For this tendency, the experience of liberal democracy has relatively little to offer Cuba: "Our experience with the U.S. style political system has been mainly negative and not a point of reference," explained one high-level party official.[5] A leading philosopher warned that, "In Cuba, the multiparty project is inevitably counterrevolutionary."[6]

Indeed, Cuban revolutionaries remained somewhat isolated from the liberalization of political discourse about democracy that swept through most of

Latin America in the transitions from military to civilian rule in the 1980s. Since the collapse of the Soviet bloc a degree of economic liberalization has been imposed in Cuba by the severity of its crisis, but political liberalization has been less evident. Nonetheless, more liberal notions of democracy are emerging among some of Cuba's left intellectuals. This is particularly evident among individuals associated with the social democratic opposition, but even some reform-minded Cuban Communists look to liberal traditions as one source of ideas for improving socialist democracy. For example, a Cuban social scientist, who has studied political and social movements in Latin America for many years, observed that "Liberal thought has been much more profound [than socialist thought] in elaborating the institutional forms needed to realize its project of democracy."[7]

A liberal-leaning political perspective among Cuban revolutionaries emphasizes that existing political institutions have to be reformed and given more real authority, independent of the Communist Party and state executive branch. For example, several of those interviewed believed that the February 1993, secret-ballot elections for the National Assembly were an important advance in the process of democratization. Yet they cautioned that it remained to be seen whether the new assembly would become a forum of real debate and decision-making over real policy alternatives. Liberal-leaning Cuban revolutionaries also call for the professionalization of elected representatives, so that legislators have the time and resources to do more than meet once or twice a year to rubber-stamp policy decisions already made by the state-party's top leadership.

Liberal perspectives in Cuba also stress the need for a clearer delineation of legislative powers and oversight. A life-long Marxist, who is now a sympathizer of the social democratic current in Cuba, expressed this concern in the following terms:

> There has to be a separation between the parliament, as representa-
> tive of the popular will, and the government, so that the govern-
> ment will be obliged to constantly account for its actions. This
> aspect of bourgeois democracy, even if it may appear a little
> formal, is necessary, in one form or another, in any socialist
> model.[8]

Liberal-minded Cuban intellectuals also emphasize the need for pluralism in the political sphere, but many still believe that is possible within a single party. A common formulation is: "Pluralism does not equal a multiparty system."[9] This is one of the key points that distinguishes liberal forces still loyal to the Communist Party from the social democratic opposition within Cuba, which calls for a multiparty system. For example, Vladimiro Roca, son of legendary Communist leader Blas Roca and now an influential figure in Cuba's small social democratic tendency, argues that, "A multiparty system is preferable, even if it's imperfect, because it allows itself to be perfected and improved with the participation and the criteria of almost all strata of society."[10]

The ideas expressed in the interviews and writings just cited do not add up to any coherent, organized liberal tendency within the Cuban left. Rather, they reflect the gradually increasing influence of liberal notions about political representation, division of powers, and the acceptance of political pluralism. We will now turn to a third current emerging within the Cuban left of the 1990s, a renovative tendency that seeks to transcend the limitations of both state socialist and liberal thought.

3. Renovative Perspectives on Democracy

In Cuba, the abruptness and severity of the regime's post-Soviet Union crisis is helping to shatter old dogmas and create intellectual and political openings for new, though still tentative, thinking about democracy in a socialist society. Two quotes suggest the possibility as well as the dilemma of efforts to democratize Cuba from a renovative left perspective. The first is from Esteban Morales, political economist and director of Cuba's Center for U.S. Studies (CESEU):

> The fall of European socialism does not represent so much a crisis of Marxist theory or methodology as a crisis of politics and practice. The excessively ideologized Marxism was related to the lack of democracy and participation, including of social scientists. The experiences in the Soviet Union have led to a serious questioning of democracy in Cuba, a renewed concern with popular participation. We need a new paradigm of democracy, which is especially difficult now given the renewed hegemony of the liberal democratic paradigm.[11]

The second revealing statement about renovative perspectives on democracy is from Jorge Ibarra, an eminent Cuban historian:

Changes in the world have provoked changes in the concept of political power in socialism. But this discussion always revolves around two axes: one, market democracy with multiple parties, and, two, a single-party state. This is not the issue. The question is whether it is possible for the distinct classes to exert influence on political power through all of the existing institutions. To what extent can the people govern—that is the issue. This implies a far more radical revision of the concept of democracy than that implied by adopting a bourgeois, multiparty system.[12]

Such dissatisfaction with the old paradigms is leading to the emergence of a renovative tendency in Cuba. The term "renovators" is meant to signify those leftists who still emphasize social goals and social, even collectivist, political and economic visions, and who are critical of both state-socialist and liberal approaches. Renovators are inclined neither to expand the concept of democracy so broadly as to be virtually synonymous with Marx's utopian communism, and thus meaningless in any practical sense, nor to restrict democracy to purely formal political rights that likewise become nearly meaningless in the real world of political, economic, and social inequality.

Among Cuban leftists, a renovative perspective on democracy is critical of the statist traditions of socialism. Fernando Martínez Heredia, for example, claims that Cuba's system of government—the Organs of Popular Power—was very successful at the local level, but that "in general the political system was weighed down by ritualistic formalism, a conservative expression that tried to take over society as well."[13] Likewise, despite the importance and achievements of Cuban mass organizations—such as the Federation of Cuban Women and the Confederation of Cuban Workers—Martínez Heredia says their tendencies toward authoritarianism and paternalism have prevented civil society from becoming more than an appendage of the political system.[14]

Cuban renovators emphasize that the key issue is popular participation in decision-making at all levels of society. They see institutional innovation, like the recent emergence of some non-governmental organizations, as important, because it opens up new spaces outside of the state and the party for democratic participation in society. Several Cubans interviewed expressed optimism about the potential contribution to Cuba's democratization of the *Consejos Populares* (popular councils), a relatively new institution. According to Sergio Baroni, a renovative urban planner,

The Consejo Popular is the most important development in terms of democracy. The councils are organized at the electoral precinct level. Each precinct chooses a representative to the council for the daily government of the community. The council deals with problems like housing and street repairs and water service, the problems of daily life. There are 93 Councils in Havana, each representing about 20,000 people. Each council has a paid professional, elected by the neighborhood and important work places. Each month the representative has to give an accounting before the electorate.[15]

One interviewee saw the Popular Councils as a key mediating link between the state and civil society: "They can be seen either as the government organizations closest to the masses, or as the community organization vested with the greatest governmental powers."[16]

Renovators believe that such institutions could help deepen democracy in Cuba if they are able to assert their autonomy from the state-party. As one still loyal but critical party militant and scholar put it:

The Party is the only institutional space here. Small groups, like the one around [social democratic dissident] Elizardo Sánchez, have created a little space. Young intellectuals in the mid-1980s began to create a new space outside the party that was not oriented toward Miami—in theater, sculpture, and to some extent the social sciences. But then the Party moved in and closed that space, co-opting some and leading others to move to Mexico. The Party is very verticalist, authoritarian, statist, and militarist. One is ever less able to participate.[17]

One seemingly obvious change in the Cuban political system that would address the problem of the Communist Party's domination of all politics would be the adoption of a multiparty system. However, in the interviews conducted for this study, only the social democratic dissidents were prepared to declare themselves against the single-party model. This does not mean that renovators within the Communist Party are not concerned with issues of pluralism, dissent, debate, and alternative programs; but for the moment they call (publicly) only for democratization, perhaps even reconceptualization, of the single party. It is difficult to determine whether this position is based on principle or on a strategic assessment of the best way to push forward democratization without risking complete political marginalization.[18]

Haroldo Dilla, a renovative voice in the social sciences, does not want the critical issue of pluralism side-tracked by debates about multiparty systems, which he says "confuse the present with the future." Dilla says the bigger problem is to overcome the assumption that pluralism undermines unity, because unity has been distorted to mean a monolithic unanimity. The solution is to be found in what he describes as a simultaneous decentralization and socialization of power: "the ideal matrix for correcting what has been a deficit in Cuban politics: the maturation of pluralism understood as the recognition of the diversity and autonomy of the participant subjects, and consequently of conflict as a moment in the creation of consensus."[19] Admitting the necessity of conflict is something that distinguishes this renovative perspective from the more orthodox state socialist views on dissent.

From a renovative perspective, democratization is fundamentally about increasing the degree of real power people have over the decisions that affect their lives. A prominent but heretical Party intellectual recalled:

> After the 1960s, the capitalist ruling classes were in shock because their children rebelled. Samuel Huntington presented an analysis of the danger that people were taking democracy seriously, that the system was overloaded with demands that couldn't be satisfied. So it was necessary to lower expectations, which is what has happened since the 60s. In the 60s, democracy was associated with "power" and power was in the streets—black power, Chicano power, etc. Now democracy is all about elections. It's a big myth. What could Cuban democracy be? I don't want Cuban socialist democracy to be what Huntington suggests. Elections are a trap. The question in Cuba now is how much power will the people elected to the National Assembly [in February 1993] really have? The elections weren't really the issue. Now, are we going to pass real shares of power from the centralized, self-appointed bureaucracy to the popularly elected representatives? Will elected delegates be able to give orders to Ministers of State?[20]

Cuban renovators also reject the argument made by some that a Chinese model might be viable for Cuba; that is, economic liberalization without democratization—a formula gaining adherents within the Cuban regime. Juan Valdés Paz, a prominent Cuban sociologist, explained:

> The proposals for economic decentralization without accompany-
> ing democratization are fundamentally about the enterprises and the
> economic bureaucracy, not about greater democratization and
> popular control. . . . [But] you can't compensate for the risks
> involved in the necessary economic liberalization without a radical
> project of democratization.[21]

Along similar lines, Haroldo Dilla concedes that liberalization of the economy may be necessary but certainly not sufficient and perhaps even counterproductive if liberal economic reforms "are not accompanied by policies designed to strengthen the spaces for participation and popular control."[22]

4. The Obstacles to Democratization

However, in Cuba today, even the most renovative views on democratization are conditioned by two factors. First, there are the dangers inherent in any severe moment of crisis. As one Cuban put it, "There is a serious contradiction between the popular participation demanded by the people and the discipline required by the current crisis."[23]   Second, there is what most Cubans perceive to be an overwhelm-ingly hostile international environment. In the words of historian Jorge Ibarra, "Socialist democracy is viable in Cuba to the extent we can survive as a nation." He is referring to what many in Cuba view as a recolonization project directed from Miami. Those dangers strengthen the position of the more conservative forces who resist any democratization of the system. According to several people interviewed, the sudden disintegration of the Soviet Union seriously narrowed a democratic opening that had started in Cuba:

> Preservation of the state and of political power became the
> overriding question. There are conservative forces who might try
> to use the situation to strengthen their own positions. But there are
> also *fuerzas aperturistas* [forces supporting an opening up of the
> system] who have had to fight to make sure that the emergency is
> not used as an excuse to make no changes at all, even the minimal

changes necessary to remain faithful to the revolution's commit-
ments.[25]

Haroldo Dilla admits that many legitimate arguments—particularly the very
real threat to Cuban sovereignty posed by the U.S. and the powerful right-wing Cuban
American political machine—can be made against the viability of democratization in
Cuba today. But even taking such real contradictions into account, Dilla insists that:

> The construction of a participatory and pluralistic democracy
> appears as a condition for patriotic resistance and for the articula-
> tion of consensus around a path filled with obstacles and sacrifices.
> . . . Probably the clearest message that we have received from the
> collapse of Eastern European bureaucratic socialism is the need to
> reinterpret the relationship between democracy and governability
> in a socialist context, in which only lengthening and accelerating
> the pace of constructing democracy is capable of assuring the
> stability and governability of the system.[26]

Just how far the democracy debate has evolved in Cuba is evidenced by such
calls, from loyal revolutionaries, to recognize that democratization is a condition for
resolving the crisis and rescuing socialism, not a goal to be postponed for some
undetermined future. The emerging renovative perspective on democracy entails
doing away with the false association between collectivist, social goals and
centralized state power. A good part of the intellectual and political task of Cuban
renovators is to break the old socialism-liberalism dichotomy and to reassert the
compatibility of social equality, individual liberty, and democratic rule. That task,
unfortunately, is being made much more difficult by intransigent forces within the
Cuban and U.S. governments, as well as among the influential Cuban American
community. In an unending cycle of reaction, they tend to reinforce one another's
inflexibility and thereby rob Cuban society of the free-flow of ideas needed to assure
a peaceful, democratic transition to a new era.

ENDNOTES

1. Edward J. McCaughan (1997) *Reinventing Revolution: The Renovation of Left Discourse in Cuba and
Mexico* (Boulder: Westview Press, 1997).
2. Three Cuban scholars, for example, have written that Marxist-Leninist conceptions of democracy "surpass
the limitations of democracy [understood] in terms of government or participation in political activities and

in the superstructural sphere, to include, besides government, popular participation and citizen rights in economic activity. That is, they consider economic democracy as consubstantial to democracy and give it its most complete, real, and legitimate meaning when also extending the analysis to the liberation struggles of the oppressed peoples." Olga Fernández Rios, Romelia Pino Freyre, and Hernán Llanes, "Cuba: Socialismo, democracia y soberanía," manuscript (Havana), April 1991.

3. Herminio Camacho, Communist Youth official for Havana Province, interview with author, March 11, 1993.

4. Cristina Pedroza, president of a local Communist Youth branch, interview with author, Havana, March 9, 1993.

5. Ramiro Abreú, high-level functionary in the Central Committee's international relations department, interview with author, Havana, March 8, 1993.

6. Olga Fernández, interview with author, Havana, February 16, 1993.

7. Juan Valdés Paz, interview with author, Havana, February 25, 1993.

8. Cecilio Dimas, interview with author, Havana, February 11, 1993.

9. Aurelio Alonso, interview with author, Havana, February 23, 1993.

10. Vladimiro Roca, interview with author, Havana, March 1993.

11. Esteban Morales, interview with author, Havana, February 15, 1993.

12. Jorge Ibarra, interview with author, Havana, February 21, 1993.

13. Fernando Martínez Heredia, "Cuba: Problemas de la liberación, la democracia, el socialismo," paper presented at the Latin American Congress of Sociology, Havana, April, 1991.

14. Ibid.

15. Sergio Baroni, interview with author, Havana, February 26, 1993.

16. Fernando Barral, interview with author, Havana, February 18, 1993.

17. Anonymous source, interview with author, Havana, March 1, 1993.

18. The risk of marginalization is real and recurrent. Several of the renovative intellectuals interviewed for this study, for example, had been associated with the important Cuban journal, *Pensamiento Crítico*, until it was closed down by the government in 1971 for its unorthodox views. Later, many of these same people worked for years at the influential Center for the Study of the Americas (CEA) in Havana until it was dissolved in 1996.

19. Haroldo Dilla Alfonso, "Cuba: La Crisis y la rearticulación del consenso político (Notas para un debate socialista)," manuscript (Havana, December 1992), pp. 22-23.

20. Anonymous source, interview with author, Havana, March 4, 1993.

21. Juan Valdés Paz, interview with author, Havana, February 25, 1993.

22. Haroldo Dilla Alfonso, op cit. p. 3.

23. Niurka Pérez, interview with author, Havana, March 1, 1993.

24. Jorge Ibarra, interview with author, Havana, February 21, 1993.

25. Juan Valdés Paz, interview with author, Havana, February 25, 1993.

26. Haroldo Dilla Alfonso, op. cit. p. 20.

21

The Prospect for Democracy in Cuba

Peter M. Sanchez

This chapter examines why Cuba is not considered to be democratic and shows how the classification of Cuba as a totalitarian or authoritarian regime has been a political decision. Considering the principal factors that contributed to the loss of a democratic potential in Cuba, the discussion elaborates on the possibilities for the emergence of democracy in Cuba in the near future. It concludes by raising the prospect that a democratic transition, while practically inevitable, could come about peacefully or violently, depending largely on United States policy.

1. Introduction

If no person is an island, then neither is an island an island. The leadership in Cuba, beginning with Fidel Castro, is trying to carry out changes to save that island nation from its economic and political decline while at the same time trying to insulate its inhabitants from external pressures to substantially change the political and economic system. This requires a balancing act that is unlikely, if not impossible to sustain. The island of Cuba will not be able to hold back a global tide which, for good or ill, is rolling in with democracy and capitalism. The most important challenge for those within and outside Cuba is to find the best way for these inevitable changes to come about peacefully.

Scholars have marveled at the rapid return of democracy to Latin America, especially during the 1980s. By 1995 the authoritarian regimes of the 1960s and 1970s had been replaced by civilian governments elected by competitive popular vote in every country, except Cuba. Many of the nascent democracies in the region have serious economic, political, and social problems that mitigate their consolidation. The possibility for direct military involvement in politics in some countries—like Colombia, Guatemala, and Peru—is still high. Nonetheless, most analysts point out that there is a significant difference between the emerging democracies in most of Latin America and the Cuban regime.

2. Why Cuba is not Considered Democratic: Paradigm Lost

During the Cold War, the academic community, like the world community, was bitterly divided. The so-called West promoted democracy and capitalism while the East touted single-party rule and socialism. The Cold War was a conflict over how societies should be organized and which ideology or paradigm they should adopt. It was a geostrategic conflict between two superpowers. Each side could count on scholars who, armed with theories, defended the tenets of their preferred social model. At its base, the struggle was over which model best approximated democracy.[1] Scholars who supported Western ideals argued that only through competitive elections and economic freedom could citizens participate effectively in their political systems. Conversely, the communist perspective posited that democracy could be attained only by eliminating the inequalities inherent in private property. By virtue of its practice throughout the twentieth century, it assumed that only one dominant party, which ruled in the interest of the working class or masses, was capable of eliminating inequalities. More simply, one model emphasized economic and political freedom and the other focused on social equity and concentration of political power.

Some scholars labeled Western democracy as procedural—focusing on the process of politics—and communist democracy as substantive— focusing on the egalitarian outcome of politics. Here, we will use the term democracy to refer to the Western, procedural democracy that has achieved hegemony in both the political and academic environments. A now landmark study of democratization argued in 1986 that the "...establishment of certain rules of regular, formalized political competition deserve priority attention by scholars and practitioners."[2] We must keep in mind, however, that Western democracy is merely republican government and not democracy in the strictest sense (rule by the people). Democracy, like communism, is an ideal that will probably never be achieved.

The end of the Cold War has concluded, for the most part, both the armed and intellectual conflict. Yet Cuba's example is still relevant in a period of globalization where neoliberal policies are running rampant and ignoring the social ills that brought about the Cuban revolution in the first place: inequality, poverty, and racism. While apologists could point to results of more equal access to important social services like education and medical care, antagonists pointed out that political freedom was lost and that economic vitality was squashed. Even Amnesty International, an organization that values economic justice, has condemned the Cuban regime for human rights violations.

Cuba is one of the few countries in the world where the political leadership still contends that democracy is best attained through single-party rule and a socialist economy. Cuba no longer has the military, economic, and moral support of the Eastern bloc. But just as important, Cuba no longer has as much intellectual and moral support of scholars and policy analysts world-wide who argued that Cuba was perhaps more responsive to the needs of its citizens than Western democracies.[3] The consensus now is that Cuba is not democratic and, even more disturbing for Cuban leaders, that Cuba must change. It is only a matter of time until Cuba succumbs to world pressure and adopts a system of multiple political parties and private property. History, it seems, will not absolve Castro; ironically, it will condemn him. Rather than going down in the history books as a harbinger of progress, Castro will most likely be remembered as the last Latin American *caudillo*, precisely that which he would least want to be remembered.

3. Why Cuba did not become Democratic with Castro's Revolution

When Castro's revolutionaries overthrew the Batista regime in 1959, optimism was in the air for those who longed for democratic and uncorrupted government. Cubans were almost unanimous in their support for Castro's revolution.[4] Even the Eisenhower administration waited to see if Castro was perhaps a reformer rather than a communist.[5] Castro's small band of guerrillas was able to defeat a repressive government principally because there was nearly universal support for a regime change.[6] The unemployed, factory workers, students, professionals, and the wealthy were united in their rejection of the corrupt, brutal dictatorship of Fulgencio Batista. As one student of revolutions points out, "Revolutionary movements ... succeed only where a critical mass of most or all of the major classes in the society is mobilized in the revolutionary process."[7] Ironically, Castro was at first a savior, even to most of the Cubans who now live in the United States.

With the Batista dictatorship out of the way democracy became a possibility. The democratic potential was quickly lost, however, for two basic reasons. First, the revolutionary leadership was partial to the communist model, which emphasized substantive democracy. Second, Cuba lost a significant portion of its middle and upper classes, its economic elite. The first reason has to do with historical processes and personalities, what one scholar would term indeterminacies.[8] The second reason is structural or deterministic. A democracy, according to a long line of scholars from Aristotle to Robert Dahl, cannot function without a vibrant and autonomous civil society, which is one manifestation of a middle class.[9]

The scholarly literature on democratization has emphasized the importance of leadership and chance in regime changes.[10] It is now conventional wisdom that structural forces do not necessarily preordain the chances for democratic development. The cunning and skill of leaders have been accepted as crucial, albeit unpredictable, factors in the political processes of any country. In essence, who the leaders are and what they choose to do during a critical historical period can have paramount influence on the long-term trajectory of a particular society. Oddly, however, Cuba has been left out of most of the ever-expanding democratization literature, as if Cuba were a special, anomalous case. Yet the case of Cuba fits reasonably with current theories on democratization, particularly the new emphasis on elite choices and civil society.

The characteristics and actions of the leadership that took power in the dawn of 1959, for example, help to explain why democracy did not take root in Cuba. The *barbudos*, as Castro and his cohorts were called because they came down from the mountains sporting beards, made important choices that set the course of Cuban history down a new path. The *barbudos* did not have to adopt communism as their guiding ideology, but they did. Castro, his brother Raul, and Ernesto "Che" Guevara probably had more to do with this decision than anyone else.[11] Castro's policy was to wait until the revolutionaries had consolidated their power before revealing their true colors. Thus Castro established a "hidden government" which consolidated power and carried out leftist policies, while a more democratic government presented an acceptable facade to the outside world, and especially to the United States.[12] Had Castro not done this, the United States would have reacted to the revolution more quickly and decisively. Thus not only was Cuba's adoption of the socialist paradigm dependent on key elites, but it was also dependent on the strategy and actions of those elites at a crucial historical moment.

Once the *barbudos* decided to take the path of the socialist model, they began a process that made it more difficult for a democratic opening to emerge. Power became more and more concentrated in the hands of the revolutionary elite, and the economy came more and more under the control of the state. Political and civil rights were severely restricted, so that the regime could carry out its socialist program and bring about substantive democracy. Perhaps the most important action taken by the new, revolutionary elite was the destruction of the economic elite[13] and the traditional armed forces, sectors that would have been the regime's chief adversaries.

Many Cuban citizens made choices during the revolution that had important, if unintended, effects on Cuba's social structure as well. During 1959-1962, approximately 200,000 (roughly one in every thirty) Cubans left the island, most bound for the United States, to wait out the end of Castro's experiment.[14] Over this four-year period, Cuba lost the majority of its upper and middle classes, draining the island of its entrepreneurs and professionals. These individuals left the island principally because it became evident to them that Castro's programs were contrary to their interests and because they assumed that the United States would not allow Castro to establish a communist government in its sphere of influence. While Castro contributed to this drain through executions and arrests of the military and economic elite, large portions of the middle and upper classes in Cuba were reduced by self-imposed exile.

Assuming the correctness of numerous studies showing that GNP per capita is directly related to the level of democracy,[15] one can conclude that the significant drain in human resources had long-term effects on Cuba's social structure and political development, particularly its lack of procedural democracy.[16] The exodus of this economic elite resulted in the elimination of an economic elite that could challenge the power of the state, as is common in a capitalist and democratic society.

In summation, the chances for democracy in Cuba were lost because the *barbudos* chose and engineered the socialist and single-party model and because the most likely supporters of democracy, the bourgeoisie and autonomous middle class, were eliminated or left the island.[17] In an ironic twist of circumstances, those who hated communism the most were instrumental in an unintended way in paving a path for its success. The case of Cuba, therefore, fits very well the recent arguments made by the democratization literature. First, elite choices were instrumental in determining the prospects for democracy. Second, the absence of a middle class and an economic elite greatly assisted in the demise of democracy in Cuba. These two factors not only help to explain the lack of democracy in Cuba after 1959, but they also help to explain why Cuba has miraculously and stubbornly resisted the third wave of democracy.

4. The Prospects for Democracy in Cuba in the Near Future

As the brief analysis above suggests, two things must happen for democracy to emerge in Cuba. First, the current political leadership must adopt the Western model of capitalism and democracy or a new leadership must replace the old. Second, Cuba must generate a vibrant and autonomous civil society, supported by a powerful middle class and economic elite. While both of these transformations may be inevitable in the long-term, they will not occur soon as long as Cuba remains insulated economically and politically.

The experiences of the former USSR and Eastern Europe suggest that communist ideology is very weak in Cuba, despite Castro's ability to hang on to the socialist model. This is not to say that Cubans reject the revolution. On the contrary, there is a great deal of support in Cuba today for the gains of the 1959 revolution, even though many of those gains have been destroyed by the recent economic crisis[18] which generated what Castro calls the Special Period in Time of Peace.[19] Cubans are most proud of their achievements in education, health, and of Cuba's ability to challenge U.S. hegemony. Nevertheless, support for the revolution or Castro is not synonymous with support for socialism and single-party rule. Cubans, from all walks of life, are increasingly aware that single party rule has stifled political expression and that the state dominated economy has undermined economic growth. An increasing number of Cubans—from the top to the bottom of the social hierarchy—are beginning to blame the system, and not just the U.S. embargo, for Cuba's economic ills.[20]

If the Soviet model has lost its legitimacy in Cuba, then how has it been able to survive? The answers lie in Fidel Castro and the alternative to that model, as well as in the absence of a middle class and economic elite. Fidel Castro is hanging on to the old model because he knows that his future is bleak if he adopts the Western model. Abandoning socialism would also be tantamount to acknowledging personal mistakes and failure, something that is not in Castro's character. Additionally, and less cynically, we can assume that Castro, like most Cubans, would like to preserve the achievements of the revolution. Finally, since Castro is almost deified in Cuba, a move against his wishes by a significant portion of the political elite is a very unlikely prospect. In many ways, Castro is Cuba and he rules as a cult leader: his preaching is gospel and followers (citizens) give up their worldly possessions for the sake of the community.

Aside from Castro's personal interest and his personal appeal is the fact that for most Cubans the alternative represents uncertainty and thus generates fear. Members of the political elite in Cuba realize that a change to democracy and capitalism could result in their demise. The party could wither away and their power and status could suddenly evaporate. For others, the change could mean losing access to education and health care. Thus while political competition and economic reform would appear to be the best option for Cuba, from inside Cuba these changes look very threatening to a large number of people.

In summation, Cuba's leadership is extremely hesitant to abandon the communist model, first and foremost because Castro does not wish to abandon the model. Second, because many Cubans fear the alternative.[21] Consequently, unless something unpredictable happens, we cannot expect Cuba's political elite to abandon socialism and single-party rule in the near future.

The only other possibility for a democratic opening in Cuba is for the development of a strong civil society. Scholars have been increasingly pointing out that democratic consolidation in Latin America will require a strong and independent civil society.[22] This is an area where there has been some optimism recently with respect to Cuba. One Cuba expert has argued that a civil society is beginning to evolve in Cuba.[23] Since the fall of the Soviet bloc, circa 1989, non-governmental organizations (NGOs) have multiplied in Cuba, largely due to the need for private groups to provide goods and services that the government can no longer guarantee due to substantial losses in trade and subsidies from the Eastern bloc countries. The Cuban leadership has allowed some autonomy to the NGOs simply to reduce frustration among the population. Nevertheless, as the NGOs begin to grow, they may develop a momentum that could be difficult to stop.

Cuba at this point in time, however, does not have a well-developed NGO sector, let alone a strong civil society or a vibrant middle class. First, the NGOs are not entirely autonomous from the state, and the government can halt their operations with ease.[24] Second, at this time, the NGOs do not have sufficient resources to become major players in Cuban society. For example, Pro-Naturaleza, an environmental group composed principally of professionals, has a limited membership and a very limited budget. Resource limitations highlight the importance of a sizable middle class for the development of democracy. The PVOs (private volunteer organizations) and NGOs cannot become important socio-political actors unless members can afford to pay dues and have time to devote to their organizations. In Cuba, even professionals have virtually no discretionary income and are too busy dealing with the hardships of survival to become intensely involved in private organizations. Thus without a relatively affluent middle class the development of a vibrant civil society is virtually impossible. Without economic growth a substantial middle class cannot emerge. Without an economic elite the power of the Cuban state cannot be challenged.

Recent economic changes in Cuba, though, have prompted some analysts to suggest that an economic opening is taking place. The U.S. dollar is now an accepted

currency in Cuba and tourism is booming. The Cuban government has taken steps to
encourage foreign investments in a variety of areas such as tourism, biotechnology,
mining, and oil.[25] But this economic opening has not created the economic growth
necessary for the development of an autonomous middle class any time in the near
future. Nor has it resulted in the creation of an autonomous economic elite since the
Cuban government has significant ownership in most foreign investment.[26]
Nevertheless, a small segment of the society is gaining some economic power and
limited independence. Small businesses are emerging in Cuba in the form of family
restaurants, farmers' markets, and other service enterprises such as beauty salons. But
these individuals, while amassing a small fortune by Cuban standards, have very little
room to maneuver and are too occupied with earning a better living to become vocal
opponents of the regime. At this point, they could not be classified as an independent
economic elite.

The political and economic changes taking place in Cuba are very limited
and potentially reversible. If democracy is going to emerge in Cuba, at the current
rate, it would be a long time in coming. A regime transition that eliminates the
remnants of the Soviet model could come in the near future, but the emergence of a
stable democratic system is still distant.

5. The Importance of U.S. Policy for Cuban Democracy

The U.S. government has been calling for democracy in Cuba since 1961.
After the fall of the Soviet bloc, many scholars and analysts participated in a virtual
academic feeding frenzy as they rushed to anticipate the fall of the Castro regime.
Biographies of Castro were rushed to press to cash in on the demand for books on
Castro after his "imminent" fall.[27] Ironically, U.S. policy since that time has helped
to create conditions that work against the development of democracy in Cuba. For
several decades, U.S. foreign policy has been, at least rhetorically, guided by the
theory of developmentalism, which argues that as nations develop socio-economically
they will also develop politically.[28] Specifically, the theory posits that economic
development, particularly capitalist, will eventually yield a pluralist political system
or democracy. If this theory were actually applicable to Cuba, the U.S. should be
promoting capitalist development, trade, and cultural exchanges that would ultimately
lead to a diversification of political and economic power on the island. The U.S.,
however, has isolated itself from Cuba, permitting the Castro regime to maintain itself
in a cocoon in which it can avoid major political changes. The U.S. belligerence

toward Cuba has maintained a siege mentality among Cuba's political elite that has discouraged political diversity on the island.

As a result, reactionary U.S. policy has helped to consolidate the power of Cuba's revolutionary elite and to ensure that a strong, independent middle class does not emerge. As one analyst argued: "Every new U.S. threat gives him [Castro] another opportunity to wrap himself in the Cuban flag and another pretext for jailing dissidents."[29] If the U.S. government were to unilaterally lift the economic embargo it placed on Cuba in 1961, and allow Cuba to become politically integrated into the Organization of American States, the pressures on the Cuban system to change economically and politically would increase dramatically. To this date, support for Cuba within Latin America is based not on support for the Cuban model but on rejection of U.S. policy toward Cuba.[30] An end to the embargo would help to promote economic growth in Cuba, which, in turn, would help develop a middle class at a much more rapid rate.

Additionally, increased tourism and travel would add additional pressures on the political system to liberalize. Many Cubans in Miami would invest in Cuba, travel to Cuba frequently, and some may even move permanently to Cuba. This return migration would potentially pose problems. But, if the Cuban people on both sides of the Florida Straits look toward the future, the return of exiles from the United States could greatly assist in generating prosperity and a civil society in Cuba. The exile Cuban community for many years has been painted as a reactionary sort of Mafia. However, the views of many Cuban-Americans do not coincide with the policy positions of the conservative Cuban American National Foundation (CANF). And a far more moderate viewpoint has been gaining ground within the Cuban-American community.[31]

While this scenario may seem naively optimistic, other scenarios, like the continuation of the embargo, will produce much more negative results. While change is inevitable in Cuba in the long term, peaceful and prompt change cannot occur without stimuli to encourage both the democratic paradigm and the economic growth necessary for spawning a middle class and a new economic elite. In summation, an end to the U.S. embargo would create conditions more conducive to democratic development. First, greater economic activity on the island and international trade would help to create an independent middle class and economic elite.[32] Second, an end to U.S. hostility would disarm Cuba's political elite, in that they would be unable to point to the Colossus of the North to explain away the island's political and economic problems. Finally, while Castro remains a demon to many Cuban-Americans and some U.S. policy makers, he is the only person who can guarantee political stability on the island.[33] Take away Castro abruptly, and no one will be able to guarantee a peaceful transition. Part of the problem with U.S. policy toward Cuba is that Castro has not been offered a graceful way out. He may not accept change, but we will never know unless he is given some face-saving options.

6. Conclusion

Cuba cannot in a figurative way remain an island. Eventually, the tide of democracy and capitalism, for good or ill, will wash over that island. Change will be more predictable and less violent if Cuba is brought into a world community that includes the United States. Regime change is likely to come to an isolated Cuba in an unpredictable and violent manner, something no one should want. Only the United States has the economic and political clout to open the floodgate to Cuba, and thus the ability to promote a more rapid democratic change. If the U.S. government ends the anachronistic policy of isolating Cuba economically and politically, then it would be instrumental in helping to promote a peaceful change toward democracy in Cuba. If, however, the U.S. persists in taking draconian methods presumed to establish democracy in Cuba, then regime change could be violent and chaotic, and yet another Cuban crisis would be on the horizon.

ENDNOTES

1. Of course, this was not just an ideological contest. The struggle at the geostrategic level was over which superpower would have the greatest influence in world politics.
2. Guillermo O'Donnell and Philippe Schmitter (1986) *Transitions From Authoritarian Rule: Tentative Conclusions About Uncertain Democracies* (Baltimore: The John Hopkins University Press), p. 3.
3. Few scholars defend the notion that Cuba is more democratic than nations that have multiple political parties. For such a defense, see Joel Edelstein (1995) "The Future of Democracy in Cuba," *Latin American Perspectives*, Volume 22, pp. 7-26. Edelstein's article received several critical responses that can be found in the same issue.
4. Louis Pérez (1988 Edition) *Cuba Between Reform and Revolution*, p. 315.
5. See Cole Blasier (1985) *The Hovering Giant: U.S. Responses to Revolutionary Change in Latin America, 1910-1985* (Revised Edition) (Pittsburgh: University of Pittsburgh Press), p. 190.
6. See Timothy P. Wickham-Crowley (1992) *Guerrillas & Revolution in Latin America: A Comparative Study of Insurgents and Regimes Since 1956* (Princeton: Princeton University Press), especially pp. 186-192.
7. Thomas H. Greene (1990) *Comparative Revolutionary Movements: Search for Theory and Justice* (third edition) (Englewood Cliffs: Prentice Hall), p. 66.
8. See Guillermo O'Donnell and Philippe Schmitter (1986) *Transitions From Authoritarian Rule: Tentative Conclusions About Uncertain Democracies* (Baltimore: Johns Hopkins University Press 1986), p. 5.

9. See, for example, Robert A. Dahl (1971) *Polyarchy: Participation and Opposition* (New Haven: Yale University Press 1971).

10. See, for example, Guillermo O'Donnell, Philippe Schmitter and Laurence Whitehead (1986) (editors) *Transitions From Authoritarian Rule: Prospects For Democracy* (Baltimore: Johns Hopkins University Press), which was one of the first works to reject deterministic theories, in recent works on democratization, and promote the importance of "fortuna" and elite choices; Giuseppe Di Palma (1990) *To Craft Democracies: An Essay on Democratic Transitions* (Los Angeles: University of California Press); and John Higley and Richard Gunther (1992) (editor) *Elites and Democratic Consolidation in Latin America and Southern Europe* (New York: Cambridge University Press).

11. For an excellent account of the *barbudos*, and especially Castro himself, see Tad Szulc (1986) *Fidel: A Critical Portrait* (New York: Avon Books).

12. See, Ibid., pp. 509-526.

13. At the beginning, the regime only eliminated the wealthy economic elite, but eventually, in 1968, decided to eliminate small businesses in Cuba through the Great Revolutionary Offensive. Some analysts believe that this was a critical mistake, based more on political power considerations than economic considerations. See Susan Eva Eckstein (1994) *Back From the Future: Cuba Under Castro* (Princeton: Princeton University Press), pp. 34-41.

14. Lisandro Pérez (1992) "Cuban Miami," in Guillermo J. Grenier and Alex Stepick (editors) *Miami Now! Immigration, Ethnicity, and Social Change* (Gainesville: University Press of Florida), p. 85.

15. See, for example, Larry Diamond (1992) "Economic Development and Democracy Reconsidered," *American Behavioral Scientist*, Volume 35, pp. 450-499.

16. There is a huge body of academic literature that posits a relationship between a vibrant middle class and prosperity and the development of democracy. For a good review of much of this literature, see Seymour Martin Lipset, Kyoung-Ryung Seong and John Charles Torres (1993) "A Comparative Analysis of the Social Requisites of Democracy," *International Social Science Journal*, Volume 45, pp. 159-160.

17. Rueschemeyer, Stephens and Stephens have argued that the working class can be the strongest supporter of democracy. However, in the case of Cuba, the revolutionary regime mobilized the working classes in complete support of single-party rule. This mobilization was very effective since the new regime carried out policies that favored the working classes. See Dietrich Rueschemeyer, Evelyn Huber Stephens and John D. Stephens (1992) *Capitalist Development and Democracy* (Chicago: University of Chicago Press).

18. While discussing politics in Cuba with a variety of Cubans, I was struck by the allegiance that even the most critical Cubans have to the accomplishments of the revolutions. Even those Cubans who think that the entire political leadership is bankrupt take great pride in Cuba's accomplishments in health, education, and perhaps most importantly, in Cuba's ability to challenge the United States. Most of these gains have eroded dramatically with the loss of Cuba's major trading partner, the former USSR.

19. For a good summary of the Special Period, see Richard A. Dello Buono (1995) "An Introduction to the Cuban Special Period," in FLACSO's Lessons from Cuba's Special Period, *Carta Cubana: Interdisciplinary Reflections on Development and Society* (Habana, Cuba: Facultad Latinoamericana de Ciencias Sociales), pp. 1-11.

20. Three Cuban economists from the Center for American Studies, Havana, Cuba, Julio Carranza Valdes, Pedro Monreal Gonzalez and Luis Gutierrez Urdaneta, recently wrote a book which calls for a transition to a regulated market economy and economic decentralization. Some of these economists are now working at the Center for Studies of the Cuban Economy (CEEC).

21. Many Cubans, especially blacks, fear that a post-Castro Cuba will be greatly influenced by Cuban exiles who are predominantly white.

22. See, for example, Charles A. Reilley (1995) (editor) *New Paths to Democratic Development in Latin*

America: The Rise of NGO-Municipal Collaboration (Boulder: Lynne Rienner Publishers); and Philip Oxhorn (1995) "From Controlled Inclusion to Coerced Marginalization: The Struggle for Civil Society in Latin America," in John A. Hall (editor) *Civil Society: Theory, History, Comparison* (Oxford: Polity Press).

23. Gillian Gunn (1995) "Cuba's NGOs: Government Puppets or Seeds of Civil Society?," *Cuba Briefing Paper Series, No. 7,* The Center for Latin American Studies, Georgetown University, February 1995.

24. This point became obvious during a 10-day PAX World Service research trip to Cuba, during May 27-June 7 1995, where we met with nearly twenty NGOs. Although some NGOs have acquired some degree of autonomy, they are too dependent on the good graces of the state to be classified as independent.

25. See Andrew Zimbalist (1994) "Treading Water: Cuba's Economic and Political Crisis," in Donald F. Schultz (editor) *Cuba and the Future* (Westport: Greenwood Press) pp. 8-21.

26. At first, the Cuban government had majority (at least 51 percent) ownership in all foreign investment enterprises. Changes in investment laws allow 100 percent foreign ownership, although the state closely selects which firms are allowed such economic freedom.

27. See for example, Howard J. Wiarda (1991) "Is Cuba Next? Crises of the Castro Regime," *Problems of Communism,* VOLUME 40, pp. 84-93; Georgie Anne Geyer (1991) *Guerrilla Prince: The Untold Story of Fidel Castro* (Boston: Little, Brown and Company); Susan Kaufman Purcell (1992) "Collapsing Cuba," *Foreign Affairs,* Volume 71, pp. 130-145; Andres Oppenheimer (1992) *Castro's Final Hour* (New York: Simon & Schuster Inc.); and Donald E. Schulz (1993) "Can Castro Survive," *Journal of Interamerican Studies and World Affairs,* Volume 35, pp. 89-117.

28. For some seminal works on developmentalism, see Gabriel Almond and James S. Coleman (1960) *The Politics of Developing Areas* (Princeton: Princeton University Press); David E. Apter (1965) *The Politics of Modernization* (Chicago: University of Chicago Press); and Walt W. Rostow (1960) *The Stages of Economic Growth: A Non-Communist Manifesto* (New York: Cambridge University Press).

29. Gillian Gunn (1990) "Will Castro Fall?" *Foreign Policy,* Volume 79, p. 150.

30. See Mark Falcoff (1990) "Why the Latins Still Love Fidel," *The American Enterprise,* Volume One, pp. 42-49. Although Falcoff correctly points out that the "Latins" love Castro because of his Anti-Americanism, he treats this perspective with disdain. He does not consider the obvious fact that many people in Latin America also oppose U.S. policy toward Cuba because it is inhumane, counterproductive and violates international law.

31. There have been moderate Cuban-American groups in Miami for many years. The CANF became one of the most prominent groups principally with the assistance of the Reagan administration in the early 1980s. The U.S. government could, if it wanted, easily provide greater assistance to moderate Cuban groups.

32. See Mauricio A. Font (1996) "Friendly Prodding and Other Sources of Change in Cuba," *Social Research,* Volume 63, pp. 573-602.

33. See Wayne S. Smith (1996) "Cuba's Long Reform," *Foreign Affairs,* Volume 75, pp. 99-112.

22

Cuba Towards the Millennium:
Models for a Transition[1]

John A. Peeler

This chapter reviews five alternative models of the Cuban revolutionary regime and their projections for the future. Quite different predictions flow from (1) supporters; (2) very hostile opponents (counter-revolutionaries); (3) a scholarly range of critical supporters; (4) pro-engagement non-supporters; and (5) those transition models based on other Latin American or Eastern European countries. A great deal of attention is paid to Przeworski's framework for transition to inclusion in an integrated global economy.

1. Introduction

That the Cuban Revolution faces major challenges and important changes in the next decade may scarcely be doubted by even its most devoted supporters. The challenge of adapting to a new and unfriendly global economic order is complicated by the uncertainties of an inevitable generational transition in the political leadership. Predictions of the future of the Cuban state and economy depend on analysts' conceptions of the nature of that regime and on expectations for the evolution of conditions and policies external to Cuba. This chapter will review some alternative models of the Cuban revolutionary regime and will conclude with the author's own analysis and predictions.

2. Models for Analyzing the Cuban Revolution

2. 1. Supporters

Supporters of the Revolution of 1959, whether within Cuba or outside, tend to depict it as an organic popular revolution oriented by a Marxist-Leninist vanguard. This perspective tends to see the revolutionary people as producing their own leadership while the leadership is seen as the class-conscious vanguard of the proletariat. For example, Peter Roman, in studying representative institutions in Cuba, emphasizes that assemblies at various levels are forums for the articulation of grievances and that the authorities do respond to those grievances. In effect, he argues for the absence of fundamental contradictions between the leadership and the population.[2] For supporters of the Revolution, in short, it is an authentically popular work-in progress; it is beset, to be sure, by contradictions, but nevertheless fundamentally viable as a project for social transformation.

Without exception, Fidel Castro and the revolutionary leadership enjoy immense legitimacy in the eyes of supporters; policies of the government or the party may be roundly, explicitly criticized, but Fidel Castro and the top leadership are almost never attacked personally. It is implicitly assumed that they continue to be the natural leaders of the Cuban people, that all true revolutionaries support them, and that the vast majority of Cubans continue to be true revolutionaries. For the survival and progress of the Revolution, solidarity behind the leadership is seen as far more important than the fraudulent or illusory pluralism and individual rights of "bour-geois" democracy.

From this perspective, the generational transition in the leadership is not fundamentally problematic, because, left to itself, the revolutionary polity will produce appropriate leadership. It is external economic and political pressures that are deeply problematic, because they threaten to force the leadership off the revolutionary track or to undermine the revolutionary commitments of the mass of Cubans. The fate of Russia and Eastern Europe is a specter haunting Cuban revolutionaries and their supporters. They are determined that Cuba avoid the precipitous abandonment of socialism and prevent its tactical concessions to private enterprise and foreign investment from undermining the socialist project. Neverthe-less, the regime and many of its supporters seem inclined, cautiously, to open the political system to elements of civil society independent of the party, but committed to the revolutionary project.

2. 2. Counter-revolutionaries

Counter-revolutionaries constitute the majority of but by no means all politically active exiles, and at least a plurality of the U.S. political elite. Counter-revolutionaries tend to see the Cuban regime either as a personal tyranny under Fidel Castro or as a communist dictatorship. Either way, they accord absolutely no legitimacy to the regime and grant it no significant popular support. Counter-revolutionaries have worked tirelessly to undermine the revolutionary government, both by subversion within Cuba and, more importantly, by cultivating political support from the U.S. government. The latter stratagem has borne such fruit as the trade embargo, the "Cuban Democracy Act" of Congressman Torricelli and the Helms-Burton Act, all of which have been aimed at "bleeding" Cuba's economy.[3]

Counter-revolutionaries have been predicting the imminent fall of the revolutionary regime since 1959, and they tend to explain its continued survival largely in terms of naked coercion and intimidation. Thus, it follows that as they look to the future, they see the prospect of the long-suffering Cuban people finally rising up and overwhelming their oppressors. They say all they want for Cuba is democracy; but as the Helms-Burton Act makes clear, many also want the return of property seized after 1959. In any case, the Cuba envisioned by the counter-revolutionaries would be strongly capitalistic in its economy while its polity would either be openly authoritarian or, more likely, "democratic" with a tightly restricted political spectrum and limited liberties.

2. 3. Critical Supporters: A Scholarly Range

Between these two mutually exclusive analytical models of the Revolution, we find the majority of Latin Americanists and foreign policy scholars in the United States, Canada and Europe, and a growing minority among social scientists in Latin America. The spectrum ranges from critical support to sympathy for the ideals of the Revolution coupled with severe criticism of its practice. The former persuasion is exemplified by Carollee Bengelsdorf, Joel Edelstein, and Marifeli Pérez-Stable, all of whom explicitly support the ideals of the Revolution while criticizing the leadership for repeatedly undercutting those ideals by its contradictory actions. Bengelsdorf argues, for example, that repeated attempts to decentralize and democratize policy-making have been undercut by the unwillingness of the central leadership to surrender authority.[4]

Critical supporters sincerely hope that somehow the Revolution may survive this latest crisis as it has survived so many before, and that it will continue to be a beacon for social justice in the barren wilderness of injustice that is Latin America. The critical supporters are distinguished from the more whole-hearted supporters by their greater willingness to directly criticize Fidel Castro and the top leadership, and especially by their greater emphasis on the importance of decentralization and democracy. For example, Joel Edelstein acknowledges the importance of the Leninist model of revolutionary leadership for bringing about a revolutionary transformation in the face of external threats. He also argues the inadequacy of that model in the present circumstance. He argues that a markedly decentralized and participatory socialism is the best means of avoiding both the re-emergence of authoritarian dependent capitalism and decline into social and political chaos.[5] Critical supporters are not advocates of conventional liberal democracy which in its debased form, found in the press and U.S. government pronouncements, becomes electoral fetishism. But they do believe that the future vitality—and perhaps survival—of the revolutionary regime will depend on a much more extensive and authentic opening than has taken place heretofore.

A somewhat more jaundiced view of the Revolution and a more conventional view of democracy is expressed by Susan Eva Eckstein, arguing that Cuba must adapt to the "new world order" in a way that "strengthens its economic base, respects democratic principles, and preserves the social gains of the revolution." Eckstein appreciates these accomplishments but implicitly acknowledges that the goal of a more sweeping revolutionary transformation is really not possible. But that, for Eckstein, is no reason to surrender the good that has been accomplished.[6]

2. 4. Pro-Engagement, Non-Support

One of the best known writers on Cuban themes is Wayne Smith, former head of the U.S. Interest Section in Havana and a consistent advocate for a political opening to Cuba. However, though he is emphatically opposed to the U.S. policy of hostility and isolation, Smith is not at all a supporter of the revolutionary regime. He simply thinks that the best way to bring about liberalization and possibly democratization is through contact, rather than through isolation and punishment. He argues that, ideological differences notwithstanding, Fidel Castro may fruitfully be compared not with Ceausescu or Gorbachev, but with Francisco Franco. That is, Smith characterizes Castro as an aged dictator presiding over the twilight of an authoritarian regime that is outmoded by history. Franco, in the 1970s, was able to exercise partial control over the transition. It is Smith's contention that Cuban reforms since the mid-1980s represent a similar attempt to prepare the society gradually for a transition to a new regime. The United States, he argues, may best facilitate this transition by engaging Cuba.[7]

2. 5. Cuba and Transition Models: Latin America and Eastern Europe

More recent discussion of Cuba has taken place within the theoretical framework of transitions from authoritarian or communist rule. A basic question has been whether the transitions from authoritarian regimes to democracy that took place in Southern Europe and Latin America in the 1970s and 1980s are comparable to the transitions from communism in the former Soviet Union and Eastern Europe in the 1980s and 1990s. While Di Palma acknowledges that there are similarities, he insists that the distinction between authoritarian and totalitarian regimes is still relevant and that communist regimes are totalitarian, at least in aspiration. Hence, there can be no negotiated transition from communism to democracy, Wayne Smith notwithstanding.[8]

On the other hand, Adam Przeworski makes an explicit and extended argument that the two sets of transitions may be fruitfully compared through formal theory.[9] He suggests that any transition may be analyzed in terms of the capabilities, goals, and interactions of four collective actors: regime hardliners and regime reformers; opposition moderates and opposition radicals. Under circumstances where the reformers and moderates gain the upper hand in their respective coalitions, a negotiated transition may occur. In this situation, Regime Reformers believe they have enough popular support to compete in a democracy with guarantees, where their most vital interests are protected. Opposition Moderates may use the Radicals to enhance their leverage, but distrust them and prefer an alliance with the Reformers. Radicals may either accept democracy with guarantees or be repressed. If the opposition is too weak, no transition takes place. If the radicals are too strong, the reformers would not be able to demand concessions or guarantees in the transition.[10]

3. Transition...To What?

All but its most militant adversaries would grant that the Cuban revolution has had real and widespread popular support rooted in the fact that it has provided tangible material benefits and opportunities to the majority. Supporters are correct in emphasizing the fundamentally popular character of the revolutionary process and the importance of preserving and advancing its social and economic achievements. Moreover, for the first time in Cuba's long and difficult history, it has had a government that has given Cubans reason to be proud of their country. Thus, in spite of the evident difficulties of the present crisis, it is not unreasonable for supporters of the revolutionary regime to expect it, if left to itself, to survive and develop. Indeed, if Cuba were by some magic to be left to itself, there is little doubt that a regime deriving its legitimacy from the social and political transformations of the Revolution would continue in some recognizable form.

Supporters of the Revolution are either insensitive to, or avoid dealing with aspects of the regime that make it less sui generis and more comparable to other polities. For example, Fidel Castro's forty-plus year incumbency begs comparison with long-lived *caudillos* of Latin America. Cuba's single-party system is certainly comparable with those of other communist and former communist countries. This is not to say that Fidel Castro is merely a caudillo; or that Cuba must necessarily recapitulate the evolution of Russia, much less Romania. Rather, it is to affirm that Cuba is probably subject to the same well-known tendencies; for example, the difficulty of passing on charismatic authority, the tendency of ruling parties to bureaucratize as in other societies.

The revolutionary regime has survived this long against incredible odds; more than anything, it is the product of an iron political will, a commitment to defy the overwhelming power of imperialism no matter the cost. This spirit still animates the leadership, some significant portion of the party membership, and substantial numbers of other citizens. These Cubans will not yield easily or gracefully to that which they have spent a lifetime struggling against. We may expect, then, that the inner core of dedicated revolutionaries—some tens of thousands at least—will defend the regime and resist its transformation.

In terms of Przeworski's analysis, the inner core is comprised of hard-liners. There is no doubt that they are still thoroughly in control, as attested by the renewal of political repression in the wake of the downing of the exile planes in 1996. Then, in May 1997, the Communist Party program emphasized commitment to the socialist revolution. In late 1997, the regime showed its hard-line proclivities by denying dissidents clearance to run for the National Assembly and by emphasizing that domestic private investment would still be tightly restricted.[11] In contrast with the Przeworski transition model, the situation in Cuba now is that the revolutionary inner core is in control and that the regime reformers are subordinate. In the opposition, moderates have little scope to separate themselves from the radical counter-revolutionaries. Given this power distribution, no transition to a new regime is likely to emerge from internal Cuban processes. The regime might evolve in response to internal changes, most notably the demise of Fidel Castro, or changes in the global political-economic conjuncture. However, the regime cannot be successfully pressured to negotiate a transition.

Unfortunately for the Revolution, Cuba will not be left to itself. There is every indication that the long-standing obsession of a succession of U.S. administrations will continue as long as the island continues to resist American hegemony. Thus, in one form or another, Cubans may expect a continuation of various sorts of economic and political pressures that will drag them down and drain the country of more human resources.

Even if U.S. hostility were to end, Cuba's dependence on sugar and other agricultural and mineral exports has not been sufficiently alleviated by increasing revenues from tourism. Moreover, the growing prominence of tourism itself poses potentially subversive challenges to the revolutionary social order. Cuba needs to insert itself in the global capitalist economy on terms over which it has little or no control. Cuba has consistent difficulty in generating enough exports to pay for its imports and enough revenue to pay for its government. Under these circumstances, Cuba will have to continue eroding the social conquests of the Revolution as it makes steadily more concessions to both global capitalism and local, small-scale free enterprise.

The impossibility of isolation applies to political as well as economic affairs. The Cuban people cannot be isolated from the increasing integration of global communications, which inevitably carries the hegemonic ideas of liberal democracy and liberal capitalism. These are prevailing ideas in the countries dominating the information technology revolution and the global information system. We may thus expect to see growth in the numbers of those who, at least privately, wish for "bourgeois" liberties, both economic and political. Since the regime will be steadily less able to preserve egalitarian social benefits, its ability to retain popular loyalty is likely to erode. The majority of the people, even if they reject the counter-revolution, are probably tired and quite possibly disillusioned. Thus external pressures are likely to undermine the power of the revolutionaries. These external challenges are not, however, likely to lead to a complete breakdown (rupture) of the regime. The Party, the Army, and the associated popular organizations are too strong, too institutional- ized, to break down, and they still retain substantial popular support.

Changes are also taking place within Cuban society that will be ever harder for the revolutionary leadership to control. The economic opening has become increasingly indispensable to the survival strategy of the regime. As steadily more opportunities are made available for foreign capital to earn profits in Cuba, the regime will have to continue expanding private enterprise opportunities for Cubans in order to confront the manifest inequality between those who operate in the dollar economy and their compatriots in the peso economy, and in order simply to allow those laid off from state enterprises to support themselves. Paradoxically, to preserve its legitimacy in the eyes of its supporters, the regime must encourage them to relearn the ways of capitalist society. The more people earn their living independently of the socialist state, the stronger the economic foundation of an autonomous civil society.

The regime has indeed been deliberately fostering the growth of civil society by its opening to the Catholic Church and other religious organizations and by sanctioning autonomous, but pro-revolutionary organizations such as the *Centro Félix Varela*. The intent is to enhance support for the Revolution by fostering more pluralism and debate within the Revolution, without sanctioning any break in the Party's political monopoly. Organizations critical of the Revolution are illegal, but they do exist in spite of government repression. The scope of their support is impossible to verify. Civil society is thus segmented into an encouraged revolutionary sector and a repressed opposition sector. The regime cannot fully repress the latter without risking the loss of essential investments and tourism from Canada and Europe.

In terms of Przeworski's framework, the revolutionary civil society may be considered roughly equivalent to reformers within the regime. The opposition sector may be differentiated into moderate and counterrevolutionary (or radical) wings, with the latter closely linked to Cuban-American counter-revolutionaries. The boundary between regime reformers (revolutionary civil society) and opposition moderates is ill-defined: reformers are not actually regime insiders, and they would see themselves as working for a more or less sweeping renovation of the Revolution, rather than its negation. Should the grip of the inner revolutionary core (hard-liners) loosen, both revolutionary civil society and opposition moderates could forge a transitional alliance, leading to a democracy with guarantees to preserve essential revolutionary achievements. Such a transitional alliance would marginalize both revolutionary hardliners and radical counter-revolutionaries.

An additional complexity that is likely to promote an opening, at least for a time, is the proximate transition from Castro to post-Castro. The historical record of such transitions—whether we consider only Marxist-Leninist regimes founded by autonomous revolutionary movements, or charismatic leaders more generally—is that the leader's departure or demise may cause profound crisis and political instability but rarely leads directly to the destruction of the regime itself.

There is, in short, reason to expect that Castro's death or departure would occasion a significant crisis but not necessarily the breakdown of the regime. There would certainly be an attempt to bring about an orderly succession, most likely with Raúl Castro succeeding his brother. Raúl's command of the Army and the Party would assure him the means to achieve and keep control in the short run. However, the new rulers would have less ability than Fidel Castro to resist the external pressures and internal changes detailed above. To enhance his own legitimacy, Raúl might well mandate further liberalization; thereby enhancing the risk that he would ultimately lose control of the civil society. Any attempt on his part to tighten the reigns of power would have very high costs in terms of foreign investment and tourism, and might also push reform-oriented party members and their allies in the revolutionary sector of the civil society toward an alliance with opposition moderates.[12] Under this scenario of escalating protest and repression, the preferences of the revolutionary civil society and the moderate opposition would be highly congruent: both would reject the survival of the regime unchanged, and both would prefer a democracy with guarantees that would limit the power of the radical counter-revolutionaries.

Fidel Castro's departure might be produced by a crisis. The ongoing political-economic crisis could be further exacerbated, possibly by some scandal or blunder by the government which would undermine its credibility and provoke popular protests. Castro's personal authority could be cast into question in the course of such a crisis. It might prove easier to bring the moderate opposition on board without Castro's polarizing figure at the head of the regime. He himself, or his lieutenants, might come to realize that. Moreover, Castro or his lieutenants might perceive that U.S. hostility could be mitigated without Castro in the picture. In a context of political-economic crisis, the prospect of normalization of relations with the U.S. would be extraordinarily attractive if it could be done while preserving the revolutionary regime through the sort of expanded coalition and aperture described in the previous paragraph. The leadership might well split over the desirability of pursuing normalization under such conditions. Fidel Castro, even if he were unwilling to leave, could find himself maneuvered out of power.

The most likely exit from such a crisis would be conciliatory; taking public action to rectify the immediate grievance and opening the political arena another notch in order to reduce the pressure. This would probably alleviate the immediate crisis but also further legitimize at least the revolutionary sector of the civil society. Opposition moderates within the civil society might also gain visibility and credibility in such a crisis by publicly defending the protesters. The counter-revolutionary opposition would use the crisis to trumpet the bankruptcy of the regime, through its access to U.S.-based media. Civil society organizations would evolve toward more openly political action, and they would become de facto political parties.

At some point in such a conciliatory and liberalizing scenario, Fidel Castro and the revolutionary leadership would no longer unilaterally control a deteriorating situation. The revolutionary sector of the civil society, and perhaps important voices within the party itself, would be advocating further opening as a means of regaining the initiative and recapturing popular support. The revolutionary component of the civil society would also be in touch with the moderate elements of the opposition, which would be making much the same demands for aperture. Radicalization of the protests might strengthen the counter-revolutionary opposition. To the rest of the political spectrum, that would be the least desirable of possible outcomes. The revolutionary coalition could then be broadened to include the moderate opposition as a means to block the counter-revolutionary opposition.

The moderate opposition, however, would join such an expanded revolutionary coalition only if the leadership agreed to some substantial aperture, some further movement towards opening the political process to competition. They might even insist on tolerating the counter-revolutionary opposition, though this would be hard for the leadership to accept. But the leadership might finally have to accept it as a way of reducing pressure in a crisis that could favor the growth of the counter-revolutionary cause. However, only a crisis that is out of control appears conducive to the ascendancy of the counter-revolutionary opposition, either through opportunism under chaotic conditions, or through imposition by a U.S. invasion ostensibly for the purpose of reimposing "law and order." Neither of these contingencies is very likely.

4. Conclusion

Understanding Cuba's situation at the present time requires us to grasp something Karl Marx understood very well a century and a half ago: humans make their own history, but not with elements of their own choosing. The Cuban revolutionary leadership and the vast majority of the Cuban people have made a radically new revolutionary society over the last forty-one years, and they have done so against the steepest odds. The project is still far from complete, and it is beset by internal contradictions. However, it still constitutes a principal alternative model for Third World societies. The Cuban revolution is a monument to revolutionary political will. It would be foolish indeed to predict the demise of the Cuban revolution.

Yet the analysis in this chapter suggests that revolutionary political will may have its limits. The grand structure, the global conjuncture that confronts Cuba in the year 2000, leaves Cuban revolutionary leaders with few options. They may either defend the integrity of the revolutionary project as they define it; thereby foregoing access to resources they need or they can make varying levels of compromise that will generate resources but will also vitiate the revolutionary project. The external conundrum has its internal reflections: if they hold to revolutionary orthodoxy regardless of the cost, they would increasingly lack the means to provide the extensive benefits which undergird the legitimacy of the regime. To the extent that they compromise with global capitalism they could generate resources; but also produce inequality and injustice, undermine socialist consciousness, and promote social and political tension. As they deal with the tension by means of aperture, they increasingly lose control of the civil society. Thus some significant transformation of the revolutionary regime seems inevitable.

ENDNOTES

1. An earlier version of this article was presented at the International Congress of the Latin American Studies Association, Guadalajara, Mexico, April 17-19, 1997.

2. Peter Roman (1993) "Representative Government in Socialist Cuba," *Latin American Perspectives*, Volume 20, Number 1, p. 27.

3. In the United States, examples of counter-revolutionary thought are easy to find. See, for example, the consistently antirevolutionary reports posted on ElCubano@aol.com.

4. Carollee Bengelsdorf (1994) *The Problem of Democracy in Cuba* (New York: Oxford University Press); Carollee Bengelsdorf (1996) "Intellectuals Under Fire," in *These Times*, September 16, pp. 27-29; Marifeli Pérez-Stable (1993) *The Cuban Revolution: Origins, Course, and Legacy* (New York: Oxford University Press); Marifeli Pérez-Stable (1996) "Cuba: Prospects for Democracy," in Jorge I. Domínguez and Abraham F. Lowenthal (editors) *Constructing Democratic Governance: Latin America and the Caribbean in the 1990s* (Baltimore: Johns Hopkins University Press), pp. 185-197.

5. Joel C. Edelstein (1995) "The Future of Democracy in Cuba," *Latin American Perspectives*, Volume 22, Number 4, p. 24.

6. Susan Eva Eckstein (1994) *Back from the Future: Cuba Under Castro* (Princeton: Princeton University Press), p. 218.

7. Among his many writings on Cuba, see, for example, "Cuba's Long Reform," *Foreign Affairs*, Volume 75, Number 2, pp. 99-112 (1996). For a contrasting analysis, see the response to Smith by Susan Kaufman Purcell (1996) "The Cuban Illusion: Keeping the Heat on Castro," *Foreign Affairs*, Volume 75, Number 3, pp. 159-161; and David Rieff (1996) "Cuba Refrozen," *Foreign Affairs*, Volume 75, Number 4, pp. 62-76.

8. Giuseppe Di Palma (1995) "Totalitarian Exits," in H. E. Chehabi and Alfred Stepan (editors) *Politics, Society, and Democracy* (Boulder, Colorado: Westview Press), pp. 233-245.

9. Adam Przeworski (1991) *Democracy and the Market: Political and Economic Reforms in Eastern Europe and Latin America* (Cambridge: Cambridge University Press), pp. 69-74.

10. A good window on what may be going through the minds of U.S. policy makers is provided by Edward González and David Ronfeldt (1994) *Storm Warnings for Cuba* (Santa Monica: RAND).

11. Pablo Alfonso, "Cuba Blocks Dissidents' Election Bids," *Miami Herald* (internet edition) December 3, 1997; John Rice, "Cuban Official Signals Limits on Capitalism," *Miami Herald* (internet ed.), November 28, 1997.

12. Raúl is portrayed by Juan Tamayo as more pragmatic than Fidel Castro, and as well along in supporting an orderly process of transition. Juan Tamayo, "Raul Castro Takes on a Higher Profile," *Miami Herald* (internet edition), December 17, 1997.

23

Incentives and Impediments to Cuban National Reconciliation

Holly Ackerman

This chapter asserts that processes of Cuban national reconciliation have been underway for over twenty years. In addition to defining "national reconciliation," the chapter re-examines the history of political conflicts and challenges some of the commonly held assumptions in the United States about the nature of ongoing relations between islanders and those living outside Cuba. The major contribution of this chapter is the specification of the dimensions of incentives and impediments, not only intransigent government postures but also simplistic media images that impede the dissolution of the remaining barriers between the Cuban exile and the island population.

1. Introduction

Cuba is an unlikely case for analyzing reconciliation because of the inherent conflict that remains largely unresolved. Nonetheless, this chapter asserts that processes of Cuban national reconciliation have been underway for the last twenty-odd years. In this chapter, an effort is made to specify the incentives and impediments to national reconciliation between the Cuban exile and the island population.

Prior to 1959, Cuba had a tradition of limited exile with small groups being forced to leave the national territory after challenging the Spanish colonial government or the dictatorial regimes that followed independence. Periodic amnesties usually permitted the return of exiles within their lifetime. Cubans were not, however, inclined to exit the island en masse or for long periods until after 1959. Since then, over one-and-a -half million Cubans have left Cuba (Milán Acosta, 1995). Despite absences of forty years, about 30 percent of the post-1959 exiles in the United States have expressed their intention to return to Cuba permanently if there is a political transition to democracy. The overwhelming majority seeks the right to return periodically as full citizens (Grenier and Godwin, 1997).

Less is known about the actual number of Cubans still seeking to emigrate. Cuban officials acknowledged that one million people had registered to leave in 1980 during the Mariel boatlift (Mesa-Lago, 1995). With the social and economic crisis in Cuba since 1989, the current levels of Cubans willing to emigrate far exceed that number (Aja Díaz, 1995; Clark, 1981; Mesa-Lago, 1995). The terms for effecting a reduction in the desire for exit and reconciliation with the diaspora remain unclear.

Within the limited but expanding social science literature on reconciliation, an initial analysis of the process of reconciliation generally focuses on the perceived injustices that have produced divisions between states or within nations (Kriesberg, 1998; Lederach, 1997). In the Cuban case, the injustices that have produced this exodus and formed the basis of national disputes can be roughly divided between pre-1980 and post-1980 motivations for exit. Prior to 1980, most of those who emigrated were born before the revolution and had experienced both dictatorial and democratic forms of government. As the new regime consolidated power, it summarily executed members of the former regime or, more often, critics within the revolutionary ranks or dissenters from the revolutionary process. The new regime incarcerated tens of thousands of Cubans without due process, confiscated properties, and eventually imposed a communist system (Gordon, 1976; ICOSOVC, 1982; OAS Reports, 1961-1965). Cubans emigrated in reaction to one or more of these events. When discussing their motivations for leaving, pre-1980 Cuban emigres mention as important factors actual or impending death, imprisonment of self or relatives, the loss of homes and businesses, and/or the loss of political freedom and a way of life.

Most post-1980 Cuban exiles, however, were born under the revolution or were quite young in 1959, and they have known no other form of government. Although former political prisoners and dissidents continue to be among those leaving, a complex mix that is best described as anti-politics motivated most of the post-1980 Cuban exiles. During the 1989-1994 period, rafters entering the United States mentioned four common toxic elements of revolutionary life that were their principal motivators (Ackerman, 1996). These were (1) the necessity of wearing a mask of compliance and support for the regime; (2) the inability to know who was who in the population due to the pervasive state security and mass surveillance techniques (e.g., the Committees for the Defense of the Revolution [CDR]); (3) the necessity of involvement in illegal activity in order to survive (principally buying on the black market before free markets were legalized in 1994); and (4) the fear that acts of violent retribution might follow a change in government.

Although both the pre and post-1980 exile groups agree that it is necessary to change the form of government in Cuba in order to enable Cuban exiles to return, the type of losses imposed by exile differs between the two groups. Few in the post-1980 group had relatives or friends who were summarily executed or imprisoned for long periods, while many in the first group were so affected. The pre-1980 Cuban exiles have, however, had up to forty years in which to rebuild their lives, whereas many post-1980 exiles feel that the greatest injustice they have suffered is a loss of time when they were not free to choose the direction of their lives (Cabello, 1997).

Using a revisionist analysis of historical events and political culture, this chapter evaluates the status of national reconciliation in the case of Cuba and concludes that a conciliatory process has been underway since 1978. The chapter begins by addressing two questions: First, what is meant by reconciliation? Second, who is to be reconciled in the Cuban case? Central to the process are social and political actors within the island and exile populations that form the geographic halves of the nation. Drawing on this history and analysis, an examination is offered of the incentives and impediments to reconciliation within the divided nation. Selected factors located within the Cuban nation, particularly at the mass level, are examined in detail while major factors involved in bilateral and multilateral foreign relations are summarized.

2. What Is National Reconciliation?

The term national reconciliation carries at least two meanings. The first, which I shall call literal reconciliation, is simply the meeting of alienated parts of a national community with the intention of accommodating differences. Parties that have refused to sit at the same table or to attempt to discuss their differences are reconciled to the necessity or benefit of acknowledging and speaking directly to each other with the intent of making an accommodation.

The second definition of reconciliation, which I shall call process reconciliation, involves a mechanism for trying, in good faith, to sort out and verify past history and differences so that rancorous divisions can be concluded without destroying the life of the nation. A social space must emerge or be designated where this process can take place through more or less formal mechanisms and relationships. The nature of the relationships and the type of linkages that are most conducive to reconciliation have only recently been well conceptualized and have not been fully specified or empirically demonstrated (Ackerman, 1994; Gardner-Feldman, 1991; Kreisberg, 1998; Walsh, 1996). The process occurs among various parties at both elite and mass levels—individuals, families, small groups, government officials—and at various institutional levels—national, regional, interstate, global—and the circumstances of each case vary. There is no formula for necessary and sufficient factors in reconciliation.

Additionally, reconciliation of a nation is conceptually distinct from transition of the state. Transition is the process of changing the form and/or terms of political domination in a state. While the two may interact, and have sometimes been temporally related, they do not necessarily occur at the same time and they can be analyzed separately. National reconciliation is an accommodation among formerly divided peoples that permits restoration of the nation on peaceful terms, while transition is an alteration of the terms of power within a recognized state. Reconciliation tends to be a more protracted process.[1]

In the Cuban case, divisions are within a single ethnic group that was split following a national political insurrection in 1959. The issue of multiple ethnic groups and diverse cultures does not complicate the Cuban case as it does some cases in Eastern Europe, nor does the issue of ideology and control imposed by a foreign power. The Cuban revolution was popularly supported and was embraced more than imposed. The primary division is based on political loyalty, with those who actively or passively accept the government of Fidel Castro remaining on the island and those who challenge or reject the revolutionary regime being imprisoned, socially ostracized or, most often, choosing to abandon the national territory.[2]

3. Who Needs and Wants to be Reconciled in the Cuban Case? A Revised History Emphasizing Mass Politics and Elements of Cuban Political Culture.

A revised history is needed to give proper consideration and weight to a variety of social actors who have been ignored in previous accounts. Both journalistic and academic works have placed emphasis on the conflict between the U.S. and Cuban governments, using the beginning and the ending of refugee flows and the bilateral relations as the central issues. In the process, mass behavior such as mutual aid was undervalued as a social force.

As in other divided groups, stereotypes have played a part in promoting and maintaining the national division. In the Cuban case, it is important to clarify the current validity of popular conceptions of the exile and island populations. The media (Didion, 1987; Mankiewicz, 1975; Matthews, 1957; Rieff, 1993; Sawyer, 1993; Walters, 1977) have employed stereotypes to characterize the two portions of the Cuban nation. These media portrayals have been particularly persuasive in the United States where free travel to Cuba is prohibited for most U.S. citizens and where coverage is infrequent except during crises. Therefore, the occasional "Cuba special" or crisis coverage has been disproportionately influential in public opinion.

The Cuban exile has frequently been portrayed in the mass media as the resentful, reactionary rich in Miami. The terms *Batistianos*, *contrarevolucionarios* and *gusanos* (Batista cronies, counter-revolutionaries, worms) were used by the Cuban government and adopted by the media to define an ideal type. The image was one of a politically reactionary, wealthy landowner who was aligned with the prior dictator and who resisted all social and political change while seeking to restore his or her property rights and political control at the expense of the mass of Cuban citizens.

At the time of the Mariel boatlift in 1980 a second stereotype was briefly defined, but the original stereotype was reapplied to the entire group once the boatlift ended. The 125,000 Mariel arrivals, most of them born under the revolution, were characterized as ungrateful for the social benefits bestowed by the revolution and demonized as aberrant, violent and anti-social element who were called *delincuentes*, *lumpen* or *escoria* (delinquents, scum) (Gamarra, 1981; del Aguila, 1982). Since the late 1980s, these derogatory terms have been dropped from the official discourse and have almost disappeared from popular usage in the 1990s.

In fact, both of these general characterizations applied to only a few thousand persons among the pre-1980 cohort and less than two thousand among the post-1980 exile cohort (Ackerman, 1996; Bowen, 1980; Clark, 1981; del Castillo, 1981; Fagen, 1968; Free, 1960).[3] The image has persisted for three reasons: first, because more conservative, moneyed interests were the first to organize in exile and they have focused on lobbying the U.S. government in an aggressive and very public way. They are also readily available to the U.S. media. Groups which organized later did so using a traditional Cuban style with small multiple groups of known associates forming loose, shifting coalitions. This is a style that is difficult to follow and is unfamiliar to the U.S. media.

Second, the image persisted because it was strategically, imaginatively and actively promoted by Fidel Castro and is invariably linked with a generalized Latin American resentment of U.S. interference in the hemisphere. Cuba's success in resisting U.S. interference, surviving the U.S. embargo, maintaining control despite the demise of Soviet aid, and asserting Cuban sovereignty has been as much a source of proud identification for many Latin Americans and Canadians as it has been for portions of the island population. The exile in Miami is seen as the author and guarantor of punitive U.S. foreign policy toward Cuba and, in the process, all Cuban exiles become stereotyped. In many minds, Miami itself has become a stigmatized, political locale.[4]

Third, the charisma and dominance of Fidel Castro has held center stage for more than forty years. The U.S. press has treated him as a clever and humorous leader who has managed to out-fox the U.S. Even veteran reporters flatter him and avoid tough questions when granted interviews. As one exile commentator recently said, "Fidel has become a totem and approaching him directly, like a mere politician, is taboo."

These stereotypes are not just held by the American public. Between 1959 and 1978, the Cuban government largely closed the island to foreign influence and controlled the media. Cubans born after 1959 were heavily propagandized with negative images of those who left and of the society they entered. Maintaining contact with relatives in Miami could ruin life chances for education and work in Cuba. A Cuban colleague, born under the revolution, tells of growing up believing that her father had deserted the family during her infancy and was living with a second wife in a different part of Cuba. Only after she defected to a U.S. embassy, while on a foreign technical exchange, did her mother reveal that the father had been living all the while in exile. Admitting this sooner might have prevented her entry into the university and acquisition of a professional job. Histories of this sort, where family composition and relationships were altered in order to appear "integrated" with the revolution, abound in Cuba and in the exile community. The fact that they are coming into more open view is evidence of a process of identity clarification and personal reconciliation that bodes well for a parallel process at the national level.

A former commercial pilot, who entered exile as a rafter, describes his stereotype of the society he was entering:

> In the movies in Cuba, over and over, we saw the same newsreel footage of a German shepherd dog attacking blacks in a civil rights demonstration. We made jokes about the dogs because they were used over and over. The news events changed but it was always that one clip of the same dogs and the same protesters. I knew that it was exaggerated but when I arrived in the U.S., I still feared that people might attack me. You grew up thinking it was a daily event all over the U.S.

Most of the rafters of the 1989-1994 period grew up with a second and post-1978 stereotype of "the North American dream." Following the opening of return visits by "non-hostile" Cuban exiles in 1978, Cubans heard about and received the material benefits of the exiles as relatives and friends returned bearing gifts and telling of opportunities unimagined in Cuba. Those who had no relatives and no possibilities for legal emigration--most of the rafter population and higher percentages of people outside of Havana--spent years dreaming of exaggerated material possibilities.

Fortunately for the prospects of reconciliation, the reality is that the Cuban exiles are more complex and dynamic than the stereotypes that still predominate in the media. It is also an attitudinal group experiencing gradual change. Since 1991 Florida International University has conducted an annual opinion survey of Cuban exiles in Florida and New Jersey (Grenier & Godwin, 1991-1997). Three general points can be deduced from these surveys. First, both punitive and reconciliatory solutions are supported by most exiles. For example, most Cuban exiles support both the current policy prohibiting trade with Cuba and a policy of direct negotiations with the present government to re-establish normal relations. Some authors have interpreted the support for punitive positions as evidence of a vindictive, irredentist position within the exile community. Taken together, the support for both punitive and reconciliatory positions is more likely to indicate an overall desire to end the division of the nation by whatever means will be most expeditious. Second, the number of exiles supporting reconciliatory solutions is growing annually among all generations. Third, recent arrivals and those Cuban-Americans born in the U.S. are the most committed to reconciliatory solutions and the least supportive of punitive measures. Mortality rates will cause an accelerating shift toward more conciliatory solutions.

Space constraints do not permit an exhaustive review, but the demographic diversity of the exile community by income, occupation, education, sex and age is well documented (Ackerman, 1996; Bach, Bach & Triplett, 1981; Boswell, 1995; Fagan, 1968; Portes, Clark & Lopez. 1981). The stereotype of a wealthy enclave is simply inaccurate. It is, however, accurate to say that each wave of Cubans who have emigrated has been disproportionately more educated and comprised a higher percentage of whites than the population remaining on the island. Less discussed is the political diversity that will be considered below.

Within the exile community, the popular view of the island population and of recently arrived Cuban exiles is also stereotyped. The predominant image is of a morally deficient, youthful population that lacks initiative and has lost the capacity to tell right from wrong as a result of years of feigned political compliance and dependence on the state for sustenance. This stereotype is belied by the collective achievements of the 1980 exiles, raised under the revolution who, in the last U.S. census, had nearly pulled even with their exile compatriots on collective economic and social achievements (PUMS, 1993). Nonetheless, as each new group of exiles is incorporated into the Cuban community in the U.S., they seem to view those who remain on the island as somehow damaged by their extended term of residence.

On the other hand, the national media image is of an island population still supportive of the historic revolutionary leadership and committed to socialism. This view ignores the hundreds of dissident groups that have been organized since 1989 (Altuna de Sanchez, 1996), the continuous existence of a political prison population since 1959, and the persistence of mass efforts to leave. It also ignores cleavages within the ruling circle. During the Papal visit in January 1998, as more media representatives were present for longer periods and with less government control, a broader picture began to be broadcast in the United States.

4. Political Actors in Exile.

A truncated view has also existed on the evolution of exile political actors and the strategies they have employed. The predominant image is drawn from the 1960s, a time of armed struggle, funded and controlled by the U.S. government and organized from Miami, Florida. Simultaneously, however, a democratic and revolutionary resistance inside Cuba attempted to stimulate a general insurrection using funds and supplies acquired by their counterparts in exile (Ackerman, 1998; Blight and Kornbluh, 1998). This effort to "re-start" the insurrection has been called the politics of illusion since it was based on uninformed optimism that the island citizenry would rise up and that the U.S. government would provide prompt, altruistic and adequate support for their efforts.

Although clandestine groups continued to operate from exile through the 1960s, they were effectively defeated on the island at the 1961 Bay of Pigs invasion and eliminated entirely by 1965. The 1,200 persons captured from the Bay of Pigs invasion brigade were imprisoned for a year and then ransomed and returned to the U.S. However, suspected resistance members inside Cuba, numbering in the tens of thousands, were also rounded up at the time of the invasion and given prison sentences of 10-30 years. They were not included in the ransom sponsored by the U.S. government. These political actors did not reemerge until the late 1970s, when they were released as a result of the first literal reconciliation of the exile and island communities.

The 1970s and early 1980s saw the consolidation and rise to prominence of a conservative exile element, led by the Cuban American National Foundation (CANF). The strategy of the CANF was to control the U.S. policy agenda rather than to be controlled by it. The CANF's policy was an effort to isolate the island, maintain preferential immigration status for Cubans, insist on the property rights of the few affluent Cuban exiles, and reimpose a market economy after the fall of the Castro brothers. The end of the regime was felt to be imminent if the embargo were tightened and enforced. This nonviolent strategy occurred together with the organization of terrorist groups that attacked individuals, groups and governments that approved of or consorted with the Cuban government—an approach known as *La guerra por los caminos del mundo* (war through the paths of the world). During the 1970s Miami witnessed 200 bombings involving Cubans (*Miami Herald*, October 10, 1988). Together with the highly visible presence and conservative policy accomplishments of CANF, the bombings and acts of civil disobedience by terrorist groups reinforced the stereotype mentioned above.

Simultaneously and without publicity, more progressive individuals and organized groups worked quietly for the release of thousands of political prisoners in Cuba.[5] In 1978 these efforts were rewarded in the first literal reconciliation of exile and island political actors. The "dialogue," held in Havana, consisted of two meetings between Fidel Castro and over 100 Cuban exiles. The meetings were organized by the Cuban government, using the good offices of individual members of the Cuban exile communities in Miami, Spain, and Caracas. The meetings served as the ceremonial means to release results of secret negotiations conducted during the prior year among exile intermediaries, the U.S. and Cuba (Gonzalez, 1987; Smith, 1987). Over the next two years, 3,600 political prisoners and their families were to be released into exile in the U.S. (Benes, 1994; *Granma Weekly Review*, September 11, 1978), with an additional 7,000 going to Venezuela (Garcia Moure, 1997; Herrera Campins, 1998; Perez, 1998; Rodriguez Iturbe, 1998).[6] Although participants in the meetings were attacked, bombed and boycotted in Miami, the literal reconciliation of 1978 brought a new set of political actors into the diaspora and produced an agreement for direct contact between citizens of the divided nation through family visits to Cuba. Quietly, over the next decade, hundreds of millions of dollars in Cuban exile remittances would be sent (*The Economist*, July 24, 1993) and tens of thousands of families visited Cuba (Mesa-Lago, 1994). Thus process reconciliation had begun at the popular level.

By the start of the 1990s, as former prisoners reestablished their lives in exile, they reemerged politically as leaders or participants in organized, centrist political parties and labor groups.[7] They adopted a strategy of being open to dialogue with the Cuban government and of affiliation with European and Latin American based international political parties, thus avoiding the U.S. government and the thorny issue of U.S. control of their organizations. The strategy had the additional advantage of creating contact and solidarity between exiles and Latin American political activists. At the same time, they recognized that leadership for political change had to originate on the island and began to seek alliances with island dissidents calling for a plebiscite. These groups have come together in *La Plataforma Democrática* (the Democratic Platform), one of the first exile coalitions to espouse nonviolent political action aimed at national reconciliation and a transition to democracy. Many other groups have followed, with an array of exile and island alliances, nonviolent strategies and political perspectives slowly emerging (Espinosa, 1998).

In May 1995, when President Bill Clinton ended a thirty year policy of nearly unconditional acceptance of Cuban refugees, the nonviolent strategy for political action swept the exile and island dissident groups. Whereas a cache of guns and speedboats were de rigeur among the 1960s exile activists, the 1990s exile activists groups have seminars on nonviolent citizen action, establish contact with island counterparts. and open web pages to broadcast the latest messages from their island partners. This is not to say that belief in armed struggle has ended within the exile community or that moderate forces predominate, only that the balance has begun to shift.[8]

Ironically, shortly after public opinion in the Miami Cuban community began to shift away from punitive policy, the Clinton Administration tightened the embargo following the Cuban government's downing of two exile aircraft in 1996. The shift toward a hostile stance had been fueled by the rafter crisis in the summer of 1994 when President Clinton met with leaders of CANF and gained their endorsement to deny entry to the tens of thousands of rafters headed toward South Florida. The immigration door was closed to Cubans for the first time and popular opinion blamed CANF for giving it a push. This endorsement reduced support for CANF in Miami. Popular support had been conditioned on the belief that the conservative forces would assure refuge for those leaving the island. Families that had been closed-mouthed about their remittances and family visits to Cuba no longer felt the need to hide. When forced to choose between starving the regime through embargo and denying their compatriots entry, most members of the exile community came down on the opposite side from the right-wing political activists.

The right-wing has been further affected by the death of CANF's founding leader, Jorge Mas Canosa. In a political culture that believes in strong, charismatic leadership and personal control of institutions, the death of a leader could mean the eclipse of a political position. The CANF's public image has been further eroded by recent indictment of some CANF leaders and the implication of others in the supply of weapons to terrorist action groups or individuals (*The Miami Herald*, August 13, 1998). Tactical miscalculations and a leadership vacuum on the right-wing of the exile community opened political space exactly when centrist forces such as *La Plataforma* were stabilizing.

About 28 percent of persons claiming Cuban ethnic background in the 1990 census were second-generation Cuban-Americans born in the United States (PUMS, 1993). They too have been politically active. As is discussed below under incentives to reconciliation, these groups draw from a pluralist model of interest group politics learned in the U.S., not from the conspiratorial model of 1959 Cuba. At the same time, they maintain the concept of a generational responsibility to contribute to national, public life - a prominent feature of pre-revolutionary Cuban political culture.[9] As one youth leader said, "Our parents have no faith in institutions. They have faith in individuals based on shared values and personal experience. We believe in the possibility of institutions that work." Whether these groups will successfully incorporate young members of the exile community born in Cuba and dissidents living in Cuba, remains to be seen. Like the *Plataforma* they have focused on building international alliances, largely to raise consciousness about conditions of daily life in Cuba (*El Nuevo Herald*, July 31, 1997).

5. Political Actors on the Island.

The principal problems on the island are lack of a space where social and political action can emerge in an organized, collective form and a new social diversity without direction created by the dissolution of the Cuban welfare state. While tight control of political space and social anarchy benefits the government in the short run, it reduces the chances of reconciliation and heightens the possibilities for violent confrontations when change does come. The regime-controlled, mass organizations in Cuba that formerly comprised a universal system of citizen-on-citizen surveillance tied to *la economia de prebendas* (an economy of small favors)—by which one advances by criticizing and reporting on co-workers and neighbors—were replaced by selective intervention in acute cases during the Special Period. Dissidents effectively identify themselves by making declarations, petitioning the government, issuing press releases and the like. Individual intervention by mass organizations can then be organized and rewarded by the government. Hence, dissident organizing is very difficult even though mass surveillance is less vigilant. Most rebellious acts in Cuba are still acts of individual defiance rather than organized acts of dissent.

In the past, the regime had employed mass organizations to preventively monitor the level of discontent and used what had been called an escape valve to periodically release dissenters from the island population. A patterned interaction has existed since the early 1960s between citizens seeking exit and the Cuban government (Ackerman, 1996). The pattern begins with a buildup of action by ordinary citizens, who are ineligible for immigration, making illegal exits by sea independently (1960-1965 and 1989-1994) or entering foreign embassies to ask for asylum (1977-1980). As the number of Cuban citizens seeking to emigrate increases, there is public recognition of the social phenomenon. As the phenomenon becomes common knowledge and the numbers increase, the government acknowledges and invites augmentation of the numbers—through Camarioca in 1965, through Mariel in 1980 and by homemade rafts in 1994. The state then demonizes those who are emigrating, labeling them as counterrevolutionary, anti-social elements trying to gain entry to the U.S. The greatly expanded wave of emigration that follows the government opening produces an immigration crisis for the United States. This results in negotiations between the U.S. and Cuban regimes to normalize and liberalize immigration accords. It then becomes mutually advantageous to both governments to shut down the illegal exits, making it difficult for ordinary people to emigrate. The net effect is to provide a barometer for the Cuban government to identify the level of domestic discontent and to rid itself of dissenters.

Following the 1980 Mariel boatlift, U.S. military advisers recognized that these cycles would continue unless the U.S. President refused entry to refugees as the crisis intensifies (Larzelere, 1988). The official refusal came in 1994 when rafters were denied entry and sent to camps at Guantánamo Naval Base. As a result, there is now a lid on the escape valve.

One could interpret the January 1998 Papal visit as the domestic equivalent of the escape valve cycle described above. As dissent has grown, with more than 300 dissident groups organized on the island in two years (Altuna de Sanchez, 1996), the regime invited people to participate in an event, observed by the entire world, that opened limited political and social space—the Pope's visit. Rather than inviting malcontents to leave, they were appeased. The historic leadership tolerated a temporary and limited increase of religious organization and participation, while simultaneously refusing further concessions after the Papal visit and maintaining harassment and imprisonment of the current crop of internal dissenters.[10] This is an oblique form of negotiation among the Cuban government, the Cuban dissidents, and their allies in exile. The regime is able to cede small areas of social and political space and to control the speed of change while simultaneously obtaining positive, international media coverage.

Only time will tell if it is a pattern that will be repeated and expanded in domestic use as it was in foreign policy. Although it has undoubtedly allowed the regime to siphon off dissent, maintain political control and improve its press image, each time the cycle occurs, increased number of people seek release from the demands of loyalty to the Cuban state. Essentially, the absolute power of the state is eroded through each round of the cycle, and the social space is opened. There is a gradual use of this space to express opinions openly on the island and to encounter the other half of the Cuban nation. Nonetheless, the elaboration of alternative institutions is very slow in coming, and most people face an increasingly complex and decentralized social reality without laws, institutions, or clear work roles to anchor them.

6. Incentives and Impediments to Reconciliation.

Given the history and actors described above, what are the most prominent incentives and impediments to national reconciliation? The incentives include: (1) prior experience with literal reconciliation that has, in the long run, proved beneficial to all parties; (2) a shared sense of *Cubanidad* including a strong tradition of mutual aid; (3) a widening political spectrum with an increasing social space and gradual tolerance for contrary views; (4) heightened commitment to non-violence at the mass level both in exile and on the island. The impediments include: (a) continued use of simplistic media images; (b) intransigence of U.S. policy toward Cuba and Cuban policy to the U.S; and (c) discontinuities and dysfunctional elements of social and political culture both on the island and in exile.

7. Incentive: Prior Experience with Reconciliation

When members of the exile community met with Fidel Castro in 1978 a formal process of reconciliation began. Over twenty years later, the impact of the historic meetings is still remembered by many of the 1994 rafters as a turning point in their lives.[11] The return of Cuban exiles to the island brought a new vision of who the exiles were, what life outside Cuba was like, and demonstrated that the regime would alter its rigid rejection of the exile community when financial necessity dictated. As a result, citizens on the island began to reevaluate what they had in common with the extended Cuban community.

The dialogue also promoted increasing demand for exit from the island. Fear of acknowledging and contacting relatives receded, as did the most harsh and dehumanizing characterizations of the two portions of the exile community. A more civilized language of description was born. Eduardo Garcia Moure, a principal facilitator of the dialogue in Venezuela, evaluates the Cuban government's response to the dialogue differently. "Fidel became frightened by dialogue. It didn't turn out as he'd expected. He actually thought that many more young Cubans would want to come back to Cuba. He underestimated the effect that exile success would have on the island and he got Mariel as a result."[12] This continues to be the contradiction of reconciliation in the Cuban case. The major material resources of the Cuban nation are now found outside the Cuban state in exile. The imbalance is such that the Cuban state is threatened by a wider reconciliation and, consequently, has applied small "doses" of dialogue rather than attempting a wider opening. Still, the net effect has been to reduce negative stereotypes and to create personal and institutional channels for periodic discussion between the two communities.

8. Incentive: A Shared Sense of *Cubanidad* Including a Strong Tradition of Mutual Aid

Both the U.S. and Cuban governments impose limitations on direct exile aid to the island and the U.S. sometimes stops financial aid entirely, depending on the status of foreign relations. Humanitarian aid goes through a tedious and lengthy bureaucratic process of "licensing" that must be repeated for each shipment. On the other side, Cuba requires that all aid be turned over to the Cuban government, often refusing distribution rights to churches, non-governmental organizations (NGOs) and the like. Yet mutual aid abounds both within the exile community, between the exile and island communities, and among islanders.

The mutual aid tradition is a very individual issue and is not necessarily tied to institutions. For example, when 2,000 rafters were being held in a refugee camp on the Cayman Islands in 1994, an exile housewife made an independent decision to fly down to the camp to see what was happening. She then devoted the next two years of her life to providing for the material needs of the desperate camp population and assuring their safe settlement in the U.S. or third countries. She became an institution in order to meet the needs of her compatriots. Through appearances on

Miami radio stations, she was able to solicit the aid needed to provide basic assistance for the Cayman refugees (Navarette, 1995). This is a Cuban tradition. Social networks grow up spontaneously based on a shared sense of Cubaness (*cubanidad*). Similarly, hundreds of Cuban exiles in Miami began calling the public phones installed on Guantanamo to send aid during the raft crisis of 1994-1996. A recent study conducted by the *Comision Economica para America Latina y el Caribe* (CEPAL) and the Cuban government estimated exile remittances to the island at 800 million dollars for 1996.[13] While this figure seems inflated, it is clear that mutual aid is thriving.

The tradition is not limited to Cuban exiles in the United States. The Cuban community in Valencia and Caracas, Venezuela, is currently engaged in similar efforts to settle exiles who arrive in Venezuela by crossing borders from Colombia, Brazil, and Guyana. Those who receive aid are not necessarily relatives, nor do they have to share a particular political perspective—they just need to be Cuban. In the Cuban case, mutual aid is tied to national identity. The image of Cubans as people who "go on and get ahead" despite adversity is a living tradition that is supported by the community in general. Longstanding traditions of this sort have obvious implications for a progressive reconciliation if the social space continues to open. The small widening of space for religious activity following the Pope's visit is a potential institutional anchor for expanding mutual aid and for reconciling differences in the informal way that characterizes Cuban culture. The Cuban people are quite literally taking care of each other. This is a tradition that augers well for reconciliation though it is not without contradictions as discussed below.

9. Incentive: A Wider Political Spectrum

The 1978 reconciliation meetings served the Cuban government by removing political prisoners from the country who might otherwise have threatened the regime. In exile, they have been instrumental in providing a center within diaspora politics. For example, most of the officers and organizers of the *Coordinadora Social Demócrata* and a sizable portion of the leadership of the *Partido Democrática Cristiano* are former political prisoners who came into exile during the 1970s and 1980s. Together with the *Partido Liberal* these groups have formed a coalition that has been remarkably stable, politically mature and long-lived by the standards of Cuban politics. In Cuban political history, coalitions have often been temporary, superficial and strained. They illustrate the mistrust of formal institutions felt by many pre-1980 exiles and their tendency toward small, conspiratorial groups. By setting a different course that also avoided U.S. involvement and the baggage of neo-colonial discourse, these groups validated the worth of institutions that could serve the needs of reconciliation. Like the younger generation of Cuban Americans who are working in coalition with island groups to try to secure release of political prisoners, these more stable institutional arrangements indicate political learning and maturity that make reconciliation more likely. Still lacking, however, are cross-generational alliances either on the island or in exile and cross-issue alliances. That is, exile elements insist on a political agenda while islanders struggle to put food on the table. An agenda that focuses on social conditions is needed.

10. Incentive: Heightened Commitment to Nonviolent Action at the Mass Level Both in Exile and on the Island.

Contrary to media images, the acceptance of nonviolent action at a mass level is now widespread both in Cuba and in the exile communities. The uses and objectives of nonviolent action vary, however. Some groups view nonviolent action as a mechanism for provoking mass protest within Cuba. The Democracy Movement exemplifies this approach. The group tries to stimulate protest on the island through bringing exile flotillas to the twelve mile limit off the Cuban coast and staging various protest actions. To date they have failed to provoke much interest or even to arrive at their destination. It is worth noting, however, that the leaders of the organization were previously strong supporters of armed struggle and then of terrorist activity. Their conversion to nonviolent action, even as an opportunistic and instrumental response, is significant for the prospects of reconciliation. They have joined in coalition efforts supporting nonviolent groups on the island.

For other organizations, such as the younger generation of Cubans and *La Plataforma* (in exile) and groups such as The Christian Liberation Movement and the Cuban Democratic Project (in Cuba), nonviolent action has meant pacifism, human rights monitoring, petitioning the Cuban government for a plebiscite, and the U.S. Congress for an end to the embargo. The overlapping concerns of these organizations build mutual trust and linkages between the island and exile communities. In some cases, family visits and professional conferences have also served as opportunities to build organizational linkages. The mutual threat that characterized individual rhetoric in the 1960s and 1970s has changed. A dialogue of peace and nonviolence has begun outside official channels.

11. Impediment: Continued Use of Simplistic Media Images.

The extraordinary charisma of Fidel Castro, his ability to stimulate nationalist sentiments and the continuing obstinacy of the U.S. embargo have worked against reconciliation. Castro continues to be portrayed as a Latin Robin Hood and the Cuban exile as a monolith of reactionaries, racists, and exploiters. The complexity of Cuban politics with its multiple small action groups - both on the island and in exile - make it difficult to understand and follow developments. This does not seem to be changing despite the expanded presence of news bureaus in Havana for several years. News bureaus fear closure if they report items unfavorable to the Cuban government, and so distorted story lines and stereotypes continue. This changed somewhat during the Pope's visits when dissidents were freely interviewed and large numbers of journalists sought alternative stories. On balance, however, the stereotypes continue to predominate. The density of Cuban politics makes it unlikely that knowledgeable, in-depth reporting will arise any time soon or that the media could sort out the complexities in a time of crisis. This state of affairs lends itself to political manipulation and works against the forces of reconciliation.

12. Impediment: Intransigence of U.S. Policy Toward Cuba and Cuban Policy to the U.S.

The largest impediment to reconciliation is the intransigence on both sides of U.S.-Cuban foreign relations. Passage of the Helms-Burton Act made it impossible for the U.S. President to exercise usual executive authority in easing relations with Cuba. The only advantage to be found in this situation is that the international sanctions contained within Helms-Burton have prompted European leaders to act as a political counterweight. Both the European Union and individual governments have acted to restrain the U.S. from fully implementing the more oppressive aspects of the Helms-Burton Act and to offer financial incentives to the Cuban government if democratic openings are made.

The Cuban government has refused these openings and responded with *el antidoto* an anti-Helms Burton Law that tightened limits of expression and essentially conflated criticism of the United States. During the lifetime of its founding leader, it seemed unlikely that substantial reconciliation would occur through government initiative. The Cuban government has been reactive in its openings—basically chasing the misery curve to avoid mass revolt but titrating concessions to maximize political control and preserve elite illusions. Citizen demand will probably be a pre-condition to further opening.

13. Discontinuities and Dysfunctional Elements of Political Culture on the Island and in Exile.

Cuban political culture promotes a total commitment to core values. Extremism has often been seen as a virtue. Although the use of violence, intimidation and intolerance for diversity have diminished, they are not by any means gone. The possibility of violent struggle continues to be a threat to reconciliation. Growing social disparities are a particular concern.

As the informal economy expands and remittances flow in, disparities of income increase in an economy that is stagnant. It has been estimated that the median monthly income in 1995 was $6.40. Hence, a family receiving $50 per month from relatives in Miami was earning 800 percent more than an average worker. Those who could rent an extra room to tourists for $25-50 dollars per day were doing well, even if they registered their business and paid the state taxes of $225 per month. Less discussed is the racial tension inherent in the situation. Only 3 percent of members of the exile community is of Afro-Cuban descent while 30-50 percent of the island is Afro-Cuban. Remittances, then, are consequently feeding both racial and material inequality. This is the flip side of the mutual aid phenomenon— *remesas generando rencor* (remittances generating rancor). To date, the Cuban government has exploited the racial divide rather than healing it, and members of the exile community have failed to acknowledge the need for a strategy that addresses popular needs as well as those of family and friends.

14. Conclusions

Despite media pictures of a people intractably divided by political beliefs, there has been reconciliation within the Cuban nation since 1978. Traditions of mutual aid have been at work both institutionally and individually. At an institutional level, linkages have been difficult to create and sustain partly because of the Cuban government's demands for control and partly because of a cultural preference for individual or small group action. Cuban exiles have resources that are needed on the island and large segments of the community have been willing to share them.

Opinions in exile communities have moved gradually toward support for peaceful solutions to the political issues dividing Cuban exiles and those on the island.

World religious leaders and European political leaders have promoted reconciliation while constructive and multilateral pressure for resolution continues. Some of the most influential leaders and organizations opposing reconciliation present a diminished threat due to shifts to nonviolent tactics, death of leaders, and reduced support for their organizations. The new generation is more tractable and less aggrieved. The most serious injustices of the revolution have abated although political incarceration continues to be a major mechanism for controlling dissent. Overall, at the level of public opinion and political action, there is cause for optimism.

The possibility of reopening an escape valve on the island has been severely limited by the U.S. rejection of further mass immigration. The Cuban government has shown that it will make concessions to maintain domestic political control. Each concession creates further social space where citizens can act. The concessions come slowly and are carefully titrated to be as small as possible. How the island population maneuvers collectively will be the most crucial element in advancing the process of reconciliation. More important, as the regime erodes, there will eventually be a substantial political opening. That will be the critical test of the goodwill and solidarity that have been produced by mutual aid and struggle for human rights. The tendency to fragment into old patterns of conflict will arise. The lack of an emerging set of collective values and the expansion of racial and generational inequalities is most threatening.

The path to Cuban reconciliation remains long and uncertain. The uncertainty can be attributed in no small part to U.S. policy and the inordinate power of Fidel Castro. Castro seems more concerned with maintaining personal control than with inserting the nation into the post-Cold War world on favorable terms. The U.S. policy remains at once punitive and ill-considered as a force for reconciliation. Cuban policy has been a priority only in times of crisis and, even then, has been heavily influenced by small, conservative segments of the exile community. Reconciliation of the U.S. and Cuba has not been on our collective minds.

ENDNOTES

1. Recent examples that illustrate this point include the apologies offered by the U.S. and Japanese governments for some state policies during World War II-the U.S. bombing of Hiroshima and Nagasaki, and the Japanese forced use of Korean women as sexual servants to their military. These efforts at reconciliation occurred decades after the events. However, it is an incomplete process. Regional conflicts from the Civil War in the United States still arise in discussion between Southern state officials and the Federal government over the issue of "Yankee control." By contrast, in the Southern Cone the transition to democracy included simultaneous creation of commissions to establish the truth of official practices regarding disappearances,

torture, and systematic state murder of political adversaries. In the succeeding decade, the process of deepening democratic institutions has been accompanied by continued revelations and conciliatory action regarding these human rights violations. In the case of U.S. civil rights violations, Bill Clinton recently commented that the time was still not ripe for an official U.S. apology to African-Americans for the imposition of slavery and segregation. Factors governing the timing and continuation of the process are not well defined.

2. Approximately 10 percent of the present Cuban nation is located in a diaspora whose principal locus is the United States, with approximately 55 percent found in South Florida and with sizable populations in New Jersey, New York, and California. The second largest site is Venezuela, followed by Spain and Puerto Rico. However, Cuban communities exist in all Latin American countries and in many parts of Europe. A few Cubanitos are sprinkled in all parts of the world. Telling stories of "the strangest place I ever met another Cuban" is a conversational pastime among Cubans. For further demographic information see Ackerman, 1995 and 1996; Boswell, 1984 and 1994; Ríos de Hernández, 1996 and Cobas & Duany, 1997.

3. Many authors classify 4 or 5 waves of immigration since 1959 based on significant events in U.S. and Cuban bilateral relations. In this article I will use a more global division into pre-1980 and post-1980 groups to emphasize the relative size and political formation of groups born before and after the revolution: 1959 to 1979 equaled 680,000 and 1980-1994 equaled 325,000.

4. For a debate on this subject, see "The Great Cuba Debate," *Peace Magazine* (May-June) 1997; "An Interview with Holly Ackerman," *Catálogo de Letras*, Volume 3, Number 13, (January) 1998.

5. For a description of the political prison population since 1959 and analysis of its political significance, see Holly Ackerman (1998) "Five Meanings of Cuba's Political Prisoners," *Cuban Studies Association Occasional Paper Series*, Volume 3, Number 1 (February), University of Miami, Coral Gables, Florida.

6. Political infighting between the National Security Council and the State Department prevented prompt settlement of the 3,600 political prisoners in the U.S., although most of them eventually gained entry despite years of delay. Venezuela kept its agreement.

7. For a more complete description of the centrist groups and their leaders, see Manuel Ramon de Zayas (1991) "Who's on First?" *Post-Modern Notes* (Spring).

8. During the recent *Cumbre de los Presidentes* de Latino America held on Margarita Island, (Venezuela) a group of activists with roots in armed struggle traditions of the 1960s tried to sail to the island with the avowed intent of assassinating President Castro. Their equipment has been linked to officials of CANF, reinforcing the belief that nonviolent strategy has been embraced by right-wing groups only as a publicity expedient but which does not represent a real philosophical shift.

9. Focus group conducted by the author with representatives of organized groups of young Cuban-Americans, Miami, August 14, 1997, Written transcript in author's possession.

10. Following the Pope's visit, President Castro released some of those political prisoners on a list presented by the Pope. But the most visible and effective of the current dissident leaders who were on the list were not released. In this process the regime gained domestic and international goodwill for its release of prisoners but was still able to repress the current political opposition and set limits on popular protest. Like the escape valve, this domestic scenario can be repeated as needed for domestic control and international goodwill.

11. Since 1994, the author has conducted over 100 interviews with rafters. In response to the question, "Do you remember the very first time you ever thought of leaving Cuba?" many respond that it was the Dialogue meetings or the effects of meeting Cubans from exile that first started them thinking about exiting.

12. Eduardo Garcia Moure, Interview by author, Caracas, Venezuela, October, 1997.

13. In order to reach this amount every Cuban exile in the world (1.5 million) would have to send about $550 per year to the island. It is well known that the earlier, richer exiles no longer have relatives on the island and many conservative exiles refuse to send anything at all. Thus, Cubans with average incomes are sending

most of the remittances and they usually do this through extended family contributions. While some families are sending "investment capital" for illegal purchases in Cuba (homes, artwork, etc.), most families send modest sums to friends and relatives as they can afford. Mesa-Lago's (1998) estimate of $400 million for 1996 seems more realistic.

REFERENCES

Ackerman, Holly (1998) "Five Meanings of Cuba's Political Prisoners," *Cuban Studies Association Occasional Paper Series*, Volume 3, Number 1 (February).
_____ (1997) "Protesta Social en la Cuba Actual: Los Balseros de 1994," *Encuentro*, Volume 3, pp. 125-132.
_____ (1996) "An Analysis and Demographic Profile of Cuban Balseros: 1991-1994," *Cuban Studies*, Volume 24.
Ackerman, Holly and Juan Clark (1996) *The Cuban Balseros: Voyage of Uncertainty* (Miami: The Cuban-American National Council).
Ackermann, Alice (1994) "Reconciliation as a Peace-Building Process in Postwar Europe," *Peace and Change* (July).
Aja Díaz, Antonio (1995) "La Emigracion Cubana de Cara al Futuro," in *Memorias de Centro de Estúdios de Alternativas Políticas* (La Habana: Universidad de Habana).
Altuna de Sánchez, Amaya (1996) *Estudio Sobre la Situación Actual en Cuba* (Miami: Partido Demócrata Cristiano de Cuba).
Bach, Robert L., Jennifer B. Bach and Timothy Triplett (1981) "The Flotilla Entrants Latest and Most Controversial," *Cuban Studies*, Volume 11, Number 2 (July), pp. 29-54.
Benes, Bernardo (n.d.) "Memorias de Mis Conversaciones Secretas con Fidel Castro," *Private diary of Bernardo Benes* (Miami Beach).
Benes, Bernardo (1995) Interview with author (January).
Blight, James G and Peter Kornbluh (1998) (editors) *Politics of Illusion: The Bay of Pigs Invasion Reexamined* (Boulder: Lynne Rienner).
Boswell, Thomas D. and James R. Curtis (1984) *The Cuban-American Experience: Culture, Images and Perspectives* (Totowa: Rowman and Allanheld).
Boswell, Thomas D. (1994) *A Demographic Profile of Cuban Americans* (Miami: Cuban American National Council).
Bowen, Robert (1980) *Final Report of the Cuban-Haitian Taskforce: November 1, 1980* (The Cuban-Haitian Taskforce, U.S. Department of Health and Human Services, Washington).

Cabello, Julio Túpac (1997) "El exilio apaciguado," *Primicia*, Volume 5, pp. 38-40 (December).

Clark, Juan (1981) *The 1980 Mariel Exodus* (Washington: The Council for Inter-American Security).

Cobas, José and Jorge Duany (1997) *Cubans in Puerto Rico: Ethnic Economy and Cultural Identity* (Gainesville: University Press of Florida).

de Zayas, Manuel Ramon (1991) "Who's on First?" *Postmodern Notes*, Volume 1 (Spring).

del Aguila, Juan M. (1982) "An Analysis of the Cuban Detainee Population in Atlanta's Federal Penitentiary," A paper delivered at the Latin American Studies Association 10th International Congress, Washington (March).

del Castillo, Siro (1981) "A Plea to Destigmatize Mariel," *Caribbean Review*, Volume 13, Number 4.

Didion, Joan (1987) *Miami* (New York: Simon and Schuster).

Fagen, Richard R., Richard A. Brody and Thomas J. O'Leary (1968) *Cubans in Exile: Disaffection and the Revolution* (Palo Alto: Stanford University Press).

Free, Lloyd A. (1960) *Attitudes of the Cuban People Toward the Castro Regime in the Late Spring of 1960* (Princeton: Institute for International Social Research).

Gamarra, Eduardo A. "Comment: The Continuing Dilemma of the Freedom Flotilla Entrants," *Cuban Studies*, Volume 12, Number 2, pp. 87-91 (July).

Garcia Moure, Eduardo, Interview with author, Caracas, Venezuela, 1997.

Gardner-Feldman, Lily (1995) *The Concept of Reconciliation* (Washington: U.S. Institute of Peace Press).

Gonzalez, Reinol (1987) *Y Fidel Creo el Punto X* (Miami: Saeta Ediciones).

Gordon, Michael (1976) *The Cuban Nationalizations* (Buffalo: Hein & Company).

Grenier, Guillermo and Hugh Godwin (1997) *FIU Cuba Poll 1997; Executive Summary* (Miami: Florida International University).

Herrera Campins, Luis, Interview with author, Caracas, Venezuela, June 1998.

ICOSOV (1982) *El Presidio Politico en Cuba: Testimonio* (Caracas: ICOSOCV Ediciones).

Kreisberg, Louis (1998) "Reconciliation: Conceptual and Empirical Issues," A paper presented at the International Studies Association Meeting, Minneapolis, Minnesota.

Larzelere, Alex (1988) *Castro's Ploy—America's Dilemma: The 1980 Cuban Boatlift* (Washington: National Defense University Press).

Lederach, John Paul (1997) *Building Peace: Sustainable Reconciliation in Divided Societies* (Washington: United States Institute of Peace Press).

Mankiewicz, Frank and Kirby Jones (1975) *With Fidel: A Portrait of Castro and Cuba* (Chicago: Playboy Press).

Matthews, Herbert (1957) "Cuban Rebel is Visited in Hideout," *New York Times*, February 24, p. 1 (A).

Mesa-Lago, Carmelo (1995) *Cuba's Raft Exodus of 1994: Causes, Settlement, Effects and Future* (Coral Gables: The North-South Center of the University of Miami).

_____ (1994) *Are Economic Reforms Propelling Cuba to the Market?* (Coral Gables: North-South Center of the University of Miami).

Milán Acosta, Guillermo C. (1995) "Estimado de los Cubanos Residentes en el Exterior," in *Memorias de Centro de Estúdios de Alternativas Políticas* (La Habana: Universidad de Habana).

Navarette, Lourdes, Interview with author, Miami, January 1996.

Organization of American States (1961) *Inter-American Commission on Human Rights. Report Concerning the Situation of Human Rights in Cuba* (OEA/Ser .L/V/II.4, Doc 30, November 7).

Perez, Carlos Andres, Interview with author, Caracas, Venezuela, June 1998.

Portes, Alejandro, Juan Clark & Manuel M. Lopez (1981) "Six Years Later, The Process of Incorporation of Cuban Exiles in the United States: 1973-1979," *Cuban Studies*, Volume 11, Number 2, pp. 1-23 (Fall).

Rieff, David (1993) *The Exile: Cuba in the Heart of Miami* (New York: Simon & Schuster).

Ríos de Hernández, Josefina and Amanda Contreras (1996) *Los Cubanos: Sociología de una Comunidad de Immigrantes en Venezuela* (Caracas: Fondo Editorial Tropykos).

Rodriguez Iturbe, Jose, Interview with author, Caracas, Venezuela, May 1998.

Sawyer, Diane (1993) "Fidel Castro in Cuba," *An ABC Primetime Live Broadcast*, March 4, 1993.

Smith, Wayne (1987) *The Closest of Enemies: A Personal and Diplomatic Account of U.S.-Cuban Relations Since 1957* (New York: Norton).

Walters, Barbara, "Fidel Speaks," An ABC Special Report, June 9, 1977.

24

Off-Shore Politics: Changes Within The Cuban Exile Community

Sara Lulo

Almost one million Cuban-Americans reside in the United States, making it the largest Cuban population outside of Cuba. Not unlike other immigrant groups, Cuban-Americans came to the United States as a result of (and in reaction to) political circumstances in their country of origin. However, Cold War politics and the United States' disdain for the proximate communist regime set an immediately distinctive tone to the Cuban immigration waves following the 1959 Revolution. The U.S. government's rhetoric hailed Cuban exiles as champions of freedom and democracy—against Castro's revolution. Forty-one years later the Revolution is still intact on the island, and what was once expected to be a temporary Cuban exile community in the United States has instead developed into an economically and politically prominent American constituency. This economic and political clout, commensurate with Cuban-Americans' vested interest in Cuba's future, make the exile community an intrinsic factor in U.S. discussions of twenty-first century Cuba. Indeed, many international policy makers deem the "psychological civil war" between Cubans living on the island and Cuban exiles as a "core issue to understanding Cuba."[1] This chapter will provide an overview of the Cuban-American immigration experience and discuss the pertinence of the community to U.S. relations with Cuba.

1. Turbulent Waves of Immigration

"The hardest part about leaving Cuba was not knowing if I ever would see my mother again."
—Nena Perez de Núnez, Cuban exile as of 1970

"If I were to have one wish, it is that not one more Cuban has to go into exile."
—Uva de Aragon, Cuban exile
Assistant Director of Cuban Research
Institute, Florida International University

Though Cuban exiles have established communities and networks throughout the United States, the two highest concentrations of Cuban-Americans settled in Miami, Florida and Union City, New Jersey. Strong Cuban-American constituencies influence politics in both Florida and New Jersey, and they are represented in the United States Congress by fellow Cuban-Americans Robert Menendez (Democrat-New Jersey), Ileana Ros-Lehtinen (Republican-Florida), and Lincoln Diaz-Balart (Republican-Florida). However, it is the Cuban enclave in Miami and its surrounding Dade County that indubitably serves as the anchor of the exile community and the epicenter of the Cuban-American immigration experience.

A popular joke claims that one of the advantages of living in Miami is that "it's so close to the United States." Indeed, the "Cubanization" of large parts of Miami, Dade County and nearby South Florida counties is evident in virtually all aspects of everyday life—from the multitude of Cuban restaurants and Cuban-owned businesses flying Cuban flags, to niches named after Havana neighborhoods, to commonplace politically-charged bumper stickers boasting slogans such as: "No Castro, No Problem" and "Cuba Libre." Over a dozen Spanish-speaking radio and television stations, as well as a Spanish version of the area's major newspaper, the Miami Herald (*El Nuevo Herald*), likewise contribute to making Miami a veritably bilingual—and bicultural—city. Indeed, while Miami is also home to large populations of Nicaraguans, Salvadorans, Haitians, and other "non-Anglo" immigrant population, it is the Cuban concentration and prominence in the area that has earned a section of the city its telling nickname, "Little Havana."

To contextualize the process by which Miami became "Cuba's second Havana," it is helpful to consider the unique historical affiliation between Miami and Cuba. Prior to the Cuban Revolution in 1959, Miami had long been the destination of choice for both exiled Cuban political figures and well-to-do Cuban jet-setters. In fact, Cuba's direct socio-political association with Miami dates back to the last century: national hero and icon José Marti and the Cuban Revolutionary Party organized a political force from the shores of the Florida Peninsula, prior to launching Cuba's War of Independence from Spain in 1895. Though less revered on their own home shores, a line of ousted Cuban heads of state, including the dictator Machado (1933), President Carlos Prio (1952), and General Batista (1959), also came to live in Florida during their exile years. Even Fidel Castro spent time in Florida in the 1950s, organizing support for the revolution, before going to Mexico and teaming up with Che Guevara to spearhead the Cuban Revolution. Additionally, Miami was also a popular vacation destination for upper and middle-class Cubans throughout the 1940s and 1950s. While U.S. tourists flocked to Havana's casinos and resorts, wealthy Cubans were likewise traversing the Florida Straits to spend a week, weekend, or simply an evening in Miami hot spots. Hence, Miami's proximity to Cuba, commensurate with the island's established ties, exchange, and familiarity with the city, made Miami a natural focal point for the large exodus that would follow the 1959 Revolution.

Since Castro's rise to power, Cuban immigration to the United States has occurred in waves largely dictated by international and domestic politics. The first wave of Cuban immigrants came on the tail of the revolutionary change in power, and this group had the most influence in the formation and mobilization of the exile community. Not surprisingly, in 1959, a large number of ousted Batista-insiders left the island, effectively trading places with the pro-Castro exiles who had been in Miami.[2] This first immigration wave lasted from January 1959 to 1961, and it brought a largely affluent and professional 135,000-person Cuban populace to Florida—many of whom had previously vacationed regularly in Miami.[3] In 1962 tension stemming from the Cuban Missile Crisis made emigration from the island increasingly difficult, and Cubans entering the United States had to do so through a third country—a bureaucratic and often lengthy procedure which slowed Cuban emigration to the United States. Three years later, in 1965, the Johnson administration's "Memorandum of Understanding" facilitated the arrival of 340,000 new Cuban immigrants on U.S. government-sponsored "freedom flights."[4] This second major wave of immigrants was overall educated and middle class, with a lower black and mulatto ratio than the island's population.[5]

The Mariel exodus in 1980 marked a major turning point in Cuban emigration. Prompted by the public demonstration of thousands of Cuban citizens seeking asylum at an unguarded Peruvian embassy in Havana, Castro ordered the unprecedented opening of the Mariel port for the voluntary exodus of anyone who wanted to leave the island.[6] Invited to help expedite the escape of family members and compatriots, the Cuban-American exile community funneled thousands of dollars to aid the U.S. government-sponsored boatlift of 125,000 refugees. Outrage followed, however, when Castro smugly announced that the released group contained mental patients, prisoners, criminals, homosexuals and other "undesirables." Though the number of felons included in the exodus proved lower than popular claims, the two governments subsequently reached an immigration pact whereby Cuba agreed to accept the return of the so-called "undesirables" to the island. In the U.S., however, confusion, fear, and anger associated with the Mariel debacle generated protest, controversy, and heightened popular wariness towards refugees. This hostility seemed to resurface again in 1994, with the influx of 30,000 *balseros* (boat refugees) from Cuba. This time, less than half the refugees (12,000) were allowed to be processed for admission to the U.S.

2. Bittersweet Beginnings

"To Cubans, being American does not mean closing the door on your past.. They retain their Cubanness."
—Maria Cristina Garcia, Historian, Texas A&M[7]

In spite of misgivings and bitterness lingering after the Mariel incident, Cuban exiles still represented potent allies in the American "fight against communism," and thus received a degree of special consideration from the U.S. government. In contrast to historical immigration procedures, Cuban immigrants were not only welcomed into the United States but they were literally brought over on federally-funded missions, granted immediate U.S. residency, and even benefitted from direct federal stipends. This perceived preferential treatment came under intense scrutiny and criticism by other immigrant groups contending that while Cubans were literally escorted by the U.S. government to "safer waters," other nationalities were summarily turned away before they could even reach the shore.

A dramatic example of this double standard lies in the dichotomous treatment of Cuban Mariel refugees and Haitian boat refugees. American television captured and broadcast the simultaneous arrival of thousands of boat refugees fleeing the regimes of Castro in Cuba and Baby Doc Duvalier's dictatorship in Haiti. The U.S. government's embrace of Cubans (and these immigrants' inherent advantage of entering an established Cuban exile community) stood in marked contrast to the deportation of thousands of Haitian refugees who had likewise risked life and limb for asylum on American shores. The U.S. actions drew widespread criticism and attack, including intimations by Senator Edward Kennedy that immigration policy was "racially biased."[8] Though the U.S. government justified this juxtaposition by categorizing Haitians "economic migrants" versus Cubans' status as "political refugees," the pervasive negative media attention fueled resentment towards immigrants and helped portray Cuban-Americans as U.S. government cronies.

The stigma on Cuban-Americans resulting largely from Mariel compelled the exile community to mobilize in order "to invent a 'new Miami' in which their own role was both central and positive."[9] With the realization that their exile status was likely to continue indefinitely or, at best, longer than anticipated, Cuban-Americans made a concerted effort to make Miami a true "home" by taking a more active role in local politics, and further expanding and strengthening financial networks and investments. Shared culture, language, and circumstance drew loyalty to Cuban businesses and personal networks, creating a strong economic base for the Cuban-American community, as well as a united "moral community" centered on anti-Castro sentiment.[10] The Cuban experience in Miami redefined assimilation insofar as it created an economic system parallel to—and eventually surpassing—the dominant Anglo hierarchy.[11] A comparative edge in accessibility to loans, housing, and other benefits helped the Cuban-American community foster new investments, expansive development, and flourishing businesses; thereby propelling the city of Miami into its emergence as a major American metropolis.[12]

3. Exiles in Action

"You get crucified in Florida [elections] if you do anything nice for... the Castro Cubans."
—Eleanor Clift, *Newsweek*[13]

With the strongest personal ties to Cuba, and with arguably the highest vested interest in fostering a democratic Cuba, it is not surprising that the exile community has been very active on issues pertaining to Cuba. Indeed, the opinions of the Cuban-American community—particularly the important voter blocs in Miami and New Jersey—have been central to U.S. foreign policy decisions. With impressive numbers and financial resources, the Cuban-American constituency is effective in attracting the attention of U.S. politicians.

Founded in 1980, the Cuban-American National Foundation (CANF) is the largest, most visible and wealthiest Cuban-American organization in the United States, with "each of its many directors contributing free time for political lobbying plus $10,000 per year."[14] The CANF is widely regarded as the most powerful lobbying group on Cuban issues, largely due to the efforts of its late founder Mas Canosa, though critics accuse the foundation of metaphorically holding U.S. politicians prisoners to its hard-line views with promises of campaign contributions and votes. Additionally, while many are quick to applaud CANF initiatives such as Radio Marti, TV Marti and the Cuban Exodus Relief Fund, CANF's dogmatic anti-Castro message is criticized for intimidating diverse opinions and viewpoints within the Cuban-American community and even making Miami an environment hostile to free speech on issues pertaining to Cuban policy.

Though Cuban-American voting patterns are historically aligned with the Republican Party—with older exiles, in particular, associated with the right wing[15]—CANF's founding principles enunciate seeking "a broad bipartisan consensus on U.S. policy toward Cuba."[16] As a formidable lobbying force, CANF has thrown its support behind candidates of both major political parties sympathetic to its stance on Cuba. Forging "close political ties to every President since Ronald Reagan," CANF has donated over $1 million to both Republicans and Democrats.[17] The signing of the Cuban Democracy Act by President Bush on the eve of the 1992 presidential election and President Clinton's subsequent tightening of sanctions with the Helms-Burton Act in 1996 are largely attributed to courtship and appeasement in search of Cuban-American support and votes.[18] Susan Kaufman Purcell, Vice President of the Americas Society/Council of the Americas, underscores the importance of the Cuban-American vote to policy considerations:

> The Clinton Administration will not press for any significant changes in the Helms-Burton legislation before the presidential election of 2000...[The] fact [is] that there is still substantial support for the embargo among Cuban-Americans in Florida and New Jersey. The electoral votes of both states will be needed by Al Gore or whoever is the Democratic nominee in 2000.[19]

If some have argued that the U.S. government was initially using Cuban exiles as trophies or pawns in the Cold War, others might argue that it is most recently Cuban-Americans—and CANF, in particular—who "wag the dog" with their political muscle. While CANF makes no apologies for its successful lobbying efforts, the group scoffs at accusations that CANF's efforts manipulate policy making and are the sole driving force behind U.S.-Cuba relations. In response to such allegations, CANF President Alberto Hernandez defends the group's political involvement as its "[rightful] participation in the American political process."[20] Furthermore, when the magazine *New Republic* ran a cover story on its October 3, 1994 issue headlining the CANF leader Jorge Mas Canosa as "Clinton's Miami Mobster," the organization filed and won a libel suit against the magazine. Though the magazine subsequently issued an apology for its inference of criminal activity, the occurrence nonetheless demonstrates a negative perception of CANF activity. Such a perception is not unique to the *New Republic's* article.[21]

More recently and severely damaging to CANF's credibility are its alleged role in terrorist actions which have killed one innocent tourist and caused physical damage inside Cuban hotels, and an on-going Federal investigation of a thwarted October 1997 assassination plot on Fidel Castro.[22] Both sets of events allegedly involved top ranking members of CANF. "If the Federal inquiry establishes that

[CANF] leaders supported commando activities against Mr. Castro or the Cuban Government, that would weaken the organization's credibility on Capitol Hill and leave an opening for those who favor a less confrontational approach to Cuba," opined two *New York Times* reporters.[23]

4. A Spectrum of Viewpoints

"As a Cuban American, I am embarrassed that non-Cubans might think that we are all of narrow mind."
—Gloria Estefan, Cuban exile, Grammy Award-winning performer
(commenting on protests to the participation of visiting Cuban
artists in a Miami music festival).

Some Cuban-Americans consider CANF's high profile and political prowess as a double-edged sword. Because of CANF's visibility and pronounced hard-line policy views, a broader American public often perceives the CANF platform as the viewpoint of all Cuban-Americans. However, Cuban-Americans are clearly not an homogeneous or monolithic group; in fact, they speak to a variety of policy preferences and priorities. As Dr. Modesto Maidique, President of Florida International University rightly contends: "It is very clear that CANF doesn't speak for all Cuban-Americans. It is unthinkable for any organization at this point in exile history to represent a clear majority."[24]

Many cite Miami as an environment which is particularly hostile to and intolerant of dissenting viewpoints towards Cuban policy. "On the local [Miami/Dade County] arena, there is strong evidence that a defining characteristic of the Cuban-American community in Dade County is a high level of intolerance towards groups and/or individuals believed to be supportive of the present Cuban government."[25] This sentiment is embodied in the highly-charged controversy surrounding the sponsorship of Cuba-based performers and artists. In Miami, a county arts board member was fired in 1997 because she advocated ending a ban on visiting Cuban artists for a popular annual festival. Several Cuban performers who have visited the Miami area in recent years have likewise been met with public protest and animosity from Cuban-American exiles who consider the musicians and other artists as "ambassadors of Castro's revolution." Even Cuban-American performers who support free cultural exchanges have come under attack.[26].

In actuality, hundreds—perhaps thousands—of exile groups reflect a wide spectrum of viewpoints on diverse issues ranging from human rights, to refugee aid, to fostering peaceful democratization on the island. Through organizations such as

La Junta Patriotica, the Free Cuba Foundation, *Hijos del Exilio Cubano and La Unidad*, Cuban-Americans underscore their chief objective: "that they be heard—and not just as simple spectators or voters —in the process shaping the fate of the Cuban nation into the next century."[27]

In the meantime, divisions within the Cuban exile community continue to foment around three central issues: political dialogue with the current Cuban regime; personal contact between Cubans in exile and those on the island; and, not surprisingly, the Helms-Burton Act (the U.S. embargo). The most divisive issue among Cuban exiles concerns whether or not the U.S. should engage in dialogue with Fidel Castro. The split on the issue is reflected in a 1995 poll of 1,500 Cuban exiles in Florida and New Jersey, with 46 percent of respondents favoring a U.S.-Cuba dialogue.[28] Exiles who view the Cuban leadership as nothing more than a "rogue regime" resent the acknowledgement of Castro as a legitimate leader, and they dismiss hypothetical negotiations with him as pointless, ineffective, and unreliable.[29] The nearly half of Cuban exiles who favor dialogue consider a free exchange of ideas as the only means of fostering a stronger civil society within Cuba and expediting meaningful democratic reform on the political level.

A second debate surrounding national dialogue with Cuba is the highly sensitive issue of personal contact between Cuban exiles and family or friends on the island. In previous years, those who expressed interest in returning to Castro's Cuba were considered traitors while the self-proclaimed "moral community" refused to see their homeland again until Castro was gone. Due to several changes including changes in sentiments—and the increasing number of tourists visiting Cuba—many of Cuba's former residents and their children are taking steps to visit Cuba. Furthermore, a 1998 change in the U.S. law now allows Cuban-Americans to send up to $1,200 per year in remittances to family members still living on the island, making remittances an increasingly significant portion of the distressed Cuban economy. Many argue that such monetary and social capital flows forge an important "transnationalization," whereby Cuban exiles exercise potentially pivotal cultural and economic influences on the island and its economy.[30] Uva de Aragon, Assistant Director of FIU's Cuban Research Institute articulates, this viewpoint: "U.S. policy has been mistaken all along...the more people communicate, the more dollars circulate, the stronger and faster the bridges are built to democracy."[31]

A third point of contention within the exile community is the U.S. embargo. Though the majority of Cuban-Americans seem to support the embargo, dissenting exile voices have been competing, perhaps more quietly, within the policy making and academic circles.

Economic sanctions have long been an international relations tool employed by the United States, and they are not unique to the U.S. Cuban policy. The U.S. sanctions against Cuba predate the existence—much less the prominence—of any Cuban-American political action committee. The original embargo was imposed on Cuba by the Eisenhower Administration in 1960, and it was subsequently tightened by the Kennedy Administration in 1962, the Bush Administration in 1992 and, most recently, the Clinton Administration in 1996. Supporters of the embargo insist that sanctions are the most effective way of replacing the Castro regime through a stranglehold on the Cuban economy. Theorizing that economic implosion is the necessary catalyst for major reform in the current Cuban system, such arguments assume a correlation between economic performance and regime change. According to this view, Castro's continued legitimacy depends on a marked improvement in economic performance; conversely, economic collapse would bring about the regime's collapse. As such, the argument goes, the United States' best course of action is to continue the embargo on Cuba's already failing economy.[32] Congressman Robert Menendez, co-author of the Helms-Burton legislation, attributes the policy choice to the U.S. lack of options: "There are only a few policy tools available to us in times of peace: use of our aid and our trade...and denial of our trade and our aid."[33]

However, the efficacy of sanctions—and Helms-Burton in particular—remains largely disputed. Importantly, the U.S. embargo against Cuba has taken on more significance and impact since the loss of Soviet support and subsidies. Compelling anti-embargo arguments point out that, even after forty years, U.S. sanctions have been ineffective in bringing about their stated objectives in Cuba. Furthermore, current U.S. policy is criticized as most negatively affecting the Cuban populace while affirming and validating Castro's contention that the U.S. is imperialistic, inhumane, and hypocritical. Sanction opponents further argue that ending the embargo could prove a proactive move to foster democracy and capitalism in that it would deprive Castro of a critical cornerstone of his ideological and political legitimacy. Simultaneously, a taste of capitalism in Cuba could have a "snowball" political effect in fostering demands for change from below.

As an alternative solution to the embargo, some maintain that swift, calculated military action is the most effective method of dealing with Castro. For example, Richard Haas, Director of Foreign Policy Studies at the Brookings Institution, hypothesizes that:

...[Instead] of tightening sanctions—which increased the misery of
the Cuban people...the Clinton administration might have been

wiser to launch a cruise missile salvo or use stealth aircraft to take
out the MiGs that in 1996 shot down the unarmed plane flown by
Cuban exiles from the group Brothers to the Rescue.[34]

Perhaps a surprisingly high number of Cuban-Americans in recent years have also indicated their support for U.S. military action to displace Castro: 57 percent of Cuban exiles polled in 1995 favored U.S. military intervention in Cuba, and 70 percent supported an armed internal rebellion to overthrow the Castro government.[35] Though these sentiments and Haas' suggestion may seem severe to those wishing for a peaceful democratic transition, the point is made, nonetheless, that the current embargo policy is indefinite, inherently speculative, and counter-productive; therefore, alternative options might be considered.

Despite powerful anti-embargo arguments and the often painful ethical dilemma associated with inflicting economic hardships on island Cubans, the majority of Cuban-Americans endorse the embargo. In 1991, 87 percent of Cuban-Americans polled in the FIU Cuba Poll supported tightening the embargo.[36] Following such a move by the U.S. in 1996, 75 percent of respondents to the 1997 FIU Poll maintained that Helms-Burton "is a good idea to bring around change in Cuba," and an overwhelming 1997 majority of 78 percent expressed strong support for continuing the embargo.[37] These polls were all taken before the 1998 visit to Cuba by Pope John Paul II, an historic event that many saw as changing hearts and minds in Miami and Union City since many Cuban exiles returned for the first time to Cuba and saw the effects of the embargo on concrete aspects of daily life.

It is interesting to note the geographic and generation variances consistently reflected in the bi-annual poll, which originated in 1991. Cuban exiles in New Jersey and younger respondents in both areas are more likely to favor strategies emphasizing negotiations. Younger respondents, in particular, show preference for negotiations. Furthermore, "respondents who left Cuba after 1979 are more likely to support negotiated solutions than those who arrived during the 1960s. In fact, the more recent the departure from Cuba, the more likely that the respondent will support negotiated solutions."[38] This dynamic is evident in the views espoused by self-proclaimed members of "Generation Ñ," American-born descendants of Cuban exiles who strongly identify with their Cuban heritage, and, overall, favor improved relations and communication between the U.S. and Cuban governments.[39]

Such trends in attitudinal change are noteworthy indications of the exile community's future direction. These trends also point to a need for reconciliation within the Cuban-American community. As more and more voices are speaking up within the exile community, there is a call for greater negotiation and understanding among Cuban-Americans. As Julia Sagebien aptly urges, "It behooves the Cuban-American community to be part of Cuba's transformation, not just debate about it."[40]

5. Cuban-Americans in the Twenty-first Century

"Whatever happens in Cuba, Miami will continue to exercise influence on life in Cuba."
—Alejandro Portes, Princeton University

Cubans widely recognize their "history of generational changes in political views, and many anticipate an increased trend of flexibility in policy preferences among Cuban-Americans.[41] There is increasingly " ... a steady generational shift toward a less confrontational position."[42] Many see the change in leadership within the CANF as a crucible for new leadership within the Cuban-American community as a whole. Often named as a viable presidential candidate in a democratic Cuba, the passing of Jorge Mas Canosa has left a noted power vacuum within CANF and the exile community itself. Ninoska Perez de Castellon, Director of CANF's *La Voz de la Fondacion*, described Mas Canosa's unique place within the exile community: "Mas Canosa created an institution which has no parallels. No one elected Mas Canosa as leader or spokesperson for the Cuban-American community. Mas Canosa obviously won that space."[43]

Who will fill that void—or with what degree of efficacy—remains dubious. Though CANF insists that it will remain steadfast in its multitude of initiatives, Mas Canosa's loss "significantly weakens CANF," and "may herald a new type of leadership...which may argue for collective [representation of Cuban-American views]."[44] However, policy makers argue that exile leadership change alone is unlikely to compel the U.S. to alter its Cuba policy in the short-term. Congressman Menendez asserts that:

> Those who believe that the death of Jorge Mas Canosa has left an open flood gate [for the U.S. to re-evaluate Helms-Burton]...are sadly mistaken. This policy is not the work of one person....[It] represents a cross-section of...widespread support for the policy.[45]

In spite of policy preferences, Cuban-Americans are able to reach consensus on two central issues: (1) support for human rights in Cuba; and (2) a desire for democratic governance to replace the current system. Since its inception in 1991, the bi-annual FIU poll of Cuban-Americans reflects a consistent majority of over 90 percent of respondents favoring support for human rights in Cuba.[46] The most recent FIU poll in 1997 reflects "...an increasing frustration about the lack of political change occurring on the island and the growing realization that desired changes are not likely to occur anytime soon."[47]

However, the possibility of a democratic Cuba carries with it important political and social implications for the exile community in the U.S. Several questions arise: (1) What becomes of the exile community if the goal of a democratic Cuba is achieved?; (2) Would Cuban-Americans' *raison d'être* as a political constituency cease to exist in the absence of Castro as its nemesis?; (3) Would the U.S. see an exodus of Cuban-Americans returning to the island or are the exiles already too rooted with children, grandchildren, and lifestyles in the U.S.?[48]; (4) Would the U.S., in turn, see an influx of Cuban immigrants during a transition process?[49]; and (5) What would be the role of former Cuban exiles—both collectively and as individuals— during a political transition in a democratic Cuba?

Despite speculation that the Pope's visit would help bring about democratization in Cuba, most Cuban-Americans believe that Cuba will not see "real" change until Fidel Castro is dead. Only 11 percent of Cuban-Americans polled in 1997 expressed confidence that the political situation in Cuba would change within one year.[50] Sebastian Arcos, a former political prisoner and Cuban human rights activist living in exile in Miami since 1997, embodies both the cynicism and optimism shared by many Cuban exiles: "Everything [in Cuba] hinges on one individual. Once he is out, things will change."[51]

ENDNOTES

1. Mark Entwistle, former Canadian Ambassador to Cuba, speaking at the Cuba Project's International Symposium: "Reintegration into World Society: Cuba in International Perspective." The symposium was held at City University of New York on September 28, 1998.
2. Portes, Alejandro and Alex Stepick (1993) *City On The Edge: The Transformation of Miami* (Berkeley: University of California Press), pp. 99-102.
3. Portes, Alejandro and Robert L. Bach (1985) *Latin Journey: Cuban and Mexican Immigrants in the United States* (Berkeley: University of California Press), pp. 85-89.
4. Portes and Bach, op. cit., p. 86.
5. Portes and Stepick, op. cit., p. 104.
6. The Mariel Exodus was often called the "Gusano Exodus.," referring to dissidents of the revolution as *gusanos* or "worms." The pejorative term of *gusano*/worm has not been part of the official revolutionary discourse for the past decade.
7. As quoted in Clary, Mike (1987) "A City That Still Is Consumed by Castro," *Los Angeles Times*, January

1, 1997. On-line. Available http://www.cubanet.org/Cnews/y97/jan97/2city.hml.

8. Portes and Stepick, op. cit., p. 54.

9. Ibid., p. 50.

10. Portes and Stepick

11. Conversation with Lisandro Perez, Professor of Sociology and Director of the Cuban Research Institute (CRI) at Florida International University, December 16, 1997, in New York, as Research Fellow at the Russell Sage Foundation.

12. Perceived preferential treatment also contributed to domestic racial tensions with native Black communities in the Dade County area, which suffered a double marginalization by both native Whites and, secondly, by Cuban immigrants. The federal Small Business Administration (SBA) "favored [Cuban-owned small firms] disproportionately," contributing over $1million in loans in 1968 to Cuban transplants, while extending only $82,600 to Black businesses. Furthermore, almost half of SBA Dade County loans between 1968 and 1980 went to Cuban and Spanish-origin businesses versus less than 10 percent to black-owned firms.

13. Eleanor Clift, speaking as a guest commentator on The McGlaughlin Group, CNN, January 18, 1998.

14. Portes and Stepick, op. cit., p. 148.

15. According to the 1997 FIU Cuba Poll, of registered voters responding to the survey, 70 percent were registered Republicans.

16. "CANFNET," On-line, October 11, 1997. Available http://www.canfnet.org/english/canf.htm.

17. Bardach, Ann Louise and Larry Rohter, "A Plot on Castro Spotlights A Powerful Group of Exiles," *The New York Times*, May 5, 1998, p. A-1.

18. The passage of Helms-Burton was signed into law following the shooting down by Cuba of an airplane carrying two U.S. civilians. The two victims aboard were members of the "Brothers to the Rescue" exile organization, which sponsors rescue missions of Cubans attempting to leave Cuba.

19. "Today's Question," *Latin America Advisor*, December 5, 1997.

20. "CANF Slams 'Sham' Report on U.S.-Cuba Relations..." Press Release, Cuban American National Foundation. On-line, November 6, 1997. Available http://www.CANFNET. htm.

21. "New Republic, Cuban-Americans Agree on Settlement in Libel Suit." On-line. November 9, 1997. Available: http://www.LatinoLink/news.htm.

22. Bardach and Rohter, *The New York Times*, July 12, p. A-1 and pp. A-10-11.

23. Bardach and Rohter, *The New York Times*, May 5, 1998, p. A-10.

24. Conversation with Dr. Modesto Maidique, President, Florida International University, January 14, 1998.

25. Grenier, Guillermo, Hugh Gladwin, Douglas McLaughen, "The 1993 FIU Cuba Poll: Views on Policy Options Toward Cuba Held by Cuban-American Residents of Dade County, Florida," (1993: Florida International University).

26. Drummond, Tammerlin (1997) "Turning The Beat Around: Right-Wing Cuban Exiles Suddenly Focus Their Ire On One of Their Favorites, Superstar Gloria Estefan," *Time*, October 20.

27. Font, Mauricio (1996-1996) "Shift in U.S. Policy Towards Cuba," *Cuban Affairs/ Asuntos Cubanos*, II (3-4), On-line. Available http://www.soc.qc.edu/cuba/fontwwm.html.

28. Grenier, Guillermo, et al (1995) "The 1995 FIU Cuba Poll.."(Florida International University).

29. "The Honorable Robert Menendez., U.S. House of Representatives, on U.S. Policy Towards Cuba," Americas Society: Edward Larocque Distinguished Visitor Series. Lecture given at the Americas Society, New York, New York, December 10, 1997.

30. Alejandro Portes, speaking at the Cuba Project's International Symposium, "Reintegration into World

Society: Cuba in International Perspective." Symposium was held at City University of New York, on September 28, 1998.

31. Conversation with Uva de Aragon, Assistant Director, Cuban Research Institute, Florida International University, January 14, 1998.

32. For more detailed discussion of this pro-embargo argument, see Juan Lopez, "Implications of the U.S. Economic Embargo For A Political Transition in Cuba." Forthcoming in *Journal of Interamerican Studies and World Affairs;* and Gonzalez, Edward (1996) *Cuba: Clearing Perilous Waters?* (Santa Monica: RAND National Defense Research Institute).

33. "The Honorable Robert Menendez..." Lecture to the Americas Society, New York, New York, December 10, 1997.

34. Haas, Richard N (1997) "Sanctioning Madness," *Foreign Affairs* (November/December)

35. Grenier, Guillermo, et al. "The 1995 FIU Cuba Poll."

36. Ibid.

37. Grenier, Guillermo (Draft) *Executive Summary: 1997 FIU Cuba Poll,*" On-line. Available http://www.fiu.edu/orgs/ipor/cubapoll/report.htm.

38. Ibid.

39. For more information on Generation ~N, see http://www.gen-n.com.

40. Julia Sagebien, speaking at the Cuba Project's International Symposium: "Reintegration into World Society: Cuba in International Perspective." Symposium was held at City University of New York, New York. September 28, 1998.

41. Conversation with Sebastian Arcos, January 14, 1998. Mr. Arcos is a former Cuban political prisoner and human rights activist. Mr. Arcos has been in exile since 1997.

42. Navarro, Mireya, "As Older Cuban Exiles Die, Young Pragmatists Emerge," *The New York Times*, December 6, 1996, p. A-1.

43. Conversation with Ninoska Perez de Castellon, Director, *La Voz de la Fondacion*. January 13, 1998.

44. Conversation with Dr. Modesto Maidique, January 14, 1998.

45. "The Honorable Robert Menendez... Lecture to the Americas Society, New York, New York, December 10, 1997.

46. Grenier, Guillermo, et al. "The 1993 FIU Cuba Poll".

47. Grenier, Guillermo (Draft) *Executive Summary: 1997 FIU Cuba Poll,*" On-line. Available http://www.fiu.edu/orgs/ipor/cubapoll/report.htm.

48. According to the 1997 FIU Cuba Poll, 49 percent of respondents said they would be (very likely 28 percent, and somewhat likely 16.6 percent) likely to return to live on the island if the economy and the government improved.

49. According to the 1997 FIU Cuba Poll, 36 percent felt that relatives on the island would come to the U.S. to live if Cuba had a democratic government.

50. Grenier, Guillermo (Draft) *Executive Summary: 1997 FIU Cuba Poll,*" On-Line. Available http://www.fiu.edu/orgs/ipor/cubapoll/report.htm.

51. Conversation with Sebastian Arcos, January 14, 1998.

25

Canadian-Cuban Relations
A Model for the New Millennium?

Peter McKenna and John M. Kirk

Given the rigid and anachronistic nature of United States policy toward Castro's Cuba, Canada's favorable relations with the revolutionary government provide an interesting contrast in style and approach to the so-called "Cuba problem." Canada has emerged as one of Cuba's most important trading partners and Canadians represent the single largest number of tourists visiting Cuba. This chapter analyzes the nature of developments in Canadian-Cuban relations since 1993. Bilateral relations are discussed in the context of political, trade, economic, and diplomatic issues. The chapter emphasizes the new approach of "constructive engagement" by Prime Minister Jean Chrétien and the Liberal government. Some of the issues examined are expanding trade relations, opposition to the U.S. Helms-Burton law, the March 1997 human rights accord between the two countries, and Ottawa's call for Cuba's reintegration into the Organization of American States (OAS). The chapter also examines the prospects for Canadian-Cuban relations in the new millennium.

---

1. Introduction

At the turn to the twenty-first century, Canada's cordial relations with Cuba stand as a model of "constructive engagement" and "principled pragmatism," which other countries may wish to emulate. Rather than seeking confrontation, exclusion and viewing the situation as "the Cuban problem," the political leadership in Ottawa has opted for strengthening relations with Havana in a wide range of policy areas. Unlike the United States, Canada's Cuba policy has moved beyond the Cold War dynamic, recognized the reality of globalized markets, and has sought to bring about constructive changes in revolutionary Cuba through dialogue and interaction—without any U.S.-like pre-conditions. Indeed, the Liberal government of Jean Chrétien, since assuming political office in October of 1993, has accorded more high-level political attention to Cuba than any previous Canadian government in recent memory. The clearest manifestation of that interest was demonstrated by Prime Minister Chrétien's late April 1998 official visit to Cuba—marking the first time in some twenty-four years that a Canadian prime minister had set foot on Cuban soil.

The Castro government, for its part, has always been interested in improving and expanding ties with Canada. Now, perhaps more than ever before, enhanced Cuban-Canadian relations have taken on a new and significant meaning and urgency. As Cuba goes through arguably the greatest period of far-reaching and wrenching change—in the social, economic, and political domains—the struggling island country needs to solidify contacts with western countries such as Canada. From a political-diplomatic, commercial-investment, and technological-administrative standpoint, Canada represents a key link in the evolution of Cuba's revolutionary process. Cubans also realize that favorable relations with Canada, as a notable example for the rest of the world, send out an important message to both their supporters and detractors.

Because this bilateral relationship does take on a very unique character, it is important to critically examine its full nature and extent. This chapter, then, begins with a brief historical overview of the Canadian-Cuban dynamic to help in contexualizing the recent transformation in the overall relationship. Second, it details what has happened in the relationship since 1993 and how it has changed dramatically from previous decades. Third, it seeks to outline the various factors and reasons that explain why relations between the two countries have moved to newer heights. Lastly, it provides some general observations and conclusions about Canadian-Cuban relations and it projects what direction the relationship is likely to take in the future.

2. Historical Overview of Canadian-Cuban Relations

More than fifty years ago, in March of 1945, full diplomatic and political relations between Canada and Cuba were established—and with little fanfare. While the overall relationship has remained consistently positive and cordial, it has experienced its share of difficulties and problems over the years; for example, the Cuban Missile Crisis and the Cuban presence in Angola. Still, Canada was actually one of only two countries—Mexico being the other in the Americas—not to sever political and economic relations with Havana in 1962. As a non-member of the Organization of American States (OAS) in the early 1960s, it did not participate in

Cuba's "exclusion" from that body. Notwithstanding intense U.S. pressure, and veiled threats of retaliation, officialdom in Ottawa has steadfastly maintained its relations with Castro's Cuba, opposed the U.S. economic embargo, and has been outspoken in its criticism of any attempts by Washington to isolate Cuba in the Americas.[1]

It is important to recognize that Canada's long-standing position on the U.S. embargo not only sets apart Canada's approach toward Cuba from that of the United States, but it also helps to explain, in part, why relations between Ottawa and Havana are on such a solid footing. From the beginning, officials in Ottawa have made it clear to their U.S. counterparts that they agreed with Washington's overall quest to bring about constructive change in Castro's Cuba, but they have disagreed strongly over the means of achieving this objective. Imposing an economic embargo against the Cuban government, Canadian officials pointed out, would prove ineffective and only succeed in tightening Castro's grip over the country. It was also believed at the time that Canada stood to benefit economically should the U.S. go ahead with the embargo.[2] In addition, they argued that Canada could not support such a punitive step because it would contravene its commitment to an open and liberal international economic and investment system—which greatly benefitted a trading country such as Canada.[3] Successive Canadian governments, then, have consistently expressed their dissatisfaction with Washington's repeated attempts to act unilaterally against Cuba—as witnessed most recently by the Chrétien government's firm opposition to the Helms-Burton law.

Clearly, Canada's policy toward Cuba has been radically different from that of the United States—although it is not something which Canadian governments wish to publicize. As a small to middling power, and one with no historical baggage of intervention or superpower interests to protect, Canada has been able to temper its Cold War preconceptions with respect to Cuba. In addition, because of its geographical distance from the Caribbean island and the absence of a vocal and influential Cuban exile community, governments in Ottawa have crafted a more pragmatic and less ideologically-driven position toward Castro's Cuba. Neither country, of course, has ever felt threatened by the other—while both share a deep concern and vulnerability about the United States—and thus have been able to conduct their relations in a mutually respectful and constructive manner. Havana has adopted a positive attitude toward Canada and the level of political dialogue has been largely civilized, even when fundamental differences do exist between the two countries.

Furthermore, the cordial nature of Canadian-Cuban relations can be partly explained by the fact that both countries share a common foreign policy problem since both have to contend with living next door to a superpower giant. Undoubtedly, both countries are significantly—and often adversely—affected by what happens in the United States or, as former Canadian Prime Minister Trudeau once said, by the "twitches" and "grunts" of the U.S. elephant. Canadian and Cuban sovereignty—whether of the political, economic, diplomatic or cultural type—are constantly being threatened, albeit to different degrees, by the superpower reach of the United States. As a result, the political leadership in Ottawa and Havana have sought to reduce their vulnerabilities by devising a host of political and economic strategies, for example, Trudeau's "Third Option" and Castro's "Rectification Program" to bolster their countries' respective positions vis-à-vis Washington. For this reason, both Canada and Cuba have been able to locate some common ground, underscored by a strong anti-U.S. sentiment among their populations, upon which to construct a mutually beneficial bilateral relationship.

Since the 1959 Cuban revolution, then, relations between the two countries have been productive and solid; and they have even demonstrated a certain uniqueness over the years—including their share of controversy. From a political standpoint, Ottawa and Havana have experienced a strangely "on-again-off-again" type of relationship. Progressive Conservative prime ministers, such as John Diefenbaker and Brian Mulroney—and to a lesser extent Liberal prime minister Lester Pearson—tended to be less endeared or rather cool toward revolutionary Cuba. During the years of Pierre Elliot Trudeau's Liberal governments, however, the political relationship seemed to flourish—even to the embarrassment of some Liberal cabinet ministers at the time. Trudeau and Castro developed a very close personal rapport, and this obviously set the tone for the overall relationship. Perhaps the highlight of this period was Trudeau's visit to Cuba in 1976, marking the first time that a NATO Head of Government ever set foot on Cuban soil. Two years later, though, a disappointed Trudeau would suspend development assistance to the country over Cuba's continued involvement in the war in Angola. Interestingly, the Liberal government of Jean Chrétien and his globe-trotting Foreign Minister Lloyd Axworthy—both of whom have visited Cuba—seemed to have moved beyond the coziness of even the Trudeau years.

3. Canadian-Cuban Relations During the Chrétien Years

From the very beginning, it was clear that the new Liberal government of Jean Chrétien was going to adopt a Cuba policy which was very different from the Mulroney years. In point of fact, Prime Minister Chrétien insisted on crafting a foreign policy approach and style—particularly with respect to the United States—which was noticeably different from that of his Conservative predecessor. In contrast to the nine-year Mulroney period, Liberal government ministers, including then-Fisheries Minister Brian Tobin, and Christine Stewart, then-Secretary of State for Latin America and Africa, would visit Havana within a year of the new government assuming political office. At the June 1994 annual General Assembly of the Organization of American States (OAS) held in Brazil, Ms. Stewart pointedly called for Cuba's reintegration into the inter-American family and stated boldly that "the isolation of Cuba is unhealthy."[4] Two weeks later, while attending an investment conference in Havana organized by *The Economist* magazine, she announced that Canada would—after having suspended government to government aid to Cuba in 1978—resume an official development assistance program for the country. With an eye to the U.S., limited development assistance has been mainly funneled through Canadian non-governmental organizations (NGOs) rather than directly to the Cuban government.

The Chrétien government approach to Cuba, then, is based partly on Ottawa's desire to distance itself from the U.S. position on Cuba as well as urging the Clinton Administration to significantly alter its badly out-dated Cuba policy. Canada's then Foreign Minister André Ouellet clearly underscored Ottawa's changing policy when he argued that "the people of Cuba are suffering from food shortages brought on by the economic crisis, and Canadians want to help them."[5] More strikingly, he went on to say in a terse fashion: "It is time to turn the page on Cuba. The Cold War is over."[6] Prime Minister Chrétien himself, during a November 1994 meeting with Mexican president-elect Ernesto Zedillo, criticized U.S. policy toward Cuba and called for a normalization of relations between Havana and Washington. When asked by a reporter how long he thought it would take before this rapprochement would take place, he responded curtly by saying that "the sooner the better in my book."[7]

One month later at the Summit of the Americas in Miami, Chrétien once again took issue with the U.S. position on Cuba. He was troubled by Cuba's exclusion from this meeting of hemispheric countries and the intrinsic value of Cuba's absence. Speaking to a clutch of reporters, he noted: "We have a right to disagree with that position. For us, it is the normalization of relations that will lead to more democracy."[8] Even more outspoken was Christine Stewart, who commented that Canada "would hope that when other summits are held in the hemisphere that Cuba be present at the table. We as a nation will work to see that happens, and we will work with others in the hemisphere to see that happens."[9]

Since the spring of 1995, Canada's Cuba policy—though committed to Cuba's reintegration—has become entangled and complicated by the February 1995 introduction of the "Cuban Liberty and Democratic Solidarity (LIBERTAD) Act," commonly referred to as the Helms-Burton law—named after its co-sponsors in the U.S. Congress.[10] From the outset, senior members of the Canadian government expressed their serious opposition to this law and have called upon the White House to ensure that Canadian interests are not adversely affected by its extraterritorial reach. Following an April 1995 meeting with his Mexican counterpart, then-Foreign Minister Ouellet indicated that the two ministers were deeply displeased with the Act. He went on to state: "We will work together with others to make sure that such legislation does not have consequences on third countries."[11]

Two years later, the political leadership in Ottawa continued to attack the Helms-Burton law as a violation of international trade and investment principles. Notwithstanding President Clinton's repeated use of a waiver of Title III provisions of the law, which enables U.S. citizens (and naturalized citizens) who previously owned property or assets in Cuba to sue the current owners for damages in U.S. courts, Canada remains steadfast in its opposition. During Prime Minister Chrétien's first official visit to Washington in April of 1997, more than three years after he was elected into office, he and President Clinton politely agreed to disagree over the law. But in his discussions with top Congressional leaders, he was even more blunt in his criticism. He told Senate majority Leader Trent Lott: "If you want to have an isolationist policy, that's your business. But don't tell us what to do. That's our business."[12]

Prior to Chrétien's visit to Washington, his Cuba policy experienced a dramatic development reminiscent of the heyday of Mr. Trudeau. In January of 1997, Canada's new Foreign Minister, Lloyd Axworthy, undertook a two-day visit to Havana—marking the first time since 1959 that a Foreign Affairs Minister from Canada had visited Cuba. While the visit was in response to an earlier invitation by Cuban Foreign Minister, Roberto Robaina—and followed an October 1996 visit to Canada by Carlos Lage, the vice-president of the Cuban Council of State—this did little to diminish criticism from official Washington. Indeed, U.S. State Department spokesperson Nicholas Burns, in unusually critical diplomatic language, sternly criticized Minister Axworthy for undertaking the visit: "It doesn't make sense to reward a dictator in our hemisphere who is completely behind the times. You reward him by sending your foreign minister down to visit, by having visits as usual, by trading. And we think that's wrong."[13]

In a subsequent effort at damage-control, and evidently trying to rein in the State Department, President Clinton entered the fray. In a White House press conference, he noted the following: "I'm skeptical, frankly, that the recent discussions between the Canadians and the Cubans will lead to advances. I believe that our policy is the proper one, but I'm glad that the Canadians are trying to make something good happen in Cuba."[14] In sharp contrast, however, virulent anti-Castro Senator Jesse Helms compared the visit and Canada's dealings with Cuba as the 1990s equivalent of British Prime Minister Neville Chamberlain's appeasement of Hitler's Germany in 1938:

> You had someone named Neville Chamberlain, he went over and sat down with Hitler and came back and said, `We can do business with this guy,' and you saw what happened. Now, if we're going to forget all principle and let Fidel Castro get by with all of his atrocities, then we [had] better look at the status of our principles and Canada certainly should look at hers.[15]

Notwithstanding Helms' ridiculous comments and President Clinton's skepticism, the Chrétien government hailed the visit as an important breakthrough. According to Foreign Affairs Minister Axworthy, the visit marked "a good beginning, a good start." He went on to explain: "It is a work in progress, but opened up all kinds of possibilities."[16] With respect to U.S. policy toward Cuba, he commented that the reality is that "I think we've gone further than anything they have been able to accomplish, by building those bridges."[17] Axworthy's bridge-building began with a series of meetings with senior members of the Cuban government, including Foreign Minister Robaina, and a late dinner with President Castro himself. Reportedly, President Castro was quoted by the Canadian Press news service as saying, "Canada has a lot of prestige. What it says and what it thinks has great meaning for us."[18]

The bilateral discussions themselves focused on a wide range of issues, from economic cooperation and foreign investment to drug interdiction and terrorism. Reference was also made to the fact that Canada would continue to maintain a modest development assistance program in Cuba.[19] Much was made, however, of a 14-point "Joint Declaration" or agreement by both sides which pledged Canada and Cuba to work together in opposing Helms-Burton and on broadening cooperation on a variety of areas -- including human rights. This latter measure was touted by Ottawa as a major accomplishment and was the end result of more than a year of previous bilateral discussions and deliberations. Among other things, the two sides agreed to hold joint seminars on human rights issues in both Canada and Cuba as well as promoting reciprocal exchanges of judges, legislators, academics, and other professionals. Having said that, there was no specific agreement on improving political freedoms in Cuba, on releasing political dissidents, or on introducing a multi-party political system -- other than a Cuban commitment to discuss these and other concerns in the future.

Still, this commitment from the Cubans should not be easily dismissed as "meaningless crumbs," as one editorial from the *Toronto Globe and Mail* suggested.[20] Brushing this aside, Axworthy simply pointed out that Canada's policy of engagement was already more successful than the U.S. approach of merely "holding a megaphone in a Senate committee room."[21] Subsequently, the thorny issue of human rights was placed on the agenda of the recently established Canada-Cuba Joint Committee on Human Rights, which is comprised of Canada's ambassador to Cuba and the director of North American affairs in the Cuban Foreign Ministry. In May of 1997, Canadian officials went to Havana to participate in the first Canada-Cuba seminar on children's rights.[22] One month later, Foreign Minister Axworthy and Diane Marleau, Minister Responsible for International Co-operation and la Francophonie, welcomed a Cuban delegation to Ottawa to engage in a two-day session on women's rights.[23]

The Cuban delegation was comprised of representatives from the Cuban Foreign Ministry and the Federation of Cuban Women, and they dealt with issues concerning the advancement of women, the application of provisions of the UN Convention on the Elimination of Discrimination Against Women, and women and sustainable development.[24] In November 1997, a high-level Cuban delegation of National Assembly members visited Ottawa as part of a Canada-Cuba parliamentary exchange program—which was a follow-up from a late 1996 visit to Cuba of a group of Canadian parliamentarians including the Speakers and the Clerks from both Houses of Canada's Parliament.[25] For the most part, the Cubans were interested in learning more about Canada's parliamentary system and the various support and administrative services which are available to Canadian legislators.

As part of the continuing dialogue and bridge-building process between the two countries, Cuban Vice-President Carlos Lage visited Canada in mid-February 1998. In addition to signing a new Canada-Cuba air transport agreement and renewing an anti-hijacking treaty, both sides held discussions on the state of the fourteen-point Canada-Cuba Joint Declaration. Two weeks later, and in the wake of the Pope's historic January 1998 visit, Canada agreed initially to accept nineteen Cuban political prisoners.[26] While the Cuban authorities were adamant that Canada accept all of them, Ottawa rejected some of the names on the list for apparently security reasons. In the end, Canada agreed to accept fifteen Cuban prisoners of conscience, and they began arriving in early April 1998.[27] Not surprisingly, Canadian officials were quick to point out that the release of these Cuban prisoners was a vindication of Ottawa's policy of "constructive engagement."

Arguably, the highlight of the Liberal government's Cuba policy first materialized unexpectedly from a news leak at the April 1998 Santiago Summit of the Americas. For reasons unknown to Canadian officials, the U.S. delegation to the Summit leaked the news to the Cable News Network (CNN) that Prime Minister Chrétien would be making an official visit to Cuba in late April. While Chrétien was noticeably perturbed by the leaked report, he received the strong endorsement of his impending trip from most of the other country delegations. President Clinton, although briefed about the visit ten days before the Summit gathering, was reported to be highly skeptical of Chrétien's chances of making any major breakthroughs in Cuba. President Clinton's National Security Advisor, Sandy Berger, was even more blunt than the President when he stated: "We have not seen much evidence that constructive engagement with Cuba has produced any material results with respect to human rights or democracy."[28]

In any event, the high-level meetings between Chrétien and Castro in late April 1998 were substantive, wide-ranging, and, at times, reportedly testy—especially over the issue of human rights. In addition to discussing trade and investment issues, international terrorism and drug smuggling, Prime Minister Chrétien presented Castro with the names of four political prisoners whom he wanted released immediately. He also discussed with the Cuban leader some of the changes that would have to take place in Cuba before the hemisphere would be prepared to welcome Cuba back into the wider inter-American family. In the end, the Prime Minister came away with no appreciable progress on the human rights front, but he did make headway on a foreign investment protection treaty with Cuba and an agreement that would see the Cuban government pay $12 million to Confederation Life Insurance Company, which had its assets expropriated after the 1959 revolution.

Critics and supporters alike would sharply disagree over the success or failure of the two-day visit, but there was no doubt that Canada derived certain tangible benefits from the visit. In addition to strengthening a long-standing diplomatic and political relationship, the high-profile visit further cemented Canada's trade and investment position in Cuba. Furthermore, it highlighted Canada's growing involvement in hemispheric affairs, improved its standing in Latin American and Caribbean capitals, and clearly contrasted Canada's policy of constructive engagement with the confrontational and isolationist approach of the Clinton Administration.

Finally, the visit sent a potent message to officialdom in Washington of Canada's continued displeasure with the anti-Cuba Helms-Burton law, and scored some domestic political or electoral points in the process.

By mid-1998, then, Canada's Cuba policy undoubtedly continued to emphasize dialogue and constructive engagement as the best means of facilitating political and economic change in Cuba. As a result, future discussions between the two countries are likely to take place on a wide variety of issues, including the controversial question of human rights (under the guise of the fourteen-point Joint Declaration). As a follow-up to the Prime Minister's visit, the government will likely attempt to accelerate an expansion and strengthening of the overall economic side of the relationship. Of course, officials in Ottawa will maintain their firm opposition to Helms-Burton and continue their efforts to have the Clinton Administration amend or repeal the law. Lastly, Prime Minister Chrétien will remain committed to securing Cuba's "re-inclusion" into the OAS and its full integration into the wider hemispheric community.

4. Explaining Canada's Cuba Policy in the 1990s

When one sets out to explain the key driving forces of Canada's policy toward Cuba in the late 1990s, it is not easy to weigh those factors in terms of their explanatory value or to rank them in order of importance. It is true that some of the factors which were present from the early 1960s still carry some explanatory value today. Accordingly, economic, trade, and investment considerations continue to underscore or drive Canada's overall policy response toward revolutionary Cuba, and this has been the case since the imposition of the U.S. embargo. Clearly, officialdom in Ottawa has consistently maintained its interest in continuing political relations with Havana as the key to expanding trade and investment opportunities in a Cuban market which is essentially closed off to the United States. Having said that, Canada's Cuba policy cannot be solely understood in economic terms, but must also take into account a variety of historical, idiosyncratic, political-symbolic, and external variables such as the policy of the United States.

While it is admittedly difficult to assess its exact importance, it does seem plausible that "historical linkages" have factored into the Chrétien government's approach to Castro's Cuba. Stated differently, what has happened in the past with respect to Canada-Cuba relations has helped influence or shape what is currently happening with the relationship. Efforts by the Chrétien Liberals to strengthen the bilateral relationship in a wide variety of policy areas all flow from a previous policy approach which has eschewed severing diplomatic ties with Havana, criticized any tightening of the U.S. economic embargo, and opposed isolating Cuba in this hemisphere. To have undertaken initiatives to undercut relations with Cuba would have marked a sharp departure from a previous pattern of Canadian foreign policy behavior. The fact of the matter is that Canada's present Cuba policy is partly a product of a position that has been adopted for 40 years. The Chrétien government has built on a pre-existing historical foundation while adding its own specially-crafted brick and mortar.

In some ways, of course, the Chrétien approach to Cuba reflects a desire on the part of the Liberal government to carve out a role for itself on the world stage and to give Canada some international recognition and profile. Like Canada's leading role in banning the manufacturing, stockpiling, transportation and use of anti-personnel land mines, it has sought to establish itself as distinctly different from previous Canadian governments on the Cuban question. In fact, a frequent criticism of Canadian policy during the Mulroney years was its constant imitation of Washington's policy and, in view of strong Canadian nationalism, it is an approach that Prime Minister Chrétien has been exceedingly careful to avoid. Canada's relations with Cuba, then, have provided the Chrétien government with an opportunity to put its own unique stamp on Canadian foreign policy—and one which will likely be reflected in any written history of the Chrétien years.

Furthermore, Foreign Minister Axworthy has made a point of raising the profile of the Cuba file within the Department of Foreign Affairs and International Trade. Unlike previous Foreign Ministers, Axworthy has taken almost a personal interest in things Cuban, perhaps signifying his reputation as being on the left-wing of the federal Liberal Party. His visit to Havana in January of 1997, even in the face of stiff U.S. opposition, was an obvious testament of his commitment to strengthening ties with Castro's Cuba. With ministerial interest and direction, the overall Department is certain to accord more bureaucratic attention and resources to the Canada-Cuba relationship. It clearly has not hurt from a bureaucratic standpoint that the political leadership in Canada has been so outspoken in its criticism of Helms-Burton. Simply put, the personal interest of key political figures like Chrétien and Axworthy helps to explain why the bilateral relationship has generated more attention in Ottawa than in the last twenty years or so.[29]

The Canada-Cuba relationship has also taken on a greater significance in Ottawa because of its relation to the larger issue of international respect for human rights. Both Chrétien and Axworthy have been stung by harsh criticism from human rights campaigners, non-governmental organizations, churches, and opposition parties for their willingness to jettison human rights considerations for the sake of exports—as witnessed by the November 1997 Asia Pacific Economic Community (APEC) summit held in Vancouver. High-profile visits by Chrétien and Axworthy to China, Indonesia, and Mexico have left the Liberal government vulnerable to public criticism over its failure to press the issue of human rights with these offending countries.[30] Cuba, then, has become important from a public opinion standpoint since it allows the Liberal government to identify Cuba as an example of just how seriously it does take human rights considerations and how effective a policy of "constructive engagement" can be. In short, the human rights accord with Cuba becomes a means of deflecting criticism from domestic human rights groups on the "company that the government has been keeping", while at the same time scoring some political points at home by "tweaking the nose" of the U.S. government.

Significantly, Canadian governments in the past have not shied away from using the proverbial "Cuba card" in the larger context of Canada-U.S. relations—and the Chrétien government is certainly no exception. In fact, the political leadership in Ottawa has been quick to point out, largely for domestic political consumption, that Canada's Cuba policy differs substantially from that of officialdom in Washington—as Prime Minister Chrétien's visit to Cuba starkly illustrated. Of course, by identifying this major difference, Canada finds itself in a more comfortable position to make the argument that it has a truly independent foreign policy—and not simply one formulated exclusively by U.S. foreign policy-makers. Ottawa's "Made-in-Canada" Cuba policy, especially since it raises the ire of the United States, not only reassures Canadians about their political sovereignty and independence but also plays to their sense of pride and national identity. For obvious reasons, this show of political independence has clear domestic political importance.

As a veteran politician, Prime Minister Chrétien was determined, even before he took over the reigns of political power, to differentiate himself and his government from his Conservative predecessor, Brian Mulroney. When he was campaigning in the fall of 1993, Chrétien often joked about the fact that Mulroney used to say "yes" to the Reagan-Bush White House before the phone actually rang. Not wanting to be seen as too cozy with our U.S. neighbors, Chrétien has used the "Cuba card" to create some political and symbolic distance between Ottawa and Washington. Yet Chrétien is reported to speak with President Clinton by telephone every week or so and to have a warm and personal rapport with the president. Obviously, the Chrétien Liberals see their new approach to Cuba as a political winner in Canada, and thus useful in terms of any future electoral contest. In an April 1996 public opinion survey, some 71 per cent of Canadians wanted Ottawa to ignore the

Helms-Burton law and to maintain trade relations with revolutionary Cuba.[31] Clearly, Canada's Cuba policy is not based solely on electoral considerations, but it has not been lost on the Chrétien government that its progressive approach to Havana has been seen as politically popular at home.

While political motivations are always present, they do not tend to supersede economic considerations—which clearly underscore the overall bilateral relationship. By having cordial relations with Havana since 1959, the political leadership in Ottawa has calculated correctly that this will open up trade and investment doors in Cuba. Furthermore, because of the U.S. embargo, it has created a number of opportunities for Canadian companies to exploit. In this context one should not dismiss the impact that the Canadian business community has had on Ottawa's Cuba policy of engagement, especially from an economic standpoint. By supplying spare parts, high-tech equipment, and machinery, Canadian businesses have been able to fill a void left by U.S. companies.

Moreover, the Chrétien government—more than any other Canadian government in recent memory—has made trade policy and increased exports the centerpiece of its foreign policy. Two-way trade between Canada and Cuba amounts to more than $600 million, with most of Canada's exports comprised of manufactured goods.[32] More important, Cuba has become an attractive destination for Canadian investment—with more than 30 companies intimately involved in various sectors of the Cuban economy.[33] Toronto-based Sherritt International, for instance, is the largest foreign investor in Cuba, involving more than $1 billion.[34] The future potential for Canadian investors in Cuba—especially in the tourism, energy, and mining sectors—looks very promising.

Indeed, when one arrives in Cuba, it is impossible not to be aware of Canada's growing trade and investment presence on the island. The airport at Varadero and the new terminal at José Martí International airport's expanded facility, which was inaugurated during Prime Minister Chrétien's April 1997 visit, were both constructed by Canadian companies. Sophisticated landing equipment at Cuban airports and hotel reservation systems, McCain's french fries, President's Choice Cola, auto parts, and compact discs are all being supplied by Canadian businesses. A number of other Canadian-based companies are providing everything from foodstuffs to paper products, engineering equipment, paint, medical technology, and a variety of items for the tourism industry. Finally, the number of joint ventures between the two countries has increased dramatically since the early 1990s, particularly in the mining sector where Canadian companies now dominate.

Logic dictates that sooner or later, the United States is going to normalize relations with Cuba. Given its economic dominance, its proximity to the island, and its long-standing personal ties, this normalization is not going to spell good news for Canadian business people. What is now somewhat of a "captive" market for Canada would eventually become one where fierce competition prevails—and a competition in which, in many areas, Canadians would likely lose out. If Canadian business interests are to survive the inevitable American onslaught, they would do so largely on the strength of their existing arrangements and on the accumulation of Ottawa's political capital in Cuba. This helps to explain, in part, why Foreign Minister Axworthy was anxious to visit Havana in January of 1997. In fact, his visit, along with Prime Minister Chrétien's late April 1998 trip, were both intended to strengthen political relations as a means of trying to safeguard whatever "niche market" Canadians have carved out for themselves in Cuba since 1959.

While trade and domestic factors are obviously important—and perhaps paramount—in explaining the nature of Canada's Cuba policy, external determinants should also be taken into consideration. In part, then, Canada's expanding ties with Cuba are a product of an enhanced political and economic focus on Latin America as a whole. The end of the Cold War, the return to democratically-elected governments, and the end to long-standing civil wars in Central America have all created important stimuli which have enabled Canada to expand relations with a number of countries in Latin America. Moreover, the onset of globalized markets and the fact that governments have introduced wide-ranging neo-liberal economic reforms have opened the eyes of officialdom in Ottawa to the region's economic potential. Not surprisingly, especially given Canada's dependence on securing new trade markets, Canadian officials have been at the forefront of promoting a Free Trade Area of the Americas (FTAA) by the year 2005.

Since the early 1990s, the region has clearly become an important component in the conduct of Canadian foreign policy. The Chrétien government's early January 1998 "Team Canada" trade mission to Mexico and South America—comprised of provincial premiers and high-powered Canadian business people—was indicative of this growing interest. Indeed, since Canada joined the Organization of American States (OAS) in January 1990, negotiated the North American Free Trade Agreement (NAFTA) and recently concluded a bilateral trade deal with Chile, the region has taken on greater saliency in official Ottawa.[35] Issues such as democratic development, trade expansion, and human rights have become a major part of the government's policy focus in the region. These issues, of course, coincide with what now constitutes the core of contemporary Canadian-Cuban relations.

5. Cuban Motivations for Closer Bilateral Relations

When one examines the Cuban side of the equation, the proximate motivations or explanatory factors are similar in some respects and different in others. But it is important to understand that the Canada-Cuba dynamic is very much a win-win situation for the Cubans—with few, if any, major costs or risks involved. For instance, the Cubans are obviously interested in increasing trade relations with western, industrialized countries like Canada. Since the demise of the Soviet Union in 1991, and the collapse of the Eastern bloc, the Cuban economy has teetered on the brink of collapse. Only recently has the economy shown some signs of improve-ment—registering a 7.8 per cent growth rate for 1995 and 2.5 per cent in 1996—after more than five years of devastating hardship, power outages, lay-offs, and food shortages. While the country has not turned the corner economically, trade linkages with countries like Canada have been very important during the so-called "special period." Canada has become not only an important supplier of high-tech and consumer goods, which the Cubans desperately need, but also a crucial source of much-needed foreign investment. Indeed, the more than 40 joint ventures with Canadian investors have been instrumental in enabling Cuba to survive this incredibly difficult period of readjustment and transition.

For political and symbolic reasons, it is important for the Castro government to showcase its relationship with a member of the exclusive Group of 8 industrialized countries, one that is prepared to work with the Cubans. The high-profile manner in which Foreign Affairs Minister Axworthy was received during his January 1997 visit—with the full Cuban media present, meetings with senior members of the Cuban government, and a major photo-opportunity with President Castro—reflected the symbolic importance that Cuba attaches to the partnership and the message that it wants to send out to the rest of the world. In a world where the only remaining superpower, the United States, has made life exceedingly more difficult for Cubans, it helps to have a friend in Canada—especially when it is known to have a very close relationship with Washington. Solid relations with Canada, then, codify a legitimacy on the Castro government, which it can turn around and use for domestic as well as external purposes. Struggling Cubans can feel somewhat reassured, and perhaps heartened, by ties with Canada; and the international community can plainly see that Cuba is receptive to change and indeed open for business.

When President Castro greeted Prime Minister Chrétien on the tarmac at Havana's José Martí International Airport in late April 1998, which was broadcast live on Cuban television, he attempted to tap into some of these very sentiments. However, in a badly miscalculated public relations move, Castro wasted no time,in an over-the-top though characteristic welcoming speech, in condemning the U.S. economic embargo as tantamount to "genocide," as a visibly uncomfortable Canadian prime minister looked on. Still, the Cuban government was no doubt pleased with an opportunity to enhance its political, commercial and technological linkages with a major western industrialized country like Canada. This, in turn, provided the Castro government with an immediate injection of international legitimacy and credibility and built upon the favorable press coverage from the Pope's January 1998 visit. More importantly, at least from a domestic and external standpoint, was the fact that the visit underscored the absurdity and outmoded nature of U.S. policy toward Cuba.

Clearly, Cuban authorities are interested in strengthening political and economic relations with Canada out of sheer necessity. With a small number of "friendly" countries around the world, Cuba's partnership with Canada is seen as very important. It does not hurt that Canada is Cuba's number one market for tourism, with some 175,000 Canadians every year—or about 7,000 a week—travelling to Cuba and bringing much-needed U.S. currency into the country. Not only is Canada important from an investment standpoint, but it also provides the Cubans with valuable development assistance and technical expertise. For example, Canadian officials have been involved in improving Cuba's banking system, its tourism sector, its economic planning, and its overall tax regime.[36]

Furthermore, Canada's close and extensive relationship with the United States is not something that is lost on the Cubans. In fact, government officials recognize the possibility of Canada serving as a mediator between Havana and Washington. The Cuban government, it should be noted, is very appreciative of the fact that Canada has been at the forefront with the Europeans in attacking the anti-Cuba Helms-Burton law.[37] Maintaining cordial relations with Canada, then, could prove beneficial should Cuba see an opportunity to normalize relations with the United States or to become more integrated with the overall inter-American system. As a leading member of the Organization of American States (OAS), Canada could be useful in facilitating Cuba's "re-inclusion" into the hemispheric body. Additionally, as a full-fledged member of NAFTA and a major proponent of expanding free trade southward, Canada could be an important ally if Cuba decides to seek some form of "associate status" with any future Free Trade Area of the Americas (FTAA).[38] In sum, the Cubans derive a significant number of benefits from their relations with Canada— without having to contend with any onerous pre-conditions attached.

6. Conclusions

As Canada and Cuba approach the new millennium, the future direction of the relationship is not likely to change significantly from what it is today. Simply put, the overall Canada-Cuba dynamic will continue at the same level of interaction, friendliness, and tone unless some external developments were to unsettle relations and thereby necessitate a reevaluation. Prime Minister Chrétien's April 1998 visit to Cuba was most assuredly a confirmation of this point.

However, should the political leadership in Washington decide to alter dramatically its current policy toward Cuba, and seek some form of rapprochement with Havana, this could precipitate a change in Canadian-Cuban relations. It would likely open up some new space for improving relations between the two countries even further—especially from an economic and political standpoint. Officials in Ottawa, fearing the prospect of closer U.S.-Cuban trade relations, would be quick to seek assurances from their opposite numbers in Havana that Canadian business people would not be unjustly squeezed out of the Cuban market by American competitors. Conversely, if the political situation in the United States becomes more virulently anti-Cuba, this could also affect the bilateral relationship. Canadian officials, certainly more than their Cuban counterparts, would have to reassess the bilateral relations—and probably downgrade or downplay them in an effort not to offend openly the United States. To be sure, Ottawa will not sacrifice its overall relationship with the United States for the sake of the Cubans, as has historically been the case. To put this in stark commercial terms, two-way trade between Canada and Cuba in a year is less than Canada's trade with the United States for a single day.

Similarly, if the domestic political situation changes in Cuba, then it could have major implications for the bilateral relationship. For instance, when Fidel Castro decides to step down, the change in political leadership would bring about a rethinking of Canadian-Cuban relations—which could place them in a temporary holding pattern until the transition was complete and the situation on the ground was seen as stable. Obviously, if the Cuban government decides to take on a more "activist" international role, or to ratchet-up its anti-American rhetoric, Ottawa would certainly view these developments in a negative light. If economic conditions should deteriorate to a crisis level in the country, and the people become further disillusioned, officials in Ottawa may attempt to press the Cuban government to implement a more radical reform program. However, if the Cubans opt to accelerate political reforms and economic liberalization, Canadian officials would encourage these moves and seek to take advantage of them.

Barring these changes, though, the bilateral relationship should continue along at the same steady, if unspectacular, pace. Irrespective of the political stripe of the government in Ottawa, the trade side of the relationship is likely to intensify—but still remain small in terms of Canada's overall trade with Latin America as a whole. Politically speaking, there is unlikely to be any significant change here—despite a wish by the Cubans to augment this aspect of the bilateral ties. There will not, for instance, be any new or substantive political initiatives in the coming years—such as a major push to have Cuba reintegrated into the OAS or to have President Castro pay a return visit to Canada.

At the same time, Canadian authorities will not push the Cuban government too hard on the democratic and human rights front. Even in the face of U.S. pressure, Ottawa will continue to avoid attaching "conditions" to the functioning of the relationship, even though privately they would dearly love to see some movement by Havana. Adherence to the notion of "principled pragmatism," with its emphasis on building bridges with small successes in the area of human rights without sternly lecturing the Cuban government, will not be soon discarded. The Cubans, for their part, will continue to have a dialogue with the Canadians on a variety of is-sues—including human rights—without making any dramatic or iron-clad commit-ments. Both sides have basically agreed that this is a sensitive area, and that neither side should operate under the assumption that fundamental changes are going to take place in Cuba overnight. While Washington maintains its "Trading With The Enemy Act"—with Cuba being the enemy—it is unlikely that much political liberalization will take place in Cuba.

It is possible, however, that the thorny issue of human rights could eventually lead to some tension in the relationship in the short term. There is a risk factor here for the relationship should the recent arrangement on human rights not show any appreciable progress. Officialdom in Ottawa is not going to wait too long to see meaningful results on the human rights front. In fact, Canadian officials had planned on reassessing or reviewing after a year or so the human rights initiative agreed to by both governments during Axworthy's January 1997 visit. Knowing full well that the United States will be watching this issue very closely, especially in the wake of Prime Minister Chrétien's high-profile visit, Ottawa needs to demonstrate some "pay-off" or dividends in this area.[39] The release of additional political prisoners, and a vague promise by Fidel Castro to "consider" signing the International

Covenant on Economic, Social and Cultural Rights, is not likely to placate officialdom in Ottawa or Washington. A failure to do so could complicate bilateral discussions in other areas, place some strain on relations at the political level, and perhaps even discourage further improvement in the overall relationship itself.

That said, the Canadian-Cuban relationship clearly represents an important model of co-operation for the rest of the international community. Both countries have shown that it is possible to have political differences and still have a productive and profitable bilateral relationship. By setting aside differing ideological philosophies and replacing them with a calculated pragmatism, Canada and Cuba have developed a framework for achieving progress on a host of issues. The two countries recognize that hostility, high-pitched rhetoric, and isolation of Cuba only serve to reinforce old stereotypes and actually reduce the likelihood for substantive change in Cuba. Through constructive engagement and dialogue, officials in Ottawa believe that they will—over a period of time—bring about positive political and economic reforms in Cuba. Since these are some of the same objectives that other countries around the world share, they may wish to learn from the Canadian approach. The old-style confrontational and isolationist approach has clearly not worked in the past, and perhaps it is now time to try a new approach.

ENDNOTES

1. Having said this, Canadian officials have frequently expressed to their Cuban counterparts their disapproval with Cuba's human rights situation and the country's lack of political liberalization.
2. See, John M. Kirk, Peter McKenna and Julia Sagebien (1995) "Back in Business: Canada-Cuba relations after 50 years," *The Focal Papers* (March), p. 9.
3. See, Kim Richard Nossal (1997) *The Politics of Canadian Foreign Policy*, Third Edition (Scarborough, Ontario: Prentice-Hall Canada), pp. 73-74.
4. See Christine Stewart, Secretary of State for Latin America and Africa, "Address to the 24th General Assembly of the Organization of American States," Belem, Brazil, June 7, 1994, p. 6.
5. See Mimi Whitefield (1994) "Saying the Cold War Is Over, Canada Restores Aid to Cuba," *The Miami Herald* (June 21).
6. Ibid.
7. See Jeff Sallot (1995) "Congress Worries Chrétien, Zedillo," *The Globe and Mail* (November) p. A3.
8. See "Cuba's Absence at Americas Summit Skirts Formal Agenda," *CubaINFO*, Volume 6, Number 16 (1994), p.3.
9. Ibid., pp. 3-4.
10. For more on this subject, see Peter McKenna (1997) "Canada and Helms-Burton: Up Close and Personal," *Canadian Foreign Policy*, Volume 4, Number 3 (Winter 1997), pp. 7-20.
11. Cited in Gord McIntosh, "Canada, Mexico Oppose U.S. Bill," *The Halifax-Mail Star*, April 28, 1995, p. B.16.
12. Robert Russo, "PM Rebukes Cuba-bashers," *The Halifax Chronicle-Herald*, April 9, 1997, p. A1.

13. Laura Eggerston and Paul Knox, "Cuba Law Swaying Canada, U.S. Says," *The Globe and Mail*, January 22, 1997, p. A1.

14. "Cuba Visit Likened to Appeasing Hitler," *The Globe and Mail*, January 24, 1997, p. A8.

15. Ibid.

16. Douglas Farah, "Cuba Signs Broad Pact With Canada," *The Guardian Weekly*, February 2, 1997, p. 15.

17. "Cuba Visit Likened to Appeasing Hitler," op. cit., p. A.8.

18. Paul Knox, "Canada, Cuba Agree on Trade and Aid," *The Globe and Mail*, January 23, 1997, p. A1.

19. In late August of 1997, Canada had announced that it would donate some $3.5 million in edible cooking oil to Cuba. "Canada Makes Food Donation," *The Globe and Mail*, August 27, 1997, p. A8.

20. "Canada's Gift to Mr. Castro," *The Globe and Mail*, January 23, 1997, p. A.20.

21. Farah, op. cit.

22. The release of Cuban writer, Celelio Sambra, in May was applauded by Minister Axworthy. According to the Minister, Sambra's release was "a result both of PEN Canada"s efforts and Canada's policy of engagement and dialogue that allows us to discuss a wide range of issues with Cuba." Apparently, Axworthy had raised the issue of Mr. Sambra's detention with the Cuban leadership when he visited the country in January 1997. Department of Foreign Affairs and International Trade, "Axworthy Welcomes Release of Cuban Writer," *News Release*, No. 86 (May 12, 1997).

23. Keith Christie was named Canada's new ambassador to Cuba in July, replacing the highly effective Mark Entwistle. This was a high-profile appointment since Christie was formerly Canada's chief trade negotiator in bilateral talks with Chile.

24. Department of Foreign Affairs and International Trade, "Axworthy and Marleau attend Canada-Cuba Seminar on Women's Rights," *News Release*, No. 105 (June 17, 1997).

25. Interview with a Deputy Principal Clerk of the Canadian Senate, November 24, 1997.

26. Paul Knox and Jeff Sallot "Cuba to Exile 19 to Canada," *The Globe and Mail*, February 27, 1998, p. A1.

27. Government of Canada "Cuban Political Prisoners Arrive in Canada," *News Release* No. 87 (April 6, 1998).

28. Janice Tibbets "Chretien to visit Castro," *The Sunday Herald*, April 19, 1998, p. A19.

29. Axworthy was under the impression that Canada could make a "difference" on the Canada-Cuba file-- especially after the downing of the two Cessna aircraft by two Cuban fighter jets in February of 1996 and the strain which this had placed on an already tense U.S.-Cuban relationship. Confidential interview with a senior official in Canada's Department of Foreign Affairs and International Trade, 12 December 1997.

30. At the late November gathering of the Asia-Pacific Economic Co-operation (APEC) forum in Vancouver, Prime Minister Chrétien was on record as saying that he would not press the issue of human rights at this meeting to deal with trade, economic and financial questions. Jeff Sallot, "Axworthy warns APEC of irrelevancy," *The Globe and Mail*, November 24, 1997, p. A1.

31. "Canadians Oppose Cuba Sanctions," *The Globe and Mail*, April 3, 1996, p. A4.

32. John M. Kirk and Peter McKenna (1997) *Canada-Cuba Relations: The Other Good Neighbor Policy* (Gainesville, Florida: University Press of Florida), pp. 159-164.

33.. It is also worth noting that two-way trade for the first nine months of 1997 indicated a further increase of roughly 25 per cent.

34. Ibid., pp. 163-167.

35. The importance of the region to Canada has also been highlighted by President Clinton's failure to secure "fast track" authority for future trade negotiations and the recent financial and economic troubles buffeting a number of Southeast Asian countries.

36. Confidential interview with a member of Canada's Department of Foreign Affairs and International Trade, December 12, 1997.

37. Most recently, Canada has sought to diminish the impact of Helms-Burton, if not to prevent the repetition of such a law, through the ongoing Organization for Economic Co-operation and Development (OECD) negotiations of Multilateral Agreement on Investment (MAI), which is intended to create a new package of rights for multinational corporations and a new set of obligations for national governments.

38. However, one senior official in Canada's Department of Foreign Affairs and International Trade made it clear that he did not think that the Canadians would be interested in championing the Cuban case on hemispheric trade matters. Confidential interview on December 11, 1997.

39. Confidential interview with a senior member of Canada's Department of Foreign Affairs and International Trade, December 11, 1997.

NAME INDEX

SUBJECT INDEX

A

Abacuá, 253
ACINOX S.A., 216
Acquired Immune Deficiency
 Syndrome (AIDS), 57
Africa, 139, 159, 161, 355
African, 158
African Americans, 78, 96, 97
African, Caribbean and Pacific (ACP)
  countries (Lomé Accord), 218
African War, 33
Afro Cubans, 80, 92, 93, 94, 96, 97, 124,
  128, 129, 130, 131, 158, 330
Agrarian reform, 251
Agrarian Reform Laws, 251
Agricultural Products Markets, 184
Amazon, 261
Americas, 351, 352
American Public Health Association, 229
Anglo (s), 5, 75, 78, 81, 82, 341
Angola, 139
Argentina, 38, 240
Arkansas, 226
Asamblea Nacional del Poder Popular
(People's Power National Assembly),
  21, 36, 37
Asia Pacific Economic Community
  (APEC), 362
Association for Free Arts and the
  National Civic Union, 86
Association of Caribbean States (ACS),
  208, 211, 212
Australia, 262
Austria, 225

B

Baden-Baden, 226
Bahamas, 209
Bahamas, 210, 212, 215, 216, 217, 218,
219, 225
Bahamian immigrants, 81
Bahamians, 81, 210
Banco Agro-Industrial y Comercial, 185
Banco Financiero Internacional (BFI), 185
Banco Internacional de Comercio SA),
  (BICSA), 185
Banco Metropolitano, 185
Banco Nacional de Cuba (BNC), 171, 185
Banco Popular de Ahorro, 185
Banco de Inversiones, 185
Barbados, 205, 210, 212, 216, 217, 218,
  219, 266
Barbudos, 292, 293
Batista Regime, 20, 102, 117, 291, 316
Batistianos, 317
Baton Rouge, 103
Bay of Pigs, 81, 320
Beijing, 4,
Belize, 218
Biodiversity, 259, 260, 261, 267, 268
Biotechnology, 3, 296
Brasilia, 4
Brazil, 37, 80, 85, 159, 161, 261, 327, 355,
Brazzaville, 4
British Overseas Trade Board, 188
British West Indies, 205
Brothers to the Rescue, 346
Bush Administration, 345

C

Cable New Network (CNN), 1, 359
CADECA, 185
Calle Neptuno, 34
Camaguey Province, 232
Camarioca, 324
Camilo Cienfuegos, 232, 233, 234
Campephillus principalis, 263
Canada, 7, 60, 210, 215, 234, 303, 308
Canada-Cuba Joint Declaration, 358